W9-CFF-474

EX
LIBRIS

SAINT
JOSEPH'S
COLLEGE
RENSSELAER
INDIANA

Foreign Policy Making in the Middle East

R. D. McLaurin
Mohammed Mughisuddin
Abraham R. Wagner

The Praeger Special Studies program—utilizing the most modern and efficient book production techniques and a selective worldwide distribution network—makes available to the academic, government, and business communities significant, timely research in U.S. and international economic, social, and political development.

Foreign Policy Making in the Middle East

Domestic Influences on Policy in Egypt, Iraq Israel, and Syria

PRAEGER SPECIAL STUDIES IN INTERNATIONAL POLITICS AND GOVERNMENT

DS
63.1
.M25

Praeger Publishers   New York   London

Library of Congress Cataloging in Publication Data

McLaurin, Ronald De, 1944-
    Foreign policy making in the Middle East.

    (Praeger special studies in international politics
and government)
    Bibliography: p.
    Includes index.
    1. Near East—Foreign relations. 2. Egypt—
Foreign relations. 3. Israel—Foreign relations.
4. Iraq—Foreign relations. 5. Syria—Foreign
relations. I. Mughisuddin, Mohammed, joint
author. III. Title.
DS63.1.M25   327'.0956   76-24360
ISBN 0-275-23870-9
ISBN 0-275-65010-3 pbk.

PRAEGER PUBLISHERS
200 Park Avenue, New York, N.Y. 10017, U.S.A.

Published in the United States of America in 1977
by Praeger Publishers, Inc.

789 038 987654321

All rights reserved

© 1977 by Praeger Publishers, Inc.
Printed in the United States of America

Perhaps no area remains as critical to global security and as much the focus of international attention as the Middle East. Yet, of the thousands of pages that have been written on the Arab-Israeli conflict, it is difficult to locate analyses that place the critical regional conflict within the context of the foreign policy processes of the respective states. It is the authors' contention that the dynamics of the Middle East in the mid-1970s is a function of personalities, interactive pressures, and policy processes. The present work brings together analyses of the dynamics of foreign policy in the Middle East by three authors, each with an emphasis on specific regional states. The authors shared in the writing of Chapters 1 and 7. Chapters 3 and 4 were the responsibility of Mohammed Mughisuddin; Chapter 5, of Abe Wagner; Chapter 6, of Ron McLaurin; and Chapter 2, of McLaurin and Mughisuddin.

Many individuals, both in the United States and the Middle Eastern states considered, have made significant contributions to the authors' understanding of the problems involved. In the Department of Defense the authors have had the benefit of discussions with Robert Ellsworth, deputy secretary of defense; Maj. Gen. Clarke Baldwin, Robert H. Kubal, Jerrold K. Milsted, and Richard Peyer, all of the Office of the Assistant Secretary of Defense (International Security Affairs); and Lt. Gen. Gordon Sumner, chairman of the Inter-American Defense Board. The authors wish to express their gratitude to each of these individuals.

The research and preparation of this work also have benefited from the aid and counsel of Preston S. Abbott, Paul A. Jureidini, and William Hazen of Abbott Associates, Inc.; and of Carol K. Wagner, Paul Y. Hammond, and Marcy G. Agmon of Analytical Assessments Corporation. The authors also would like to express their appreciation to Andrew W. Marshall, Office of the Secretary of Defense; Anthony H. Cordesman, Office of the Deputy Secretary of Defense; Lt. Col. Alfred B. Prados, Jr., U.S. defense attaché to the Yemen Arab Republic; Lt. Col. Thomas Pianka, National War College; Commander Gary G. Sick, National Security Council staff; Sally Skillings, Resources for the Future; Abdul Aziz Said and Alan Taylor of the American University; Kerim K. Key, Howard University; Phebe A. Marr, University of Tennessee; Peter A. Gubser, the Ford Foundation; Edward E. Azar, University of North Carolina at Chapel Hill; Thomas J. Sloan, Kansas State University; Jeffrey Richelson and Lee E. Dutter, University of Texas; Amnon Sella, the Hebrew University of Jerusalem; J. Thomas McAndrew, Department of State; and Alaeddin S. Hreib, Sami Khoury, and Charles H. Wagner. The manuscript was typed with patience and skill by Maureen Ham, Joan Flood, Cathie Love, and Ellena Vitanov.

While each of these individuals has made a contribution to this work, the authors bear sole responsibility for any errors of fact or judgment.

CONTENTS

LIST OF TABLES AND FIGURES

LIST OF ABBREVIATIONS

OAPEC	Organization of Arab Petroleum Exporting Countries
AJC	American Jewish Committee
ALF	Arab Liberation Front
ANM	Arab Nationalist Movement
AOLP	Action Organization for the Liberation of Palestine
CFAS	Committee on Foreign Affairs and Security
ICP	Iraqi Communist Party
IDF	Israel Defense Forces
INOC	Iraqi National Oil Company
IPC	Iraq Petroleum Company
KDP	Kurdistan Democratic Party
KRP	Kurdistan Revolutionary Party
MENA	Middle East News Agency
NPF	National Progressive Front (Syria)
NRP	National Religious Parties (Israel)
PAO	Palestine Arab Organization
PFLP	Popular Front for the Liberation of Palestine
PLO	Palestine Liberation Organization
PSF	Popular Struggle Front
RCC	Revolutionary Command Council (Iraq)
SSNP	Syrian Social Nationalist Party
WZO	World Zionist Organization

Foreign Policy Making in the Middle East

1

BACKGROUND

The modern political history of the Middle East could be given any one of many starting points, from the late nineteenth century to the post-World War II era. Whichever initial point is chosen, it is safe to state that since then the region has been characterized by substantial political change and spasmodic outbreaks of political violence.

Developments in the Middle East raise a number of significant questions for the future of both that region and others. What is the impact of violence on foreign policy? To what extent does impending war alter alignment patterns? How is the cost-benefit calculus of the many action options available in each set of a nation's bilateral relations affected by the imminence of war in one set? How do the course of hostilities, ally behavior, and the political/military aftermath of war influence postwar policies?

The four countries considered in this book provide good cases to use in the search for answers to these and similar questions. It is clear, for example, that Middle East political relations are affected by imminent war. Previous study has found noticeable variations in Arab national political behavior just prior to the outbreak of hostilities. It is interesting to speculate on the degree and type of perturbations of regional political relations that the Arab-Israeli conflict has constituted for almost three decades.

This book is not intended as a political history of Egypt, Iraq, Israel, or Syria.[1] Even less is it a regional history.[2] Still, it is important to give at least some recent historical perspective to our analysis of the four states' foreign-policy processes, and that perspective must of necessity revolve around what have been two principal elements since the late 1940s—the continued growth and importance of Arab nationalism and the creation of Israel as an independent state.[3]

No attempt is made to provide an analysis or synthesis of Arab nationalism here, a task that has been ably performed by others.[4] It is, however, necessary to underscore the importance of this elusive and potent force in postwar Arab political development. In each of the Arab states considered here, for example, Arab nationalism has played a major role and is intimately associated with the revolutionary experience each has undergone. Because this book is concerned with societal and related pressures on foreign-policy decision making, the Arab nationalist Weltanschauung is directly relevant to our subject.

Similarly, Jewish nationalism in Palestine, Zionism, and the history of Israel's creation have been chronicled elsewhere.[5] Apart from their importance in understanding current Israeli policy, they have had a far-reaching effect on the evolution of the Middle East, particularly the Levant area. Israel's existence and its military strength also have had significant effects on the nature of bilateral relations between various Arab states and foreign powers external to the region.

For a variety of reasons, the process by which Israel was established as a modern state (or reborn, from the Israeli viewpoint) was not accepted as legitimate by any Arab state. This perceived illegitimacy was, however, only in part a function of the "Palestine problem." That Israel was viewed as a foreign creation, a dagger in the heart of the Arab nation—and thus an enemy of Arab nationalism—was also a critical consideration. In the Arab view, Israel was a price the Arabs were forced to pay for the sins of the Nazi holocaust in which the Arab states had had no part. Because of all Israel represented, because of the presence of 3 million Palestinians without their own "national home," and because of the perceived "indecisive" military outcome of the 1948 war, the hope that the Israeli state could be eradicated was virtually universal among Arabs. Even after the 1956 rout of Egypt by British, French, and Israeli forces, there was still no consensus in the Arab world that Israel's military power was preponderant over any likely coalition of major Arab forces.

The 1950 Tripartite Agreement on arms transfers to the Middle East was negated by the Soviet arms deals with Egypt and Syria in 1955–56. In 1955, a major regional arms race began that continues to the present.[6] When the June 1967 War broke out, few believed Israel would be able to overwhelm the Arabs as totally or as quickly as it did.

The political and military lessons of the 1967 conflict in the Middle East have been analyzed by many writers—Arab, Israeli, Western, and Soviet. But the most important conclusion Arab elites were to draw from the 1967 conflict crept into their consciousness only subtly over the succeeding six years—Israel was there to stay. Whatever the changes in the details of the regional military equation, no combination of Arab forces would be able to disestablish Israel as a regional state in the foreseeable future. The development of an Israeli nuclear weapons capability—never completely confirmed but widely believed to exist—served to underscore the accuracy and impact of this conclusion.

At the same time, the June War created a set of new facts. It was one thing for Egyptians, Lebanese, Syrians, Jordanians, Iraqis, Moroccans, and other Arab citizens of extant states to "accept" the inevitability of the existence of Israel on "Palestinian land" held by Israel since 1948, but quite another for Egyptians, Syrians, and Palestinian-Jordanians to accept indefinite occupation by Israel of Egyptian, Syrian, and (Palestinian) Jordanian land never allotted to Israel under the UN partition plan and never claimed by Israel. Even beyond the merits of the Palestinian claims perceived by Arab governments, those regimes supported the Palestinian resistance movement for their own political ends. By 1970, the primary Arab issue in Arab-Israeli relations had passed from recognition of "Palestinian rights" to return of Arab lands (in the Sinai, West Bank, and Golan Heights) captured in 1967. This was demonstrated by the various exchanges of Gunnar Jarring's unsuccessful "mission"; the circumstances surrounding the proposal, consideration, and collapse of the Rogers Peace Plan; and Arab strategic planning preceding the 1973 October War.[7]

As we shall see, although the years from 1967 to 1973 seemed to be characterized by stagnation in terms of Arab-Israeli bilateral developments, they were a period of major political change within several Arab countries, including all of the Arab confrontation states and Iraq. In Egypt, Iraq, and Syria, ideological rhetoricians gave way to more pragmatic leadership that has laid the groundwork and given the impetus for economic development, political institutionalization, and perhaps, in Iraq and Syria, greater political stability. Meanwhile, in Jordan, the civil war of 1969–70 led to the eviction of most of the activist Palestinian elements from that country.[8]

The death of Gamal Abdel Nasser in 1970 brought Anwar Sadat, another pragmatist, to the Egyptian presidency. Only a few weeks before Nasser's death, Syria's leadership had passed from Salah Jadid to Hafez Assad in a coup that was merely the final act in a transfer of power begun more than a year earlier. Over the next two and a half years, Syria, Egypt, and Jordan watched the 1967 cease-fire become a no-war, no-peace political "fact," with the appearance of permanence more firmly established with the passing of each day.

Sadat's expulsion of most of Egypt's Soviet technicians in 1972 was but one of several Egyptian attempts to break the stalemate.[9] Within some six months, after it had become clear that nothing short of war could bring about movement toward a return of the occupied territories, Sadat decided on such a course.[10] Egyptian-Syrian coordination proceeded well at the national strategic level, but progressed only minimally from the point of view of detailed military coordination.[11]

The October War and the events surrounding its outbreak and aftermath have been chronicled even more widely than the 1967 conflict.[12] For both wars, we refer readers to the extant literature on the war rather than add to it. At the same time, like the June War, the October conflict gave rise to a new set of realities. Whereas by virtue of Israel's overwhelming victory in 1967, most Arab elites grudgingly accepted the fact of Israel's existence and permanence as a state in the Middle East, Israel learned in 1973 that the costs of not achieving some sort of settlement with the Arab states were high militarily and politically. Both sides, at least as far as the confrontation states were concerned, perceived important benefits to be derived from a settlement in the modern history of the Middle East.

A second new development involves the regional positions of Egypt, Syria, and the Palestinians. The October War reestablished the importance of Egypt in the Arab world, secured the position of Hafez Assad in Syria, and thereby created conditions that would subsequently lead to the removal of the Palestinians as an independent element in the Arab-Israeli conflict—ironically, at a time when the Palestinian issue and the Palestine Liberation Organization (PLO) finally attained substantial worldwide recognition. After the October War there were determined efforts by both Egypt and Syria—often at odds with each other over the most effective means—to bring about circumstances conducive to an Arab-Israeli settlement. Both countries absorbed substantial costs in these efforts, and each was opposed by much of the Arab world (often including the other) for a variety of reasons. Yet by 1975, the key Arab countries in the conflict were clearly Egypt and Syria, and the most important nonconfrontation Arab state was Iraq. (The process by which this constellation of forces formed is examined in Chapter 2.)

But is the set of post-1973 facts sufficient to serve as a basis for peaceful settlement? If states behave as rational actors attempting to maximize their objective national interests, the answer should be "Yes." That no overall settlement has been achieved suggests that the matter is not this simple. Evaluation of the points of conflict indicates that the issue has gone well beyond the merits of the specific areas of disagreement. As the Arab-Israeli conflict has become institutionalized, the roles of people and of processes have been increasingly apparent as key factors in the dynamics of the conflict.

It is our belief that the governments of the Middle East, like the democracies of the West, cannot be analyzed, nor their actions understood, without reference to the publics they speak for and answer to. While it is certainly true that Middle East politics differs in many respects from the politics of the West —in the nature of the issues, the role of culture and religion, the forms of interest articulation, and the types of representation—interests, interest groups, and interest articulation are at the heart of the political process in both environments.

The countries we shall be studying here, like almost all the other states of the Middle East—Iran and Turkey are the only exceptions—are relatively new. Although Egyptian, Iraqi, Israeli, and Syrian traditions go back to some of the earliest recorded civilizations, the modern nationstates we now call Egypt, Iraq, Israel, and Syria all occupy territory that for many years prior to World War II was under some form of foreign control. Each has expended considerable effort in developing a sense of nationhood, of national identity. Each has minority groups and subcultures whose relationships to the nation as a whole are important both to the national identity and to national policies. Indeed, minority issues in Iraq, Israel, and Syria have been among the most important problems facing those countries.

Today's Middle East is, then, a vast complex of publics or constituencies; and national leaders' decisions must be placed in the context of their need to maintain their domestic power positions by influencing constituent alignments, as well as in that of their intentions to realize Egyptian, Iraqi, Israeli, Jordanian, Syrian, or some other "national interest." This book discusses these critical regional actors in terms of the publics and processes that shape national policies.

ORGANIZATION

This book is presented in seven chapters. Chapter 1 has consisted of a general sketch of historical background that seeks to place the subject matter of the rest of the book—people, pressures, and policies—in the context of overall Middle East actions and interactions.

Chapter 2 addresses the external environment with which Egypt, Iraq, Israel, and Syria must deal. In the first section of this chapter, we consider the nonregional international constraints to which the four countries must be responsive, including U.S. and Soviet interests, policies, and activities in the region. In addition, Chapter 2 addresses the regional environment, Middle East countries and interaction patterns that influence the foreign and military policies of the four countries we are studying.

Chapters 3 to 6 analyze the foreign policies of Egypt, Iraq, Israel, and Syria, respectively. Recognizing that there are major differences in the structure of and influences on the four governments, we have nevertheless attempted to retain an approach to the four that allows maximum comparability. Each chapter therefore has three primary sections. The first part is a discussion of the internal environment of national security policy that describes the structure of government, the operation of the political system, and the main interest groups or publics. The second section identifies the major issue areas as they are perceived within each country. Finally, the political and military objectives and policies of each government are described.

Chapter 7 places the conclusions of Chapters 3 to 6 in the context of an analysis of the role of groups and pressures in the political evolution of the Middle East.

NOTES

1. Among the many works on recent Egyptian political history are R. Hrair Dekmejian, *Egypt Under Nasir: A Study in Political Dynamics* (Albany: State University of New York Press, 1971); Mohamed Heikal, *The Road to Ramadan* (New York: Quadrangle, 1975); Peter Mansfield, *Nasser's Egypt* (Baltimore: Penguin Books, 1969); and Anthony Nutting, *Nasser* (New York: E. P. Dutton, 1972). Fewer studies of recent Iraq have been published. Two that should be consulted are Majid Khadduri, *Republican Iraq: A Study in Iraqi Politics Since 1958* (London: Oxford University Press, 1969); and Kent Lorenzo Kimball, *The Changing Pattern of Political Power in Iraq, 1958 to 1971* (New York: Robert Speller and Sons, 1972). Israel, like Egypt, has attracted considerable attention from political analysts. Five of the best books on recent Israeli political developments are David Ben-Gurion, *Israel: A Personal History* (New York: Funk and Wagnalls, 1971); Michael Brecher, *The Foreign Policy System of Israel: Setting, Images, Processes* (New Haven: Yale University Press, 1972); Yair Evron, *The Middle East: Nations, Superpowers and Wars* (New York: Praeger, 1973); Chaim Herzog, *The War of Atonement: October 1973* (Boston: Little, Brown, 1975); Terence Prittie, *Eshkol: The Man and the Nation* (New York: Pitman, 1969). There are no books on Syria under Assad. Itamar Rabinovich's *Syria Under the Ba'ath 1963–66: The Army-Party Symbiosis* (Jerusalem: Israel Universities Press; New York: Halsted Press, 1972) gives helpful background on the Ba'ath; and Tabitha Petran's *Syria* (New York: Praeger, 1972) has a number of interesting insights into recent Syria. The older, standard accounts—Patrick Seale, *The Struggle for Syria: A Study of Post-War Arab Policies, 1945–1958* (New York: Oxford University Press, 1965); and Gordon H. Torrey, *Syrian Politics and the Military, 1945–1958* (Columbus: Ohio State University, 1964)—can be profitably read.

2. See Paul Y. Hammond and Sidney S. Alexander, eds., *Political Dynamics in the Middle East* (New York: American Elsevier, 1972); Malcolm H. Kerr, *The Arab Cold War, 1958–1967: A Study of Ideology in Politics,* 3rd ed. (London: Oxford University Press, 1972); Majid Khadduri, *Arab Contemporaries: The Role of Personalities in Politics* (Baltimore: Johns Hopkins University Press, 1973); George Lenczowski, ed., *Political Elites in the Middle East* (Washington, D. C.: American Enterprise Institute, 1975); Dana Adams Schmidt, *Armageddon in the Middle East* (New York: John Day, 1974); and Frank Tachau, ed., *Political Elites and Political Development in the Middle East* (Cambridge; Mass.: Schenkman, 1975).

3. The irony—and significance—of Israel's emergence (as a function of Jewish nationalism) in the period during which Arab nationalism resulted in an "Arab world" of sovereign states in place of the Arab dependencies that existed prior to World War II has been addressed by a number of authors. Certainly, Israel has fortified the potency of the Arab nationalist cause, even as it is seen to be anathema to Arab nationalists.

4. George Antonius, *The Arab Awakening* (Philadelphia: Lippincott, 1938); Sylvia Haim, *Arab Nationalism: An Anthology* (Berkeley and Los Angeles: University of California Press, 1962); Albert H. Hourani, *Arabic Thought in the Liberal Age, 1798–1939* (New York and London: Oxford University Press, 1962); and Zeine N. Zeine, *The Emergence of Arab Nationalism: With a Background Study of Arab-Turkish Relations in the Near East* (Beirut: Khayats, 1966).

5. See David Ben-Gurion, *Israel: Years of Challenge* (New York: Holt, Rinehart and Winston, 1963); Ben Halpern, *The Idea of the Jewish State* (Cambridge, Mass.: Harvard University Press, 1961); Walter Z. Laqueur, *A History of Zionism* (New York: Holt, Rinehart and Winston, 1972); and Chaim Weizman, *Trial and Error* (New York: Schocken, 1966).

6. In the 1950s and 1960s the arms race was quantitative. In the 1970s, it has become qualitative.

7. The Jarring mission exchanges appear in various UN documents and in *Journal of Palestine Studies* 2, no. 4 (Summer 1973). The essence of the Rogers peace initiatives of 1969 and 1970 is framed in Rogers' speech of December 9, 1969, reprinted in U.S. Senate, Committee on Foreign Relations, *A Select Chronology and Background Documents Relating to the Middle East,* 2nd ed., rev. (Washington, D.C.: U.S. Government Printing Office, 1975). There is a wealth of literature on the strategic and tactical prelude to the October War. See especially Chaim Herzog, *The War of Atonement.* The point the reader should note is that each of these demonstrates the policy primacy of securing the return of the occupied territories. The goal of mainstream Arab political thinking after about 1972 was to restore and maintain movement toward a settlement that would secure the return of the occupied territories to Egypt, Syria, and Jordan (or a Palestinian entity) and would defuse the Palestinian problem. If this should involve, as an outcome, some form of acceptance of Israel, including recognition and minor territorial modifications, such a result was acceptable.

8. See Paul A. Jureidini and William E. Hazen, *The Palestinian Movement in Politics* (Lexington, Mass.: D. C. Heath, 1976), pp. 41–76.

9. See Abraham S. Becker, "The Superpowers and the Arab-Israeli Conflict, 1970–1973," RAND Corporation paper, December 1973; and Heikal, *The Road to Ramadan.*

10. Charles Wakebridge, "The Egyptian Staff Solution," *Military Review* 55, no. 3 (March 1975): 3–11.

11. Ibid. The nature of the Egyptian and Syrian attacks was totally different, and coordination was poor beyond the timing of the initial assault. Indeed, considering the similarity of their training experience, the degree of difference is surprising.

12. J. S. Arora, *West Asia War 1973: That Shook the World and Brought Us to the Brink of the Third World War* (New Delhi: New Light Publishers, n.d.); Yeshoyahu Ben-Porat et al., *Kippur* (Tel Aviv: Special Edition Publishers, 1973); Riad N. el-Rayyes and Dunia Nahas, eds., *The October War: Documents, Personalities, Analyses and Maps* (Beirut: An-Nahar Press Services S.A.R.L., 1974); Heikal, *The Road to Ramadan*; Herzog, *The War of Atonement:* Walter Laqueur, *Confrontation: The Middle East War and World Politics* (London: Wildwood House and Abacus, 1974); Louis Williams, ed. *Military Aspects of the Israeli-Arab Conflict* (Tel Aviv: University Publishing Projects, 1975); D. K. Palit, *Return to Sinai: The Arab Offensive, October 1973* (New Delhi: Palit and Palit, 1974); Zeev Schif, *October Earthquake* (Tel Aviv: University Publishing Projects, Ltd., 1974); Lester A. Sobel, ed., *Israel and The Arabs: The October 1973 War* (New York: Facts on File, 1974); Sunday Times Insight Team, *Insight on the Middle East War* (London: Times News, Ltd., 1974); and Lawrence L. Whetten, *The Canal War: Four Power Conflict in the Middle East* (Cambridge, Mass.: MIT Press, 1974). See also *Journal of Palestine Studies* 14, no. 2 (Winter 1974), special issue, "The October War and Its Aftermath." For those with the resources, the Arabic-language literature on the 1973 conflict is voluminous and rich.

2

THE EXTERNAL
ENVIRONMENT

Because the Middle East is viewed by all the major industrialized countries as important, external powers are significantly involved in the region. Given the high level of armaments, and the role of the oil-producing states in the world economy, only the United States and the Soviet Union have sufficient power to singly and significantly affect the principal political and military developments within the Middle East. Thus, in this chapter, which considers the constraints external to Egypt, Iraq, Israel, and Syria that operate on those countries' political evolution, primary attention is given to the superpowers. With the superpowers, however, regional states play a major role in affecting the four countries' actions. Therefore, in this chapter we also will give some attention to the overall tenor of, and to the key variables influencing, intraregional relations that impact on the foreign policies of Egypt, Iraq, Israel, and Syria.

THE UNITED STATES

Interests

Although American contacts with the Middle East may be traced to the formative years of the United States, relations have changed substantially since World War II. Of all Middle East actors, both regional and external, the interests and attitudes of the United States probably have been most greatly altered by the events and developments of the early 1970s. Until then, U.S. national interests in the Middle East could be viewed as marginal. These interests were the following:

denial of control over Middle East resources to hostile powers;

preservation of the assured destruction capability of the regional element of
U.S. strategic forces;

assured supply of Middle East natural resources important to American industry and military;

assured supply to U.S. allies of resources adequate to maintain their economic
and military strength;

realization of the benefits resulting from U.S. commercial investments and
operations in the Middle East;

maintenance of U.S. credibility by fully meeting American commitments;[1]

maintenance of overflight and transit rights.

It should be noted that support of Israel, or support for the existence of
Israel, is not included among traditional U.S. interests. The existence of Israel
per se is not, strictly speaking, an interest of the United States. Israel's importance to the United States has been argued even by Israelis largely in terms
either of "duty" resulting from the Holocaust or of a means to further the
interests listed above. An alternative—and far more empirically valid—reason
for U.S. support of Israel's existence is concern to maintain American credibility.

Although we shall not detail the elements in U.S. decision making on the
Middle East or the constituents of Middle East policy—these are reasonably
well known—it is necessary to have some idea of U.S. policies to the present.
These have been described in a number of books and articles, to which we refer
the reader.[2]

That the interests of the United States have changed substantially since
1970—and particularly since 1973—is a function of several phenomena.

First, the Soviet Union and the United States became the sole great
powers deeply involved in the Middle East at the time they embarked on a
broad and ambitious attempt to improve their relations. Their heightened
regional rivalry stood in glaring—and ominous—contrast with their growing
global cooperation. Some critics argued that the Soviet Union must cooperate
in the Middle East or "détente" would be meaningless.[3] We believe, on the
contrary, that there is no inherent contradiction between growing global cooperation and continued regional rivalry. Yet, clearly, the new cooperation and
the more nearly equal political strength in the area should have altered superpower goals and policies.

Second, the October War resulted in a pronounced shift in international
attitudes toward the Middle East. Virtually all of the developed countries and
the developing world alike support return of the occupied territories, recognition of Palestinian national rights, and the continued existence of Israel.

This international shift derives from the solidarity and power of Arab
oil-exporting nations, in the case of the developed countries, and from the

financial strength of the oil producers, in the Third World's perceptions. (Particularly in the latter case, the merits of the issues as perceived locally also have played a major role, but this is not a salient issue to most of the Third World.)

Moreover, Egypt and Syria, though not major oil producers, have directly benefited from the revolution in petroleum commerce. The cost of their high level of armaments is borne by the oil producers but must be matched by Israel, either through Israeli expenditures or through American grant military aid. Finally, the oil picture for the United States has changed. In 1972–73 the continuing growth in energy demand and the decline in domestic petroleum production left a shortfall of significant proportions. Moreover, whereas Venezuelan and Canadian crude had been imported to meet this shortfall in the past, the dimensions of the requirement meant that only Middle Eastern oil could fill the demand. In 1973, for example, the oil import pattern changed dramatically. Table 1 demonstrates the growth and shift in U.S. petroleum importation.[4]

The significance of this change was visible after the October War, when crude oil exports to the United States were embargoed by the members of the Organization of Arab Petroleum Exporting Countries. This action caused considerable disruption in the United States, although the net effect had greater psychological than energy availability importance. The embargo was followed by a large price rise that became effective on January 1, 1974. The magnitude of petroleum price increases has affected all oil-importing countries.

From the foregoing, it must be clear that a predominant U.S. interest in the Middle East today is oil. Moreover, the interest is no longer commercial in nature.[5] Middle East oil will continue to supply a crucial portion of America's energy requirements until alternative energy sources are developed. The United States has no major interests in Egypt, Iraq, Israel, or Syria. None of the emotional or traditional associations that characterize European-American relations or even American-Israeli relations tie most Americans to any of the three Arab states. Yet, the U.S. interest in oil for industrial and defense needs (not to mention the commercial interest in downstream operations) does confer on the Middle East as a whole a very considerable importance; and Egypt, Iraq, Israel, and Syria are key states in the evolution of the Middle East political situation. (Moreover, Iraqi oil reserves are believed to be very sizable.) Since the United States seeks, as a principal regional objective, to ensure the continued and adequate supply of oil from the Middle East, it must endeavor to bring about a political situation in which oil production and distribution will not be interrupted, either by facilitating a settlement of the conflict that threatens the oil supply—the Arab-Israeli dispute—or by reducing the role of these or other states to the extent that they may impede a resolution acceptable to the other parties.

TABLE 1

Direct and Indirect Importation of Middle East Crude Oil and Products, as Percent of Total Such Imports, 1972–76[a]

	1972 Direct	1973 Direct	1973 (Total)	1974 Direct	1974 (Total)	1975 Direct	1975 (Total)	1976[b]
Algeria	1.9	2.2	(2.4)	3.1	(3.4)	4.7	(4.8)	7.0
Bahrain	0.3	0.2	(0.2)	0.2	(0.2)	0.3	(0.3)	negl.
Egypt	0.2	0.2	(0.2)	0.1	(negl.)	0.1	(0.1)	0.6
Iran	3.0	3.6	(6.9)	7.7	(12.0)	4.8	(8.9)	6.3
Iraq	negl.	negl.	(0.3)	0	(0.2)	0.1	(0.2)	negl.
Israel	0	negl.	negl.	negl.	negl.	0	(0)	0
Kuwait	0.9	0.8	(1.0)	0.1	(0.4)	0.3	(0.5)	negl.
Libya	2.6	2.7	(4.9)	0.1	(0.7)	3.8	(5.5)	8.5
Oman	negl.	negl.	negl.	negl.	(0.1)	0.1	(0.1)	0.3
Qatar	0.1	0.1	(0.1)	0.3	(0.9)	0.3	(1.5)	0.4
Saudi Arabia	4.0	7.9	(11.8)	7.6	(11.1)	11.2	(14.1)	22.7
Syria	0	negl.	negl.	0	(negl.)	negl.	negl.	negl.
Tunisia	0.2	0.3	(0.3)	0.2	(0.3)	negl.	negl.	0.2
United Arab Emirates	1.6	1.1	(1.3)	1.2	(1.4)	2.3	(2.9)	5.2
People's Democratic Republic of Yemen	negl.	negl.	negl.	negl.	negl.	negl.	negl.	negl.

negl. = negligible

[a] Imports into the 50 states and the District of Columbia. Imports into U.S. territories, commonwealths, and trust territory are not included unless they are later sent to the United States.

[b] First-quarter preliminary figures for crude oil only.

Sources: 1972–75 — U.S. Bureau of Mines. 1976 — U.S. Federal Energy Administration, *Energy Information: Report to Congress. First Quarter 1976* (Washington, D.C.: U.S. Government Printing Office, 1976), p. 49.

From these limited but important interests flow U.S. objectives relevant to Egypt, Iraq, Israel, and Syria, which include the following:

avoidance of a military confrontation with the Soviet Union;[6]
achievement of a peaceful settlement between Arabs and Israelis;
maintenance of Israeli security;
continued and unimpeded access to oil at a reasonable price;
demonstration that alliance with the Soviet Union is unwise;[7]
demonstration that the United States will not permit a Soviet political victory
    through arms in the region;[8]
maintenance of American credibility and of the respect for the United States
    as a superpower;[9]
increased access to Middle East markets;[10]
productive use of their new wealth by oil producers.

The United States, like the Soviet Union, places preeminent weight on avoiding a superpower military confrontation in the Middle East. Obviously this priority does not exclude the possibility of such a conflict and does not mean the United States or the Soviet Union will in every case defer to the other in a sort of superpower Alphonse and Gaston routine. The concern to avoid confrontation and, it is hoped, a nuclear war is simply one among other considerations. Faced with the prospect of significant costs in terms of other objectives, the United States may challenge the Soviet Union under certain conditions. Nevertheless, the parameters within which decisions on confrontation are made seem to be reciprocal perceptions of issue salience. That is, each superpower seems understandably more willing to take a strong stand when it is certain the other will back down. Thus, positions that indicate new firmness are particularly important: they constitute the developing interstices for each power's future policy, and the superpower relationship itself, in cases of potential confrontation in the Middle East.

Because the United States seeks to avoid a confrontation with the Soviet Union over the Middle East, yet also seeks to optimize its interests there, the precise weight of its requirements is kept vague. This process is, of course, the essence of politics. For example, the achievement of resolution (acceptable to all parties) to the Arab-Israeli conflict (including the Palestinian problem) is important because such a resolution would both contribute to the security of oil supply and reduce the danger of a war between the superpowers. Yet, from this fact it cannot safely be concluded that the United States would risk a war to achieve a settlement. Nor can the contrary be presumed. Such decisions are taken on a case-by-case basis and proceed from the unique factors bearing on each instance. What will be the impact of a given course of action on U.S. credibility? on Israeli security? on consequent Soviet perceptions, conclusions, and actions?—these are the kinds of considerations involved in crisis decision making.[11]

Similarly, we cannot assess in absolute terms the importance of arriving at an Arab-Israeli settlement acceptable to both sides. We assume that a certain minimum Israeli security is a prerequisite to such a settlement; but Israel's security is also a factor of considerable importance in the calculus of American domestic politics, where Israel's supporters retain substantial influence. Thus, U.S. policy with respect to Israel's security must be viewed not only as an immanent part of any feasible settlement but also in the context of American political requirements.[12]

So, too, the continued flow of oil has a direct impact upon the domestic politics and society of the United States. Decisions, then, must be taken with reference to domestic attitudes and projected attitudes, as well as to international factors. Although most of the consideration of this issue has focused on quantity and cost, quality is also of some importance.

The United States, it is widely believed, has given up its ideas about "keeping" the Soviet Union out of, or "expelling" it from, the Middle East. Yet, this belief is not consistently supported. The secretary of state has spoken of expelling the Soviet Union, and continued movement toward a settlement has been risked in order to increase the American role at the expense of the Soviet Union. The processes of disengagement and settlement have evolved in such a way as—and to some degree in order—to minimize the Soviet role. These objectives strongly suggest that superpower interests are still viewed largely in zero-sum game terms, even if local interests are not (and after the parties to the dispute seem to have begun to extricate themselves from zero-sum calculations).

There is, of course, a substantial difference between objectives that support erosion of the Soviet presence and those emphasizing maintenance or growth of the American role. Whether American credibility should have been put on the line, whether past policies have been justified or not, whether the widely perceived American commitment to Israel is wise or necessary—are related questions; but raising them does not alter the fact that U.S. credibility and the American role in the Middle East are perceived in a certain way. To act in such a way as to violate expectations may well raise even greater questions of role in the long run. It is in the shadow of this reality that recent Middle East policy has evolved.

Finally, given the new monetary position of the oil-producing countries and the price and quantity of oil imported by the United States, the growth of commerical relations between the United States and the Arab world is an objective of new-found importance. In fact, U.S. trade with Arab countries was increasing even before the true dimensions of the shift in U.S. oil importation became clear.[13] The projected capital flow to oil-producing countries establishes beyond doubt the American and global need to channel this capital into investment and commerce. This objective suggests major changes in U.S. attitudes toward (and perhaps laws regarding) foreign investment in the United States and American investment in countries such as Egypt, Iraq, and Syria. To date, little progress has been made in implementing these changes.

Policies

Because the policies of the United States in the Middle East have been reviewed and analyzed frequently,[14] we shall address only a few of the major points in the recent period, paying particular attention to the Arab-Israeli dimension.

In pursuance of the objectives we have indicated, the United States has made a substantial effort to separate the oil supply problem and its associated considerations from the Arab-Israeli issue.[15] Indeed, the two issues were largely and surprisingly discrete before 1973. It was only in 1972 and 1973, as the United States looked to Saudi Arabia for a vast increase in its oil production to meet the new projections of American and European energy requirements, but was unreceptive to Saudi suggestions on investment, that the American fears that the issues might be mixed began to be realized. By the time of the war, the probability that an embargo might be applied was widely recognized and the possibility that the "oil weapon" might be used after the war to bring about acceptable progress toward an overall settlement was given substantial credence.

The reason that the two issues had not interacted more fully and consistently in the past is important to note here. While both centered on that region generally called the Middle East, they took place in two different parts of the area—the Arab-Israeli conflict in the eastern Mediterranean, the petroleum production around the Persian Gulf. Thus, the immediate actors in each drama were different. Today, in both cases the roles—and therefore involvement—have proliferated so that there is a considerable cross-participation even on the two issues taken individually.

The general Middle East policy issues that are clearly relevant to Egypt, Israel, and Syria are less important to Iraq. Iraq's primary focus of activity relevant to the United States is in the Persian Gulf. There, while Iraq and Iran have long maintained a state of friction, U.S. policy has encouraged Iran and Saudi Arabia to consider themselves the guardians of the Gulf. That such a role for these two powers is anathema to Iraq is scarcely surprising: Iran has long been perceived as Iraq's main threat, and the Saudi Arabian and Iraqi regimes have been antagonistic as well. U.S. recognition that Iran is the dominant power in the Persian Gulf has led to a policy of heavy arms sales to Teheran.[16] Iran has purchased more military equipment from the United

States than any other country in the world, including NATO allies.[17] It is due to receive more from U.S. military and sales programs than any other country in the world—far more.[18] The buildup of arms in Iran has coincided with a sizable weapons increase in Iraq. The U.S. policy of supplying Iran with virtually any and all equipment requested has forced Iraq to turn to the Soviet Union for more and more arms.

Since the Iran-Iraq agreement in the spring of 1975, the primary movement in the Persian Gulf has been the evolution of competing ideas regarding area security. Although Iran and Iraq seem to agree on at least the principle that Persian Gulf security should be the responsibility of the powers surrounding it (principally Iran, Iraq, and Saudi Arabia), Saudi Arabia and the many small sheikhdoms hold some private reservations concerning their own security under these conditions. The rapprochement—or at least reconciliation—between Iran and Iraq has significantly reduced the influence of outside powers to which Teheran and Baghdad had looked for support in the conflict.

In the eastern Mediterranean, U.S. policy opposes any increased influence or presence of Soviet armed forces personnel, with a view to avoiding a superpower military or nuclear confrontation and to reducing the Soviet role. Increases in Soviet military adviser levels, ship-days in the Mediterranean Sea or Indian Ocean, and activity levels at Middle Eastern facilities customarily used by Soviet forces are duly noted and frequently commented upon by spokesmen for various agencies of the executive branch of the U.S. government.

The fear of, and determination to avoid, a confrontation express themselves in several ways. For example, the secretary of state and president strenuously opposed the creation of a peacekeeping force that would include American and Soviet components.[19] During the October War, a real concern of Secretary of State Kissinger appears to have been that if the Soviets were not confronted early and at a low level with a combination of strong U.S. defense support for Israel and signals that the United States was prepared to take a more active role, they might initiate a course of action that would result in a later, far more serious, confrontation.[20] Robert Hunter succinctly captured the essence of the dilemma: "The Americans," he says, "have a difficult task. On the one hand they must continually impress upon the Russians the risks of superpower conflict if Israel is directly threatened; on the other hand, they must not allow Israel so much latitude that a super-power conflict becomes inevitable."[21]

We have already briefly discussed the effort to reduce the Soviet profile and role in the Middle East as an element in the power relations of the two superpowers in that region. It would not be accurate to suggest that the United States has attempted to bypass Moscow, for a relatively consistent element of U.S. efforts to achieve a settlement has been consultation with the Soviet Union. Certainly, American leaders recognize the necessity of securing Soviet

support for any broad-based settlement in the Middle East. We are arguing
that, as one expert has written, "it still remains for the United States to accept
in positive terms something she has so far accepted only by default—namely,
a continuing and active Soviet presence in the Arab Middle East, for the
foreseeable future."[22]

The underlying assumption of the opposition to a larger Soviet role is that
Soviet influence will grow in the Middle East and American influence will
wane as a result. Yet, a larger Soviet role does not logically require, and has
not actually had, this effect, as Sadat's actions in July 1972 illustrate. We have
suggested elsewhere[23] that the Soviet Union cannot compete on even terms
with the West as a whole or with the United States in the Middle East.
However, neither great power will be in a position to meet all of the political,
military, economic, or social needs of this diverse region by itself. Neither
superpower can be forced out by the actions of the other.

Despite all of the foregoing, the political and economic dynamics of the
Middle East continues to depend in large measure upon the denouement of the
most salient regional problem, the Arab-Israeli conflict. In that arena, U.S.
policy has demonstrated strong learning effects (perhaps "overlearning") over
time.

Current approaches bear little resemblance to any previous American
attempts in the long and tragic history of the post-1948 Middle East. Following
the June War, the United States slowly began to approach a settlement, taking
into account the new realities. No major serious efforts were made, however,
until the Nixon administration took office in 1969. In 1969 and 1970, as the
U.S. government involved itself in the Middle East problem, the primary
factors in American policy were the following:

the role of U.S.-Soviet agreement and the limits of Soviet support;
the parameters of settlement, principally some mix that would fall within
    Resolution 242—Israeli withdrawal from occupied Arab territory, the
    recognition of and establishment of security for Israel, and an acceptable
    solution to the Palestinian problem;
stability of the governments of the parties to the conflict;
the role of public opinion in the Middle East, particularly in Israel;
Congressional and U.S. public opinion;
the need for a Palestinian spokesman;
the appropriate role for the United States.

From 1969 to 1971, the U.S. government took an active role in trying to
achieve agreement among the parties to the conflict. This approach also involved the Soviet Union, and a series of discussions between the two superpowers led to general agreement on the proper ingredients of a settlement, as well
as on the shape such a settlement should take. Although several versions of

this approach were advanced, the Rogers Plan of December 1969[24] conforms to the overall tone of the discussions and agreements reached by the Soviet Union and the United States.

However, the United States was not able to "sell" Israel on the approach the superpowers agreed to. Moreover, even if Egypt and Jordan went along with the plan, Syria, in accordance with its custom, would attack those regimes for their "sellout," recognizing that she could always accede to the agreement later.[25] Israel also could make such an "imposed peace" very costly to the American administration. Finally, the absence of a real spokesman for the Palestinians complicated the issue of negotiating a formula along the lines of the Rogers Plan.[26]

One of the most important levers at U.S. disposal was its post-1969 role as the sole major military supplier of Israel. Major debates arose within the executive branch of the U.S. government over the proper use of arms to support American diplomacy in its efforts to bring about a settlement. The competing philosophies were the "incentive" technique and the "cushion" approach. Both schools agreed that the United States must carefully weigh Israeli arms requests. The "incentive" supporters, however, believed the United States should supply major end items only when, and to the extent that, Israel cooperated with American peace initiatives. The "cushion" argument took a different line, maintaining that Israel must be supplied with a sufficient amount of military hardware to feel secure. Only then could Israel afford to consider compromises.

Skillful Israeli diplomacy and use of its domestic U.S. resources ended in a victory for the cushion approach when the U.S. initiatives of 1969–71 failed. After 1971, the State Department assessed the "lessons learned" from the 1969–71 efforts, and concluded that peace could not be imposed, that the outside powers should not identify themselves with a preferred settlement outline that in effect invalidates their role as neutral mediators. Thus, after 1971, U.S. efforts awaited action "by the parties." In reality, the new policy, largely (and perhaps unfairly) identified with Assistant Secretary of State Joseph Sisco, its best-known proponent, was scarcely more than a rationalization for taking no active role at all in the Middle East.

> [S]uperior Israeli military strength, backed by American support, could enforce the status quo on a long-term basis; . . . The Arabs, recognizing their military helplessness . . . would do nothing to shake the status quo and would either resign themselves to it . . . or eventually undergo a fundamental change of attitude and sue for peace; . . . the United States . . . could turn this [new] partnership [with Israel] into a positive asset, with Israel as its policeman in the Middle East; and . . . the Soviet-American detente . . . could be counted on to confirm the continued freezing of the Middle Eastern status quo.[27]

The October War took the United States by surprise and established the Middle East as one of the major focuses of American diplomatic initiative.

> For the United States a diplomatic role in the Middle East [became] not a preference but a matter of vital interest:
> • Because of our historical and moral commitment to the survival and security of Israel;
> • Because of our important concerns in the Arab world, an area of more than 150 million people and the site of the world's largest oil reserves;
> • Because perpetual crisis in the Middle East jeopardizes the world's hopes for economic recovery, threatening the well-being of the industrial nations and the hopes of the developing world; and
> • Because tension in the Middle East increases the prospect of direct U.S.-Soviet confrontation with its attendant nuclear risk.[28]

Rather than following a new set of "lessons learned," however, the United States undertook a bold, new approach based on the personal diplomacy of the secretary of state. The unique aspects of the effort were its mixture of personal (Kissinger) and global (Geneva Conference) diplomacy; the focus on building momentum toward a general settlement through step-by-step moves tied directly to the general settlement; the bilateral nature of what is at base a multilateral approach; the emphasis on trust—and on building it—as the major ingredient in the process; the well-managed mixture of publicity and secrecy (no small task); and the admirable U.S. disregard of public statements by the parties to the conflict.

While it has long been axiomatic that when fundamental requirements are in conflict, no agreement can be reached, American policy assumes that the essentials of each party are not in conflict, that a settlement meeting the minimum requirements of each side can be achieved. The major issues can be subsumed under the rubric "political independence and territorial integrity," and for each side a substantial portion of the minimum requirements deals with aspects of status—for Israel, recognition, the end of the state of belligerency, peace treaties, and diplomatic relations; for the Arabs, return of the occupied territories, establishment of a Palestinian state, and international or Arab control of at least the Arab part of Jerusalem. These needs are not contradictory.

Prerequisites to a lasting peace go far beyond the minimum requirements for a settlement. The focal point of these prerequisites is trust, the belief that the other parties intend to fulfill the commitments into which they entered in order to bring about the settlement agreement. Clearly, American policy is directed toward building this trust en route to a settlement that meets the minimum requirements of both sides. To date, the persuasion to which the United States has resorted has been aimed at Israel. This is true for several reasons. First, greatest U.S. influence lies there. Second, Israel, as the preeminent military power in the region, is in a position to make certain types of military concessions the Arab states cannot make. Third, Israel's physical position (in control of the occupied territories) is unique: of all the parties to the conflict, only Israel possesses something tangible that is both vital to peace and negotiable—the Arab territories taken in 1967. The security guarantees Israel may require will be offered only if the territory should be returned and can be employed only under those circumstances. Thus, it is to Israel that the United States looks for most of the important initial concessions. The problem is that Israel, like Syria (and Egypt to a lesser extent), does not speak with one voice. Israeli leaders, too, answer to a diverse constituency that perceives— with alarm, in many cases—the machinations preliminary to the settlement with views and values very different from those of the prime minister and his immediate advisers. Arab governments are more effective at communicating to selected audiences in other Arab states than in communicating to Israeli audiences. Similarly, Israel has not been adept at communicating to diverse audiences in Arab countries. The United States seeks to bridge this gap by restricting the public communications role to rumor.

The secretary of state described the post-1973 approach as follows:

> . . . [F]or 30 years it proved nearly impossible even to begin the process of negotiation. Every attempt to discuss a comprehensive solution failed—from the partition plan, to the Lausanne conference, to the Rogers plan and the Four Powers talks of 1969 and 1970, to the U.N. Security Council deliberations. To discuss simultaneously issues of such complexity, between countries whose deep mutual mistrust rejected even the concept of compromise, was futile until a minimum of confidence had been established. In the long history of the Arab-Israeli conflict, it is a new and relatively recent development that opinion in the Arab world has begun to think in terms of recognizing a sovereign Israel and that Israel has begun to see peace as a tangible goal rather than a distant dream.
>
> The United States therefore concluded that instead of seeking to deal with all problems at once we should proceed step by step with the parties prepared to negotiate and on the issues where some room for maneuver seemed possible. We believed that once the parties began a negotiating process, they would develop a stake in success. Solutions to problems more easily negotiable would build mutual confidence. On each side a sense would grow that negotiations could produce benefits and that agreements would be kept— agreements that could become building blocks for a final peace. Ultimately we expected that the step-by-step process would bring about, for the first time, the basic political conditions needed for the overall settlement called for by Security Council Resolution 338. This remains our goal.[29]

Thus from 1973 to 1975, "step-by-step" diplomacy, as it came to be known, characterized the administration efforts. The gains seemed modest— a few kilometers in the Golan Heights and Sinai that represented only small steps toward Israeli withdrawal; passage through the Suez Canal of nonmilitary cargoes bound to or from Israel; certain stipulations regarding the non-resort to the threat or use of force; and de facto Egyptian recognition of Israel. But the value of "step by step" lay in the opportunity given all parties to reassess the attitudes of the other parties; the opportunity to awaken American public opinion and the U.S. Congress to a broader and more up-to-date perspective on the Middle East; and the opportunity to build or maintain strong bilateral relationships between the United States and each of the regional governments.

"Step by step" scored victories in the preliminary disengagement agreements in the Sinai and on the Golan Heights and again in the Egyptian-Israeli agreement of September 1975. It can be said as well that Israeli perceptions of both Egypt and Syria changed, though attitudes toward Syria changed less —and probably as a result of Syrian activities in the Lebanese crisis of 1975-76 rather than as a result of U.S. diplomacy. Certainly, the secretary of state was able to bring about much more evenhanded U.S. public and Congressional attitudes. And U.S. bilateral relations with Egypt and Syria improved markedly, though American ties with its traditional friends in the region— Israel and Jordan—suffered to some extent.

"Step by step" is built on recognition of the importance of the Soviet Union. It emphasizes a role for the parties and the need for the governments concerned to lead public opinions within each country. While "step by step" assumes that a settlement must take place within the parameters of Security Council resolutions 242 and 338, the United States generally has avoided taking concrete positions (except to break last-minute deadlocks), in order to preserve American credibility as an honest broker between the two sides.[30]

As we have indicated, U.S. "step-by-step" diplomacy recognizes the need for Soviet support. However, U.S. policy initiatives generally have left little room for superpower partnerships. They have been, almost literally, a "one-man show." That continued Soviet support will accompany efforts almost publicly advertised as being aimed both at a settlement and, through settlement, at ultimately reducing Soviet influence in the region is highly dubious.

THE SOVIET UNION

Objectives

Although there have been changes in Soviet objectives and policies vis-à-vis the Middle East since 1967, the degree of change reflects the necessary global and regional role of the Soviet Union more than it does conscious modification of priorities on salient issues. We have cursorily traced the history of Soviet interest in the Middle East elsewhere.[31] The important point to note is that the Middle East was largely peripheral to Soviet interest—and influence in the Middle East was beyond Soviet capabilities—before 1955.[32]

Soviet Middle East regional objectives continue to center on avoiding conflict with the United States, minimizing Western influence in the Middle East, and increasing Soviet southern security and regional influence. Changes in objectives from before 1973 to after 1973 have been subtle, of degree rather than of substance in most areas.

Avoiding a Superpower Confrontation

The goal of avoiding conflict has been an imperative of Soviet policy in the Middle East; and if current actions vis-à-vis the United States seem to manifest greater self-confidence, the change is marginal. Indeed, Arab expectations and perceptions now incorporate a recognition of Soviet unwillingness to risk a superpower confrontation over the Middle East.[33]

In view of the importance of the Middle East in international politics, its increasing salience to the United States, and the larger and more potent Soviet presence, the need to reach some understanding with the United States on respective regional roles was evident at least by the late 1960s. This requirement coincided with the superpower détente and therefore became a part of it. The two great powers' attempts to ensure that they were not drawn into a nuclear conflict as an outgrowth of their involvement in the Middle East were viewed with considerable suspicion within the region. Because the United States flexed its muscles in Jordan in 1970 and was still deeply involved in Vietnam—a war that may have been unpopular around the world but that, if nothing else, demonstrated the willingness of the United States to take military action far from its own shores—Arab states continued to feel that the United States would back Israel, if necessary.[34] On the other hand, Soviet willingness to confront the United States on behalf of the Arabs was not credible. Thus, when the United States and the Soviet Union negotiated their regional roles during President Nixon's visit to Moscow in late May 1972, the common Arab view was that the two superpowers were perpetuating the "no peace, no war" status quo that left Israel occupying the West Bank, Jerusalem, the Golan Heights, and the Sinai. At least some of the Soviet problems in Egypt and elsewhere may be attributed to the force of this perception.[35]

Caught between the possible need to intervene and the constant demands to provide advanced military matériel—both of these necessary to maintain its role as the primary external Arab "friend"—and the more vital need to avoid a strategic confrontation with the United States, the Soviet leadership saw important potential advantages stemming from an Arab-Israeli settlement. Since the benefits were limited and the costs of settlement options varied,

Soviet support for settlement was limited. Still, the Soviet Union has supported the concept of Arab-Israeli settlement on a limited basis since at least the late 1960s. We believe this support is based to some extent upon the cost to the Soviet Union of the conflict, but primarily upon the fear of a superpower confrontation. This possibility appeared all the more realistic after the American alert of October 1973, which almost certainly took the Kremlin by surprise.

Minimizing Western Influence

Despite the end of the Cold War and the general relaxation of East-West tensions within Europe, the Soviet Union has continued to try to reduce the European presence and influence in the Middle East. At the same time, Soviet actions suggest a reluctant acceptance of some Western presence as a function of the historic interaction of Europe and the Middle East. The factors that give rise to this policy ambivalence are themselves conflicting.

First, the economic, social, political—and even military—actions of the major Middle East countries closest to the Soviet Union—Egypt, Iraq and Syria—in 1973–76 have reinforced Soviet fears that, given the choice, Arab peoples and governments prefer to deal with Western countries.[36] (In some respects, of course, Arab countries have no realistic alternative to turning to the Soviet Union or other socialist states. The barter terms of Soviet commercial agreements and economic assistance appear to be a clear-cut advantage to capital-poor Arab states,[37] while the political and military exigencies of the arms trade—including Western public opinion, spares availability, cost factors, and interchangeability potential, as well as the constraints resulting from current weapons inventory—foreordain a continued level of substantial Arab-Soviet interaction.)

Second, however, the magnitude of Arab international commercial, financial, political, military, and social needs far exceeds the Soviet capacity to provide resources. Moreover, the capital resources of the Middle East have recently grown as a consequence of the great increase in petroleum revenues. The Soviet leadership recognizes that its nation can no longer aspire to more than a marginal role in most economic relations in the Middle East. Its political and military resources are much greater than its economic resources, and allow a unique role that optimizes the impact of limited resources.

An additional ambivalence characterizes the Soviet view of the West, particularly in the Middle East. On the one hand, the West is no longer seen as a monolithic threat to the socialist commonwealth and no longer speaks with unity or uniformity on many issues. This evolution is especially evident on matters affecting the Middle East, because European governments see their immediate, vital interests affected by largely abstract policy statements. Under the circumstances, it would be truly surprising if they were to agree to the American view.[38] On the other hand, from a strategic point of view, Western Europe is still allied with the United States; and European influence in the Middle East must be considered as at least potentially hostile.

Broadening Relations

The channels through which the realization of Soviet objectives is sought have not changed appreciably. The movement away from intensive focus on several "progressive" states—an approach Communist ideologues worked assiduously to defend by means of complicated doctrinal rationalizations—and toward a less intensive and more broadly based presence throughout the region was well under way after the June War. Such barriers as arms procurement patterns and elite religious and sociological fears in the more backward Arab countries in the Arabian Peninsula, Persian Gulf, and North Africa tended to extend Soviet exclusion from a number of Arab countries.[39] However, when Soviet policy began to lean toward the development of at least cordial relations with all the regimes of the Middle East, some progress was achieved, although for reasons as diverse as the following:

the refusal of the United States to provide certain types of weapons systems;
the feared effects of the influx of Western technicians and their families on the
    social structure of conservative states;
Soviet willingness to provide arms and technology at low cost;
regional political rivalries.

This broadening of the Soviet Union's relations across the region, which we have described in more detail elsewhere,[40] was reinforced by the deterioration in Egyptian-Soviet relations following the death of Nasser in 1970. The Soviet investment in Egypt, economic as well as political, was as large as any Soviet involvement outside Eastern Europe. The decimation of the Soviet-oriented clique in Cairo, the expulsion of the Russian advisers in 1972, and the gradual elimination thereafter of the extraordinary privileges built up and enjoyed by the Soviet Union in Egypt probably were viewed in Moscow as further evidence against overcommitment. Although the radical reorientation of Egypt's external relations brought about an inevitable reallocation of investment priorities, it is unlikely that the Soviet Union will soon allow itself to become committed to any Middle East regime to the extent it was in Egypt. Thus, later Soviet attempts to expand relations with Jordan and to conclude a surface-to-air missile (SAM) agreement with the once-anathema Hussein regime were consistent with the more recent approach. Manifestly, the broadening of relations also allows for (and requires) considerably more flexibility.

Soviet Security

We have discussed the issue of Soviet security elsewhere.[41] No major developments took place after 1973 to further imperil security in the south from a military, naval, or air perspective.

So far as ground forces are concerned, strategically oriented American (and often Western) ground forces were present in sizable numbers only in Turkey. Although the number of American military and other advisory personnel in Iran and Saudi Arabia was on the increase,[42] these were almost exclusively military assistance personnel. As a NATO member, however, Turkey hosted a number of NATO and U.S. facilities with uniquely strategic missions.

Until the early 1970s, Soviet-Iranian relations had been improving for some years. However, about 1969–70 the United States began to provide, seemingly without question, virtually all the military equipment Iran requested. Apart from its unfortunate regional implications, the open-ended supply relationship cooled—at least temporarily—the growth in Soviet-Iranian cooperation, which largely stagnated from about 1970.

The Cyprus problem, meanwhile, continued to bedevil American-Turkish relations. Since U.S. bases in Turkey could be seen only as enemy facilities, the American-Turkish problems were very much in Moscow's interest and were greatly accelerated following the Cyprus conflict of 1975.

Soviet naval power in the Mediterranean grew substantially beginning in the mid-1960s but leveled off—except during crises—around 1973. The Soviet squadron in the Mediterranean is a large force, but is vastly inferior to Western naval forces there in both size and firepower. In addition, it is hostage to the Western forces, since its only lines of communication with the Black Sea or Pacific fleet are through narrow straits that can easily be closed by the West. Nevertheless, the growth of the Mediterranean Squadron and the fragility of the U.S.-Turkish relationship have slightly enhanced Soviet security.

Soviet Influence

Originally viewed in the Kremlin as a means to the end of increasing Soviet security, Russian influence in the Middle East has become an end in itself related to Soviet perceptions of their nation as a superpower of stature and power equal to the United States. Whatever the post-1972 change in Soviet rhetoric relating to the balance of global forces[43] may mean, it certainly is based on the view that the Soviet Union and the United States are preeminent powers of equal status.

That the Soviet Union has long manifested an "insecurity complex" concerning its stature as a great power has been widely noted. The United

States, seeking to exclude and then remove the Soviet Union from the Middle East[44]—an objective wholly incompatible with Soviet power, proximity,[45] and interest—contributed in no small way to this "complex." However, Soviet Middle East behavior in 1972–76 evidences greater confidence and less concern with image. We believe that the Soviets recognize the inevitability of their presence and influence in the Middle East now; indeed, we believe they may overestimate their staying power in a postsettlement environment.[46] So long as Soviet regional influence is assured, it will be a less powerful stimulus in policy. Once threatened, however, status will again become a key policy force.

Policy

A dominant theme in Soviet Middle East policy has been the avoidance of superpower conflict. As American spokesmen have frequently pointed out, a great power cannot let its desire to avoid confrontation deter it from taking all actions important to the realization of other goals.[47] This observation applies with equal force to the Soviet Union, which has been relatively active in the Middle East-North Africa region and has substantial economic and political investments to protect there.

Moreover, the factors impelling Moscow to avoid a confrontation with the United States are not limited to considerations of immediate military security. Mutual superpower perceptions and the relationship of these perceptions to détente are clearly relevant in this regard.

That the United States should continue to pursue a policy of détente is clearly in the interest of the Soviet Union, yet the Kremlin cannot sacrifice its many regional interests and strengths to this one end. The willingness to absorb specific tactical losses in order to preserve détente is manifest, but no great power can afford to subordinate every tactical opportunity to such vague, uncertain—however important—and perhaps ephemeral developments.

Since the principal Soviet need is to avoid a superpower conflict, and since the possibility of such a conflict arising from the Middle East is marginal except for the Arab-Israeli problem, we shall consider this arena of Soviet behavior first and in the greatest detail as a principal issue area of Soviet foreign policy.

Soviet policy regarding the Arab-Israeli conflict has involved a hierarchical sequence of three principles:

contain the problem and keep it from exploding;
control hostilities (and consult with the United States, where necessary) should they occur;
work toward a settlement.

Containment of the Arab-Israeli Problem

Containment of the primary regional powder keg, the Arab-Israeli conflict, is a difficult task for either of the superpowers because of the limited
number of participants to which their influence extends and the limited degree
of that influence. Before 1973, the Soviet Union and its East European allies
were virtually the sole military suppliers of Egypt, Iraq, and Syria,[48] while the
United States (and, to a lesser extent, its West European allies) filled the same
role for Israel and Jordan.[49] Thus, neither Moscow nor Washington was in a
position to influence the key antagonists on either side. After the October War,
the military supply picture changed only in degree and to the extent that Egypt
forsook its Soviet supply relationship—at least for a while—in favor of establishing military relations with Western suppliers. This major change could
prove to be quite significant in the long term, depending upon the success of
Egypt's search for arms in the West, the tenure of the Sadat regime, and the
progress made in settlement talks on Israel's northern and eastern fronts.

The attempt to control hostilities has taken several forms. Most promi-
nently, while Russian diplomats have not consistently supported specific peace
initiatives (any more than their American counterparts have), the Soviet Union
has counseled against war with what appears to be consistency.[50] A second and
perhaps more significant manifestation of the effort to keep the conflict from
erupting into full-scale hostilities has been the types of armaments sent by the
Soviet Union to its Arab clients. The third example is in the move toward
settlement, which is considered below.

We have little direct evidence of Soviet restraints on the Arabs concerning
recourse to war. Apart from undertakings made to U.S. officials in this regard,
we must look largely to Arab revelations, which usually are well after the fact,
and to American intelligence resources (to the extent that they are reflected
in the public statements of U.S. officials). The sum of evidence generally points
toward Soviet restraint. Certainly, it is the feeling of Arab elites that the Soviet
Union has counseled against war.[51]

Arms transfers from the Soviet Union to key Arab clients generally have
resulted in the provision of equipment that is advanced by regional standards
but one to two generations behind similar equipment provided to Israel.[52]
Contrary to many press reports, the Soviet Union has not sent its most advanced weaponry to Egypt, Iraq, and Syria. Even in the field of ground-based
air defense, the SAMs, air defense artillery, and associated equipment provided
to the Arabs do not encompass the full range of Soviet weapons systems.
Moreover, in other fields, such as aircraft, the export versions of jet combat
aircraft frequently are modified in important respects.[53] As the October War
made clear, another weapons area in which some control can be exercised is
ammunition, spare parts, and replacement equipment.

It should be noted that the approaches to conflict containment mentioned above are not intended to suggest that the Soviet Union will actually prevent Arab states from going to war, even if the capability to do so is available. Before the October War, the Soviet Union was warned by Egypt of a likely crisis with Israel, although Moscow was informed neither of the exact timing nor of the magnitude of the action.[54] Nevertheless, available reports do not indicate a serious effort to defuse the crisis. With the record to date, it appears that the Soviet Union will counsel in the future, as in the past, against recourse to war, but will not attempt to interfere with a firm Arab decision to begin hostilities.[55]

Control of Hostilities

There have been four Arab-Israeli wars—in 1948–49, 1956, 1967, and 1973. In the first of these, the Soviet Union can hardly be thought to have been involved, since apart from its diplomatic support for and recognition of Israel, and its role in multilateral peacekeeping efforts, its sole concrete activity was the sending of some arms (via Czechoslovakia) to the new Israeli state. Similarly, as a new actor in the area, the Soviet Union had little influence in or impact on the 1956 crisis.[56] Indeed, one might argue that the greatest impact of Soviet behavior in the Suez crisis was on the NATO allies in their relations with each other rather than on the Middle East actors or British or French policy.

In 1967 and 1973, U.S.-Soviet agreement was universally recognized to be a major prerequisite to achieving a cease-fire. Moreover, the magnitude[57] and duration of hostilities were directly affected by Soviet (and American) actions. In both conflicts, the initial outbreak of hostilities was followed almost immediately by efforts to impose a cease-fire.[58] The common ground of the superpowers in the early stages of Arab-Israeli wars seems generally to be very limited: both wish to see something of the course of the conflict before committing themselves to approaches that concede too much. Yet, both are intensely interested in avoiding a confrontation with each other. In October 1973, the United States and the Soviet Union maintained contact from a time soon after hostilities broke out. Although this contact was primarily concerned with the discovery of a possible basis for a cease-fire, it is reasonable to assume that both superpowers used the same (and other) channels to explore perceptions about their own roles and problems relative to the conflict. There seems to have been an early, tacit understanding that neither would take direct military action beyond resupplying its clients. Both powers seemed to accept the necessity of letting the battlefield dictate the political parameters within which a cease-fire agreement was to be constructed.[59]

Achievement of a Settlement

The final element of the Soviet approach to the Arab-Israeli problem is the search for a settlement. We believe this aspect of Soviet policy to be ambivalent and complex, subject not only to the interplay of various factions and interests in the Kremlin, but also to cyclical and self-limiting forces generated by trends within the Middle East.

Soviet policy regarding a Middle East settlement has stirred frequent debate in the United States. In academic circles, supporters of détente have tended to see the Soviet Union as favoring a settlement and acting reasonably and responsibly to bring about a resolution to the Arab-Israeli conflict, while those who see the Soviet Union in a more irrevocably hostile pose have generally stressed Soviet foot-dragging or, in some cases, reported Soviet impediments to the evolution of a settlement. Because of the secrecy surrounding details of Soviet diplomacy, academic experts can pick the facts that support their position and refute the opposition, disregarding contrasting points of view as unsubstantiated speculation. Interestingly, State Department officials' views seem to vacillate.

We do not feel this divergence and fluctuation are without meaning. They reflect the ambivalence inherent in Soviet policy. Our concept of the Kremlin's approach to an Arab-Israeli settlement could be diagrammed as shown below.

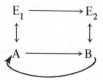

A is the Soviet policy manifesting a determination to achieve a settlement, B is Soviet policy manifesting resistance to settlement, E_1 is the regional environment at the same time as A, and E_2 is the regional environment a later time.

Since 1967, existing Arab states have had tangible objectives related to the Arab-Israeli conflict: the return of the occupied Golan Heights, West Bank, and Sinai. In addition, a resolution to the Palestinian problem has gained greater acceptance since the June War, as the parameters of realism have become narrower. Return of the occupied territories is a goal at the intergovernmental level, where the Soviet Union must deal. (By contrast, the subnational and transnational pressures of the Palestinian problem are less salient.) As Arnold Horelick and others have pointed out,[60] the occupied territories constitute an unprecedented problem for Soviet Middle East relations. Since their return is a sine qua non for settlement, and since settlement is probably a sine qua non of their return, the Soviet Union must move toward a settlement if it hopes to maintain close, cooperative relations with these countries. Put differently, if Moscow can't deliver, the Arabs will go elsewhere.

Under these circumstances, it is not surprising that the Soviet Union is disposed to make visible efforts toward settlement. However, as we have pointed out, the possibility of superpower conflict is a principal consideration of Soviet policy makers. Thus, also from the perspectives both of maintaining a détente relationship with the United States and of avoiding a conflict, the Soviet Union is inclined to favor and move toward the establishment of a settlement.

However, when there is a visible movement that suggests progress toward a general settlement in the Middle East, much of the activity involves the United States. Partly because the United States is the only state with potential leverage over Israel—the country that holds the tangible keys to peace (the occupied territories)—partly because the United States has chosen to follow a highly personal approach to its negotiations with Arab governments, and partly because the current Arab and Israeli leaders are inclined to improve their relations with the United States[61] and to place considerable faith in at least certain types of American undertakings, the United States has been the *primus inter pares* in superpower-led peace initiatives. Thus, as the process evolves, Soviet leaders increasingly see the possibility that a settlement may be achieved that gives only lip service (and, worse, lip service that is credible to no one) to Soviet participation;[62] that substantially improves the American position in bilateral relations with key Arab states;[63] and that creates conditions that appear to seriously threaten the major regional role the Soviet Union has come to play. As the shape of a settlement begins to become visible, the Soviet leadership is able to see more clearly its vulnerabilities to Western, and particularly American, economic, military, and political competition.[64] This mechanism is conducive to an increasing reticence to cooperate as a settlement nears, then to a positive attempt to block settlement.

These, then, are the tensions that drive Soviet foreign policy with regard to a Middle East settlement, a dilemma that at once causes and explains the ambivalence of Soviet policy.

Notwithstanding the foregoing—and indeed emerging from it—the contention of the authors is that the movement toward settlement has been the stronger of the two contradictory themes in Soviet policy toward the Arab-Israeli conflict since 1969–70, and more particularly since 1973. The dominance of the settlement motif is explained by the relative sense of Soviet security, based on the level of Soviet presence and activity across a number of countries and in diverse fields; by the primacy of the determination to avoid a superpower confrontation that might lead to nuclear war, especially after the tense period of late October 1973; to a lesser extent, by the related policy to preserve détente; and perhaps by the inability to see the contradiction between regional nationalism and the concept that Soviet influence will replace an inevitably eroding Western role.

Recent Soviet Policy on Settlement

Others have chronicled in more detail the fluctuation of Soviet settlement policy in the Middle East during the period from the War of Attrition (September 1968 to September 1970) to the October War and immediately following the 1973 hostilities.[65] We need not restate their accounts—which we suggest, however, should be placed in the framework sketched above.

The concrete aspects of the policy fluctuation described here take predictable forms. During periods in which the settlement objective dominates the Soviet approach, the Palestinians have been advised to articulate limited goals, the Syrians encouraged (and bribed) to be forthcoming and patient, the Iraqis and Libyans counseled at least to moderate or mute their criticism.[66] When progress toward a settlement begins to evoke clearer perceptions of Soviet costs, Iraqi irreconcilables are not discouraged, the Syrians are advised to be wary of U.S. and Israeli objectives—a warning Syria can hardly afford to take lightly—and Moscow's support for the Palestinians is given greater visibility and fewer conditions.[67]

When and to the extent that Soviet policy favors a settlement, as has been the case for most of the period since 1970, the form this settlement should take is similar in its essentials to the points made by Secretary of State William Rogers in 1969:

> a peace agreement between the parties . . . based on clear and stated intentions and a willingness to bring about basic changes in . . . attitudes and conditions;
> demilitarized zones and related security arrangements;
> changes in the pre-existing lines [that is, borders] . . . confined to insubstantial alterations required for mutual security;
> just settlement [of the Palestinian problem taking] into account the desires and aspirations of the refugees and the legitimate concerns of the governments in the area;
> Jerusalem . . . a unified city within which there would no longer be restrictions on the movement of persons and goods [and should be] roles for both Israel and Jordan in the civic, economic, and religious life of the city.[68]

The Rogers Plan is now viewed in the State Department as the height of shallow thinking and ingenuousness. It is considered to have been a serious error to publicly advance specific proposals, thereby alienating one or both sides and foreclosing later mediation. Indeed, many today question the realism of any policy that publicly places the United States in front of Israel in negotiation, thus opening the way for Israeli use of effective domestic American pressure to blunt the U.S. initiative. The post-Rogers Plan view (that the most effective role for outside powers lies in creating conditions for settlement and "encouraging" the parties to establish and discuss their own settlement policies) still dominates American policy.[69]

The Soviet Union, however, views the situation differently. Soviet diplomats have emphasized that their nation has never wavered from the area of agreement reached in 1969–71, that the Soviet Union still supports the principles and ideas on which the superpowers had seemed to reach an accord then.[70] They have expressed disappointment that the United States seems to have turned its back on the 1969–71 talks. Soviet diplomats in late 1975 stressed that they were even cooperating with U.S. step-by-step diplomacy, in the sense that they were not actively opposing it, although they had serious reservations concerning the Kissinger step-by-step approach.[71] That the Soviets have been periodically discomfited by their isolation from the center of the negotiation process while the United States took center stage has not been a secret.[72]

By the spring and summer of 1976, Syrian policy in the Lebanese conflict began to create additional pressures relevant to Soviet policy on an Arab-Israeli settlement. The virtual elimination of the Palestinians as an independent force in the conflict, taken together with the radical shift in Egyptian relations with the superpowers; the continued vacuum in Soviet relations with Israel, Jordan, Lebanon, and the Persian Gulf oil-producing states[73] (whose subsidies are important to the Arab confrontation states); and the uncertainty of Syrian inclinations have evoked concern in the Kremlin lest the Soviet position throughout the Middle East be endangered.[74] Thus, from June to September 1976, Moscow took various initiatives to support the Palestinians, and thereby Soviet relations with Iraq and Libya, with minimum risk to Syrian-Soviet relations.[75]

The events of 1976, then, suggest the necessity of reopening the basic question of what a settlement would mean to the Soviet position in the Middle East.

Resolution of the principal aspects of the Arab-Israeli conflict—territorial boundaries, peace treaties and recognition, Jerusalem, and the Palestinian problem—to the extent it reduces the threat of war that has been constant in the Middle East for almost three decades, will greatly diminish the role of the Soviet Union in the confrontation states. Unable to compete effectively with the West in technology and commerce,[76] and even less able to compete in cultural matters,[77] the Soviet Union has relied principally on economic and military assistance to effect and continue its presence.[78] While economic assistance will still be welcome, we think it likely that Syria in particular will reduce its arms procurement levels in order to increase economic and social development. Moreover, Syria will be able to diversify its weapons purchases and probably will take advantage of that opportunity.

This is not to say that the Soviet Union will be excluded from the region. In an area of such diversity, there will always be intraregional conflicts; and the parties to these conflicts will look outside the area for superpower support. We do feel, however, that a settlement would end the prospects of dominant Soviet influence in the Middle East for the foreseeable future.

Indeed, mediating conflicts or maintaining neutrality between feuding states that are the objects of its attention has been a major problem for the Soviet Union in the region, and will continue to be a principal constraint on the dominance of any external power.[79]

Because we believe that it is not in the Soviet regional interest to see the achievement of a settlement in the Middle East, we expect a rise in Soviet-supported resistance to such a settlement if and when its realization nears. In that event, the United States must be prepared not only to offer, or have offered, concrete and important "sweeteners" for the Syrians, but also to provide some global compensations to the Soviet Union for its perceived Middle East losses.

REGIONAL ENVIRONMENT

Since the June War, the subsystemic environment has undergone substantial qualitative and quantitative changes that clearly reflect, and are caused by, foreign and domestic policies of the major regional actors—Egypt, Iran, Iraq, Israel, Saudi Arabia, and Syria. These environmental changes can best be understood by delineating them into several broad categories: ideological, economic, and military.

Ideological Factors

In the early 1960s, when Egypt promulgated a series of socialist decrees, the ideological "mood" of the masses seemed to favor a socialist path to economic development. Being the most influential Arab state, Egypt could sway a substantial portion of the Arab masses to accept its version of socialism as the panacea of the Arab world's political, social, and economic problems.

In accepting the theoretical aspect of socialism, Egypt was joined by Syria and Iraq, whose governments used the socialist slogans as an effective means to legitimize their authority among the masses, who had been informed that "Arab socialism" was founded on the Islamic principles of brotherhood and help for the needy. Furthermore, in the mind of the Arab masses, the ideology of socialism was closely linked with the Soviet political and social system, a system these masses "admired" because of the scientific and social achievement it purported to have brought about in the Soviet Union within the brief period of 40–50 years.

Thus, it is fair to say that ideologically the Arab world was divided between those who accepted socialism as a model for economic and social changes and those who maintained that these changes must be induced by indigenous traditional values. This bifurcation of the eastern Arab world manifested itself in informal political blocs of the so-called radical and moderate Arab states. This inter-Arab rivalry began to take a physical form in the fighting over Yemen between 1962 and 1967; over Oman since 1964; over Jordan in 1970–71; and over Lebanon between 1974 and 1976. In the Yemen civil war, the iman's royalist forces were supported by Saudi Arabia and Jordan; his opponents, the republican forces, were aided by the presence of more than 40,000 Egyptian troops in the country. In Oman, the royalists are aided by Jordan, Iran, and Saudi Arabia; and the guerrillas are supported by Iraq, Libya, and the Soviet Union. In the Palestinian-Jordanian civil war in 1970–71, the Jordanian government was supported by Saudi Arabia, Kuwait, and Iran; the Palestinians, by Syria.

In the Lebanese civil war between the right-wing Phalangists and the coalition of the left-wing Palestinians and Lebanese, the 30,000 Syrian troops that were sent into Lebanon in June 1976, ostensibly to prevent partition of the country between the two factions, turned against the Palestinians and leftists, who apparently were winning military battles against the Phalangists. The Phalangists also were supported by Israel, which provided military aid and training for the Christian military and patrolled the Lebanese coast to prevent supplies from reaching the Palestinians. The Palestinians and the leftist Lebanese were aided by Iraq, Libya, and, to a limited extent, Egypt. Jordan supported the Syrian military intervention in Lebanon. Although Saudi Arabia had acquiesced to Syria's military intervention in Lebanon, Riyadh later expressed displeasure at the Syrian military's overzealousness in its operations against the Palestinians by suspending economic aid to Syria and withdrawing a Saudi military contingent that had been stationed in Syria for several years as a symbol of Saudi commitment to Syria's stand against Israel.

Although in the earlier inter-Arab conflicts the opponents played their roles more or less according to their respective ideologies—the monarchies supported the royalists and the republics aided the revolutionaries—in Lebanon the lines were not so clearly drawn. Here, a self-styled revolutionary regime aided the extreme rightist faction in the civil war! Although the Syrian military action against the leftists in Lebanon might be construed as contrary to the Ba'athist ideology, it clearly showed that the men at the helm of affairs in Damascus were adept at bending with the wind—the wind of conservatism that is gradually displacing the revolutionary forces in the area.

This trend toward conservatism, however, should not be taken as obscurantism on the part of the decision makers, who are pragmatic in their approach to development and international relations. Today the Arab world, though as divided as ever, is not ideologically bipolarized. It can no longer be separated into "radical" and "moderate" blocs. Today, the most salient Arab states—Egypt, Syria, Saudi Arabia, and Iraq—are governed by pragmatists and not by ideologues. Perhaps ideology was never a real issue in Arab politics

—it was more often than not used as a legitimizing instrument by the various regimes. Today ideology, especially the ideology of the left, is a discredited, almost useless, factor in the Arab world.

Economic Factors

If the Arab world is gradually moving toward pragmatism or conservatism, the primary force in this evolution is the fabulous oil wealth that is filling the coffers of oil-producing Arab states much faster than these states are capable of investing in their own economies. The sudden and dramatic increase of revenues of the oil-producing states is creating far-reaching attitudinal and economic changes in the area. The Middle Easterners seem more self-confident and more optimistic about their future than was the case before the October War (as a consequence of which the oil-producing states increased the price of oil). The new oil wealth of the Arabs and the Iranians, and their determination to cooperate within reasonable limits in the Organization of Petroleum Exporting Countries (OPEC) deliberations, have placed them among the financial leaders of the world. For the Arabs, this newly acquired status will produce favorable effects on their most salient international problem—the Arab-Israel conflict. Already, a number of European states and Japan are actively engaged in competition for the Arab markets and transfer of technology to the Arab states.

The two non-Arab Muslim states—Iran and Turkey—have moved closer to the Arab world. Iran has done so primarily because without close cooperation with the Arabs, especially Saudi Arabia, Tehran could not assure the high level of its oil income. And Turkey has done so because of its disillusionment with the United States for placing an arms embargo against Ankara after the 1974 Cyprus crisis. Turkey has begun to realize that Europe and North America no longer hold a monopoly on the surplus capital needed by the Turks for economic development projects. The Turks realize that some of their financial needs can be more easily met by such Arab states as Libya, Iraq, and Saudi Arabia, and to some extent by Iran. Thus, they see no reason to toe the U.S. line in Middle Eastern affairs.

Military Factors

Military cooperation among the Arab states and between them and non-Arab Muslim states of the Middle East has been steadily increasing since the June War. In this respect, Pakistan, and more recently Iran, have been selectively active in providing military training to Egypt, Syria, Jordan, Saudi Arabia, Abu Dhabi, Kuwait, and Oman.[80]

Before the October War, Iran transferred 80 Patton tanks, 12 F-105s, 14 helicopters, and a number of mobile radar units to Jordan. In August 1973, it was alleged that Iranian air units would be stationed at al-Mafraq air base in Jordan.[81]

During the October War, Iran airlifted medical supplies to Jordan and reportedly sent pilots and transport planes to Saudi Arabia for moving its combat troops to the front line on the Golan Heights. During this period more than 100 Iranian pilots were said to have participated in airlifting military equipment and personnel from Saudi Arabia to the front line states.[82]

Within the Arab world, military cooperation improved significantly between June 1967 and October 1973. Notwithstanding the political differences that divided them into separate ideological blocs, the Arab states showed remarkable unity during the October War. Although a similar spirit of military cooperation was manifested by the Arab states during the June War, the number of combat units contributed by the Arab states in 1967 was much smaller than their contribution in 1973, when nine Arab states provided over 50,000 ground troops and air units to Syria and Egypt. Troops and matériel were sent by Algeria, Iraq, Jordan, Morocco, Kuwait, Libya, Saudi Arabia, Sudan, and Tunisia. Suddenly and dramatically, the Iraqi-Syrian "ideological" dispute was buried; and the Kurdish revolt in Iraq was "suspended" with the help of the shah of Iran, who promised not to create border problems for Iraq while over 30,000 Iraqi troops, 400 tanks, and a squadron of jets were fighting on the Arab-Israeli front.

Since the end of the October War, the Arab states and Israel have escalated their arms race; both sides are acquiring modern and highly sophisticated weapons from a variety of foreign sources. As a result of the Soviet-Egyptian rift, the Egyptian military today is less well-armed than it was before the October War. The armed forces of other Arab states, especially Saudi Arabia, Kuwait, Syria, Iraq, and Jordan, are perhaps slightly better equipped than they were before the conflict. Israel, from all available accounts, is far superior in military terms today than it was on the eve of the October War, thanks to the generous financial and military aid provided by the United States since 1973.

NOTES

1. See U.S. Congress, Senate, Committee on Foreign Relations, *National Commitments*, Report 91–129, 91st Cong., 1st sess., 1969 (Washington, D.C.: U.S. Government Printing Office, 1969), pp. 50, 65–67.

2. John C. Campbell and Helen Caruso, *The West and the Middle East* (New York: Council on Foreign Relations, 1972); Harry N. Howard, "The United States and the Middle East," ch. 5 in Tareq Y. Ismael, ed., *The Middle East in World Politics: A Study in Contemporary International Relations* (Syracuse, N.Y.: Syracuse University Press, 1974); Robert Hunter, "The United

States in the Middle East," in Peter Mansfield, ed., *The Middle East: A Political and Economic Survey* (London: Oxford University Press, 1973), pp. 90–100; Amos A. Jordan, "Les États-Unis à la recherche d'une politique mediterranéenne," *Politique étrangère* 36, no. 5–6 (1971): 501–18; Marvin Kalb and Bernard Kalb, *Kissinger* (Boston: Little, Brown, 1974); Don Peretz, "The United States, the Arabs, and Israel: Peace Efforts of Kennedy, Johnson, and Nixon," *Annals of the American Academy of Political and Social Science* no. 401 (May 1972): 116–25; William R. Polk, *The United States and the Arab World*, rev. ed. (Cambridge, Mass.: Harvard University Press, 1969); Robert J. Pranger, *American Policy for Peace in the Middle East, 1969–1971: Problems of Principle, Maneuver and Time* (Washington, D.C.: American Enterprise Institute, 1971); William B. Quandt, "The Middle East Conflict in U.S. Strategy, 1970–1971," *Journal of Palestine Studies* 1 no. 1 (Autumn 1971): pp. 39–52; and "United States Policy in the Middle East: Constraints and Choices," in Paul Y. Hammond and Sidney S. Alexander, eds., *Political Dynamics in the Middle East*, (New York: American Elsevier, 1971), pp. 489–525; Barry Rubin, "U.S. Policy, January-October 1973," *Journal of Palestine Studies* 3, no. 2 (Winter 1974): 98–111; and John C. Campbell, "American Efforts for Peace," in Malcolm H. Kerr, ed., *The Elusive Peace in the Middle East* (Albany: State University of New York Press, 1975), pp. 249–310.

3. Kalb and Kalb, *Kissinger*, p. 466.

4. Cf. R. D. McLaurin and Mohammed Mughisuddin, *The Soviet Union and the Middle East* (Washington, D.C.: American Institutes for Research, 1974), p. 318.

5. See ibid., pp. 316–18.

6. Quandt, "The Middle East Conflict," p. 40; Stephens, "The Great Powers and the Middle East," *Journal of Palestine Studies* 2, no. 4 (Summer 1973): 79.

7. Stephens, "The Great Powers," p. 79.

8. Kalb and Kalb, *Kissinger*, pp. 471, 512.

9. Ibid., p. 471.

10. Polk, The United States, p. 316; "American Business in the Middle East and North Africa," remarks of Deputy Assistant Secretary of State Sidney Sober at a seminar sponsored by the Middle East Institute, May 14, 1976.

11. We are suggesting here only some of the conscious inputs. Equally—some believe more —important are bureaucratic politics, organizational process, biological-psychological effects of stress, and the like.

12. The directness of the transfer of Israeli perceptions into American attitudes is less clear and may be changing. See Godfrey Sperling, Jr., "Sympathy Ebbing in U.S. Congress for Israel's Position," *Christian Science Monitor,* February 24, 1975, pp. 1, 3. Also see Kenneth Rich, "Percy Works Hard to Explain Himself," Los Angeles *Times,* February 16, 1975, sec. S 1–A, pp. 4–5.

13. Alaeddin S. Hreib, *American Trade with the Arab World* (McLean, Va.: U.S. Middle East Service Ass., 1972).

14. See note 2. Several of these studies are unusually rich in detail.

15. See, for example, Leslie H. Gelb, "Arab Chiefs Send 2 to Washington to See Kissinger," New York *Times,* February 17, 1974, pp. 1, 2.

16. U.S. sales to Iran amount to a de facto determination to sell to the shah whatever he wishes. For an interesting analysis, see Michael Getler, "Long-term Impact of Arms Sales to Persian Gulf Questioned," Washington *Post,* January 30, 1975, pp. A–1, A–14.

17. U.S. Defense Security Assistance Agency, *Foreign Military Sales and Military Assistance Facts* (Data Management Division, Comptroller, DSAA, 1975), pp. 14–15.

18. Ibid., pp. 14–15, 24–25.

19. Ultimately, such a force may be the only way to establish a viable peace settlement in the Middle East. Some of the difficulties of an effort along these lines have been examined in Paul A. Jureidini, R. D. McLaurin, and Mohammed Mughisuddin, ed., *The Prospects for Joint U.S.-Soviet Peacekeeping in the Middle East: A Conference Report* (Kensington, Md.: American Institutes for Research, 1973). See Kalb and Kalb, *Kissinger,* pp. 489, 494, 512.

20. Kalb and Kalb, *Kissinger,* p. 471.

21. Hunter, "The United States," p. 93.

22. Ibid., p. 94.

23. McLaurin and Mughisuddin, *The Soviet Union and the Middle East,* esp. ch. 11.

24. See Rogers' statement before the Galaxy Conference on Adult Education, Washington, D.C., December 9, 1969. The most detailed analyses of the Rogers period are Campbell, "American Efforts for Peace"; Robert O. Freeman, *Soviet Policy Toward the Middle East Since 1970* (New York: Praeger, 1975); and Lawrence L. Whetten, *The Canal War: Four Power Conflict in the Middle East* (Cambridge, Mass.: MIT Press, 1974).

25. This characterization of Syrian policy patterns was concisely described by Nadav Safran in "Arab Politics, Peace and War," *Orbis* 18, no. 2 (Summer 1974): 377–401.

26. The "Palestinian spokesman" emerged in 1973 as the Palestine Liberation Organization (PLO), but by 1976 Syria was trying to end the independence of the PLO. See Paul A. Jureidini and William E. Hazen, *The Palestinian Movement in Politics* (Lexington, Mass.: D.C. Heath, 1976); Paul A. Jureidini, "The Abiding Threat of War," forthcoming article; Paul A. Jureidini and William E. Hazen, *Lebanon's Dissolution: Futures and Consequences* (Alexandria, Va.: Abbott Associates, 1976); and Fehmi Saddy, *The Eastern Front: Implications of the Syrian/Palestinian/Jordanian Entente and the Lebanese Civil War* (Alexandria, Va.: Abbott Associates, 1976). See Chapter 6 of this book.

27. Malcolm H. Kerr, ed., *The Elusive Peace in the Middle East,* p. 4.

28. Speech by Secretary of State Henry A. Kissinger before the Cincinnati Chamber of Commerce, September 16, 1975 (reprinted by U.S. Department of State, Bureau of Public Affairs), pp. 3–4.

29. Ibid.

30. Regarding the three principal elements that must make up any settlement, only on the Palestinian issue does the United States seem to have made a clear-cut movement. By 1975, U.S. spokesmen were even willing to agree with what many Arabs had long stated, that "The Palestinian dimension of the Arab-Israeli conflict is the heart of that conflict" (statement by Deputy Assistant Secretary of State Harold H. Saunders before a subcommittee of the Committee on International Relations, U.S. House of Representatives, November 12, 1975). Ironically, even as the United States seemed to be moving toward an accommodation with the PLO, the latter was coming under the pressure—and would succumb to the dominance—of Syria.

31. R. D. McLaurin, *The Middle East in Soviet Policy* (Lexington, Mass.: D.C. Heath, 1975), ch. 2.

32. Although McLaurin (ibid.) and Hannes Adomeit ("Soviet Policy in the Middle East: Problems of Analysis," *Soviet Studies* 27, no. 2 [April 1975]: 288–305) have pointed out that the "Russian historical interest" in the Middle East and Persian Gulf bears no resemblance to post-1955 interests, objectives, and activities, many analysts continue to perpetuate the notion of a grand historical design. Moreover, included in the latter group are those who should certainly know better, such as Abe Becker ("Oil and the Persian Gulf in Soviet Policy in the 1970s [RAND Corp., Santa Monica, Calif., December 1971]) and, surprisingly, Stephen Page, whose otherwise excellent book, *The U.S.S.R. and Arabia: The Development of Soviet Policies and Attitudes Towards the Countries of the Arabian Peninsula, 1955–1970* (London: Central Asian Research Centre, 1971), is a model of sound content analysis and historical research. Since the 1940 German-Soviet discussions continue to serve as a key element in those writers' conclusions about Russian historical ambitions, we shall remind the reader that it was the Germans, not the Russians, who proposed directing Soviet ambitions toward the Persian Gulf—for reasons that are, as Adomeit has pointed out, quite obvious.

33. See R. D. McLaurin, "The Soviet-American Strategic Balance: Arab Elite Views," forthcoming article; Mohamed Heikal, *The Road to Ramadan* (New York: Quadrangle, 1975), passim.

34. R. D. McLaurin, "Arab Perceptions of the Superpower Military Balance," paper presented at the International Studies Association annual meeting, Toronto, Canada, 1976. During the October War a variety of interventionist fears and scenarios were articulated in the Arab world. See William A. Rugh, "Arab Media and Politics During the October War," *Middle East Journal* 29, no. 3 (Summer 1975): 310–28. Heikal's *Road* is a source of endless and sometimes uniquely picturesque examples of Arab perceptions (as is his previous English-language book, *The Cairo Documents* [New York: Doubleday, 1973]).

35. See Heikal, *Road,* pp. 160–84, and the series of editorials written by Heikal in *Al-Ahram* in the summer of 1972 ("The State of No Peace and No War: Who Is Responsible?" June 16, p. 1; "The State of No Peace and No War: America's Role and Responsibility," June 23, p. 1; "The State of No Peace and No War . . . and the Soviet Union," June 30, p. 1; "The State of No Peace and No War . . . and Egypt," July 7, p. 1; "The State of No Peace and No War: Backgammon and Chess," July 14, p. 1; "The State of No Peace and No War: What Is To Be Done?" July 21, p. 1); and the entire issue of *An-Nahar Arab Report* 3, no. 30 (July 23, 1972).

36. See McLaurin and Mughisuddin, *The Soviet Union and the Middle East,* passim. Most observers familiar with the Middle East recognize Arab preference for interacting with the West.

37. There are some important disadvantages to accepting the barter agreements with the Soviet Union, including loss of traditional markets and Soviet reexport history. Developing countries with small foreign exchange resource bases generally have found bilaterally balanced barter agreements with the Soviet Union very attractive as a way of conducting trade. That capital influx greatly affects these perceptions is clear, as in Iraq.

38. See U.S. Congress, House, *United States-Europe Relations and the 1973 Middle East War,* hearings before the Subcommittee on Foreign Affairs, 93rd Cong., 1st and 2nd Sess., November 1, 1973, and February 19, 1974.

39. See Lilita Dzirkalis, "Present Soviet Policy Toward Third World States," paper presented at Southern California Arms Control and Disarmament Seminar, November 1971; and Jaan Pennar, *The U.S.S.R. and the Arabs: The Ideological Dimension* (New York: Crane, Russak, 1973).

40. McLaurin and Mughisuddin, *The Soviet Union,* pts. II and III.

41. McLaurin, *The Middle East,* passim.

42. Robert M. Brodkey and James Horgen, *Americans in the Gulf: Estimates and Projections of the Influx of American Nationals into the Persian Gulf, 1975–1980* (Washington, D.C.: American Institutes for Research, 1975).

43. See Leon Gouré, "Soviet Perceptions of the Strategic Balance in Relation to the Soviet Concept of the Correlation of World Forces," paper presented at Conference on Perceptions, RAND Corporation, Washington, D.C., April 21, 1976. The paper was presented on behalf of the Center for Advanced International Studies, University of Miami.

44. As late as 1972, Henry Kissinger, special assistant to the president for national security affairs, spoke of "expelling" the Soviet Union from Egypt.

45. Some argue that the Middle East is "pretty far away" from the Soviet Union (Herbert Dinerstein, in U.S. Congress, *United States-Europe Relations,* p. 9). However, as we have pointed out elsewhere:

> The borders of the U.S.S.R. are very close to the Mediterranean; the Black Sea coast of the U.S.S.R. is vulnerable to naval operations from the Mediterranean; more graphically, the oilfields of Baku are closer to Iraq's, the Persian Gulf's, and far closer to Iran's oilfields than Cairo is; and Cairo is closer to Soviet territory than it is to the capitals of the Sudan, Saudi Arabia, either Yemen, Oman, the Union of Arab Emirates, Qatar, Bahrain, or Iran, not to mention Libya or the rest of the Maghreb.

McLaurin, *The Middle East,* p. 15.

46. McLaurin and Mughisuddin, *The Soviet Union,* ch. 11.

47. For example, see the press conferences of Secretary of State Henry A. Kissinger, December 23, 1975, and February 4, 1976, as well as his address before the Commonwealth Club and the World Affairs Council of Northern California, San Francisco, February 3, 1976.

48. See McLaurin, *The Middle East,* pp. 109–11; and Jon Glassman, *Arms for the Arabs: The Soviet Union and War in the Middle East* (Baltimore: Johns Hopkins University Press, 1975), passim.

49. McLaurin, *The Middle East,* pp. 109–11.

50. Even such Cold War analysts as the Center for Advanced International Studies at the University of Miami point out that although "the Soviet Union affirmed the right of the Arabs to resort to 'other means,' this had not been matched by the advice Moscow gave its clients or the Soviet arms aid program." Foy D. Kohler et al., *The Soviet Union and the October 1973 Middle East War: The Implications for Detente* (Miami: Center for Advanced International Studies, University of Miami, 1974), p. 40.

51. See, for example, Mohammed Heikal, *The Road to Ramadan* and *The Cairo Documents.*

52. McLaurin and Mughisuddin, *The Soviet Union.*

53. However, it should not be supposed that conflict control is the only reason for restraint in providing equipment. Soviet military leaders are understandably concerned about the possibility that the most advanced Soviet military equipment might fall into American hands, thus compromising security considerations. The capture of SAM-6 systems intact by the Israelis will—or so it is widely presumed—lead to the development of effective electronic countermeasures much more rapidly than if their development had taken place without the Soviet systems.

54. To date, the best public record on this point is Heikal's *The Road to Ramadan.*

55. Soviet behavior in the June War is considerably more ambiguous than that of the October War. Most observers believe Soviet behavior in 1967 was characterized by a poor understanding of Israeli perceptions, expectations, and strategic policy, as well as by an exceedingly poor grasp of the limits of Soviet influence.

56. Some question whether the Suez conflict can legitimately be included among Arab-Israeli wars.

57. The record rates of expending equipment and ammunition necessitated the kind of supply and resupply practices actually used. These rates were only in part a function of strategic and tactical planning (such as in artillery and ground-based air defense); they also resulted from important weaknesses in support personnel and logistical systems that put many repairable vehicles out of combat. Another factor was training, both sides stressing heavy fire volume: the Arabs, to compensate for inadequate gunnery training; the Israelis, as a function of very good training.

58. After the October War, most American writers criticized the Soviet Union for being unresponsive to American calls for a cease-fire (see Kohler et al., *The Soviet Union,* p. 58). In this respect, American histories differ markedly from other accounts. Arab writers (and Egyptian President Anwar Sadat) have criticized the Soviet Union for having attempted to bring about, by ruse, a cease-fire from the very first day of the conflict. Moreover, it was commonplace during the war for American commentators to remark that the U.S. government was "in no rush" to establish a cease-fire, feeling that another resounding Israeli victory might hasten a better-founded peace and the reduction of Soviet influence.

59. At the same time, the Soviet Union did urge all Arab states to support Egypt and Syria. Some observers see this behavior as contradictory to "controlling hostilities." We disagree. The point of hostilities control is not to reduce the level of conflict, but to maintain some influence over it and, ultimately, to keep regional hostilities from leading to a superpower military confrontation. While no one was in a position to assess precisely the Arab-Israeli balance of forces, the Russians, through intimate involvement in the military programs of both Egypt and Syria, must surely have been aware of at least some vague outside limits on the capabilities of the two principal Arab antagonists to sustain offensive military operations. Consequently, Moscow was well aware that initial victories would not—could not—lead to an effective military invasion of Israel proper.

Without direct Soviet involvement or any real threat to the existence of Israel—a threat that, in any event, exceeded Egyptian and Syrian objectives—the United States was not likely to intervene. If additional Arab states heeded the Soviet call to assist Egypt and Syria, their contributions (even those of Jordan and Iraq) could only marginally affect the ultimate outcome of the hostilities. Thus, the costs of such a course of action to the Soviet Union were minimal. The benefits were somewhat greater, since the Soviet appeal was further evidence of support for the Arab cause and could only be contrasted with American behavior, which appeared to support the Arab enemy.

60. Arnold Horelick, "Soviet Policy in the Middle East," in Paul Y. Hammond and Sidney S. Alexander, eds., *Political Dynamics in the Middle East* (New York: American Elsevier, 1972), p. 600.

61. R. D. McLaurin and Mohammed Mughisuddin, *Cooperation and Conflict: Egyptian, Iraqi, and Syrian Objectives and U.S. Policy* (Washington, D.C.: American Institutes for Research, 1975).

62. "Half-Way Meeting," *An-Nahar Arab Report* 6, no. 6 (February 10, 1975): 1.

63. "Soviet Apprehensions," *An-Nahar Arab Report* 5, no. 4 (January 28, 1974): 2–3.

64. McLaurin and Mughisuddin, *The Soviet Union*, ch. 11.

65. See, for example, Lawrence L. Whetten, *The Canal War: Four-Power Conflict in the Middle East* (Cambridge: MIT Press, 1974), pp. 1–232; and Robert O. Freedman, *Soviet Policy Toward the Middle East Since 1970,* passim.

66. "Kremlin Briefs Arafat on Its Mideast Peace Plans," *Christian Science Monitor,* April 29, 1975, p. 4; Joseph Fitchett, "Soviets Reported Urging Arafat to Adopt Peaceful Procedures," *Washington Post,* December 11, 1974, p. A–15; Marilyn Berger, "Russians Shift on Mideast," ibid., November 26, 1974, p. A–12.

67. "Soviet Conditions," *An-Nahar Arab Report* 5, no. 17 (April 29, 1974): 1; "Soviet Reservations," idem., no. 21 (May 27, 1974): 2. Also see idem., no. 23 (June 10, 1974): 1–2; no. 28 (July 15, 1974): 1; and no. 48 (December 2, 1974): 3.

68. Statement of U.S. Secretary of State William P. Rogers before the Galaxy Conference on Adult Education, Washington, D.C., December 1969.

69. This State Department view was asserted in strong terms to one of the authors by several senior officials in December 1975.

70. R. D. McLaurin, memorandum of conversation, December 3, 1975. Participants: Mr. Tarasienko, Soviet embassy; Mr. Vikulov, Soviet embassy; Mr. Semakis, Department of State; R. D. McLaurin, Abbott Associates. (Hereinafter, McLaurin memo.) This memcon is on file at the Alexandra, Va., Office of Abbott Associates. Also see "A Slow Process," *An-Nahar Arab Report* 6, no. 21 (May 26, 1975): 2–3.

71. McLaurin memo. Also see Marilyn Berger, "Gromyko, Kissinger Confer," *Washington Post,* February 18, 1975, p. A–11.

72. McLaurin memo.

73. The Soviet Union has consequently tried to improve relations with Jordan, most recently through an attempt to sell Soviet SAMs to that country after the initial breakdown in Jordanian-U.S. negotiations aimed at establishing Hawk missile sites in Jordan. Similarly, there were several Soviet efforts to sell or give military equipment to Lebanon from 1970 to 1975. The Soviet Union moved to establish at least under-the-table relations with Israel in 1975 ("Renewed Contacts," *An-Nahar Arab Report* 4, no. 17 [April 28, 1975]: 2–4), a development that continued more openly into 1976 (Don Oberdorfer, "Russians Talk with Israelis," *Washington Post,* May 27, 1976, p. A–1; Bernard Gwertzman, "Soviet-Israel Talks Held by Envoys in Washington," *New York Times,* May 24, 1975, p. 1). Some preliminary steps were made toward improving contacts, and establishing relations, with Saudi Arabia (Dev Murarka, "How Moscow Is Countering Sadat's Tilt toward the U.S.," *Christian Science Monitor,* June 4, 1975, p. 15) and other traditional Persian Gulf states (R. D. McLaurin, "Soviet Policy in the Persian Gulf," in Mohammed Mughisuddin, ed., *Conflict and Cooperation in the Persian Gulf* [New York: Praeger, forthcoming]).

74. "Soviet Apprehensions," *An-Nahar Arab Report* 5, no. 4 (January 28, 1974): 2–3.

75. "Revision of Strategy," *An-Nahar Arab Report* 5, no. 28 (July 15, 1974): 1–2; "Anti-U.S. Front," ibid. no. 32 (August 12, 1974): 1; "Rewards of Success," ibid. no. 48 (December 2, 1974): 3; "One More Time," ibid. 6, no. 6 (February 10, 1975): 2; Dana Adams Schmidt, "Kremlin Tries New Tactics in Tug of War over Syria," *Christian Science Monitor,* June 1, 1976, p. 1; Christopher S. Wren, "Setback for Soviet," New York *Times,* June 12, 1976, p. 5; John K. Cooley, "Soviets Held Unwilling to Estrange Syrians," Washington *Post,* July 16, 1976, p. A–8.

76. McLaurin and Mughisuddin, *The Soviet Union,* ch. 5.

77. McLaurin, *The Middle East,* ch. 7.

78. Ibid., chs, 5 and 6; Glassman, *Arms for the Arabs,* passim.

79. "The Soviet Dilemma," *An-Nahar Arab Report* 7, no. 15 (April 12, 1976): "Backgrounder"; Cooley, "Soviets Held Unwilling ."

80. Mohammed Mughisuddin and James Horgen, *Regional Military Cooperation in the Middle East: 1970–1975* (Washington, D.C.: American Institutes for Research, 1975). Turkey and Pakistan also provided military training to Libyan officers. See Juan de Onis, "Iran and Turkey Widen Arab Support," New York *Times,* January 20, 1975, p. 4.

81. Voice of Palestine [clandestine], April 3, 1973—FBIS, April 4, 1973, p. D-1; Baghdad INA, August 2, 1973—FBIS, August 7, 1973, p. D-1; Radio Jerusalem—FBIS, January 10, 1975, p. N-3; Jim Hoagland, "Iran Gives U.S. Jets to Jordan," Washington *Post,* January 8, 1975, p. A-1.

82. R. K. Ramazani, "Emerging Patterns of Regional Relations in Iranian Foreign Policy," *Orbis* 18, no. 4 (Winter 1975): 1059; Damascus, MENA to Cairo, November 22, 1973—FBIS, November 23, 1973, p. E-4.

3

EGYPTIAN FOREIGN POLICY

EGYPTIAN POLICY ENVIRONMENT

Like any other society faced by the challenges of modernization and industrialization, the Egyptian society, though racially and linguistically homogeneous, is divided into a variety of ideological, class, professional, religious, and ethnic segments, each seeking to protect, as well as to promote, its vested interests. The existence of this division has been recognized by the Egyptian constitution, which prescribes representation of the workers, farmers, intelligentsia, soldiers, and the "national capitalists" in the People's Assembly (the country's legislative body) as well as in the Arab Socialist Union (ASU), the sole political organization permitted to function in the country. Having recognized this division, the constitution goes on to state that "social solidarity" is the basis of society. In other words, it is an ideal and a goal that the constitution urges the Egyptian policy makers to achieve by means of reconciling ideological, class, and other salient divisions that may exist in the country. Thus, the Egyptian policy makers must make decisions in an environment that assumes the existence of social conflict. In addition to the interest groups recognized by the constitution, there are others that, although not given the same merit, play an important role in the decision-making process of the country. It is evident that the Egyptian decision makers, whose responsibility it is to try to synthesize the often conflicting interests of the competing groups in the country, face a highly challenging task whose success under the existing circumstances cannot always be guaranteed.

The nonrecognized groups include the bureaucracy, the *ulama,* and the newly formed *minbars* that are supposed to reflect the ideological views of the Egyptian left, right, and center. Most, if not all, of these groups are theoretically subsumed under one or another of the interest units recognized by the constitution. In practice, however, the nonrecognized affiliations endeavor to articulate their respective interests as separate units rather than as components of such categories as the intelligentsia or workers. For example, it would be difficult to place the *ulama* in the category of intelligentsia, peasants, workers, or soldiers. Under the Egyptian system recognized by the constitution, the *ulama* fall in the category of intelligentsia, which also subsumes leftist and socialist writers and revolutionaries whose perceptions of Egyptian interests and goals are inherently opposed to that of the *ulama*. Traditionally and educationally, the *ulama* is a conservative force committed to maintaining traditional religious values in the country. Thus, neither the *ulama* or the leftists intellectuals are content with the coexistence imposed on them by the constitution. Therefore, each group, seeking ways and means to advance and consolidate its interests, is involved in political activities at the various levels of the Egyptian decision-making system.

Similarly, the military, which is recognized as a separate interest group, has many internal factions based on personality conflicts as well as on differences of opinion concerning military tactics and strategy and the sources of weapons acquisitions. This means that no single group of military men can confidently claim to speak for the armed forces. Therefore, the dissident groups endeavor to seek independent methods of influencing the decision-making process of the country. These methods have included threats and attempted use of violence as well as public airing of differences. Although newspaper reports occasionally indicate the existence of military groups that are allegedly pro-Soviet Union, pro-America, pro-Libya, or pro-Iraq, it would be counterproductive to classify them as such. These military groups are composed of young Egyptian nationalists who grew up during the era of Nasserite fervor for Arab unity, Arab pride, and Arab manifest destiny. The so-called pro-Soviet or pro-American military officers are in reality pro-Egypt. They would like to acquire weapons from one superpower or the other in an effort to achieve an Egyptian goal of recovering the lost Arab territories and to become a preponderant military power in the Middle East.

Although the Egyptian constitution continues to recognize the military as a salient interest group whose views must be considered by the country's decision makers, President Sadat has endeavored to limit its role primarily to the territorial defense of the country, claiming that he wants to end the era of a "revolutionary legitimacy" and inaugurate an era of "constitutional legitimacy" in the country. Sadat has tried to change the armed forces from an ideological group that had been considered a defender of the "socialist gains" to a nonideological force answerable to the constitutionally legitimate government of the country. In other words. Sadat believes that the armed forces ought to owe their allegiance to the constitution and not to a particular model of national development.[1]

Before proceeding further, we would like to point out that neither the constitutional recognition of the salient groups in Egypt nor the existence of informal but highly influential groups in the country should be construed to mean that the country maintains a multiparty system under the umbrella of the ASU. We should remember that terms such as "interest groups" are being used here to facilitate our understanding of the decision-making system, which did not come into existence through evolution and tradition but was imposed from above. These interest groups have not yet crystallized into cohesive and cogent classes capable of clearly defining and articulating their interests. The role of interest articulation rests with a handful of persons who have limited access to their constituents. These constituents, furthermore, do not always readily associate themselves with the interest groups to which they are officially assigned.

Neither the awareness of the existence of the interest groups nor the knowledge that these groups are recognized by the constitution, nor that they interact in certain ways, can provide a clear picture of the Egyptian policy environments unless we supplement our knowledge through a discussion of the degree of freedom afforded these groups to pursue their perceived interests, the degree of political and economic freedom enjoyed by the population, the degree of freedom allowed to the media, and the degree of respect and support commanded by the government.

It would not be inaccurate to say that the freedom of most of these groups is limited to expressing their views within the context of ASU's charter. Even the three *minbars* (platforms), created after a long and often bitter debate initiated by the conservatives, who sought a return to a multiparty system, do not enjoy a significant degree of autonomy outside the ASU. Although the creation of these *minbars* was meant to alleviate the leftist and rightist pressures on the government and to give an illusion of freedom of association, opposition groups have not found the political climate conducive to open challenge of the government's foreign and domestic policies. Consequently, the opposition groups—the Nasserites, the Communists, and the groups connected with a former editor of *Al-Ahram,* Mohammed Heikal, and Hatem Sadeq; the organization of Kemaluddin Rifaat and Abdul Karim Ahmad; a group linked with Ali Sabri and Farid Abdul Karim; and several student organizations at the universities of Ain Sham, Alexandria, Cairo, and Assiout —have been engaged in covert activities designed both to weaken the government and to create a leftist unity in the country.[2]

It is significant that although a popular plebiscite had approved the formation of several "forums" within the ASU, President Sadat's opposition to this concept, based on his and the country's disillusioning experience with a multi-party system, caused him to refer the matter to a select committee for further study and recommendations. As a result of the deliberations by this committee, composed of representatives of all shades of opinion, it was recommended that the forums be limited to three. The Committee on the Future of Political Action in Egypt reportedly arrived at the following conclusions: that the Egyptian people accept the principle of the alliance of the forces of working people and the formula of representation that gives the workers and the peasants at least 50 percent of the seats in every elected body in the country; that public opinion in the country had been moving away from the idea of forming too many new political parties and groups; and that public opinion should be crystallized around platforms. In March 1975, the ASU Central Committee accepted the recommendations of the Committee on the Future of Political Action and adopted a resolution calling for the creation of three platforms representing three "ideological" blocs within the ASU.[3]

The *minbar* (the Arabic word for the lectern used by the *imam* in the mosque) of the left is headed by Khaled Mohieddin, one of the original members of the 1952 coup that ousted King Farouk. The center *minbar* is headed by Abou Wafia, President Sadat's brother-in-law, and Mamdough Salem, the prime minister. This group reflects the orthodoxy of the government.

The *minbar* of the right is headed by Mustapha Kamal Mourad, who had been one of the junior officers of the coup group. He has since been the foremost administrator of the public sector of the economy, and favors more of a free enterprise system.

In conjunction with these changes, and to provide a channel of communications between the leadership of each *minbar* and its adherents, the government has "assigned" two newspapers and a weekly to these three platforms. *Al-Akhbar al-Youm* is identified with the right; *Al-Ahram* with the center; and the weekly *Rose al-Youssef* with the left *minbar.*[4]

In terms of freedom of expression and freedom to know, the Egyptian press is more limited in the area of foreign relations than it is in domestic affairs. After decades of censorship during the monarchy and the Nasser regime, the Egyptian press was given "full" freedom by President Sadat. This freedom, however, in reality is "unlimited" in domestic affairs and "limited" in foreign affairs. Within the realm of domestic politics, the Egyptian press has been allowed to express opposing views even on such sacred subjects as Nasser and the one-party system, and favorable views on a multiparty system, monarchy, aristocrats, and the Communist party.

In the field of foreign affairs, however, the Egyptian press is restricted to expressing favorable-to-neutral opinion on the administration's major foreign policy. In this field, the press usually expresses the administration's views. If, however, an independent and strong-willed editor—a Heikal, for example— dares to oppose the government's foreign policy, he is promptly removed from his position of influence. Only the Egyptian government can, and does, use the media for expounding its views on the country's foreign-policy. Interest groups have little means of conveying their foreign-policy views to the public. They may, through their elected representatives, express their views in the ASU or the People's Assembly; but they have little chance to make them known in the media, particularly when those views are opposed to that of the government. This, however, should not be construed to imply that the Egyptian government can or does ignore views of important interest groups or individuals in the country. Rather, it means that the government, for both domestic and external policy reasons, wants to give the impression of unity in foreign policy. In terms of foreign-policy goals, this impression of unity would not necessarily be a distorted one.

Hardly any Egyptian groups or individuals of consequence differ significantly with the foreign-policy goals of the government: the recovery of Arab lands from Israel, the settlement of the Palestinian issue, Arab unity, and neutralism in the East-West conflict. Admittedly, a dissonance between the government and certain interest groups exists in the selection of appropriate means to achieve the foreign-policy goals, but there are very few disagreements on the state's foreign-policy goals. For example, several generals of the Egyptian military have opposed President Sadat's heavy reliance on U.S. diplomacy in resolving the Arab-Israeli conflict. This opposition is based not on ideological but on strategic considerations that clearly argue against closing the Russian armament door before obtaining either a peace settlement or another source of sophisticated weapons. Similarly, certain groups might be involved in a mutual struggle to affect Egyptian relations with regional powers—for example, Saudi Arabia vs. Libya, and Iraq vs. Syria.

In conclusion, it may be stated that several interest groups actively participate in the Egyptian decision-making process and that the bureaucratic and political elites are duly responsive to significant demands of these groups.

Linguistically, religiously, and ethnically, Egypt is a relatively homogeneous society. More than 98 percent of the population speak Arabic; the rest speak Nubian or Berber. About 90 percent of the population are adherents of Sunni Islam; the remaining are divided among a variety of Christian churches, the native Coptic Church being predominant.[5] Although a handful of Jews still live in Egypt, they do not play a significant role in the country. Generally, the relationship between the Copts and the Muslims has been cordial, although occasional friction and even violent clashes have taken place. These clashes, however, have not been as intense or serious as, say, the Kurdish-Arab conflict in Iraq or the friction between the Alawits and the Sunnis in Syria.

Economically and socially, Egypt is not as homogeneous as it is linguistically and ethnically. Although the official line denies the existence of a class struggle in the country, at least two Egyptian leftist intellectuals analyze their society from a Marxist perspective that sees the country engaged in an "inevitable" class struggle between the proletariat and the bourgeoisie.[6] In an effort to create social cohesion and to alleviate economic disparity between the superrich and the wretchedly poor, the Nasser administration instituted a series of reform laws that, although denying the existence of a class struggle, called for a redistribution of the national wealth through minimum and maximum wages, social security benefits, profit sharing with workers, and nationalization of all major means of production, distribution, transportation, and international trade and commerce.

Nasser had hoped that through these methods, which he called Arab Socialism, Egypt, while industrializing and modernizing its economy, would avoid the class and social conflicts that arise in the process of redistribution of national wealth and political power. Nasser realized that without domestic peace and social cohesion, Egypt would not be able to meet the challenges posed by industrialization. It was this desire for social cohesion that strengthened Nasser's and Sadat's determination to prohibit a multiparty system in the country. This system, in the prerevolutionary period, was held directly responsible for governmental instability and the consequent failure of a parliamentary system. Thus, the Egyptian leaders have sought to create and maintain social cohesion by means of consensus, theoretically reached through discussions and compromises between competing groups represented in the ASU.

Although the utility of this concept (consensus, *ijma*) as a method of making laws in Egypt cannot be readily ascertained, it is evident that, because of its close association with the Islamic law, it is more acceptable to most Egyptians than a purely Western political way of making laws.[7] The Egyptian government has endeavored to make this connection between consensus and the Islamic law clear to the populace, thus winning their approval of the system.[8]

Although many anti-government demonstrations by students and workers have taken place since the late 1960s, the Egyptian government seemingly commands the respect and popular support of the people. As a result of the October War, which evidently restored the self-respect and confidence of the people, the Egyptian government has further consolidated its control of the country and has received more popular support than previously considered possible. It should, however, be noted that this support is primarily for President Sadat as the leader credited with the success of the Egyptian military in the initial stages of the war. Since he has become the focus of public support as well as criticism, the future stability and course of action of the Egyptian government will depend on the success or failure of his current policies. If he fails and loses his legitimacy and support, the Egyptian governmental system might undergo a radical change in both substance and personnel.

Structure of the Government

Egypt is governed by a republican form of government, with executive powers concentrated in the presidency (see Figure 1). He is the commander-in-chief of the armed forces as well as commander of the national police force —in other words, he controls the state's monopoly of coercive power. In

FIGURE 1

Structure of the Egyptian Government

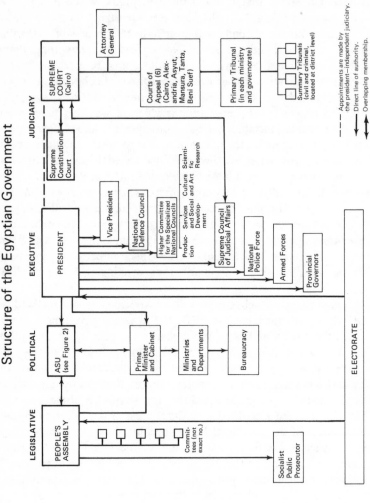

Source: Constitution of the Arab Republic of Egypt.

48

formulating and implementing the state's policies, the president is assisted by the Council of Ministers, which he appoints, under a prime minister. The Council of Ministers, including the prime minister, is confirmed by the People's Assembly. The president is nominated for a six-year term by a two-thirds vote of the People's Assembly and confirmed by a national plebiscite in which he must receive an absolute majority of the votes of those participating. He may be reelected for a second term.[9]

The Egyptian constitution provides for an independent judicial system with four tiers: summary tribunals, primary tribunals, courts of appeal, and the Supreme Court. In addition, there is the autonomous Supreme Constitutional Court, with jurisdiction over matters relating to the constitutionality of new laws and bills.[10]

The legislative branch of the Egyptian governmental structure is headed by the People's Assembly, whose members are directly elected through general elections and secret ballot. Although it is not specifically prescribed in the constitution, the ASU has traditionally controlled the nomination and election of Assembly members, all of whom have been "active" members of the ASU. The constitution requires that the People's Assembly must have at least 350 members, 50 percent of whom must be workers and peasants. The Assembly is elected for a term of five years. Although it is empowered to approve or reject the state's general budget, it cannot amend the draft budget except with the approval of the government.[11]

The People's Assembly has a number of permanent and *ad hoc* working committees that hold hearings on matters pending before the Assembly. Based on the discussions of the issues with suitable spokesmen, the committees make their recommendations to the Assembly, which then takes appropriate action. The task of implementing the decisions of the Assembly, the Cabinet, and other top decision-making bodies, such as the National Defense Council and the Specialized National Councils, is assigned to the various ministries and departments of the central government. The People's Assembly supervises the activities of the public prosecutor, who is responsible "for taking measures guaranteeing the rights of the people, insuring the safety of the society and its political system, safeguarding socialist gains, and enforcing socialist conduct."[12] The armed forces, in addition to their traditional role of defense, also are assigned the task of protecting the socialist gains of the people's struggle.[13]

Although the 1971 constitution had provided for the creation of Specialized National Councils, these councils did not come into being until June 1974, when a republic decree brought them into existence and defined their powers and their relationship to other organs of the government. These councils are for production and economic affairs; services and social development; culture, arts, literature, and information; and education, scientific research, and technology.[14] The Higher Committee for the Specialized National Councils has the task of coordinating the activities of these councils and of preparing reports on studies, proposals, and recommendations made by the councils. With the help of these studies, reports, and recommendations, the Egyptian government draws up stable, long-term national policies and plans. In coordination with the Higher Committee, these councils also have been empowered to assess the work accomplished by, and approve the annual plans of action of, the departments and ministries. The president is obliged to chair the annual meetings scheduled to adopt and recommend policies and plans for the country.[15]

OPERATION OF THE EGYPTIAN POLITICAL SYSTEM: INTEREST GROUPS

The Arab Socialist Union

As indicated earlier, the Arab Socialist Union (ASU) is the sole political party sanctioned under the Egyptian constitution. Although Article 55 of the constitution permits Egyptian citizens to form societies within limits of the law, the scope of their political activities is practically nonexistent, because only the ASU is entitled to act politically. In other words, a politically active group must keep its activities within the prescribed limits and the organizational structure of the party that is said to represent the "alliance" of the peasants, workers, soldiers, intelligentsia, and national capitalists; the peasants and workers are entitled to at least 50 percent of the membership in all the organizations of the ASU. In 1971, the ASU was reported to have approximately 6 million members.[16]

In 1976, after a long and bitter debate between the rightists, who favored a return to a multiparty system, and the leftists, who supported a single-party system, President Sadat created three ideological platforms (*minbars*) within the ASU. Although some people might interpret this event as a first step toward establishing a multiparty system in Egypt, the political activities of these *minbars* have been too insignificant and restricted for one to make a categorical statement.

The ASU consists of a National Congress of 1,700 delegates elected by the people (see Figure 2). The Congress elects a 150-member Central Committee, which in turn elects the 11-man Higher Executive Committee. The Central Committee is divided into functional subcommittees that draw up and, theoretically, direct the country's domestic and foreign policies.[17] Both Nasser and Sadat have held key positions in the ASU: chairmanship of the Union, chairmanship of the National Congress, and chairmanship of the Higher Executive Committee. Other key positions, such as secretary-general of the National Congress and chairman of the Central Committee and of functional subcommittees, are often, if not always, held by close associates of the president.[18]

FIGURE 2

ASU Organizational Chart

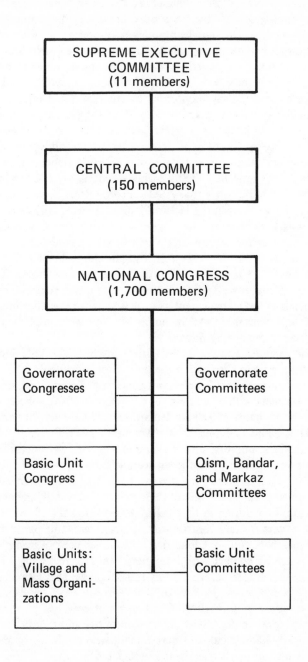

Source: Charter of the Arab Socialist Union.

Although we are not certain about the degree and effectiveness of control these subcommittees exert over the bureaucracy in its routine work, it is evident that they play a significant role in resolution of social conflict by reconciliation and compromise and in eliminating the opposition from positions of responsibility. Purges of prominent but "undesirable" members of the ASU take place in these subcommittees, whose recommendations for disciplinary action are almost always confirmed by the National Congress. After the May 1971 affair (an abortive attempt by Sadat's opponents to force him out of office), the ASU was reorganized by Sadat, who also ordered new elections for the political party. These steps allowed him to consolidate his hold on the country's popular organization by eliminating his opponents from key positions in the ASU hierarchy. The following examples are cited to indicate the degree and scope of influence that ASU subcommittees exert in Egyptian life. In August 1971, workers at the Helwan Iron and Steel Works went on strike, causing serious dislocation in the production schedule of this industrial complex. After suppressing the striking workers, who demanded better working conditions, Sadat asked the ASU to investigate the labor union, the management, and the ASU basic unit committee at the Helwan Works. The recommendations of the investigating committee involved disciplinary actions against officials of the management as well as those of the labor union and the ASU basic unit committee. All recommendations were implemented by the executive branch headed by Sadat.[19]

Another manifestation of Sadat's firm control of the ASU and the party subcommittees' role in eliminating the opposition was the expulsion from the party of 89 prominent middle-echelon leaders, for alleged "deviationism" and for having contacts with foreigners. The key figure of the subcommittee was reported to be Mohammed Osman Ismail, an anti-Communist rural landlord who served as Sadat's adviser for parliamentary affairs.[20] During this purge, several journalists, authors, film makers, and actors were deprived of their membership in the ASU. All of them were known for their "leftist-Communist" leanings. Half of those purged were in the field of communications. This meant, for most of them, the loss of their jobs, because ASU membership was a prerequisite for working in that field. Despite Heikal's efforts to protect a number of writers for and contributors to *Al-Ahram*, this paper lost at least eight staff members and contributors who were accused of being "deviationists" and of having contact with foreigners. Jim Hoagland suggests that one reason *Al-Ahram* was so severely hit by the purge was that Osman Ismail and Heikal were in conflict on the issue of Sadat's expulsion of the Russian technicians and advisers in July 1972. The two reportedly had clashed during a debate on the issue in an ASU Central Committee meeting in August 1972. Heikal allegedly had ridiculed Osman Ismail, who retaliated by purging several of Heikal's journalist friends and associates.[21]

The organizational network of the ASU extends in pyramid fashion throughout the country, with the Executive Committee its apex and the basic units at the bottom of the configuration. Between the two extremes are, from the top: the Central Committee, the National Congress, the governorate and district committees, and the basic units (located in factories, communities, and villages).

Because the top leadership of the ASU—the People's Assembly and the executive branch, including the Council of Ministers—overlaps, there are visible signs of meaningful cooperation between the political party and the executive and the legislative branches. It would not be uncommon to see the Executive Committee of the ASU, which has as its members Cabinet ministers and key legislators, make a statement of goals that would later be adopted as a government policy to be implemented by the bureaucracy. Also, a Cabinet decision might as easily be accepted and adopted by the ASU Executive Committee or the Central Committee, which might then advise its political and administrative machinery to disseminate the information for a "popular" response to the government's policy.

This, however, should not be construed to imply that the ASU is a vanguard for recruiting top political leadership of the executive branch. R. H. Dekmejian's study shows that of the 131 ministers who served in the Cabinet between 1952 and 1968, only three held positions in the political organization prior to becoming ministers, while more than 80 held a party position either during or after their term as minister.[22] Thus, we tend to agree with the statement that describes Egyptian political alliances as "personal," "ad hoc," and "lacking in solemn commitment to the movement of the party." This system has appropriately been called a "collaboration" movement that conceptually rests on the "principle of power concentration and dispersion." It allows concentration of power at the national level and permits subnational leaders residual powers dealing primarily with local and community affairs. This prevents the subnational leader from building a national image and from challenging the top echelon.

This cooperation, however, does not seem to extend fully to either the subnational level or to the various levels of the national and provincial bureaucracies, which tend to show resentment toward "outside" interference in their work. This resentment is usually expressed in the form of delays and obstacles to the carrying out of orders from above. Realizing the existence of this rift between the party functionaries and the middle-to-upper level echelons of the bureaucracy, the ASU and its predecessors, the National Union and the Freedom Rally, have endeavored to enlist the sympathies and cooperation of key civilian bureaucrats at these levels; the ASU has placed an increasing number of these bureaucrats in significant positions in the party hierarchy.[23]

The Military

Although the ASU claims to represent the peasants, the workers, the intelligentsia, and the soldiers, the party's relationship with the armed forces has not been delineated. The armed forces generally have been represented in the ASU hierarchy by retired officers, who have defended their constituents against attacks by the leftists. Although the task of defining the ASU-military relationship was assigned to the Executive Committee of the party, the committee was unable to reconcile the differences between those who wanted to radicalize and politicize the armed forces and those who opposed such an indoctrination on the ground that it would alienate the officer corps, hurt their morale, and thus weaken and divide the forces into mutually hostile ideological groups.

After the June War and the subsequent relaxing of the press laws, the Egyptian military came under heavy public criticism led by the leftist elements in the ASU. This group, which had been in favor of opening the military ranks to ASU recruitment, urged the government and the military hierarchy to eliminate the "exclusiveness" of the officers corps and to find effective methods by which links could be forged between the armed forces and the proposed popular defense army. It was a leftist conviction that without devising and implementing such a program for the armed forces, the country would not be able to resist foreign aggression and to recover the lost territory and prestige.

Initially, both Nasser and the military high command resisted these pressures, but finally they had to concede some ground to the critics of the armed forces. The student demonstrations in favor of creating a popular defense army and the Israeli attack on electrical installations in 1968 forced Nasser to approve creation of a popular defense army. In January 1969, he set up a committee, composed of three ex-officers—Foreign Minister Mahmud Riyad, Interior Minister Sharawi Jomaa, and National Guidance Minister Muhammad Faiq—with the task of finding effective means to strengthen the ties between the popular forces, as represented by the ASU, and the armed forces. This committee reportedly met with high-ranking officers of the armed forces and elicited their views on the issue. As a result of these discussions and, more important, as a consequence of the 1967 defeat, the armed forces started a program of self-reform that emphasized, among other things, "the need for cohesion in each fighting unit between officers and men, and the imperativeness of ideological unity."[24] Despite this declaration of intent on the part of the armed forces, the military ranks were not allowed to be an overt target of ASU indoctrination. The committee, having failed to find an acceptable solution to the problem of how to represent the armed forces in the ASU, again left the issue to the discretion of the party's Executive Committee, which has not yet, to the best of our knowledge, given its verdict.

The *Ulama*

At an international conference on the modern history of Egypt, held at the London School of Economics in 1965, an Egyptian professor at the American University of Cairo, Afaf Loutfi el-Sayed, said: "Once nationalism replaced the overall concept of the Muslim community as the focus of loyalties, the political influence of religion waned. When the modern Muslim relegated religion to the realm of the spiritual, and admitted that society could be ruled by a civil code of law, his dependence on the *ulama* as other than religious teachers disappeared, and their influence on him in matters other than religion disappeared likewise."[25]

We must agree with the above statement and concede that the Egyptian *ulama* no longer occupy the prestigious position they held in the era of the *sharia* courts, which for 1,300 years governed every aspect of Muslim social life and which, after the introduction of civil courts, functioned side by side with them until January 1, 1956, when all courts were centralized in the civil courts.[26] Granted that their official functions have substantially diminished, that they no longer are called upon to express their opinion on legislation, and that they have lost administrative and financial control over the *awkaf* (endowments) that had provided them financial security and independence from governmental control, the *ulama* nevertheless remain among the most influential opinion makers in the country.

In contrast with other groups that interact on more or less equal ground —that is, none assumes to be morally superior to the others—the *ulama* assume moral and philosophical superiority over all other groups; and, being religious scholars, their members project the image of being the most faithful practitioners of the Islamic tenets. What makes their role unique? Basically, their knowledge and practice of the principles of Islam places them in the center of the Muslim-Arab society whose behavior and social conduct continues to be regulated by Islamic principles. Therefore, despite a decline in their official position, the *ulama* continue to receive respect and even veneration from the Muslim masses whose lives have not yet been deeply affected by the modernization process. Even some "modernized" Muslims show deep respect to the *ulama.*

For the twentieth-century Western man, who has learned to analytically compartmentalize his activities into religious, personal, community, state and other affairs, this description of the role of the *ulama* might seem antiquated and unworthy of serious analysis and discussion. For millions of Muslims in the Middle East, however, the *ulama* are still an important part of their social, religious, and even political life. A key reason for this behavior is that the Muslims have not accepted the "artificial" division between the religious and secular activities of either the individual or such corporate entities as the state.

Since the advent of Islam in the seventh century and the *ulama's* subsequent attainment of a central role in the Muslim society, the *ulama's* political and religious significance has been recognized by all local and foreign powers interested in the world of Islam. Because of their unique role in the society, the *ulama* have customarily been respected by the rulers; on occasion they have been a target of the ruler's wrath; but the *ulama* have never been completely ignored or eliminated from a position of influence in the society. Historically, the degree of the *ulama's* influence on the masses and the government has occasionally changed, depending on the political and economic circumstances of the country. The *ulama* often were able to shield the masses against a ruthless ruler by warning the ruler that his actions were un-Islamic and, therefore, could be construed to free the population from the oath of allegiance—and thus deprive him of the legitimacy to rule. This powerful instrument was used only in extreme cases. The strong ruler who manifested obeisance to the religious traditions used the *ulama* either to legitimize his actions vis-à-vis the community or to help him rule the people, for in a society dominated by religion and tradition, the moral influence of the *ulama* was great and their right to participate in matters of government recognized.

It seems that after a few years of keeping a low profile in the social and political affairs of the country, the Egyptian *ulama* are again endeavoring to take a more active role in keeping the country on "the right path." A recent curb on the drinking of alcohol, Al-Azhar University's restrictions on Western dress for its faculty, and the reported reemergence of the Muslim Brotherhood are only the most obvious indications of the "return of Islam" in Egypt and other Middle Eastern states.[27]

ISSUE AREAS

In addition to the interest groups discussed above, which seem to divide the society vertically, there are several significant "issue areas" that cut across these interest groups horizontally and cause shifts in alignments and alliances of Egyptian elites and their constituents. Since most interest groups tend to be rather amorphous, the intensity of competition appears less emotional and personal than it is in the struggle between the exponents of the various issues confronting the country. Political, ideological, and economic issues tend to generate more emotional support than such formless interest groups as the intelligentsia, workers, and peasants. A particular political issue, such as Palestine, elicits wider and more demonstrative support than almost any aspect of the interests of workers and peasants, the two groups that are officially assigned 50 percent of the seats in the People's Assembly and the ASU. Similarly, the intelligentsia is not an ideologically cohesive group; thus, its members tend to show deeper commitments to significant national issues than to their own amorphous interests.

The task of identifying certain groups of people with issue areas over an extended period of time is rendered more difficult when we observe interest contradictions in the political behavior of Egyptian individuals and groups participating in the system. For example, an educated Egyptian may simultaneously be an exponent of rapid economic development, a supporter of the Qaddafi variety of Islam, an advocate of closer ties with the Soviet Union and the socialist world, an opponent of Communist ideology, an anti-imperialist, a proponent of Arab unity, and a champion of a secular state in Palestine. Although some scholars have recognized the futility of dividing the Egyptian and Arab populations into neatly defined groups of leftists, rightists, and moderates, others continue to discuss the Middle East regimes and publics in these terms.[28]

Since the Egyptians, along with other Arabs, have been so incessantly preoccupied with the problem of Palestine and Israel, it becomes doubly difficult to separate the "true believer" from the pragmatist—especially in the politico-ideological field, an area of concern that has a direct bearing on the problems of Palestine and the Israeli-occupied Arab territories; on Egyptian relations with the Soviet Union, the United States, the regional actors, and Europe; and on a host of related issues confronting Egypt.

As far as the territorial issues are concerned, there is unanimity among the Egyptians: they are firmly committed to a complete recovery of the Arab lands occupied by Israel since 1967. This unanimity, however, does not extend to the means of achieving this goal. Nor is there a consensus on such questions as should Egypt concentrate its energy on recovering the Sinai first? should Cairo insist on a simultaneous withdrawal from the Sinai and the Golan Heights? what about the West Bank and Jerusalem? should Jerusalem be internationalized?

These questions have not only created domestic dissension in Egypt but also have caused an occasional deterioration of its relations with Syria, Libya, Jordan, Iraq, and the Palestine Liberation Organization (PLO). Neither the charismatic Nasser nor the pragmatic Sadat has been able to create a domestic or a regional unity on these issues, which have remained the most agonizing concern of the Egyptian people and their policy makers. These and the related issues of economic development, military expenditure, and regional and systemic alliances have given birth to several ideological movements that claim to offer panaceas for the country's social, economic, and political problems. Since the late 1940s, Egyptians have been attracted to such ideologically opposed movements as the Muslim Brotherhood, communism, Arab socialism, and pan-Arabism.

Although it is obvious that none of these movements, ideologies, or approaches could possibly have resolved the country's complex domestic and foreign policy issues, Arab socialism and pan-Arabism alone must bear full responsibility for the pathetic failure of the government's policies, because these were the only movements that had been officially encouraged, sanctioned, and chosen by the government, especially under Nasser. Other significant movements with their own strategies and methods for achieving the country's domestic and foreign-policy goals were not allowed to function as legitimate organizations within Egypt's political system. For example, the Communist party of Egypt, which never won the respectability of being a legitimate political party, was forced to dissolve itself "voluntarily" in the 1960s. Similarly, the Muslim Brotherhood was proscribed in December 1954, following an abortive attempt on Nasser's life, allegedly by a member of this organization. The considerable popularity of the Brotherhood at the grass-roots level and its opposition to the military junta during the incipient stage of the military regime caused Nasser to use repressive measures against its leadership and cadre. Despite its trials and tribulations under the Nasser regime, however, the Brotherhood, with the help of its sympathizers in the military, in the bureaucracy, and among the college students, managed to survive Nasser's death. Although a ban against the organization still exists, the Brotherhood leaders and its sympathizers have fared better under Sadat. Faced by a strong challenge from the pro-Soviet faction of the regime, which was led by Vice-President Ali Sabri, Sadat, after assuming power on October 15, 1970, released scores of members of the outlawed Muslim Brotherhood who, in return, provided the president with substantial support during a critical period of his struggle against a coalition of personal and ideological foes.[29]

Sadat's behavior toward the Brotherhood was not an isolated action, but part of an orchestrated program that he wished to implement. This program called for a substantial change in the economic and political orientations of the country and in its foreign policy. Having realized that the ideology of Arab socialism and pan-Arabism has not achieved its stated domestic objectives and that it often has proved to be counterproductive in the country's foreign affairs, Sadat began to introduce modifications into the policies formulated by Nasser. For example, his approach to Arab unity is based on coordination of action and on reaching a consensus through consultation. There are no implied threats in Sadat's plea for Arab unity, as had often been the case during the Nasser regime. Similarly, Sadat has introduced tangible changes into the economic system of the country. Being a pragmatist, he no longer seems to subscribe to the proposition that socialism is the panacea for Egypt's economic and social maladies. Also, in respect to relations with Israel, the pragmatic Sadat has shown much more flexibility in Egyptian willingness to reach a peaceful solution to the Arab-Israeli conflict than had been the case with most Arab leaders since the beginning of the dispute. His willingness to recognize Israel as an independent state, provided the Jewish state gives up "every inch" of Arab territory, is clearly a significant departure from the course adopted by President Nasser.[30]

Since the June War, the recovery of the Arab territory under Israeli occupation has been an undying goal of most Egyptians and Arabs. Nasser was firm about this, and Sadat has reiterated this goal time and again. There is, however, one major difference between Nasser's and Sadat's policies vis-à-vis the occupied territories: Before he would agree to enter into negotiations with Israel, Nasser wanted a prior commitment that all Arab territories would be evacuated by the Israelis; he also was unwilling to make concessionary statements to assuage Israeli apprehensions about Arab designs on the Zionist state. Sadat modified Egyptian policy by declaring his willingness to recognize Israel's existence as an independent state if Tel Aviv would return "every inch" of UAR territory captured in the June War. In addition, he offered to enter into negotiation for Israel's "right to passage" through the Strait of Tiran and the Gulf of Aqaba, provided Israel settled the Palestinian refugee problem.[31]

While pursuing his diplomatic efforts to recover the Sinai and to find an amicable solution to the refugee problem, Sadat endeavored to strengthen the Egyptian armed forces, on which he would later depend to achieve a partial success in forcing Israel to withdraw from a small portion of the Sinai along the eastern bank of the Suez Canal. Through his own foreign minister, King Hussein of Jordan, President Yahya Khan of Pakistan, and other mutually friendly diplomatic channels available to him, Sadat let the Nixon administration know that Cairo would be prepared to settle the Arab-Israeli conflict by peaceful means, provided Egypt would not be asked to "surrender one inch of our land. . . ."[32] Sadat had come to realize that only the United States had the power to exert sufficient pressure on Tel Aviv to obtain a reasonable degree of flexibility in the negotiating stance of the Israeli government. Although his military options were still available to him, he initially tried to resolve the dispute without resorting to force.

Despite Sadat's plea and a warning that failure to resolve the dispute by peaceful means would inevitably constrain Egypt to use force, the Nixon administration was unable to get Israel to the negotiating table. Having exhausted his diplomatic efforts in Washington, Sadat moved to strengthen Egypt's military ties with Syria, Libya, Sudan, and Algeria. Realizing that these military arrangements alone would not suffice to meet the country's strategic and economic needs, he endeavored to enlist the economic and moral support of King Faisal of Saudi Arabia and other Arab oil-producing states of the Persian Gulf. In the initial stages of planning for the October War, Sadat was unsuccessful in obtaining a Saudi commitment that oil would be used as a weapon against Israel's supporters. Saudi Arabia, though committed to providing financial assistance for Egypt to acquire modern weapons, was reluctant to accept the principle of using oil as a weapon in international diplomacy.

Because of this disagreement, Egyptian relations with Saudi Arabia were beginning to cool at the end of 1972. In view of this and other considerations, Egyptian Prime Minister Aziz Sidqi visited several Arab states on the Persian

Gulf, endeavoring to counter the Saudi stance on oil diplomacy.[33] The Saudi-Egyptian disagreement was, however, quickly "resolved" when Saudi Arabia failed to obtain "preferred access" to the American energy market in return for assured Saudi oil supply to the United States. Angered by the Nixon administration's refusal to accept a special bilateral arrangement with Riyadh, Saudi Arabia abandoned the idea of maintaining a superficial separation between oil and political affairs.[34] By the middle of 1973, it was apparent that the Saudi government had made a change in its long-standing oil policy and that it was using all available means of communication to let the major oil comsumers know about the change.[35]

Before Egypt and Syria launched a coordinated attack on the Israeli forces in the Sinai Peninsula and Golan Heights in October 1973, Sadat was successful in creating a united Arab front against Israel. Although this strategic unity provided him with political, military, and economic support for the execution of the war, he paid an onerous price for this ephemeral cooperation. Before, during, and after the October War, Sadat was under intense pressure from his allies to make ideological changes in Egypt's domestic and foreign policies. For example, Saudi Arabia sought the expulsion of the Soviet advisers and technicians, suggested the abolition of certain of the socialist decrees issued by Nasser in the early 1960s, and asked for firm guarantees of its future investments in the country. Although Sadat's decision to expel the Soviet military advisers cannot be attributed solely to Saudi pressure, there is no doubt that King Faisal's profound and abiding distrust of the Soviet Union and communism played a significant role in this Egyptian decision, especially since the Saudi monarch was reported to have offered substantial financial aid for converting the Egyptian armed forces to Western European arms.[36]

Similarly, Sadat came under pressure from President Qaddafi of Libya for an immediate union between Egypt and Libya. This was the price Libya asked for providing military and economic aid to Sadat during a future conflict with Israel. For several domestic and regional reasons, Sadat was reluctant to accept Qaddafi's proposal for an immediate union. Domestically, it would have been impossible for him to reconcile the social and political views of the salient Egyptian elites with those of the Libyans; the former are a mix of various contemporary and traditional ideas, and the latter are derived from an ideology based on pristine Islam. Another factor that caused Sadat to hesitate to fully endorse the Libyan proposal for an immediate union was that the Libyan president was perceived to be a "militant" and a "radical" leader who firmly rejected the idea of coexistence between the Arabs and the Zionist state and who supported radical movements against the conservative regimes in the Middle East. On both counts, Sadat found himself in disagreement with Qaddafi. Sadat had already indicated his willingness to recognize Israel within its pre-1967 boundaries, and he was opposed to fomenting discontent and social disorder in the Middle East, especially in those monarchies—Saudi Arabia,

Iran, Kuwait, and the Persian Gulf emirates—that were financing his economic development and military plans. On the regional level, the choice before him was between Saudi Arabia and Iran, on the one hand, and Libya, on the other. Sadat, who wished to keep all his options open for an optimal use of the resources available, chose a compromise solution of a "phased union" with Libya. Thus, during the October War, Egypt received military and economic aid from a variety of ideologically diverse Arab states.[37]

In addition to the political and ideological pressures discussed above, Sadat was faced with several tactical and strategic disagreements with Syria that had to be ironed out before the October War.[38] Although most of these disagreements were finally resolved by the two heads of state, often arbitrarily and against the advice of their respective counselors, there are no indications that Hafez Assad and Anwar Sadat either discussed or reached an agreement on a method by which they would coordinate their postwar policies and behaviors. Consequently, such significant questions as the legitimacy and necessity of signing separate military and political agreements with the adversary were not spelled out. In the post-October War period, this lack of clarification caused a serious rift between the two wartime allies that had not been healed by September 1976.

This military coordination with Syria and diplomatic coordination with other Arab states rendered Sadat's foreign policy less flexible than it seemed to be in 1970–71. After the October War, Sadat could no longer afford to talk about merely recovering "every inch" of territory taken from the UAR in 1967. As the senior partner in the Syrian-Egyptian military alliance, Sadat was expected to insist on a concurrent recovery of the Sinai Peninsula, the Golan Heights, and, in the post-Rabat period,* the West Bank of the Jordan for the Palestinians. These expectations, however, were not made operational in the postwar period because they were beyond Egypt's military and economic capabilities. Militarily, Egypt could not force Israel to withdraw either from the West Bank or from the Golan Heights. Economically, it could not afford to reject a partial withdrawal of the Israeli forces from Sinai, which would return its oil fields along and in the Gulf of Suez to Egypt. Under these circumstances, it was prudent for Sadat to accept what he could get through the good offices of Secretary of State Kissinger. As a nationalist Egyptian leader, it was incumbent upon him to place Egyptian state interests above the perceived interests of the Syrians and the Palestinians.

---

*This refers to the Seventh Arab Summit Conference held in Rabat during October 26–29, 1974. The summit confirmed, among other things, that the PLO was the sole legitimate representative of the Palestinian people and that any part of the West Bank recovered from Israel would be given to the PLO.

His failure to place the Egyptian interests at par with the interests of Syria and the Palestinians brought Sadat under heavy attack from several Arab capitals and Palestinian organizations. For a while after the second Sinai agreement of September 1975, Egypt appeared to be isolated in the Arab world, for in contrast with the Syrian behavior toward Israel, that of Egypt seemed soft and compromising. The four major Palestinian groups—the Popular Front for the Liberation of Palestine (PFLP), the Popular Front for the Liberation of Palestine-General Command (PFLP-GC), the Arab Liberation Front (ALF), and the Palestinian Revolutionary Front for the Liberation of Palestine (PRFLP)—and the governments of Iraq and Libya formed the "rejection front" that sought to discredit Sadat's foreign policy. Domestically, opposition to his policy came from the Sabri-Mohieddin group as well as from individuals such as Mohammed Heikal, the former editor-in-chief of the influential *Al-Ahram,* and the little-known leader of an obscure Egyptian student group, Saleh Abdullah Sareya, whose activities in Egypt allegedly were financed by Libya.[39]

The "radical" groups and countries in the Middle East were not the only ones to oppose Sadat's policy of "compromises," as reflected in the Sinai II agreement, which failed to make any reference to Israeli withdrawal from the Golan Heights or any mention of the need to resolve the Palestinian problem.[40] Egypt remained diplomatically isolated in the Arab world until June 1976, when Syria, pursuing its own national interest, committed military forces against the Palestinians in Lebanon. Suddenly Syria, the "uncompromising" champion of the PLO, notably of Yassir Arafat, became a vulnerable target of wrath of the major Palestinian organizations (one notable exception being the Syrian-sponsored al-Sa'iqa) and their supporters. This situation provided Sadat with a breathing period during which he succeeded in mending fences with the PLO. The Lebanese civil war that still raged in early October 1976 diverted the Arab world's attention from Egypt and its "compromises" to Syria and its "cooperation," directly with the United States and indirectly with Israel, in the Lebanese civil war.[41]

Economic Development

As in the case of territorial issues, so in the context of the issues pertaining to economic development, the Egyptians, like most peoples of the Third World, are in complete agreement on the necessity and urgency of raising the standard of living of the masses through rapid industrialization. The disagreements here, as in many other areas, stem from the opposing methods proffered by the proponents of various models of economic development: the Russian model, the Chinese model, the mixed model, the capitalist model, and the Arab socialist model. Beginning with the socialist decrees of 1961, the Egyptian government embarked on a number of large-scale development plans financed entirely by the public sector: it promulgated new laws and regulations designed to narrow the income gap between the top and bottom income brackets by establishing a maximum-minimum income scale for all private and public income earners in the country; put into effect a profit-sharing plan for most profit-making industries; and placed worker-leaders on the management boards of the nationalized industries. These and similar measures evidently satisfied the demands of the workers and trade unions and that of some socialist elements in the country who had been urging the government to institute reforms in these and other areas.

Although they moved Egypt toward a state-capitalist economy, these steps did not completely satisfy the proponents of the Soviet model of development and alienated the private capitalists, who found it increasingly difficult to sustain growth under new laws and regulations. Despite the dissatisfaction expressed by the opponents of the Egyptian government's economic and industrial policies, the country showed a sustained growth in the industrial sector —an impressive annual rate of 16 percent during the 1960s. As the country progressively moved toward establishing a series of heavy and medium industries, the direct contribution of the state to industrial finance, in the form of new investments, grew from E£83 million (December 1957-June 1960) to E£ 516.5 million (July 1960-June 1965). The June War forced the Egyptian government to divert a larger portion of public funds to the military sector, thereby reducing its direct contribution to the industrial sector to E£507.2 million between June 1965 and June 1970.[42] Despite the difficulties faced by Egypt in attracting large-scale foreign investment from the Western industrial states, there has not been, and probably will not be, any significant departure from the heavy reliance on the public sector in the country's development planning. Both the Transition Plan (July 1, 1974-December 31, 1975) and the Ten-Year Plan (January 1, 1973-December 31, 1982) clearly show that the public sector will continue to dominate the country's economic development planning. During that period, private investment probably will not total more than 10–15 percent of a total investment of E£8,400 million ($19.2 billion).[43]

In an effort to stimulate foreign investments, the Sadat government announced a new code that gives special guarantees to Arab and other foreign investors against expropriation and take-over, facilitates the import of machinery and equipment required for projects, permits the repatriation of a portion of the profits, and establishes industrial and financial free zones in certain parts of the country. These and other "liberal" actions elicited both favorable and critical comments from domestic and foreign opponents of these measures. In an effort to discredit the government for its "liberal" policies, Sadat's critics charged that the new laws, designed to attract foreign capital, were aimed at eradicating the socialist gains achieved during Nasser's regime. Leading Egyptian leftists, such as Lewis Awad and Lutfi Kholi, who are alleged to have encouraged student demonstrations against the government, were leading critics of President Sadat's new policies. Kamal Chatilla, secretary-general of the Union of the People's Working Forces, Lebanon's largest Nasserite organization, expressed public displeasure at the appearance of anti-Nasser articles in the government-controlled Egyptian press.[44] The General Federation of Egyptian Workers was reported to have issued a statement condemning Sadat's reforms, but the censor allegedly suppressed it.[45]

In an effort to persuade its critics that the policies being followed were not only not anti-Nasser but were, in fact, a continuation of Nasser's policies, the Egyptian government issued statements designed to show its continuous adherence to the principles of Egyptian socialism as envisaged by Nasser. In this connection, President Sadat met with Kamal Chatilla and other prominent Nasserites, and personally assured them of his determination to keep Egypt on the development path set by Nasser.[46]

The Soviet Union, with which Sadat's relations have been less than cordial since he ousted the Russian advisers in July 1972, also was reported to have expressed anxiety about the introduction of foreign private capital into the Egyptian economy. Such capital, the Soviets feared, would weaken the Egyptian public sector which had been expanding with the help of Soviet credits since the mid-1960s. Abdel Aziz Higazi, deputy premier and minister of economy, denying the reports that under the new laws the public sector would retreat in favor of the private sector, endeavored to reassure Moscow that foreign private capital would work in harmony with the Egyptian economic plans designed to achieve socialism in the country.[47] In an address to the People's Assembly, Higazi said that there was no contradiction between permitting foreign capital investments and socialist ideology, because the country's socialist system recognized various types of capital ownership—public ownership, private ownership, and the investment of foreign capital in the form of aid, loans, or direct investments.[48]

Related to the problems of industrialization and development are education and training programs for the country's youth. These issues in turn are linked with the country's ideological orientations, perceived needs, relationships with foreign powers capable of meeting its educational and technological requirements, and many other tangible and intangible factors. Although educational reform has not recently surfaced as a major national issue, the country's high school and university students have often participated in street demonstrations supporting or opposing the government's economic, educational, and foreign policies. Egyptian disagreements in this area occasionally have surfaced in the form of student riots and of public debates between the exponents of various schools of thought on education and training of the country's youth for the military and civilian services.

Since this and other issue areas are substantially linked with larger political and economic factors, the debate on these subjects usually assumes ideological and political coloration. Even student demands for educational reforms often have divided the students into ideological groups—usually identified as the leftist, rightist, and moderate groups. These groups are supported by powerful nonuniversity groups, individuals, and, in some cases, by foreign governments. In the early days of the Sadat administration, when the leftists were still considered a viable threat to the new president's authority, his private secretary, Ashraf Marwan, was reported to have been active in establishing a secret student organization as a counter force to the leftist student organization in the country. Concurrently, Mohammed Osman Ismail, assistant secretary of the ASU, was reported to be involved in the formation of a secret rightist student body, members of which were given military training in Libya.[49]

The leftist student groups were linked with such national leaders as Ali Sabri and Khaled Mohieddin, and with the leftist press. Since the Egyptian students are highly politicized and their intragroup struggles often manifest ideological motivations and foreign support, one may ask whether they represent authentic nationalist sentiments. Although the Egyptian students who participated in the anti-government riots of January 1972 have been accused of receiving foreign monetary aid and of being influenced by Marxists, Leninists, and Palestinian students in Egypt, the leaders of the student riots have rejected these charges, insisting that their organizations reflect true nationalistic concern about the economic and political conditions in the country.[50]

A cursory look at the student manifesto published in January 1972 would confirm our earlier statement that most of the issues in which Egyptian students are actively involved have little to do with education. All of their demands were political. For example, the manifesto demanded that the Egyptian government give "wholehearted" support to the Palestinian commando organizations and release the four commandos charged with murdering Jordanian Prime Minister Wasfi Tal; asked for an end to censorship and domestic Secret Service activity; urged a ban on American imports; demanded nationalization of American companies in Egypt; and opposed expansion of the tourism industry.[51]

Although this manifesto did not express any opinion on Egyptian-Soviet relations, later reports indicated that some student groups voiced apprehension about the country's total reliance on the Soviet Union for the acquisition of sophisticated weapons systems and the training of military personnel in the use of these weapons.[52] The right-wing student groups have occasionally displayed open hostility toward the Soviet Union and often have accused it of encouraging subversive activities in the country. This wing of the student movement is closely associated with such national leaders as Abdul Latif Baghdadi, Kamaluddin Husain, Hasan Ibrahim, and Zakaria Mohieddin.

These students, however, were not alone in criticizing the government for its "excessive" reliance on the Soviet Union, for its defense policy, and for maintaining press censorship. In December 1972, a group of "right-wing" deputies made an attack on the policies followed by Premier Aziz Sidai, whose "presence in power" was considered to be "the sole guarantee for a minimum level of relations with the Soviet Union. . . ."[53] During this period, a committee of the People's Assembly declared that "to strike at local American concerns is an inevitable measure in view of the escalated U.S. aid to Israel and the hostile attitude to our cause."[54] This committee urged Egypt, Syria, and Libya to take the lead in this direction.

It should be reiterated that the student demands had nothing to do with academic affairs or campus life in general; these were political demands for effecting personnel and policy changes in domestic and foreign affairs. The student demonstrations and strikes during 1972 and early 1973 were given publicity in the Egyptian press, which generally tended to be pro-student in its editorial comments. The student strikes and the press comments critical of the government's policies provoked Sadat into taking strong disciplinary measures against the student leadership, as well as against a number of anti-government journalists, who were arrested. With the exception of a student— Issam Ghazzah—who was reputed to have Muslim Brotherhood connections, all others arrested were allegedly leftist students and Communist writers and journalists. The detained students included a number of Palestinian and pro-Palestinian individuals active in the Egyptian student movement.[55]

Military Training

The issue of military training is of course tied to a political decision on the source of weapons acquisition and the willingness of the supplier to provide adequate in-country or foreign training for the officers of the recipient state. In Egypt, this question acquired significance soon after Nasser's decision to purchase Soviet weapons, effective use of which required training of military personnel by Soviet instructors. Although a significant number of ranking officers reportedly resisted the idea of exposing the noncommissioned and junior officers to Soviet training, for fear of political indoctrination that might weaken military discipline, military needs and political imperatives forced them to withdraw their objections. As a result, thousands of Egyptians were given military training, initially by Russian and later also by Cuban and North Korean instructors. After the June War, thousands of Russian military instructors and advisers were brought into Egypt to train troops and also to maintain the new equipment in operational condition. Because of its sensitive nature, this issue did not receive as much publicity in the Egyptian press as, for example, Soviet weapons did. It seems to us that it was much easier for the Egyptian government to create a consensus on the need to acquire Soviet weapons than on the need to provide Soviet military training for Egyptian military personnel. The more conservative elements in the military and the political spheres apparently opposed the presence of a large foreign military contingent on Egyptian soil and the sending of a large number of Egyptians to the Soviet Union for training, apparently fearing political and ideological indoctrination contrary to Egyptian political and religious values. In arguing against the presence of a foreign military contingent in the country, the opponents of this aspect of Soviet-Egyptian ties reminded the public of the perils the country faced during the British military presence in Egypt.[56]

Despite this opposition and the early surfacing of a conflict between Russian instructors and Egyptian officers, there were 15,000 Soviet personnel in Egypt at the height of the Soviet-Egyptian military cooperation, which began to decrease after the Soviets failed to supply the weapons systems that the Egyptian high command considered essential. Although the training issue was not a major consideration in Sadat's expulsion decision of July 1972, the civilian and military leaders who supported Sadat's decision included those who had opposed Soviet presence in Egypt. Gen. Mohammed Ahmad Sadeq, Gen. Saaduddin Shazli, and Air Force Commander Ali Baghdadi were reported to be among those who opposed closer collaboration with the Soviet Union. In this opposition, they were supported by Vice-President Husein Shafi; Sayyed Mirei, secretary-general of ASU; and former Revolutionary Command Council members Zakaria Mohieddin, Abdul Latif Baghdadi, and Kamaluddin Hussain, all of whom called for abrogation of the Soviet-Egyptian treaty and the expulsion of Soviet experts from the country.[57] It was this coalition of civilian and military leaders that played a leading role in the liquidation of the pro-Soviet wing represented by Ali Sabri, Sami Sharaf, and Sharawi Jomaa. Neither the expulsion of the Soviet advisers and technicians nor the liquidation of the pro-Soviet wing in Egypt, however, reduced the degree of Egyptian dependence on the Soviet Union for military equipment. The military imperatives again forced Sadat to curtail the growing anti-Soviet sentiments by firing Gen. Mohammed Ahmad Sadeq, who had become a focus for opposition to the Soviet presence.[58]

Since the October War and the subsequent U.S. involvement in the peacemaking efforts, pro-Soviet sentiments have suffered new setbacks in Egypt. Prominent among the factors that seem to have adversely affected the Soviet-Egyptian ties are the following:

Sadat's allegation that the Soviet ambassador in Cairo deliberately tried to split the Egyptian-Syrian military front during the October War by misinforming him that Syria had asked for an immediate cease-fire six hours after the beginning of hostilities;

the Soviet refusal to replace all Egyptian matériel losses suffered during the October War, especially the 120 planes reportedly lost by Egypt;

the Soviet-U.S. "understanding" on Jewish emigration from Russia to Israel.

A survey of the Egyptian and Arab press during the post-October War period indicates that these were the most salient points in the Egyptians' criticism of their Soviet ally. While one segment of the civil-military leadership has been critical of Soviet policies, another equally influential leadership group has expressed a keen awareness of Egyptian dependence on Soviet goodwill for both military and industrial equipment. For military and economic expedience alone, the latter group, which includes a significant number of Egyptian technocrats, bureaucrats, and civilian and military elites (for instance, such former critics of the Soviet Union as Mohammed Heikal and General Saaduddin Shazli), were unwilling to weaken the Soviet-Egyptian ties.[59]

Foreign Relations

This issue area covers such intangible factors as the Egyptian perception of the country's role in the Middle East, what constitutes national prestige, and Egypt's relations with the super-powers and other nations. (The last subject is more fully discussed under the "External Environment.") Here we may briefly recapitulate what has already been stated. For historical, religious, political, and ideological reasons, Egyptians are divided on the question of the country's ties with Europe and the two superpowers. In their opposition or support, each group offers cogent and convincing arguments that show that, for most of these seemingly opposing groups, the real issue of disagreement is not so much the goals to be achieved as the means to achieve them.

As far as Egypt's role in the Middle East is concerned, there appear to be two major schools of thought in the country. One group actively seeks Arab cooperation under Egyptian aegis; the other shows signs of isolationism and resents the human and material losses sustained by Egypt for the Arab cause. Although the isolationist trend appears to be growing, the pan-Arabists continue to be in the ascendancy. The pan-Arabists, however, are not unanimous on the kind of Arab unity that should be sought: some Egyptians support the Qaddafi approach that calls for an immediate federal union of "revolutionary" Arab states. This group, which has attracted a number of former members of the Muslim Brotherhood, tends to take a chauvinistic approach to almost all "Arab" causes from the Persian Gulf in the east to Spanish Sahara in the west. The spokesmen and leaders of this group in Egypt cannot be easily identified because the Cairo-Tripoli rift has caused them to keep a low public profile, lest they be accused of subversion. Another pan-Arab group seeks Arab unity through a series of anti-monarchist revolutions that would usher in an era of Arab socialist states dedicated to a set of common economic, political, and social goals that would bind them in a common struggle against the "imperialist and reactionary" forces. This group draws support from the Popular Front for the Liberation of Palestine, the Popular Front for the Liberation of Oman, and other leftist-oriented revolutionary groups in the Arab world.

Because of Sadat's opposition to these approaches to Arab unity, the pan-Arab groups have not drawn popular support from the masses, who currently seem to favor the pragmatic and evolutionary approach to Arab unity, which promises a better financial and political return than the approaches advocated by other groups. This, however, does not mean that the pragmatists have abandoned Egypt's leadership role in the Arab world. Rather, it means that they have come to realize that Nasser's method of inciting the Arab masses against their legitimate rulers proved to be counterproductive to his stated goal of Arab unity; that many "monarchist" rulers enjoyed a respectable degree of support based on such tangible factors as tribal and religious loyalties, which they were unable to readily abandon in favor of a less personal object, such as the Arab nation; and that an approach to Arab unity from below was not a viable approach and that it must be abandoned in favor of Arab political and economic cooperation and coordination in resolving the problems of the area. Since his accession to power in 1970, Sadat has endeavored to follow a more Egyptian than pan-Arab goal; time and again in his public speeches, he has reiterated his determination to make independent decisions that would be "in the interest of Egypt alone—decisions based on values only we, the people of Egypt, feel."[60]

Although these remarks were made in the context of Egypt's relations with the superpowers, and did not deal directly with the country's relations with the Arab states, there are ample indications that before the October War, Sadat wanted to turn inward and away from pan-Arab issues, such as Palestine, in order to concentrate his efforts on solving Egypt's social and economic problems. The pan-Arab issue, he believed, had deprived Egypt of vital resources desperately needed for domestic development. Malcolm Kerr maintains that the "politically conservative Egyptian Muslim, much more than his counterpart in the Fertile Crescent countries, does possess an isolationist streak...."[61] While the Arab agreements, alliances, and understandings forged before, during, and after the October War may have deprived him of the option of seeking purely Egyptian solutions to the country's domestic and international problems, Sadat, who is by no means an isolationist, would prefer to expend his nation's scarce resources and energies in strengthening the economy rather than in encouraging the overthrow of regimes deemed unfriendly to Egypt. In intraregional politics, he sees Egypt's role as a judicious mediator and conciliator rather than as an imperial arbiter, as seemed to have been the case under Nasser.[62]

EGYPTIAN OBJECTIVES AND POLICIES

For the purposes of our discussion and analysis, Egyptian objectives and policies may be grouped into four categories: political, military, economic, and social. This classification, however, should not be construed to mean an independent existence of these categories. The military, economic, and social objectives and policies are generally formulated to achieve a set of political goals that provide the *raisons d'être* for all other objectives and policies pursued by the state. And often the success or failure of the military, economic, and social policies is a direct reflection of the success or failure of political objectives and goals. For example, in 1960 Nasser established a set of economic goals to be achieved during the next two decades. Although some of these goals were considered to be economically unrealistic, in political terms they were essential for the continuous existence of the regime, which wanted to establish its credentials as a revolutionary socialist state.

Egypt, however, failed to achieve its economic goals—not necessarily because they were economically unrealistic but because Nasser's political goals and policies at the systemic and regional levels proved to be incompatible with the country's economic needs. A successful completion of the economic projects depended largely on a massive infusion of foreign capital and technology and a sharp reduction in defense expenditure. Egypt failed to attract enough foreign capital because the country's new laws, promulgated under the socialist decrees, did not provide enough incentives and guarantees to private foreign capitalists. Also, Egypt could not reduce its defense expenditure because of its conflict with Israel and its military involvement in the Yemen civil war. Although the socialist decrees were designed to broaden the regime's popularity, they proved to be a serious impediment to achieving the country's economic goals—which in turn would have strengthened its political objectives and policies. In other words, it may be said that the politically essential goals may prove to be politically difficult to achieve. That was essentially true of Nasser's Egypt.

Objectives

In addition to such general and obvious objectives as maintaining territorial integrity, political independence, and national defense—goals that all independent states are obliged to pursue—Egypt's current policies are formulated with a view to achieving the following political objectives:

recovering the Egyptian (the Sinai Peninsula) and other Arab lands (the West
    Bank of the Jordan, including the Arab section of Jerusalem, and the
    Golan Heights) under Israeli occupation since the June War;
restoring the political and territorial rights of the Palestinian people;
accelerating the rate of economic and industrial development;
modernizing political, economic, and social institutions;
strengthening inter-Arab ties that have recently been forged on the basis of
    political consensus and economic cooperation among the Arab states;

enhancing Egypt's regional and extraregional prestige and role in international affairs.

The above objectives are being pursued by means of political, military, economic, and social programs.

Political Policies

Although the Egyptian political objectives have changed little since the July 1952 revolution, Egyptian policies under President Sadat have shown remarkable differences in substance and style compared with those of Nasser. Unlike his charismatic predecessor, whose rhetoric and alleged intrigues often created apprehension and militancy among his Arab opponents, Sadat has adopted a pragmatic approach to resolving the major problems confronting the country. Recognizing Egypt's military and economic inadequacies for regaining the Egyptian and Arab lands, Sadat offered, as early as December 1970, to recognize the existence of Israel as an independent and sovereign state if it would return the Sinai Peninsula to its rightful previous owner. Sadat was the first Arab leader of stature to publicly indicate his willingness to recognize Israel and to resolve the conflict by peaceful means. It should be noted that at this stage Sadat linked his willingness to recognize Israel only with the recovery of the Sinai Peninsula. This was his first condition for resolving the Egyptian-Israeli dispute. In addition, he offered to enter into immediate negotiations with Israel on the question of the freedom of passage for Israeli ships through the Strait of Tiran. This was Sadat's "step-by-step" approach to resolving the Arab-Israeli dispute. The second step in this process, he indicated, would involve the settlement of the Palestinian problem, which he linked with a promise that a just solution of this issue would give Israeli ships the right to use the Suez Canal.

While offering a unique opportunity to Israel for a peaceful settlement of the dispute, Sadat took a number of steps designed to strengthen Egypt's military and diplomatic support in the Arab-Israeli dispute. In acquiring Soviet weapons and training, Egypt spent about E£ 5 billion (E£ 100=$225.56) between 1967 and 1973. In addition, Sadat rapidly moved to mend his fences with Saudi Arabia and to strengthen his ties with Syria, Sudan, Kuwait, the United Arab Emirates, and, for a brief period, with Libya. Having consolidated his relations with his immediate Arab neighbors, he concentrated his efforts on the African, the nonaligned, and the Muslim states of the Third World. Simultaneously, Sadat embarked on a concerted effort to convince Western Europe that Egypt was ready for a peaceful settlement of the Arab-Israeli dispute and Israeli unwillingness to part with the conquered territory was responsible for the continued stalemate between the disputants. Perhaps the most important change in Egyptian foreign policy took place when Sadat, piqued by the Soviet refusal to equip the Egyptian military with more sophisticated weapons, asked the Russian advisers and technicians to leave the country.[63] In addition to satisfying domestic anti-Soviet critics and placating such new regional allies as Saudi Arabia and Libya, both of which had expressed their disapproval of the Soviet presence in Egypt, Sadat's action was deemed to be a conciliatory step toward the Nixon administration.[64] Sadat wanted to end the polarization of the Arab-Israeli conflict by developing better and more congenial ties with the United States, which alone, he concluded, could oblige Israel to withdraw from the Arab territories. However, he was informed that U.S. pressure against Israel would not materialize as long as Soviet military influence remained strong in Egypt. The United States, through a Saudi Arabian intermediary, informed Sadat that the Nixon administration would be prepared to undertake a new initiative in the Arab-Israeli conflict as a quid pro quo for a change in Soviet-Egyptian ties.[65]

Sadat's concessions to Israel (promise of recognition and negotiations) and to the United States (the expulsion of the Soviet technicians and advisers), however, did not bring any reciprocal concessions to Egypt, whose population was becoming extremely restive under the "no-war, no-peace" situation that had existed since the U.S.-sponsored Suez Canal cease-fire went into effect in August 1970. Sadat had nothing to show for these political concessions and the heavy defense expenditure that was being incurred, except public ridicule by Israeli and Arab leaders. Even though Egypt received its share of promised financial aid from the Arab oil-producing states, some of them, like Algeria and Iraq, were highly critical of Sadat's peace efforts through Washington and of his willingness to recognize Israel.[66] The United States showed no signs of reappraising its Middle East policies, apart from a series of generalized statements about the need for a new initiative to restore peace in the region. Apparently having realized that the Zionist lobby in the United States and the Soviet-American détente would not allow any significant change in U.S. Middle East policy, Sadat apparently concluded that only a renewal of Arab-Israeli hostilities would break the stalemate and constrain Washington to renew its peacemaking activities in the region. According to Sadat's calculation, the military action would unify the Arabs, who would be obliged to use their oil resources as a political weapon against the United States and other pro-Israeli states. In addition, Sadat wanted to shatter the Israeli concept of security that called for substantial territorial changes in favor of the Jewish state.

In summary, it may be argued that Sadat's strategy achieved its main goals: it reactivated the U.S. role as a peacemaker in the Arab-Israeli conflict; it further isolated Israel from a number of European and African states; it achieved a substantial degree of Arab unity, expressed in the form of an oil embargo and increase in oil prices; and it strengthened the argument that the security Israel sought could not be obtained and maintained by military force

alone. Since the end of the hostilities and the disengagement agreement between Egypt and Israel, Sadat has endeavored to strengthen Egyptian-U.S. ties
by publicly voicing his approval of Secretary of State Kissinger's diplomatic
efforts; by reestablishing diplomatic ties with the United States; and by providing a rousing reception for President Nixon during his visit to Egypt.

Recognizing that Saudi Arabia, because of its oil and monetary resources,
is destined to play a much more decisive and significant role in regional and
extraregional affairs, Sadat has made deliberate efforts to move politically and
ideologically closer to Riyadh than to Tripoli, which has publicly expressed
disapproval of Sadat's reliance on the United States for a peaceful solution of
the Arab-Israeli dispute. Saudi Arabia, along with Kuwait, Qatar, Bahrain,
and the United Arab Emirates, has provided hundreds of millions of dollars
for Egypt's war-shattered economy; and collectively these donors have promised even larger amounts in economic and military aid. In addition, under the
terms of the 1974 Rabat Conference, the Arab oil-producing states promised
Egypt annual aid of $1 billion for the indefinite future.[67]

In addition to strengthening his ties with most Arab states (the single
significant exception being Libya), Sadat has endeavored to improve Egypt's
relations with Iran, whose industrial and military power, fed by the country's
oil revenues, is rapidly expanding to give Iran a prominent role in the region.
As a result of this reconciliation, the shah of Iran has promised to invest about
$1 billion in rebuilding the Suez Canal Zone, is establishing new industries in
the free zones, and is financing joint projects in Egypt. Furthermore, Iran is
now more forthright in giving political and military aid to the Arabs than had
previously been the case.[68] It seems that a Cairo-Riyadh-Teheran axis is being
forged with the encouragement of the U.S. government, which seeks the
continuation of political stability in the oil-rich Persian Gulf region. Some
political observers believe that during the shah of Iran's January 1975 visit to
Cairo, he and President Sadat probably discussed, inter alia, ways and means
of ending Saudi-Iranian oil rivalry—which, if not checked, could seriously
threaten Iran's industrial development.[69] It is plausible that the U.S. government is encouraging Iran to give some of its American-built weapons systems
to Egypt so that the Sadat regime will not be threatened by the Egyptian
military for its failure to replenish the Soviet armaments lost during the
October War. In addition, Iran could provide training facilities for Egyptian
pilots and radar technicians in the use of U.S. matériel that Egypt might
acquire after substantial progress has been made in resolving the Arab-Israeli
conflict.

The Egyptian-Iranian and the Egyptian-Saudi rapprochements seem to
have stimulated Iraqi interest in offering $700 million in economic aid to Cairo
and in signing a series of commercial and technical agreements.[70] Although
it is a leader of the "rejection front," the Iraqi regime has endeavored, under
internal pressure, to improve its relations with its Egyptian "brothers," against

whom it has often competed for the leadership of the Arab East. Although the Rabat Conference urged only King Hussein of Jordan to try to resolve the Iraqi-Iranian conflict, Sadat also offered his "good offices" to the two disputants. Evidently, Sadat assumes that a rapprochement between Iran and Iraq would help to create a general atmosphere of Arab-Iranian cordiality and to improve trade relations between the Arab states and Iran, whose major regional trade partner recently has been Israel.

Sadat seems to feel that a general reconciliation between Iran and the major Arab states would not only loosen the Iranian-Israeli links (a highly desirable prospect for the Arabs), but also would save Egypt from being singled out for political attacks by its adversaries, such as Libya, as acquiescent to Iran's Persian Gulf policies and its military occupation of three islands—Bani Tonb and Taob-e Bozorg, and Abu Musa—at the northern end of the Strait of Hormuz in 1971.[71] As president of the most influential Arab state, Sadat has the means to effect a reconciliation between the Arabs and the Iranians, provided Iran's regional and oil policies do not radically diverge from the policies and interests of the Arabs.

Since the creation of Israel in 1948 and the ensuing expulsion-emigration of the Arab population from the area constituting the Jewish state, Egypt has consistently supported the "inherent" right of the Palestinian people to return to their homes and lands and to establish an independent political entity in Palestine. Always unequivocal in defending the rights of the Palestinians to regain their territory, Egypt has maintained relations with the various Palestinian organizations that have oscillated between cordiality and enmity. In an effort to ensure the spread of influence among the Palestinian elites and masses, Egypt has endeavored to promote amenable Palestinians to key positions in their national councils.

During Ahmad Shuqairy's tenure as head of the Palestine Liberation Organization (PLO), Egypt's relations with the Palestinian movement were cordial and amicable; Nasser used this organization more for the enhancement of the Egyptian national interests than to promote and safeguard the national interests of the Palestinian people. The crushing defeat of the Arab armies in June 1967, the "resignation" of Shuqairy from the PLO, the emergence of more militant and nationalistic leaders within the Palestinian resistance movement, and the willingness of other Arab states to support rival Palestinian groups changed Egyptian relations with the Palestinians. While the "moderate" leaders of the resistance movement maintained close ties with Egypt, neither Nasser nor his successor, Sadat, could any longer take for granted an automatic Palestinian approval of Egyptian policies affecting their national aspirations and goals. Similarly, Palestinian leaders and organizations who refused to work within an Egyptian-approved framework of activities were immediately deprived of Egyptian financial and political support. For example, George Habash, while leading the Arab Nationalist Movement, was closely affiliated with Nasser, who provided this Palestinian leader with shelter and with financial and political support, as long as Habash did not adopt political and ideological stances unacceptable to Egypt. The Nasser-Habash ties broke after the June War, when Habash became an exponent of the Marxist-Leninist approach to the political and social problems of the Arab world. The break was so complete that the Egyptian radio, television, and the semi-official newspaper *Al-Ahram* made no mention of the Popular Front for the Liberation of Palestine (PFLP), even at the height of its popularity in 1970, when it hijacked a number of airplanes. The Egyptian media identified the hijackers merely as "members of the Palestinian resistance movement." This ostracism of Habash and the PFLP, however, was not as complete as it might sound. Egyptian newspapers of lesser standing than *Al-Ahram* did occasionally refer to Nasser's erstwhile ally.[72]

The vacuum left by the Habash-Nasser break was immediately filled by a new group of young and dynamic Palestinian leaders who, earlier in 1965, had founded the Palestine National Liberation Movement (al-Fatah). This young organization was in immediate need of an influential and resourceful sponsor who would be willing to provide military training. Egypt, which had experienced another humiliating military defeat and had lost credibility with some elements of the resistance movement, was in need of a friendly commando organization through which to regain some of the influence lost during and after the June War. In August 1967, after assuring himself of Fatah's ideology and principles through his foreign minister, Mahmud Riyad, and Mohammed Heikal of *Al-Ahram,* Nasser met with two Fatah leaders and offered them large-scale aid in arms, training, and supplies.[73]

During the next three years, President Nasser gave every indication that Fatah was nearly the only Palestinian organization that inspired Cairo's confidence and deserved its full support. Nasser was unusually generous in his statements about Fatah and let it be known that he wished to identify his regime with it. Nasser helped to build up Yassir Arafat's image by introducing him to foreign leaders, including the Soviet leaders. Although it had been engaged in anti-Israel activities since January 1965, Fatah became "the acknowledged voice" of the Palestinian resistance only after the battle of Karamah in March 1968.[74] In the same year, Fatah joined the PLO, of which Arafat was elected chairman, a position he has held since then. Thus, Nasser succeeded in enhancing Egypt's influence in the resistance organization, which in 1969 brought all commando groups within its fold.

Although Egypt's ties with Fatah and the Fatah-dominated PLO apparently remained strong, a number of influential Palestinian leaders began to manifest discontent with Cairo. Some of them opposed close cooperation with Egypt on ideological grounds, and others objected on purely nationalistic grounds. This opposition became more vocal and significant in July 1970, when President Nasser accepted the Rogers Peace Plan and a cease-fire along the Suez Canal. Kamal Adwan, a member of Fatah's Central Committee who was in charge of information, ordered Fatah's Cairo-based Assifa Radio to denounce Egypt for its approach to the Middle East conflict.[75] Assifa Radio's denunciatory broadcast caused the Egyptian government to suspend the Fatah and PLO broadcasting facilities in Cairo. The Egyptian authorities also closed down the Palestinian offices in the country and expelled 15 Palestinian guerrillas belonging to Fatah and PFLP.[76] Except for two minor Palestinian organizations—the Action Organization for the Liberation of Palestine (AOLP) and the Palestine Arab Organization (PAO)—almost all other Palestinian groups roundly condemned Egypt and Jordan for accepting the Rogers Peace Plan.[77]

Although the Palestinian-Jordanian confrontations in September 1970 and in March 1971 helped to bring the resistance and Cairo closer to each other, the Palestinian-Egyptian détente again foundered in November, when four Black Septemberists assassinated Jordanian Prime Minister Wasfi Tal in Cairo. Following this incident, the Egyptian security apparatus began to crack down on Palestinian students and guerrillas in the country. The retaliation was not to avenge the death of the Jordanian premier, for whom Sadat had little respect because of Tal's role in Jordanian-Palestinian relations, but to ensure firm government control over the activities of anti-government "centers of power," which, availing themselves of pro-Palestinian public sentiment, began to organize student committees that became the nucleus of anti-government riots in January 1972. It was surmised that the assassination took place with the connivance of the Egyptian security apparatus, with a view to embarrassing Sadat, whose control over the security police was not yet consolidated following the removal of the former security chief, Sharawi Jomaa.[78] For Sadat, the incident became a challenge to his authority, and he used both diplomacy and force to suppress it. The Egyptian police arrested a number of Palestinian students and accused the resistance of inciting anti-government demonstrations. In an effort to put pressure on the resistance leadership, to let them know that Egypt might sponsor an alternative leadership group among the Palestinians, the Egyptian government began to encourage former PLO chief Ahmad Shuqairy to come out of retirement and to take a more active role in Palestinian affairs. After consulting with a number of Palestinian leaders, Shuqairy called for a "rectification" of the resistance movement within the framework of the PLO.[79]

If the Egyptian government could use the encouragement of the long-discredited Shuqairy to put pressure on the Palestinians, the Palestinians could count on their rich and influential allies to induce Sadat to moderate his attitude and policies toward the resistance. Although Sadat could not allow the alleged assassins to escape without trial, neither could he afford to treat them as common criminals. Libyan pressure on behalf of the resistance forced Sadat to declare that the assassination of Wasfi Tal was a political act and that its perpetrators would be tried by the State Security Court rather than by the criminal court.[80] Although these actions and the presence of the pro-Egyptian leaders on the Central Committee of the PLO helped to lower tension between the two parties, Egyptian-Palestinian relations remained tense until April 1972, when, as a reaction to King Hussein's United Kingdom plan, Sadat severed diplomatic ties with Amman. Concurrently, Sadat, while addressing the Palestine National Congress held in Cairo, reaffirmed Egypt's position that the PLO was the only legitimate representative of the Palestinian people and reiterated his determination to recover Arab territory by force, if necessary. Denouncing Hussein's plan for a United Kingdom of the West Bank and the Transjordan, Sadat said that it was an American plot designed to undermine the Palestine question.[81] These actions and statements were highly appreciated by the PLO and were responsible for effecting a rapprochement between Cairo and the resistance.

These statements and diplomatic moves were, however, not directed merely toward the PLO. They were parts of a much larger political and military action program that was being formulated by Sadat. Having become disillusioned with the U.S. peace initiatives, he was forced to prepare for a military action against the Israeli forces in Sinai. For this purpose, he needed to strengthen his ties with Syria, Libya, and Algeria, among others. Because of the Palestinian-Jordanian conflict, none of these countries maintained cordial relations with Amman. Since Sadat was depending on Qaddafi for financial aid and for military equipment, it was imperative to show bellicosity toward Jordan. For Sadat, confronted by internal problems and preparing for a military conflict with Israel, it was much more beneficial to cultivate better relations with the PLO and its Libyan patron, Muammar Qaddafi, than to maintain diplomatic ties with Hussein, who had foreclosed the possibility of participation in a future military conflict with Israel.[82]

Egyptian-resistance relations again became tense during sessions of the Arab League Defense Council, which met at Cairo in January 1973. During this conference, efforts were made to reconcile the Cairo-Amman differences prior to King Hussein's visit to the United States. At the urging of King Faisal, secret contacts reportedly were made between Cairo and Amman before their representatives met during sessions of the Arab League Defense Council. The resistance reiterated its objections to improving Arab relations with Hussein and seeking a peaceful solution to the Arab-Israeli conflict. Relations between the resistance and Cairo further deteriorated when Egyptian Foreign Minister Mohammed Zayyat proposed the creation of a Palestinian state. The resistance believed that Egypt sought to create a Palestinian entity willing to negotiate peace with Israel. Although Cairo rejected this interpretation of its proposal, many Palestinian leaders remained suspicious of Egyptian motives.

After the October War, Egyptian-Palestinian relations plummeted to a new low when, in a joint Egyptian-Jordanian communiqué issued on July 18,

1974, Egypt recognized Hussein's right to speak for the Palestinians living in the Transjordan. Simultaneously, Cairo endeavored to reassure the Palestinians of Egyptian support regarding all the territory claimed by the PLO and occupied by Israel, including the West Bank and Gaza Strip. The Palestinians, furious, accused the Egyptian government of violating the Algiers declaration that had recognized the PLO as the sole legitimate representative of the Palestinian people.[83] Denouncing the Sadat-Hussein "collusion" against the Palestinians, the PLO demanded an official abrogation of the relevant statement in the communiqué, a step Cairo could hardly take because of its political and diplomatic implications. It was during this time that Faisal was trying to mollify Yassir Arafat with the promise that the Saudi monarch would prevail upon King Hussein to change his mind regarding the West Bank if the resistance leader were a little more conciliatory toward the Jordanian monarch. The Egyptian foreign minister, Ismail Fahmi, said that Jordan could temporarily represent the Palestinians on the West Bank, provided Israel pulled out of the area. This statement, which obviously went beyond the Egyptian-Jordanian communiqué, was interpreted by the resistance as the hardening of the Egyptian position toward the Palestinians. Commenting on the Egyptian-Jordanian communiqué, Farouk Qaddumi, who had the title of foreign minister of the PLO, said that a conference of leaders of Egypt, Syria, Jordan, and the PLO was out of the question. (It should be recalled that Sadat had sought to convene such a conference before the proposed Geneva Conference.)

In making this joint statement with Jordan, Sadat had taken a calculated risk, in the hope that the United States could more easily convince Israel to return the West Bank if Hussein, and not the resistance movement, were to negotiate with Israel. Fahmi's statement was designed to satisfy the Israeli objection to the prospect of immediate Palestinian control over the West Bank after the Israeli withdrawal. The Palestinians believed that the Egyptians had been deceived by the Israelis, whose tactics of negotiations again succeeded in dividing the Arab world on the issue of Palestine. The Palestinian reaction aside, it was evident that the Egyptian-Jordanian communiqué and the Fahmi statement were received with approval by the U.S. government, which, for the first time, expressed its approval of a disengagement between Jordan and Israel.[84] The Palestinians asserted that the Egyptian-Jordanian and the U.S.-Jordanian communiqués were diplomatic signals that showed the signatories' efforts to reestablish Jordanian control over the West Bank.

The Palestinian-Egyptian rift caused the PLO to fight the Egyptian-Jordanian accord with a diplomatic campaign in the Arab world. After discussing the issue at an extraordinary session of the PLO Executive Committee, Yassir Arafat sought support from King Faisal, who reportedly assured him that Saudi Arabia would oppose a Jordanian-Israeli disengagement if it prejudiced the rights of the Palestinian people and of the PLO. There were, however, no reports of Faisal's reaction to the Egyptian-Jordanian communiqué, which had given the PLO serious cause for apprehension. If there were no public pronouncements from Faisal to smoothe the Palestinians, there were indications that the failure of Israel to negotiate a withdrawal with Jordan was forcing the Arab leaders to recognize the PLO as the sole legitimate representative of the Palestinians, wherever they might be living. This recognition was accorded by the Arab heads of state meeting at Rabat in October 1974. Thus, Sadat was able to come out of the situation without serious damage to his ties with King Hussein or with the resistance. He let the Arab consensus bury the Egyptian-Jordanian communiqué that had sought to divide the legitimacy of authority over the Palestinians between Hussein and the PLO.

Sadat, in coordination with King Faisal and President Assad, was endeavoring to find a compromise formula that would assign an acceptable role to both Jordan and the PLO in the proposed Geneva Peace Conference between the Arabs and Israel. In this connection, a conference of Egypt, Syria, Jordan, and the PLO, held at Cairo in January 1975, tried to resolve the difference between Jordan and the PLO. Reports emanating from the PLO participants at the conference indicated that the Egyptian delegation had suggested that the resistance designate Jordan to carry out disengagement negotiations on behalf of the PLO. This Egyptian attitude, these sources contend, was directly connected with Cairo's continuous reliance on the American peace approach, which did not assign the PLO any role in the negotiation process. The PLO believed that Egypt was unwilling to exert any pressure on Jordan and that Cairo was more interested in creating conditions conducive to Secretary of State Kissinger's peace efforts (that would cover Jordan as well as Egypt) than in coordinating efforts with the PLO, as envisaged by the Rabat communiqué.[85]

As a compromise, in the fall of 1976 Sadat suggested the creation of a confederation between Jordan and the Palestinian state that might be formed following an Israeli withdrawal from the West Bank and the Gaza Strip. The comments emanating from the PLO sources regarding the proposal were by no means entirely favorable. Not surprisingly, the conservative faction of the PLO expressed support for the Sadat proposal, while it was rejected by the more militant groups in the organization.

Before Egypt entered the final phases of preparation for a military crossing of the Suez Canal, Cairo endeavored to mend its fences with most of its Arab adversaries and sought to enlist moral and political support for the Arab cause from several international organizations, including the Organization of African Unity, the Security Council of the United Nations, and the Organization of the Nonaligned Nations.[86] These were laudable and significant achievements on the part of Sadat and other Arab leaders.

Closer to the home front, however, Sadat was unable to resolve his differences with President Qaddafi, whose oil-rich state was scheduled to merge in a federation with Egypt and Syria before September 1, 1973. The agreement for the federation of the three Arab states had been reached in 1972, but by the beginning of 1973 serious problems had appeared regarding the questions of war and peace, the role of religion, the type of constitution to be adopted for the proposed federation, and the federation's ties with the Arab states. It seems that prior to signing the federation agreement, Sadat had failed to discuss and settle the major differences between himself and Qaddafi, who took his pan-Arab and Islamic brotherhood ideals much more seriously than most other Arab rulers. Qaddafi believed that an Egyptian-Libyan union was imperative and inevitable, even at the cost of "civil war," and that this merger would be the best means to prepare for war against Israel. Since Qaddafi believed in the "inevitability" of the union, he saw no reason for further delay of this "noble" goal. Sadat, on the other hand, while accepting the necessity of unity, believed that it should be achieved in stages.

In addition, the two leaders differed in their approaches to the Arab-Israeli conflict and the role of Islam in domestic and international affairs. On the question of the Arab-Israeli conflict, President Qaddafi was firmly against recognizing Israel; and he was convinced that only through the use of force could the Palestinians and the Arabs regain their political and territorial rights. On the question of the role of Islam in domestic and international affairs, President Qaddafi argued that the Muslims must organize their affairs according to the *sharia* (Islamic law) and that the Muslim states should cooperate and coordinate their efforts in all spheres of international activities. These ideas were not totally acceptable to Sadat, whose domestic situation and international responsibilities radically differed from those of his Libyan counterpart. Domestically, Sadat could not accept Qaddafi's suggestion about the *sharia* without alienating the Coptic Christian portion of the Egyptian population. This minority was, of course, not the only consideration for Sadat's opposition. A large number of the People's Assembly and the ASU members, along with writers, intellectuals, and officials, were opposed to Qaddafi's rigid interpretation of Islam.[87] Similarly, Sadat feared that a complete identity of views with Qaddafi on international problems would destroy Egyptian chances of recovering Arab territory. While recognizing the necessity of strengthening Egyptian armed forces, partly through financial aid from Libya, he was reluctant to close the door on peaceful negotiations through the good offices of the United States—a method urged by King Faisal, who could cover any financial deficit incurred by Egypt, should Libya stop its aid because of political disagreements.

Despite Sadat's opposition and the apparent dislike of many other Egyptians for Qaddafi's policies, there were many pro-Libyans within the Egyptian political system. Of these, the most prominent was Mohammed Heikal, who, although by no means a Muslim fundamentalist of the Qaddafi variety, supported Qaddafi's ideas on the union. In his influential weekly column, "Frankly Speaking," he criticized Sadat for his lack of enthusiasm for the union with Libya. The appearance of Heikal's criticism coincided with the Libyan unionist march on Egypt in July 1973, and with the rumors that an anti-Sadat coup was imminent. Other suporters of Qaddafi were the pro-Sadeq military officers, religiously oriented students, and the remnant of the Muslim Brotherhood.[88]

Qaddafi's contacts with these groups have been a source of concern and apprehension to Sadat, who has more than once been a target of assassination. One such attempt was reported to have been made on April 19, 1974, a day after the attack on the military academy in which 11 persons were killed and 27 wounded by a squad of "Mohammed's Youth" allegedly headed by Dr. Saleh Abdullah Sareya, a Palestinian with an Iraqi passport who was working for the Arab League in Cairo. The Egyptian government accused Sareya of contact with Qaddafi. In August 1974, President Sadat accused Libya of being involved in an attempt to blow up his house at Mersa Matruh, and to kill Ihsan Abdul Qaddos, a pro-Sadat editor. Despite these and other alleged provocations by Libya, Sadat has been unable either to ignore Qaddafi or to put an effective end to their rift.[89]

Sadat has been unable to ignore Qaddafi primarily because the Libyan leader commands considerable respect among the Arab and Muslim youth; some are attracted to him because they consider him the true successor of Nasser—dynamic, defiant of the West as well as of the East, self-assured, and highly proud of his Arab-Islamic heritage; others admire him for his pan-Islamic approach, which has extended Libyan financial support to such far-away places as the Philippines and Pakistan as well as places closer to home, such as Chad, Turkey, and Uganda; still others respect him for his revolutionary fervor that supports the Irish Republican Army against the British, the Palestinian guerrillas against Israel, and liberation movements in the Spanish Sahara and in Ethiopia; and still others like his condemnation of "reactionary" monarchies in Saudi Arabia, Morocco, and Jordan.[90]

Since Sadat's strategy was to depolarize the Arab-Israeli conflict and to neutralize the U.S. role in it, it was imperative for him to maintain close relations with Saudi Arabia because, as one of the largest oil producers in the world, it could play a significant role in influencing Washington's Middle East policies. Before the October War, the American assumption was that the Persian Gulf oil-producing Arab states would not, and perhaps could not, use oil as an effective political weapon to influence the Middle East policies of the oil-importing states of Europe, Japan, and the United States. U.S. officials made deliberate efforts to maintain this posture; during press conferences and speeches, they reiterated their conviction that the Arab-Israeli conflict was unrelated to the problems of oil nationalization and oil prices. If Sadat were to disprove this assumption, he would have to have the close cooperation of King Faisal, without whose participation and blessings no Arab oil embargo or oil price increase could be expected to succeed.[91] Libya could provide Egypt with financial aid and with some military equipment from Europe, but Tripoli could not match Saudi Arabia in its oil resources, which give Riyadh considerably more political influence in regional and extraregional affairs. Therefore, for Sadat the choice was clear. He could not afford to alienate Saudi Arabia by moving Egypt closer to Qaddafi's Libya, with which Saudi relations were less than cordial.

Military Objectives

In view of the highly sensitive nature of this subject and the unavailability of hard data, the military goals listed below had to be stated in broad general terms. Thus, the discussion that follows the list is premised on the assumption that the Arab-Israeli conflict will continue to be the major source of concern for the Egyptian government for several years. This discussion is based primarily on a number of articles that have appeared since the end of the October War and on several studies that compared and analyzed the strength and weaknesses of the Israeli and the Arab (primarily of Egypt, Syria, and Jordan) armies before the October War.[92] The goals are the following:

to raise the strength and efficiency of the armed forces so that they will become
    an effective deterrent against foreign enemies;
to assure, by acceptable political means, the availability of modern, sophis-
    ticated weapons systems for all branches of the armed forces;
to establish and expand defense-related industries within the country;
to strengthen military cooperation and coordination with the neighboring
    Arab states.

Military Policies

Since the mid-1950s, Egyptian military efforts have been directed toward maintaining a semblance of a "balance of power" between that country and Israel. It was the Israeli military pressure in the Sinai and the realization of the enemy's military superiority that forced Nasser to break the Western-imposed arms embargo and to seek Russian weapons comparable with those available to Israel.[93] For this purpose, Egypt has been spending a substantial portion of its annual budget on the defense establishment, which increased from E£80,000 in 1955–56 to E£323,000 in 1974–75.[94] Initially, the Egyptians believed that they could achieve military parity with Israel merely by acquiring massive supplies of military equipment from abroad. The June War, however, seems to have changed this attitude. The Egyptian government began to place greater emphasis on training and on attracting the better-educated citizens to the armed forces. The level of education in Egypt has been far below the education level in Israel, where over 90 percent of the Jewish population is literate; the Egyptian literacy figure is about 30 percent. Because the general level of education and health was rather low, the Egyptian draftee took much longer to be trained than his counterpart in Israel. Furthermore, there was, and is, a wide social gap between the Egyptian soldier, who generally comes from the village or a small agricultural town, and the officer, who generally comes from a middle-class urban background and has at least a high school diploma and the equivalent of a college degree from one of the three service academies. Immediately after the June War, the maximum eligible age for admission to the military academy was raised from 21.5 years to 22.5 years and the minimum grade requirement was withdrawn. This was considered necessary to meet the immediate needs of the military, which had lost thousands of officers in the Six-Day War. The previous conditions were, however, reinstated as soon as enough manpower became available in 1969. Similarly, in 1969 the Egyptian air force, recognizing the need for better-educated officers, began to accept college graduates up to 24 years of age. Almost all of the Egyptian pilots have been trained by Soviet instructors in either Egypt or the Soviet Union, especially in the Ukraine, where a special school for training Egyptian pilots was established.[95]

Although all branches of the Egyptian armed forces are continuously being strengthened, the greatest emphasis is placed on the army and the air force. The army is largely infantry. Since it operates in areas most suitable for tank warfare, the Egyptian army has procured a large number of T-54/55 and T-34 tanks. In addition, it has been receiving consignments of JS-3 heavy tanks from the Soviet Union since 1968. The total number of these tanks, however, did not exceed 50 before the October War.[96] In the June War, the Egyptian army lost the major portion of its tank force, which was estimated by the Institute for Strategic Studies to be 250. By 1973, the army's manpower strength had grown from 140,000 to 280,000 and its tank force to 2,060.

Similarly, having lost most of its MIG fighters, and all of its TU-16 medium bombers and IL-28 bombers, during the Six-Day War, the Egyptian air force began to rebuild its strength soon after the hostilities ended. By the end of 1968, it had acquired twice as many combat aircraft as it had possessed before the June War.[97] By the beginning of October 1973, the Egyptian air force had acquired 568 combat aircraft and had increased its manpower from 15,000 plus 4,000 reservists to 28,000 plus 20,000 reservists.[98] It should be noted that most of the increase in the aircraft inventory was in the interceptor fighter type (which could not be used for offensive purposes) and not in the bomber type of aircraft. It should be further noted that the number of IL-28 light jet bombers, which stood at 40 in 1968–69, decreased dramatically to 10 in 1972–73, and that after the October War there were perhaps no more than 5 IL-28 bombers in the Egyptian inventory.[99] This reduction probably reflected Egyptian realism about the impossibility of penetrating Israeli defenses in the Sinai. Therefore, in keeping with the strategy to prevent Israeli deep-penetration raids, the Egyptian air force, with the help of the Soviet Union, constructed an air defense system along the Nile Valley and acquired from the Soviet Union a number of MIG-21-Js, the radar-equipped, all-weather combat aircraft, for night interception.[100]

The acquisition of arms did not, however, solve Egypt's military problems, which were more serious in the areas of training technical personnel and developing effective strategy and tactics against Israel than in maintaining the flow of arms from abroad. An accelerated training program for pilots was initiated soon after the hostilities ended in 1967. But even three years later, President Nasser conceded that Egypt did not have enough qualified pilots to match the strength of the Israeli air force.[101] This statement was made after the first group of 200 pilots had returned from the Soviet Union in the fall of 1969. Recognizing the need to enhance the efficiency of the armed forces, the Egyptian government undertook a comprehensive program of training in the use of the highly sophisticated Soviet weapons and of developing new military strategy and tactics against the Israeli occupation forces in the Sinai. For this purpose, it acquired the services of Soviet instructors and advisers, who began to arrive in Egypt in small numbers (700–900) before the June War and later rapidly increased their strength to 15,000 by the time their mission was abruptly terminated by Sadat in July 1972.[102]

In the same vein, the Egyptian government in 1968 made it obligatory for able-bodied college students to take military training. With the exception of graduate students and undergraduates over 28 years of age, all students attending institutions of higher learning had to fulfill this obligation before they graduated. Although it is difficult to accurately assess the impact of this program, it apparently was designed more to create a patriotic spirit and to establish the fundamentals of discipline than to prepare the students for modern warfare.

While Egyptians were being trained to narrow the proficiency gap that existed between the Egyptian armed forces and those of Israel, Cairo maintained a steady pressure on the Soviet Union to provide the more sophisticated MIG-23s, which could, under appropriate conditions, match or even exceed the speed, range, and ceiling of the U.S.-made F-4. Although the Soviet Union sent a squadron of MIG-23s to Egypt in 1971, the operational control over these planes remained with the Soviet pilots. The main purpose of stationing the MIG-23s in Egypt was to provide a deterrence against Israeli deep-penetration attacks while the surface-to-air missile (SAM) network was being constructed and extended to protect strategic areas in the country. Previously, it was assumed that the Soviet refusal to provide Egypt with the MIG-23s was based on the unavailability of qualified Egyptian pilots and fear of revealing the secrets of the plane, which was one of the best combat planes available to the Russian armed forces.[103] However, it seems to us that the Russian refusal to supply Egypt with MIG-23s was based more on political factors than on technical and security factors.

Soviet relations with Sadat have not been very cordial because of his continuous efforts to depolarize the Arab-Israeli conflict, a process aimed at increasing Egyptian-U.S. contacts and at reducing Egyptian reliance on the Soviet Union. In addition, Sadat's reputation as a conservative leader, whose domestic and foreign policies seemed to favor the "rightist" elements in the region, created further problems between Moscow and Cairo. Recently, the Soviet Union has supplied an undisclosed number of MIG-23s to Syria, and Russian instructors are currently training Syrian pilots to fly the plane. This is a clear signal to Sadat that the Russians do not consider him indispensable to maintenance of their influence in the Arab world.

The delivery of MIG-23s to the Syrians could increase domestic pressure on Sadat for a more conciliatory policy toward the Soviet Union, which continues to reward its "allies" and "friends." Currently, Sadat is in an unenviable position. With the exception of some spare parts and some replacement weapons lost in the October War, the Egyptian armed forces have not received any new equipment from the Soviet Union since the disengagement agreement was signed between Egypt and Israel.[104] Israel, on the other hand, claims to be stronger now than it was before the October War. This leaves Egypt without any credible threat to resume hostilities if Israel does not agree to withdraw from the Sinai within a reasonable period of time. Sadat could, of course, resume hostilities with the equipment and the forces at his disposal. But such an action probably would cause heavy damage to the Egyptian armed forces and, above all, would undermine the confidence the Arabs had achieved as a result of the Egyptian and Syrian military gains in the initial days of the October War. These military gains have destroyed the myth of Israeli invincibility. The October War proved to the Arabs that they were capable of waging modern warfare against an Israel that held technological and scientific superiority over its Arab adversaries. Without adequate preparations, another war with Israel could destroy the psychological confidence that has allowed the Egyptians to show willingness to accept Israel's existence as an independent state.

In an effort to diversify its sources of weapons, Egypt has been seeking to purchase modern weapons from non-Soviet sources. Before the October War, Sadat had tried to buy the Anglo-French Jaguar supersonic strike fighter. His request, however, was refused because of the French and British embargo on the sale of arms to countries directly involved in the Arab-Israeli conflict. The French, nevertheless, agreed to sell 110 Mirages to Libya, 38 of which were delivered before the war and reportedly were stationed in Egypt during this period.[105] Under a military cooperation agreement with Libya, Egyptian pilots were trained to fly the Mirage before the October War.[106] Because of the Libyan-Egyptian rift, these Mirages, 100 tanks, and an artillery regiment stationed in Egypt were returned to Libya during September and October 1974.[107]

The lifting of the French arms embargo in August 1974 has opened new prospects for Egypt to acquire sophisticated French weapons either directly or through a third party willing to act on Cairo's behalf. Three such arrangements have already been reported by the press. In a dispatch from Beirut, Joseph Fitchett reported that Kuwait will be allowed to purchase the Anglo-French Jaguar and that it can be expected to give Egyptian pilots access to its Jaguars.[108] According to a story in the New York *Times*, Saudi Arabia ordered 36 Mirage Vs. Of this order, three Mirages were reported to have been delivered to Egypt in November 1974. In January 1977, France announced a multibillion dollar arms agreement with Egypt and the Arab Military Industries Organization that provides for transfer of weapons technology, weapons systems, and personnel training to Egypt and other members of AMIO. The cost of the agreement was reported as about $4 billion to be paid for by Saudi Arabia, Qatar, the UAE, and Egypt.[109]

While Egypt is seeking to acquire weapons through third parties, it also is making direct approaches to France, Britain, and the United States for a variety of weapons systems. In June 1974, *An-Nahar* reported that a U.S. Defense Department team would go to Cairo to determine Egypt's need for American weapons. Although nothing significant seems to have come of this effort, Egyptian efforts in London and Paris were more successful.[110] Britain's aircraft industry reportedly was willing to supply Egypt with means to build its own battlefield helicopters and fighter-trainer planes.[111] Similarly, the French government seems to have indicated its willingness to sell sophisticated arms directly to Egypt. According to news dispatches from Paris and Cairo, President Sadat, during his recent official visit to France, purchased large quantities of French combat planes, electronic equipment, tanks, missiles, helicopters, and radar systems. It is assumed that Saudi Arabia has agreed to share the major portion of the cost of this equipment.[112]

Even if Sadat succeeded in acquiring all the equipment he wanted from the French, the Egyptian armed forces still would not be as well equipped as those of Israel, whose U.S.-built F-4 is superior to the French Mirage. Furthermore, while Egypt is seeking to catch up with Israel at least in the quality of armament, Israel is making a quantum jump in improving its arsenal by seeking to acquire a number of F-14 and F-15 airplanes from the United States.[113] If Israel achieves an overwhelming superiority in combat planes and in electronic countermeasures that would effectively neutralize the Egyptian and Syrian missile and radar networks, Tel Aviv might not be able to resist the temptation to launch a preemptive strike against the Arabs, whose military vulnerability seems to be increasing because of Soviet refusal to supply the Egyptian armed forces with new equipment. Such an act would, of course, destroy chances of an Arab-Israeli settlement, for which the United States has been making strenuous efforts.[114]

Although the Egyptian armed forces obtain most of their major weapons systems from abroad, some of the defense needs are met locally. In addition to small arms, artillery, and mortars, the Egyptian armament industry has produced a limited number of jet trainers. In the 1960s, Egypt, with the help of German scientists, endeavored to develop three surface-to-surface missiles: the 235-mile-range *Al-Zafir,* the 375-mile-range *Al-Kahir*, and the 440-mile-range *Al-Ared. Al-Zafir* and *Al-Kahir* were test fired in July 1962 and *Al-Ared* in July 1963. All three were displayed in the Cairo military parade in 1965. But there is no evidence that these missiles have become operational. Our assumption is that the withdrawal of most German scientists from Egypt, following the crisis in Arab-German relations in 1965, brought the project to an end. It is plausible that the Egyptian government, with financial support from the Arab oil-producing states, will again focus its attention on developing domestic defense capabilities.[115]

The Egyptian government has been urging the Arab oil-producing states to give serious attention to the idea of setting up a joint armament industry that would reduce their reliance on foreign weapons. In this connection, the chiefs of staff of the members of the Arab League have recommended the investment of 2 percent of national revenues for the establishment of a joint armament industry. General Saaduddin Shazli, then the Egyptian chief of staff, contended that if the Arab states accepted this recommendation, they could overtake the Israelis in weapons production within five years.[116] While it is not yet known whether this recommendation will be accepted by the Arab states, press reports indicate that the French government might be amenable to setting up assembly plants for the Mirage in the region. Even if the Arab countries were to accept this recommendation, it would be a long time before Egypt could become self-sufficient in producing sophisticated weapons systems. In the meantime, Cairo will continue its efforts to find foreign sources to meet its defense needs. At present, it seems that France will become a major source of arms for Egypt and several other Arab states.

Economic Objectives and Policies

At the same time that it affirms the socialist character of the country and guarantees private ownership against unlawful expropriation and sequestration, the Egyptian constitution enunciates the following major economic objectives:[117]

to increase the national income through a comprehensive development plan;
to assure just distribution of the national wealth;
to raise the standard of living;
to increase work opportunities;
to link wages with production;
to narrow income differentials by guaranteeing a minimum wage and fixing a
    maximum wage;
to acquire and maintain public control of all means of production;
to secure participation of the workers in the management of public and private
    enterprises;
to implement profit-sharing programs for the benefit of the workers;[118]
to allocate to public, cooperative, and private sectors equitable responsibilities
    in the development projects of the country.

Although the permanent constitution was adopted in 1971, some of the economic goals and welfare principles that it contains have been the basis of the country's development program since the mid-1950s. After the nationalization of the Suez Canal Company on July 26, 1956, "planning," "welfare," and "nationalization" became three pillars of Arab Socialism, which was designed to create a socialist-type economic system in the country. Since then, economic policy has been aimed at self-sufficiency through import substitution, promotion of export-oriented industries, establishment of heavy industry, rural industrialization, and expansion of key industries. As the state enlarged its economic role and gradually brought all industry, transportation, banking, and import-export trade under its monopoly, the economy became more "socialized" and bureaucratized."[119] This rapid expansion of the bureaucracy is considered to be the most important institutional change in the Egyptian economy. The existence of a large bureaucracy is not a new phenomenon in Egypt, however; Egyptian rulers have traditionally depended on the bureaucracy for effective control over the country's resources. The recent expansion of the bureaucracy has been in the areas that were, at least from the middle of the nineteenth century, excluded from its control.[120]

Since the nationalization of the Suez Canal Company, Egyptian efforts at industrialization have overwhelmingly depended on financial and technological aid from the Soviet Union and East European states. As a result of this dependence, the choice of technique in industrialization has been a function of the capacity of the donors.[121]

In an effort to reduce its dependence on the Communist states, Egypt has taken a number of steps designed to increase its economic and political intercourse with the West, which, Cairo hopes, would be willing to share its technological and financial resources. In this connection, the Egyptian government under Sadat has moved toward more liberal economic policies. It has eased restrictions on business in the country and has created a number of "free zones" in Alexandria and the Suez Canal Zone where foreign investors will be allowed to import industrial machinery free of duty and to export manufactured goods. In addition, foreign investors have been promised a five-year tax holiday and permission to repatriate profits and salaries of foreign experts—and even the initial investments, after an agreed period. Furthermore, the Egyptian government has granted permission to foreign banks, including at least four American banks, to operate in the country. It hopes that the opening of these American banks will facilitate bilateral trade between Egypt and the United States.

While the American banks were being given permission to operate in the country, Egypt and the United States signed a number of other agreements designed to expand economic ties between the two countries. They agreed to do the following:[122]

form a joint Project Development Institute, to be located in Cairo, that will evaluate Egypt's economic development plans;

negotiate a tax equalization treaty to avoid double taxation of American firms doing business in Egypt;

facilitate cooperative and joint ventures among appropriate governmental and private institutions;

encourage increased trade between the two countries;

make special efforts to increase tourism in both directions;

establish a joint cooperation commission, headed by the foreign ministers of the two countries;

set up a joint working group on Suez Canal reconstruction and development, to consider and review plans for reopening the Suez Canal and reconstruction of the cities along it;

establish a joint working group to investigate and recommend measures designed to open the way for U.S. private investment in joint ventures in Egypt and to promote trade between the two countries;

set up a joint working group on agriculture, to study and recommend actions designed to increase Egypt's agricultural production;

establish a joint working group on technology, research, and development in scientific fields, including space, with special emphasis on exchange of scientists;

set up a joint working group on medical cooperation to assist Egypt in strengthening its medical research, treatment, and training facilities.

In addition to signing bilateral agreements with the United States, Egypt entered into similar arrangements with Iran, Saudi Arabia, Kuwait, the United Arab Emirates (UAE), West Germany, France, and Japan. Even before the shah's official visit to Egypt in January 1975, Iran and Egypt had entered into a number of financial and technical cooperation agreements that would assure about $800 million of Iranian investments in Egypt and would greatly expand trade between the two countries.[123]

Similarly, Egypt and Saudi Arabia have entered into a series of financial and commercial agreements designed to strengthen the economy of Egypt and its ties with Riyadh. The two countries have agreed to the following:

formation of a joint Egyptian-Saudi reconstruction company, with a capital of
    $50 million, to be shared equally—the aim of the company is to invest in
    reconstruction projects in Egypt;
formation of a joint Egyptian-Saudi industrial investment company, with a
    capital of $100 million, to make investments in industrial development
    projects in Egypt.[124]

In addition to approving a $700 million loan to Cairo, Iraq formed a holding company with Egypt called the Arab Industrial Development Company, with a capital of $350 million, on an equal partnership basis. This company will build factories for tractors, automobiles, and other engineering industries.[125]

Egypt has entered into similar financial arrangements with Kuwait, Qatar, and the UAE that will provide Cairo with about $2 billion in loans and grants until about 1980.[126]

It is evident that the new "open door" policy being pursued by Sadat, and the changed political and psychological climate in the country, have attracted considerable Arab capital to Egypt. These factors have encouraged Japan and a number of West European states to extend loans to the Egyptian government, which also is seeking technology from Europe and Japan. Japan has signed a $175 million agreement for widening and deepening the Suez Canal, a project that will take about 3.5 years. Japan, West Germany, and Brazil have jointly agreed to set up an iron and steel complex in one of the free zones near Alexandria. This project, which will cost E£ 60 million, will have a production capacity of 1.6 million tons annually. Production is scheduled to begin in the second half of 1977.

The Egyptian development strategy seems to be directed toward acquiring modern technology through triangular business and commercial agreements financed by oil-producing Arab states with surplus petrodollars available for investment abroad. Currently, France and Britain are leading all other European states and Japan in their willingness and ability to transfer modern technology to Egypt through the military and civilian projects being financed jointly by Egypt and its oil-producing Arab friends. Some of this technology —British Leyland's proposed assembly plant for Land Rovers, for example— might not be as sophisticated as what Egypt would like to acquire, but the fact that new sources of technology are now available is in itself significant. Egypt no longer need rely for technology solely on that of the Soviet Union and

Eastern Europe, which in most cases is less sophisticated than that of Europe, Japan and the United States. Furthermore, there is no reason to believe that the West European states, Britain, and Japan, given their energy and business needs, would refuse to help Egypt acquire and broaden its technological base in the more complex fields of nuclear energy, space, computers, and communications.

Egyptian economic policies, as reflected in the new liberalized laws and in the ten-year development plan (1973–82), indicate that the government is determined to alleviate the social and economic problems created by shortages of sugar, tea, meat, rice, soap, and matches.[127] While industrial plans are being implemented to make Egypt self-sufficient in consumer goods, the government has entered into bilateral agreements that will allow it to import scarce essential goods from a variety of foreign sources, including the United States, Australia, France, Japan, and other industrial centers.

Altogether, the Egyptian government spent E£ 200 million on importing consumer goods during 1974; and indications were that in order to keep the population content, it would have spend more money on importing consumer goods and basic commodities. The foreign exchange value of the consumer goods aside, the Egyptian government spends E£ 350 million annually on maintaining the stability of prices of basic consumer goods.[128]

A quick look at the main targets of the ten-year plan, given in Table 2, shows that the industrial sector is scheduled to receive by far the largest share of capital investment—E£ 2,700 million (34.06 percent) of the total sum of E£ 7,925 million—for the entire plan. Transportation and communication are projected to receive 21.45 percent of the total, followed by housing (13.88 percent) and agriculture (12.61 percent).

In terms of its physical targets, the ten-year plan is projected to achieve the following:[129]

double the real gross national income from E£ 2,867 million in 1972 to E£ 5,735 million—this would require a sustained annual increase of 7.2 percent;
raise the per capita annual income from E£ 80 in 1972 to E£ 125;
increase agricultural production by 42 percent;
create 3 million new jobs;
reach an equilibrium in the nation's balance of trade by the end of 1977, using the surplus thereafter to repay foreign debts and build up the nation's reserves (perhaps one of the most difficult goals to achieve).

Since the mid-1950s, Egypt has incurred a large debt to the United States, West Germany, the International Bank for Reconstruction and Development, and several other European and Arab countries. Moreover, although no exact figures on Egyptian indebtedness are available in public records, it is estimated

TABLE 2
Egypt's Ten-Year Plan, 1973–82

	1973–77		1978–82		Total Period	
	Million E£	Percent of Projected Total	Million E£	Percent of Projected Total	Million E£	Percent
Industry	1,000	33.27	1,700	34.55	2,700	34.06
Agriculture	400	13.31	600	12.19	1,000	12.61
Transportation and communication	700	23.29	1,000	20.32	1,700	21.45
Electric power	200	6.65	400	8.13	600	7.57
Housing	350	11.64	750	15.24	1,100	13.88
Public utilities	130	4.32	195	3.96	325	4.10
Social sciences	225	7.48	275	5.58	500	6.30
Total	3,005	99.96	4,920	99.97	7,925	99.97

Source: An-Nahar Arab Report 3, no. 47 (November 20, 1972): n.p.

that Cairo owes over $4 billion to Moscow.[130] Prior to the cancellation of Leonid Brezhnev's visit to Egypt scheduled for January 1975, there were reports that the Soviet Union had agreed to reschedule Egypt's debt. Since the cancellation, however, Sadat has disclosed Moscow's refusal to do so.[131] Although Egypt has been promised nearly $3 billion in economic aid and grants by the Arab oil-producing states and by Iran, most of this money is tied to specific projects and thus is not available for paying foreign debts. Therefore, in order for Egypt to meet its foreign debt obligations, it will have to strain its meager foreign exchange that is direly needed for defense and social projects.

Despite the Soviet-Egyptian rift, Moscow has continued to show its interest and willingness to help Cairo in the industrialization of the country. In July 1974, *Al-Ahram* reported that the Soviet Union had agreed to carry out a number of industrial projects in Egypt at a cost of 120 million rubles (about $161 million). This accord was reached during a visit to Moscow by Egypt's minister of industry, who signed three agreements with the Soviet Union. The projects included the expansion of Egypt's aluminum production from 100,000 tons annually to 166,000 tons.[132] In October 1974, the Egyptian minister of planning, Ismail Sabry Abdullah, announced that the Soviet Union had agreed to participate in two major industrial projects in Egypt—an iron and steel complex in Alexandria and an aluminum factory in Upper Egypt. The minister said that Moscow had further agreed to enlarge the Soviet-built and Soviet-financed Helwan iron and steel complex at a cost of $100 million. It also would provide Egypt with a $50 million loan to finance economic projects over the next 14 months and would reactivate long-promised economic aid.[133] In December of that year, there were unconfirmed reports suggesting that, because of the Egyptian-U.S. disagreement over the sale of a U.S. nuclear reactor to Egypt, Cairo had turned to Moscow for the purchase of that item. *An-Nahar* reported that the Soviet Union had agreed to the Egyptian request.

Although Egyptian-Soviet relations have continued to deteriorate, we believe that their economic and industrial ties will not radically change in the immediately foreseeable future. This is because technical and economic factors have tied Egypt firmly to the Soviet Union and Eastern Europe, the source of 90 percent of Egypt's imported modern industry. Furthermore, since the June War, the Soviet Union has become Egypt's principal trading partner. For example, in 1971, Egypt's imports from the Soviet Union were valued at E£ 54.0 million; in the same year, its exports to Russia were valued at E£ 136.2 million. Egypt's total imports during 1971 were E£ 400 million and its exports E£ 343.2. Although the 1972 figures showed a slight decline, the Soviet Union remained by far the principal customer for Egyptian goods and services, which in that year were valued at E£ 126.0 million (exports to Russia); Cairo imported E£ 51.9 million worth of goods from the Soviet Union. During that year, Egypt's total imports amounted to E£ 381.4 million and its exports to

E£ 358.8 million. While these figures by themselves are high enough, when we add Egyptian trade with Eastern Europe and take into consideration the categories of Egyptian imports and exports, we soon realize the magnitude of Egypt's efforts to reorient its trade relations. In 1971, Egyptian imports from Eastern Europe (Czechoslovakia, East Germany, Yugoslavia, Poland, and Rumania) totaled E£ 58.20 million and its exports to them totaled E£ 53.0 million. In other words, of its total E£ 743.2 million external trade in 1971, Egypt exchanged goods and services worth E£ 301.4 million with the Soviet Union and its five socialist allies—a little less than 50 percent of its total external trade. In 1972, Egypt's total external trade stood at E£ 740.2 million and its trade with the Soviet Union and Eastern Europe was valued at E£ 298.50 million.

It is significant that in recent years, raw materials and industrial equipment have accounted for half of all Soviet exports to Egypt, while the Soviet Union has taken about 30 percent of all manufactured goods exported by Egypt. During the heyday of Soviet-Egyptian freindship, bilateral agreements between the two countries established in Egypt a number of manufacturing units specifically designed to produce goods for Soviet markets. Some of these units reportedly are producing while others are being built under the previous arrangements. With the completion of these factories, Egyptian exports to the Soviet Union should increase and help to reduce the Egyptian debt to Moscow. It is argued that the Soviet Union will continue to provide Egypt with technical aid for industrialization. This will help the Soviet Union not only in maintaining its presence in Egypt but also in realizing the economic and commercial benefits that have been calculated into Soviet economic development plans. On its part, Egypt would be well advised to maintain good commercial relations with the Soviet Union, for Egyptian manufactured products would not find many profitable markets elsewhere.[134]

In summary, it may be recalled that the Egyptian ten-year plan, the "transitional plan," and the annual development and ordinary budgets all focus primary attention on industrialization of the country. In each case, the industrial sector receives the lion's share of the budget. It is evident that the Egyptian government is determined to carry out a rapid industrialization of the country, and for this purpose Cairo is offering liberal incentives to foreign investors willing to participate in the government's industrial endeavor. Through rapid industrialization, the government hopes to alleviate economic hardships of the people, most of whom live in thousands of villages in the ten-mile agricultural belt along the Nile. Although the government has come under strong criticism for its "neglect" of the agricultural sector, which still accounts for 30 percent of the gross domestic product, it is our understanding that Egypt has reached the limit beyond which further efforts at land reclamation would prove exorbitantly costly, and thus counterproductive to the country's goals of economic development. This is not to suggest that there is no room for increasing the agricultural yield through the widespread use of fertilizers and rotation of crops. While the Egyptian government does have extensive plans for the manufacture and distribution of fertilizers, it does not foresee opening up large new agricultural zones in the country. This is primarily because the land to be reclaimed is often arid desert, and the cost of reclamation is much higher than the short-term expected results. Therefore, the government prefers to invest in manufacturing industry, where returns to the scarce capital may well be higher than in agriculture.[135]

Although the promises of about $3 billion in economic aid and grants from the Arab oil producers and from Iran have alleviated the Egyptian deficiency in foreign capital, Egypt still needs to import technology, which she is seeking from the West and Japan. In such projects as iron and steel mills, aluminum mills, a number of others that were designed, financed, and constructed by the Soviet Union and Eastern Europe, Egypt will, of necessity, continue to rely on the socialist bloc for spare parts and for expansion of the projects. For the establishment of new industries, however, Egypt is turning to the West for technological and, in some cases, financial aid, for which Cairo is offering generous incentives to potential investors.

Social Objectives and Policies

In a major statement to a joint session of the ASU Central Committee and People's Assembly on April 18, 1974, President Sadat set down five major social goals for Egypt:

social development and the building of the individual;
entering the age of science and technology;
cultural progress based on science and faith;
an open society enjoying the currents of freedom;
a secure society in which every citizen is reassured about his present and
    future.[136]

President Sadat said that social development must take place within "our spiritual and ethical values," which alone can save the Egyptians from the adverse effects of material affluence that the "age of science and technology" would bring to the country. He went on to say that the Egyptian people "adhere to the principles of social solidarity, cohesion of the family, and the prevalence of the sentiments of love and rejection of rancor." These principles, he said, were "a fence against absolute individual whims and social irresponsibility."[137] Through the achievement of these social goals, Sadat hopes to create a "new Egyptian man" who, although immersed in national, cultural, and spiritual values, will be modern in outlook, educated, and without the fanaticism and the spirit of fatalism "falsely attributed to the people."[138]

With these goals in view, the Egyptian government would like to undertake a "comprehensive revolution in the systems and concepts of education and general culture in all their forms and at all their levels, starting with the elimination of illiteracy and then proceeding to general, technical and college education and then to scientific and technological research."[139]

The Egyptian government is striving to provide educational facilities in all sections of the country; primary education is theoretically free and compulsory for children between the ages of 6 and 12, but the rapidly increasing population is retarding the government's efforts to provide enough facilities and trained teachers to meet the demand. Tuition is also free in secondary schools and institutions of higher learning. The expansion of educational facilities at the secondary and university levels has rapidly increased the number of high school and college graduates, most of whom major in social sciences and the humanities. Despite the government's efforts to encourage vocational and technical training, that educational trend continues. This situation has created a massive surplus of college graduates with degrees in liberal arts who are automatically given jobs in the already overgrown bureaucracy. Thus, while the educational facilities have expanded rapidly, economic opportunities have not kept pace with them. On the other hand, there is a serious shortage of technicians and trained personnel at the middle level, which slows the rate of economic development.

Although the Egyptian government recognizes the need for better health and social services for the people, its annual and development budgets and its ten-year plan do not reflect significant concern with these sectors. The 1971–72 annual budget allocated less than 7 percent to health, social, and religious services.[140] The ten-year plan shows no substantial change in the percentage of allocation for this sector. Heavy defense expenditure, focus on industrialization that requires heavy capital outlay, and reconstruction of the Suez Canal Zone cities are primarily responsible for this neglect—a situation that recently came under criticism by a commission of the People's Assembly set up to examine the government budget for 1975. The commission noted with regret the government failure to appropriate enough funds for public health, education, agriculture, and rural electrification projects.[141]

Realizing the social, political, and strategic risks inherent in the concentration of population and industry in the narrow Nile Valley (which contains only 3–5 percent of the country's total area), the Egyptian government is planning new industrial parks and population centers in the Sinai Peninsula as well as in the southern part of the country. By providing job opportunities and better social services to the people in the provinces, the government further hopes to discourage the country's surplus rural labor from crowding the metropolitan areas, especially Cairo, and from overtaxing the already inadequate housing facilities, communication systems, and social services available in Cairo and Alexandria.

NOTES

1. Foreign Broadcast Information Service (FBIS), March 16, 1976, p. D–4.

2. *An-Nahar Arab Report* 6, no. 51 (December 22, 1975): 2–3.

3. President Anwar Sadat's speech to the People's Assembly Session, March 14, 1976, as reported by FBIS, March 16, 1976, pp. D–2 to D–3.

4. FBIS, March 29, 1976, p. D–29; and New York *Times*, May 3, 1976, p. 6.

5. American University, Foreign Area Studies, *Area Handbook for United Arab Republic (Egypt)* (Washington D.C.: U.S. Government Printing Office, 1970), p. viii. Coptic-Muslim relations have not always been peaceful and accommodating; the two communities have had many bloody clashes over the past decades, the latest occurring in November 1972. Despite the efforts of the Egyptian government and political parties to create harmonious relations between the two religious communities, the latent mutual antagonism between the Coptic and Muslim clergy has prevented a lasting reconciliation. A pro-Coptic view may be found in Edward Wakin, *A Lonely Minority* (New York: William Morrow, 1963); also see the statement of Shawky F. Karas on behalf of the American Coptic Association on July 24, 1974, U.S. Congress, Senate, Committee on Foreign Relations, *Foreign Assistance Authorization*, S.3394, 93rd Congress. 2nd Sess., 1974, (Washington, D.C.: U.S. Government Printing Office, 1974), pp. 371–74.

6. Anwar Abdel Malek, *Egypt: Military Society* (New York: Random House, 1968); and Mahmoud Hussein, *Class Conflict in Egypt: 1945–1971* (New York and London: Monthly Review Press, 1973). The latter writer is usually labeled as a Marxist of pro-Chinese orientation.

7. *Ijma* (consensus) is one of the four main sources of Islamic law. Others sources are the Quran (Koran), the Hadith (traditions of the Prophet Muhammad), and *ijtihad* (interpretation by qualified persons). *Qiyas* (analogy) is another source acceptable to some doctors of law.

8. See Nasser's speeches on special occasions, such as anniversaries of the July Revolution, birthdays of the Prophet Muhammad, and Eids (several days of celebrations following the month of fasting, Ramadan, and the annual pilgrimage, *hajj*, to Mecca). Nasser focused on this concept during his confrontation with the Egyptian Communists, who opposed his methods of achieving consensus by merging all political parties into a single party as an instrument of conflict resolution. See R. H. Dekmejian, *Egypt Under Nasser* (Albany: State University of New York Press, 1971); Mohammed Heikal, *The Cairo Documents* (New York: Doubleday, 1973); Anthony Nutting, *Nasser* (New York: E. P. Dutton, 1972); and R. D. McLaurin and Mohammed Mughisuddin, *The Soviet Union and the Middle East* (Washington, D.C.: American Institutes for Research, 1974), pp. 275–313.

9. For details of election procedures, presidential powers, and the council of ministers' relationship with the People's Assembly and the president, see the Egyptian constitution (1971), art. 73–152.

10. Art. 165–78. See Figure 1.

11. Art. 86, 114, and 116. For the first time, in October 1971, the ASU did not propose a list of candidates for the general election to the People's Assembly. It left the door open to any member of the party to seek election to the assembly. In this election, 1,533 candidates participated; 338 were elected and 12 were appointed by the president for the six districts in Sinai and the Suez Canal that were under Israeli occupation. Some of these candidates were not members of the ASU, but were allowed by Sadat to join the party so that they might compete in the election. Farmers and workers won 53 percent of the seats (*Record of the Arab World* [July-December 1971]: 2803–64).

12. Art. 179.

13. Art. 180.

14. The president of the republic has the discretion to create more specialized councils whenever necessary.

15. FBIS, June 3, 1974, pp. D–11 to D–12.

16. *Record of the Arab World* (July-December 1971): 2841.

17. *An-Nahar Arab Report* 1, no. 21 (July 27, 1970).

18. In the May 1971 conspiracy against President Sadat, the secretary-general of ASU, Abdel Mohsin Abdel Nur was one of the 120 accused of plotting to overthrow the regime. Three other members of the Executive Committee also were allegedly involved in the conspiracy— Mohammed Labib Shoqair, speaker of the National Assembly; Diaeddin Mohammed Dawud; and Sharawi Jomaa, minister of the interior. All were found guilty and sentenced to imprisonment; Nur received 15 years at hard labor, Dawud was given 10 years at hard labor, and Shoqair received one year at hard labor. Jomaa was sentenced to death (commuted to life imprisonment at hard labor). For a list of the accused and the sentences they received, see *Record of the Arab World* (July-December, 1971): 2837–41.

Immediately after Abdel Nur's arrest, Sadat appointed Dr. Mohammed Dakruni as acting secretary-general of the ASU; a few days later, he was replaced by Dr. Aziz Sidqi. Later, Sayyed Mirei was elected secretary-general of the ASU. Each was personally chosen by Sadat.

19. *Record of the Arab World* (July-December, 1971): 2846–47.

20. Mohammed Osman Ismail was at the time an assistant secretary-general of the ASU. In addition to his role on the disciplinary committee, he also was allegedly active in organizing a group of "rightist" students who reportedly were trained in Libya to fight against the leftist student groups. The other Egyptian said to be involved in this project was Ashraf Marwan, Sadat's adviser on information. See *An-Nahar Arab Report* 4, no. 6 (February 5, 1973); Jim Hoagland, "Egyptians Fear That Sadat Will Return to 'Rule by the Whip,' " Washington *Post*, February 19, 1973, p. A–17.

The chairman of this powerful subcommittee was Hafez Badawi, speaker of the People's Assembly. In 1971, he presided over the First Chamber of the Revolution Court, which tried the more than 100 conspirators against the Sadat regime.

Because half of its 12 members were expelled from the ASU, the Egyptian Press Syndicate was temporarily dissolved. It had supported the student demonstration and pressured for an end to press censorship; this reportedly had angered Sadat, who proceeded to take disciplinary action against the syndicate. Prominent among those accused of "deviation" and expelled from ASU were: Lutfi Kholi, editor of *At-Talia,* the leftist literary magazine published by *Al-Ahram*, and a member of the ASU Executive Committee; Ahmad Fuad Najm; Mahmoud Amin Alam; Dr. Ali Rai; Amal Dunqol; Ahmad Hijazi; Muhsinah Tawfiq; Alfred Faraj; Ali Abdul Khaleq; and Tharwat Abaza. (*An-Nahar Arab Report* 4 [February 12, 1973]).

21. Hoagland, "Egyptians Fear. . . ."

22. Dekmejian, *Egypt*, pp. 192–99.

23. Iliya Harik, "The Single Party as a Subordinate Movement: The Case of Egypt," *World Politics,* no. 1 (October 1973): 81; Leonard Binder, "Political Recruitment and Participation in Egypt," ch. 8 of *Political Parties and Political Development,* Joseph Palombara and Myron Weiner, eds. (Princeton: Princeton University Press, 1966), p. 219.

24. Dekmejian, *Egypt*, p. 256.

25. Afaf Loutfi el-Sayed, "The Role of the *Ulama* in Egypt During the Early Nineteenth Century," in *Political and Social Change in Modern Egypt*, P. M. Holt, ed. (London: Oxford University Press, 1968), p. 280.

26. Bayard Dodge, *Al-Azhar* (Washington, D.C.: Middle East Institute, 1974), p. 180.

27. Bernard Lewis, "The Return of Islam," *Commentary* 61, no. 1 (January 1976): 39–49. The implications of the title are obvious but not necessarily accurate. We believe that Islam never

really "departed" from the scene; it was only perceived to have done so by writers who based their conclusions on transitory episodes. For stories on alcohol and al-Azhar, and the Brotherhood, see New York *Times*, May 18, 1976, p. 9; May 19, 1976, p. 6; June 1, 1976, p. 2. Also see Ahmed Shawki, "Moslem Brotherhood is Reviving in Egypt," Washington *Post*, July 12, 1976, p. A–10; Richard Crichfield, "Egypt Gravitates Toward Return to Moslem Orthodoxy," Washington *Star*, June 1, 1976, p. 1; and "Egypt is Going Dry," May 18, 1976, p. A–4.

28. As a representative sampling of the former, see Michael W. Suleiman, "Attitudes of Arab Elite Toward Palestine and Israel," *American Political Science Review* 67, no. 2 (June 1973): 482–89; examples of the latter are found daily in the U.S. and European media.

29. *An-Nahar Arab Report* 2, no. 37 (September 13, 1971): 3; and 6, nos. 19, 21, 24 (May 12, May 26, June 16, 1976): n.p.

30. President Sadat's interview with James Reston, "Egyptian Leader Gives Conditions for Peace Accord," New York *Times*, December 28, 1970, pp. 1, 14. Excerpts from this interview may be found on p. 15.

31. Ibid., p. 15

32. Ibid., p. 15.

33. The *Times* (London), December 19, 1972, as reported in "Chronology," *Middle East Journal* 27, no. 2 (Spring 1973): 196. For a comprehensive discussion of Egypt's diplomatic efforts before the October War, see Mohammed Heikal, *The Road to Ramadan* (New York: Quadrangle, 1975).

34. *An-Nahar Arab Report* 4, nos. 5, 31 (January 29, July 30, 1973): n.p.

35. Ibid. nos. 39, 40 (September 24, October 1, 1973): n.p.

36. Ibid. no. 36 (September 3, 1973): 1–2.

37. Mohammed Mughisuddin and James Horgen, *Regional Military Cooperation in the Middle East: 1970–1975* (Washington, D.C.: American Institutes for Research, 1975), pp. 32–41.

38. For a comprehensive discussion of these disagreements, see Maj. Gen. D. K. Palit, *Return to Sinai* (New Delhi: Palit and Palit, 1974); and Heikal, *The Road to Ramadan*.

39. *An-Nahar Arab Report* 5, no. 18 (May 6, 1974): 4.

40. Dan Gillon, "Israel: No Time for Stalling," *Middle East International*, no. 52 (October 1975): 6–8.

41. Several press reports indicated that the United States aided the Syrian military action in Lebanon. Whether or not these reports were accurate is less important than the fact that many Palestinian and Arab elites believed that the United States and Israel were allowing, if not actively supporting, the Syrian military action against the Palestinians in Lebanon. See Henry Tanner, "Questions and Answers on Lebanon," New York *Times*, August 7, 1976, p. 2; and Douglas Watson, "Views from Behind the Gunsights," Washington *Post*, August 11, 1976, pp. A–1 and A–14; and Terence Smith, "Israel's Stepping Up Patrols in Lebanon," New York *Times*, August 3, 1976, pp. 1 and 4.

42. *An-Nahar Arab Report* 2, no. 18 (May 3, 1971).

43. Ibid. 3, no. 39 (September 25, 1972); John Waterbury, *"A Note on Egypt: 1973,"* American Universities Field Staff, *Reports*, Northeast Africa series 18, no. 4 (July 1973): 1–9.

44. *The Arab World*, March 28, 1974, p. 7. Although a number of pro-Nasserite Lebanese issued statements criticizing the Egyptian press for anti-Nasser propaganda and the Sadat regime for undoing the socialist gains in Egypt, other prominent Lebanese politicians, such as Dr. Amin al-Hafez and other pro-Nasserites, have indicated their support of Sadat's domestic policies. FBIS (quoting *An-Nahar* of April 7), April 12, 1974, p. D–4.

45. Victor Zorza, "Kremlin Firing Back," Washington *Post*, April 23, 1974, p. A–15.

46. *The Arab World*, March 28, 1974, p. 7. *Al-Ahram* also assured him that the recent calls for taking measures to correct past mistakes did not imply personal criticism of Nasser.

47. "Soviets Question Egypt's Economic Policy," *The Arab World*, March 26, 1974, p. 5.

48. *Al-yom* (April 28, 1974), as reported in *The Arab World*, April 30, 1974, pp. 9–10. Dr.

Ismail Sabry, minister of planning, made a similar statement in an interview in *Rose al-Youssef: The Arab World*, July 4, 1974, pp. 9–10.

49. *An-Nahar Arab Report* 3, no. 50 (December 11, 1972): 1. It should be noted that these organizations were being formed at the time of the Libyan-Egyptian collaboration. Since this collaboration has been discontinued, it is assumed that Libyan support of these organizations has ended and that some of the leaders no longer hold privileged positions in the Egyptian system.

50. In January 1972, President Sadat accused the striking students of having received E£ 16,000 from "foreign hands." Although he personally did not identify either the source of this aid or a specific group of recipients, Sayyed Mirei, first secretary of the ASU Central Committee, alleged that Maoists and pro-Soviet Communists had penetrated the student movement. Mirei also charged that the 12,000 Palestinian students in Egypt were behind the anti-government demonstrations. *An-Nahar Arab Report* 3, no. 5 (January 31, 1972): 1–2.

51. Ibid., p. 1.

52. Ibid. no. 8 (February 21, 1972): 2.

53. Ibid. no. 51 (December 18, 1972): 1.

54. Ibid. no. 52 (December 25, 1972): 1–2.

55. Ibid. 4, no. 3 (January 15, 1973): 1. The arrested students included Ahmad Bahaa, a founder of the Palestine Revolution Partisan Group; Ahmad Abdullah, member of the ASU National Congress; Husain Saaduddin; Siham and Mohammed Tawfiqi; Sanaa Abdul Aziz; Sayyed Awad, chairman of the Cultural Committee of the Egyptian Federation of Students; Mohammed Khalad, editor of *Al-Rababi*, published by the American University of Cairo; and Mohammed Dardiri. Twelve Palestinian students also were arrested, among them Khadri Shehadeh, a member of the Palestinian National Council, who was charged with engaging in publicity for the PFLP.

56. It should be noted that whereas the conservatives opposed the presence of a large Soviet contingent, the leftist students opposed the expansion of tourism, which would have increased the inflow of Westerners to Egypt. It seems that neither the leftist nor the rightist groups showed sufficient confidence in the inherent ability of the Egyptian to resist foreign influences incompatible with his religious and political values. This conflict between the desire to acquire modern technology and the urge to reject the foreign ideological and cultural values that often accompany the importation of technology has existed in the Middle East for many centuries, going back to the time of the beginning of European technological ascendancy over the Ottoman Empire. The Ottoman decision makers, like their modern Egyptian counterparts, were eager to acquire European military technology but were vehemently opposed to accepting European political and cultural values, which they considered inferior to their own.

57. *An-Nahar Arab Report* 3, no. 19 (May 18, 1972): 2.

58. General Sadeq was fired on October 26, 1972, a day after Premier Sidqi reported to a joint session of the Central Committee and the parliamentary group of ASU on the results of his recent conferences with the Soviet leaders in Moscow. He reportedly told the joint session that the Soviet Union had promised further military aid, provided the "rightist" elements in the country were eliminated from key positions. Ibid. no. 44 (October 30, 1972): 2.

59. For Heikal's views on the issue, see his editorials in *Al-Ahram* immediately prior to his dismissal on February 1, 1974. General Shazli told a Lebanese newspaper that the Soviet Union "was absolutely indispensable to the Arabs, and [that] it would be a mistake to imagine that the United States was a viable alternative." Ibid. 5, no. 37 (September 16, 1974): 2.

60. This quotation is from President Sadat's speech to a conference of the Egyptian Students' Federation, Alexandria, April 3, 1974, as reported by FBIS, April 4, 1974, pp. D–8 to D–9.

61. Malcolm Kerr, "The United Arab Republic: The Domestic, Political and Economic Background of Foreign Policy," in Paul Y. Hammond and Sidney S. Alexander, eds., *Political Dynamics in the Middle East* (New York: American Elsevier, 1972), p. 223.

62. Sadat has endeavored to reconcile differences between Saudi Arabia and South Yemen,

Iran and Iraq, Iraq and Kuwait, Jordan and the PLO, and the factions in the Oman civil war. He also played a key role in the recognition of Bangladesh by Pakistan in April 1974. For an example of his pre-October War approach, see James Reston's interview with the Egyptian president in New York *Times*, December 28, 1970, pp. 1, 14, 15. In his *October Papers*, Sadat elucidated his ideas on the basis of Arab cooperation, Arab nationalism, and Egyptian nationalism. FBIS, supp., May 13, 1974, pp. 1–34.

63. This was the ostensible reason given by Sadat at the time of the expulsion in July 1972. We have already discussed some other factors that might have strengthened his resolve to take the anti-Soviet steps. In Leonard Binder's view, the Soviets were expelled from Egypt because they were "too friendly with Sadat's enemies and the communist ideology is uncongenial to the ideological predilections of Sadat's propertied and religious supporters." "Transformation in the Middle East Subordinate System After 1967," in *The USSR and the Middle East*, Michael Confino and Shimon Shamir, eds. (Jerusalem: Israel Universities Press, 1973), p. 271.

64. Numerous sources have suggested that both Libya and Saudi Arabia had been urging Sadat to expel the Soviet advisers from Egypt. See William Dullforce, "Egypt Expels Russian Advisers," Washington *Post*, July 19, 1972, pp. A–1, A–14; John K. Cooley, "Cairo Hopes Washington Will Push Israeli Pullback," *Christian Science Monitor*, July 22, 1972, pp. 1, 5.

65. President Nixon reportedly told the Saudi Arabian defense minister, Prince Sultan Ibn Abdel Aziz, who visited the United States between June 18 and July 1, 1972, that the United States would be willing to take a new initiative only after the Soviets had been expelled from Egypt. "Arab Aides' Talk with Nixon Called Factor in Sadat's Decision," New York *Times*, July 24, 1972, p. 2; Rowland Evans and Robert Novak, " . . . and an Interview with Anwar Sadat," Washington *Post*, December 7, 1972, p. A–19. The Evans and Novak article says that the White House had been demanding the expulsion of the Soviet advisers and technicians since 1970.

66. Under the Khartoum agreement of August 1967, Egypt and Jordan were promised a subsidy of £135 million ($392 million) a year for the indefinite future. While this conference had authorized each state to seek a political solution, it had rejected direct negotiations and formal peace with and recognition of Israel.

67. The 1974 Rabat conference of Arab heads of state promised an annual subsidy of $1 billion each to Egypt and Syria, $300 million to Jordan, $50 million to the PLO, and $150 million to South Yemen. Citing "reliable Arab sources" in Beirut, Jim Hoagland reported that the Arab oil producers had decided to slash the proposed financial aid by 58 percent. No reasons for this were given (Washington *Post*, January 14, 1975, p. A–1). There is no accurate account of the total Saudi help given to Egypt since the October War. Press estimates have ranged between $500 million and $2 billion. On August 3, 1974, the authoritative Egyptian daily *Al-Ahram* reported that Saudi Arabia had given Egypt a grant of $1 billion "in appreciation of the sacrifices made by the Egyptian people in fighting for the Arab nation." This report said that the $1 billion gift was in addition to the interest-free loan of $500 million Riyadh had granted to Cairo. Another report said that Faisal had given a gift of $300 million to meet the requirements of reconstruction and to improve the University of Al-Azhar. It was further reported that Saudi Arabia would finance the purchase of French fighter planes for Egypt at a cost of over $500 million (FBIS, August 5, 7, and 28, 1974). Recently, Saudi Arabia signed an agreement to purchase 60 U.S.-built F-5 jet fighters, some of which might be transferred to Egypt, according to newspaper reports. Saudi sources insist that there are "no strings" attached to the U.S.-Saudi agreement (Guy Halverson, "Will F-5 Sale Bind Saudis, U.S. Closer?" *Christian Science Monitor*, January 14, 1975, p. 6).

68. In the October War, Iran was reported to have placed six C-130 cargo planes at the disposal of Saudi Arabia for the transportation of Saudi troops to Jordan. (Jim Hoagland, "Shah Visiting Jordan, Egypt," Washington *Post*, January 7, 1975, pp. A–1, A–12). As an expression of solidarity with the Arabs during the October War, the shah agreed to a "cease-fire" with Iraq so that the Iraqi troops could support the Syrians at the Golan front.

69. Jim Hoagland, "Shah Visiting Jordan, Egypt," p. A–12. Harry B. Ellis, "Why Iran's Shah Turns from Israel," *Christian Science Monitor*, December 23, 1974, p. 1, notes a rapprochement developing between Riyadh and Teheran. Joseph Fitchett, however, argues that Saudi Arabia "is likely to be suspicious of Egyptian Iranian cooperation in the Gulf." ("Egypt and Iran May Shift Middle East Balance," *Christian Science Monitor*, December 23, 1974. pp. 1, 4.)

70. *An-Nahar Arab Report* 5, no. 46 (November 18, 1974).

71. Claiming Arab sovereignty over these islands, most Arab states denounced the Iranian action as "provocative" and "imperialistic." Accusing the United Kingdom of "collusion" with Iran, the Libyan Arab Republic retaliated by nationalizing British oil interests in the country. Iraq retaliated by breaking diplomatic ties with London and Teheran. However, British oil interests in Iraq were not nationalized until June 1972 (*Record of the Arab World* [July-December 1971]: 2932, 3291). Although the issue is no longer a serious bone of contention between Iran and the Arabs, the Iranian military buildup and its military actions in Dhofar have been criticized by the Arab media.

72. *An-Nahar Arab Report* 1, no. 27 (September 7, 1970): 2.

73. Salah Khalaf (alias Abu Iyad) and Farouk Qaddumi (alias Abu Lutf) met with Riyad, Heikal, and later with Nasser in August 1967 (Riad N. el-Rayyes and Dunia Nahas, eds., *Guerrillas for Palestine* [Beirut: An-Nahar Press Services S.A.R.L., 1974], p. 97).

74. Michael C. Hudson, "Developments and Setbacks in the Palestinian Resistance Movement 1967–1971," *Journal of Palestine Studies* 1, no. 3 (Spring 1972): 64–84. This one-day battle was fought on March 21 in the town of Karamah, on the East Bank of the Jordan. Israeli armored columns, supported by the Israeli air force, attacked the town, believed to be a training center for the guerrillas. Although lacking sophisticated weapons, the Palestinian commandos, in coordination with the Jordanian forces, inflicted heavy casualties on the Israelis, who, according to a statement by King Hussein, lost 4 jets and 35 armored vehicles, and suffered 200 casualties, including 73 dead. *Middle East Journal* 22, no. 3 (Summer 1968): "Chronology," 325.

75. According to *An-Nahar Arab Report* 1, no. 27 (September 7, 1970): 2, Adwan had taken this action independently, without consulting the Central Committee, which, he believed, would have opposed his move. Kamal Adwan was a Palestinian nationalist who opposed a close identification between Fatah-PLO and Egypt. In April 1973, he was assassinated in a raid on his apartment in Beirut by an Israeli terrorist squad. Other prominent members of the Central Committee opposing close identification with Egypt were the Hassan brothers, Hani and Khaled. They are among the founders of Fatah and maintain close relations with Saudi Arabia. In the power struggle between the Nasserites and Faisalites, the influence of the Hassan brothers was temporarily eclipsed; Khaled Hassan, who had been considered Faisal's choice to succeed Arafat, was ousted from the PLO Executive Committee in January 1973. Recently Khaled Hassan has been appointed the PLO representative to the Egyptian-Palestinian Coordination Committee, whose Egyptian representative is Foreign Minister Ismail Fahmi (FBIS, March 28, 1974), p. G–5. Hani Hassan, alias Abu al-Hassan, continued to remain in the limelight and played an important role in the organization as a member of the five-man Action Committee of the PLO. The pro-Egyptian faction was led by the triumvirate of Yassir Arafat, Salah Khalaf, and Farouk Qaddumi.

76. Text of the official announcement of the closing down of the Fatah and PLO broadcasting facilities is in FBIS, July 28, 1970, p. G–1. The report of the expulsions was published by the Kuwaiti daily *Al-Rai al-Aam*, and distributed by AFP on August 4, 1970 (FBIS, August 4, 1970, p. G–1).

77. Palestinian broadcasting stations in Algeria, Syria, Iraq, and Sudan were unanimous in their denunciation of Egypt and Jordan for accepting the Rogers Plan (see FBIS from July 24, 1970, to the end of March 1971). On March 29, Sadat rescinded the suspension order during the second Jordanian-Palestinian crisis, which he was endeavoring to resolve.

78. *An-Nahar Arab Report* 2, no. 46 (December 6, 1971): 2. It should be noted that after the assassination, the Black Septemberists declared that a similar fate awaited those Arab leaders

who sought a peaceful resolution of the Palestinian problem. Since Sadat was still engaged in a dialogue with the United States, he could not afford inaction against certain elements of the Palestinians in Egypt.

79. El-Rayyes and Nahas, *Guerrillas for Palestine*, p. 100.

80. *An-Nahar Arab Report* 2, no. 49 (December 6, 1971): 2. On February 29, 1972, the four alleged assassins were released on bail of E£ 1,000 each. At the time of this release, the state prosecutor said that ballistic tests did not show that the bullet that killed Wasfi Tal came from any of the revolvers carried by the four accused.

81. Egypt broke diplomatic ties with Amman on April 6, 1972. Soon after announcing his united kingdom plan on March 15, 1972, King Hussein met with President Nixon in Washington, and acquainted him with the plan. While Sadat was telling the Arabs that he would use force to recover Arab territory, Hussein was telling his American audience that he would not enter into another war with Israel because a repetition of the 1967 disaster would "mean the destruction of the Arab world." *An-Nahar Arab Report* 3, no. 17 (April 24, 1972): n.p.

82. After several months of talks between Cairo and Amman, in which Riyadh played a decisive role, diplomatic ties between Egypt and Jordan were restored on September 12, 1973, less than a month before the fourth Arab-Israeli war began on October 6. Ibid. 4, no. 39 (September 24, 1973): n.p.

83. A three-day Arab summit was held in Algiers on November 26–28, 1973.

84. See the text of U.S.-Jordanian communiqué issued in Washington, August 18, 1974.

85. *An-Nahar Arab Report* 6, no. 2 (January 13, 1975): 3.

86. Sadat attended the Addis Ababa meeting of the OAU held in May 1973. A resolution by the OAU asked its members to sever diplomatic and trade ties with Israel; most members broke diplomatic ties by the end of the year. In July, a Security Council resolution favorable to the Arabs and supported by 14 permanent and nonpermanent members was vetoed by the United States. It was considered a moral victory for the Arabs, who were able to isolate the United States and Israel in the world organization. The nonaligned nations meeting in Algiers passed a strongly worded pro-Arab resolution that provided a further boost to Arab morale.

87. In July 1973, Qaddafi reportedly held a series of discussion sessions with the members of the People's Assembly and the ASU (*An-Nahar Arab Report* 4, no. 28 [July 9, 1973]: 3). This encounter reportedly produced a negative reaction from many Egyptian legislators.

88. Hatem Sadeq, Egyptian minister of war and commander-in-chief of the Egyptian Libyan, and Syrian joint forces, was dismissed by Sadat on October 26, 1972. Qaddafi shared Sadeq's views concerning the futility of collaboration with the Soviet Union and was reported to be angry at Sadat's decision because neither Libya nor Syria was consulted.

89. Libya and Egypt traded a long and comprehensive list of accusations pertaining to the supply of matériel, military coordination, the use of airport and seaport facilities, and similar matters during the October War. Radio Cairo, Radio Tripoli, and the Egyptian and Libyan press carried official versions of these charges. See FBIS, June-August 1973.

90. Embassy of Pakistan, Washington, D.C., *Pakistan Affairs* 28, no. 2 (January 16, 1975): 1. In response to an appeal for aid by the Pakistan government, the Arab oil-producing states contributed $40 million toward the rehabilitation of the victims of an earthquake that had struck northern Pakistan in January 1975. Of this sum, $16 million came from Libya, $10 million from Saudi Arabia, $8 million from the United Arab Emirates, and $5 million from Kuwait. During the 1971 India-Pakistan war, Libya provided indispensable military matériel to Pakistan. Similarly, during the Cyprus crisis in July-August 1975, Libya reportedly provided substantial financial aid and oil to Turkey.

91. On a number of occasions, Joseph Sisco, assistant secretary of state for Near Eastern and South Asian affairs, and Secretary of State William Rogers enunciated this assumption in their public statements and press interviews. This assumption was not based on historical evidence. In the past, Arab states had used oil as a political weapon against the West on three occasions. During

the 1956 war, oil supplies were interrupted and pipelines in Syria were blown up; during the 1967 war, several Arab oil producers inposed a temporary embargo on shipments to the United States, Britain, and West Germany; and in 1971, Libya nationalized British oil interests in retaliation for Britain's refusal to prevent Iran from occupying two islands in the Persian Gulf. For a Saudi reaction to Libyan-Egyptian relations, see John K. Cooley, "Saudi Arabia Reviews Ties with U.S.," *Christian Science Monitor*, July 10, 1973, pp. 1, 3. It must, however, be conceded that Saudi pronouncements, in 1972 and earlier, that oil would not be used as a political weapon had strengthened the American assumption. In April 1973 Saudi Petroleum Minister Zaki el-Yamani linked the possibility of raising Saudi oil production to meet the growing U.S. energy needs with Washington's ability to change its pro-Israeli posture. See New York *Times*, April 19, 1973, p. 1. In August, King Faisal, in an interview with NBC, reiterated his petroleum minister's conditions for increasing the Saudi oil production to 20 million barrels a day by 1985.

92. For example, see Colin S. Gray, "The Security of Israel," *Military Review* no. 10 (October 1973): 22–36; Ronald M. Devore, "The Arab-Israeli Military Balance," *Revue militaire générale* (March 1973), repr. in *Military Review* 53, no. 11 (November 1973): 65–71; Melvin J. Stanford, "Strategic Factors Within the Middle East," *Military Review* 53, no. 12 (December 1973): 78–91; "Middle East War," ibid. 54, no. 2 (February 1974): 48–49; Kenneth S. Brower, "The Yom Kippur War," ibid. no. 3 (March 1974): 25–33; Roger L. Crump, "The October War: A Postures Assessment," ibid. no. 8 (August 1974): 12–26; Dale R. Tahtinen, *The Arab-Israeli Military Balance Since October 1973* (Washington, D.C.: American Enterprise Institute, 1973); *The Military Balance 1971–1972* (London: International Institute for Strategic Studies, 1971); *The Military Balance 1972–1973* (London: IISS, 1972); *The Military Balance 1974–1975* (London: IISS, 1974); *Strategic Survey 1973* (London: IISS, 1974).

93. Under a tripartite declaration issued on May 25, 1950, the United States, Britain, and France undertook to impose a halt to the arms race between Israel and the Arab states. Despite this declaration, Israel managed to obtain arms from France, with whom it began to develop close political and military relations. The text of the tripartite declaration is in Ralph H. Magnus, ed., *Documents on the Middle East* (Washington, D.C.: American Enterprise Institute, 1969), pp. 163–64.

94. J. C. Hurewitz, *Middle East Politics: The Military Dimension* (New York: Praeger, 1969), pp. 136; *The Military Balance 1974–1975*, p. 32. The Egyptian defense expenditure from 1952–53 to 1966–67 may be found in Hurewitz, p. 136; annual defense expenditures since then are available in the volumes of *The Military Balance*.

95. Harvey H. Smith, William W. Cover, et al., *Area Handbook for the United Arab Republic (Egypt)* (Washington, D.C.: U.S. Government Printing Office, 1970), p. 466. Since the end of the October War, a small contingent of Pakistani air force personnel has been engaged in a training program in Egypt. A group of Egyptain air force pilots reportedly received some training in Iran.

96. According to *The Military Balance 1974–1975*, the Egyptian army possessed the following equipment: 2,000 Js-3/T-10 heavy tanks, T-54/55 and T-62 medium tanks, and PT-76 light tanks; 2,000 BTR-40, BTR-50P, BTR-60P, OT-64, and BTR-152 armored personnel carriers; 100 BMP-76 patrol boats; about 120 SU-100 and JSU-152 SP guns; about 1,200 122-mm., 130-mm., and 152-mm. guns and howitzers; 8-inch guns; 40 203-mm. howitzers; 420 rocket launchers; about 900 57-mm., 85-mm., and 100-mm. anti-tank guns; Sagger, Swatter, and Snapper anti-tank guided weapons; 18 Frog-7, and some Samlet, SSM; ZSU-23-4 and ZSU-57-2 SP guns; SA-6, SA-7. Probably these figures do not reflect the losses suffered during the October War and the replacements received since then. Tahtinen, *The Arab-Israeli Military Balance Today*, p. 22.

97. In 1967, the Egyptian air force was reported to have 220 combat planes of different types; in 1968–69, it acquired 400 planes, including 40 SU-7 fighter-bombers, which were reported to have been delivered in response to the U.S. decision of October 1968 to supply F-4E fighter-bomber/interceptors to Israel.

98. *The Military Balance 1974–1975*, pp. 32–33.

99. Tahtinen, *The Arab-Israeli Military Balance Today*, p. 5; *The Military Balance 1974–1975*, p. 33.

100. Stockholm International Peace Research Institute (SIPRI), *The Arms Trade with the Third World* (Stockholm: Almqvist and Wiksell, 1971), p. 526.

101. One qualified source estimates that Egypt, Syria, Jordan, and Iraq had a total of 600–700 qualified pilots and that Israel had between 800 and 900 qualified pilots. Egypt alone was reported to have lost 100 pilots during the Six-Day War. The four Arab states had a total of 420 combat aircraft available to them in the June War; Israel had 230 combat aircraft available during the same period.

102. The total number of the Soviet advisers in 1968 was reported to be between 1,500 and 3,000; in 1970, it increased to about 10,000; in 1971, it was estimated to be 12,000 (SIPRI, *Arms Trade*, p. 527; Smith, Cover, et al., *Area Handbook for the UAR*, p. 457).

103. Based on experience with the Syrian and Egyptian forces, this Russian apprehension is understandable. In 1966, a Syrian pilot defected to Israel with a MIG-21; and in the June War, the Israelis were reported to have captured an Egyptian SU-7 intact. Tahtinen, *The Arab-Israeli Military Balance Today*, p. 16, ftns. 27, 29.

104. On September 11, 1974, the Lebanese daily *Beirut* reported that the Soviets had airlifted new weapons, including 50 MIG-23s, to Egypt. This report, however, was not confirmed by other sources. President Sadat has continued to insist that no new Soviet planes have arrived in Egypt since the October War. *An-Nahar Arab Report* 5, no. 38 (September 23, 1974): n.p.

105. *The Military Balance 1974–1975*, p. 33.

106. Joseph Fitchett, "New Arms Race Threatened in Mideast," *Christian Science Monitor,* August 30, 1974, pp. 1, 6.

107. "Sadat Says Egypt Lost 6,000 Men," Washington *Post*, October 8, 1974, p. A–16.

108. "New Arms Race Threatened in Mideast," p. 6.

109. New York *Times*, November 20, 1974, p. 18, and *Christian Science Monitor*, January 11, 1977, p. 4, and January 18, 1977, p. 5.

110. *An-Nahar Arab Report* 5, no. 26 (July 1, 1974): n.p. Making the announcement of the forthcoming visit by a group of U.S. military officers, Pentagon officials emphasized that the U.S. team had not been given the task of establishing Egyptian military needs and that it had no authority to make recommendations on this subject. Washington *Post*, June 20, 1974, p. A–27.

111. *An-Nahar Arab Report* 5, no. 40 (October 7, 1974): n.p.

112. Washington *Post*, January 25, 1975, p. A–7. In January 1977, the French government agreed to sell weapons systems to Egypt worth $4 billion. In addition, France agreed to provide weapons technology and training to the Arab Military Industrial Organization, which includes Egypt, Saudi Arabia, Qatar, and the UAE. See John F. Cooley, "Arab Arms Industry Gets Helping Hand from French," *Christian Science Monitor*, January 11, 1977, p. 4.

113. *Christian Science Monitor*, July 8, 1974. According to this report, the Israeli air force commander, Maj. Gen. Benjamin Peled, said that while the present strength of the Israeli air force would be sufficient to meet any Arab challenge, Israel needed new planes (F-14s, F-15s) to maintain "control" of Middle East skies.

114. In addition to the combat planes, Israel reportedly is seeking the Dragon anti-tank missile, the Shrike anti-radar missile, the Lance ground-to-ground missile, and pilotless aircraft used as decoys and for reconnaissance. The Lance missile, which has a range of 30–40 miles, can also be fired from helicopters and can carry either a conventional or a mininuclear warhead. Christopher Dobson, "Is Israel Combat-ready?" *Sunday Telegraph*, November 24, 1974, excerpts in *Atlas World Press Review* 22, no. 1 (January 1975): 39.

115. SIPRI, *Arms Trade*, pp. 723–53. This section also deals with the abortive Indian-Egyptian effort to fit the Egyptian E-300 turbojet engine with the Indian HAL airframe. After the June War, the Egyptians ceased the effort to produce the jet engine. *The Military Balance 1971–1972*, p. 33.

116. *An-Nahar Arab Report* 4, no. 1 (January 1, 1973).

117. Egyptian constitution (1971), ch. II, art. 23–39.

118. In a move to attract foreign capital to Egypt, the People's Assembly passed a law in June 1974, that freed foreign companies from the law requiring worker participation and profit sharing. Washington *Post*, June 11, 1974, p. A–14.

119. According to Bent Hansen, "Economic Development in Egypt," in *Economic Development and Population Growth in the Middle East,* Charles A. Cooper and Sidney S. Alexander, eds., (New York: American Elsevier, 1972), pp. 22–89, Egyptian expenditure on bureaucracy has doubled from 1959/60, when it spent 5 percent of the gross domestic product on administration, to 10 percent in 1965/66.

120. Ibid., p. 75.

121. Ibid., p. 80.

122. Washington *Post*, July 17, 1974, p. E–1; text of Egyptian-U.S. joint communiqué issued in Cairo on June 14, 1974 in *An-Nahar Arab Report* 5, no. 25 (June 24, 1974): n. p. New Egyptian laws on foreign investments allow non-Arab foreign investors to repatriate profits made on export of goods manufactured in the country; profits made on local sale are excluded from this provision. Arab investors may repatriate all their profits, whether made on local sale or on export. On January 6, 1975, the first joint banking venture to be set up under the "open door" policy was formally created by the Bank Misr (51 percent share) and three foreign banks: First National of Chicago, Banco di Roma Holdings of Luxembourg, and UBAF Ltd. of London.

123. On November 25, 1974, Egypt and Iran signed an agreement for technical and financial cooperation. This agreement created the joint Egyptian-Iranian Investment Bank, with a capital of $20 million, for the purpose of financing projects in Egypt and Iran. Under this accord, the two parties expressed their initial agreement to establish in Suez a $300 million nitrogen fertilizer and phosphate plant that will produce ammonia, urea fertilizer, sulfuric acid, phosphoric acid, and superphosphate, utilizing phosphorus from Egypt and sulfur ore from Iran. Other agreements deal with a cotton textile project and the establishment of two joint companies for engineering investments and for installation works in the Port Said area. Iran agreed to give Egypt a loan of $250 million for the above projects. (Middle East News Agency [MENA] broadcast from Cairo; November 25, 1974, as reported by FBIS, November 26, 1974, pp. D–7 to D–8.)

124. FBIS, November 19, 1974, p. C–4.

125. Ibid., p. E–1.

126. During Prime Minister Higazi's trip to Kuwait in December 1974, the Kuwait government promised $1,300 million in aid and grants to Egypt. Earlier, Higazi had secured $1,195 million from the UAE, Qatar, and Saudi Arabia. The money will be invested in joint housing, industrial, and other projects in Egypt. *An-Nahar Arab Report* 5, no. 46 (December 2, 1974): 1–2.

127. Ibid. 5, no. 42 (October 21, 1974): 3; Henry Tanner, "Egyptian Food Shortages and Economic Ill Stir Bitter Criticism," New York *Times*, September 4, 1974, p. 12. Tanner reports that Western industrialists have been told by Egyptian officials that the "need now is for Western technology, and that money is no longer a problem."

128. Statement by Dr. Abd al-Qadir Hatim, deputy prime minister and minister of information of Egypt. Hatim said that of the E£ 350 million for subsidies, E£ 250 million are spent to maintain the low price of bread, sold for 5 milliemes but costing 25 milliemes. Other essential items being subsidized were wheat, cotton, rice, sugar, kerosene, and cooking oil. (Cairo Domestic Service, April 1, 1974, as monitored by FBIS, April 2, 1974, p. D-12). *An-Nahar Arab Report* 6, no. 4 (January 27, 1975), reports that during 1975, Egypt will spend E£ 640 million on food subsidies.

129. National Bank of Egypt, *Economic Bulletin*, 26, no. 1 (1973): 17; and Central Bank of Egypt, *Annual Report 1971–1972*, p. 2, in Albert L. Gray, Jr., "Egypt's Ten Year Plan: 1973–1982," paper presented at Middle East Studies Association annual meeting, Boston, Mass., November 7, 1974, pp. 2–3.

130. *An-Nahar Arab Report* 5, no. 40 (October 7, 1974): 3. In 1971–72, Egypt spent E£ 352.8 million in servicing and repayment of external debts, an increase of E£ 128.0 million over the previous year. Egypt's overdue debt to West Germany reached about 460 million marks in the middle of 1973—in addition to another 400 million marks not yet due. In 1972, West Germany and the United States agreed to reschedule the loans owed by Egypt.

131. According to a report in *An-Nahar Arab Report* 5, no. 50 (December 16, 1974), the Soviets had agreed to reschedule Egypt's debt, which "amounts to about $500 million." Earlier, this weekly said that the Egyptian debt to the Soviet Union was about $400 million.

132. *Christian Science Monitor,* July 26, 1974, p. 8.

133. New York *Times*, October 29, 1974, p. 7.

134. Egyptian trade figures were obtained from Europa, *The Middle East and North Africa 1974–1975* (London: Europa Publications, 1974), pp. 297–99; information on Egyptian manufactured goods came from *An-Nahar Arab Report* 3, no. 47 (November 20, 1972): n.p.

135. We do not wish to suggest that Egypt has no reclamation projects currently being carried out. We are aware of the Lake Manzola project, which is designed to reclaim about 500,000 feddans (1 feddan = 1.038 acres). The point is that Egypt has severe land and water limitations that make it extremely difficult to expand agricultural areas for the growing population. At 5.5 persons per acre, Egypt has one of the highest man/land ratios in the world. Currently, Egypt loses 25,000 feddans annually to housing; and as the population increases, this loss will increase proportionately (Europa, *The Middle East*, pp. 284–86). In the production of fertilizer, Egypt plans to be self-sufficient by 1977.

136. Text of President Sadat's *October Papers*, as reported in *Al-Ahram*, April 19, 1974, and in FBIS supp. 26, no. 93, May 13, 1974.

137. *October Papers*, p. 32.

138. Ibid., p. 31.

139. Ibid., p. 23.

140. Europa, *The Middle East*, p. 296.

141. *An-Nahar Arab Report* 6, no. 4 (January 27, 1975): n.p.

4

IRAQI FOREIGN POLICY

IRAQI POLICY ENVIRONMENT

Steeped in the tradition of confessionalism and ethnic politics, Iraq remains a mosaic of religious, ethnic, linguistic, regional, and ideological groups, most of which function as interest groups in the country's political system. Iraq's political and cultural history has created serious impediments to developing a sense of territorial nationalism (*al-wataniya*) among the masses, who continue to owe their principal allegiance to their religious and ethnic groups.

Moreover, Iraq has a long history of confessional conflicts going back to the days of Khalif Ali (656–61) who became the patron saint of the first great schismatic sect of Islam. The Shiites, the followers of Ali, have venerated him equally with, and on occasion more than, Prophet Mohammed. The Sunnites, the followers of orthodox Islamic law, have historically held the reins of power except between 1623 and 1638, when the Shia Safavid dynasty of Iran ruled most of Iraq. The Sunni Ottoman ruled the country between 1534 and 1918. The Hashemite dynasty, which ruled the country from 1921 to 1958, and most of the ruling elites of the "revolutionary" period since 1958, have been from the Sunni sect of Islam. The unwillingness of the Sunni religious minority to share power with the Shiites, who claim a 55–60 percent majority in the country, has been one of the major impediments to effecting a political rapprochement between the Shiites and Sunnites, most of whom are ethnically and linguistically Arabs.[1]

Ethnically, the Iraqi population can be divided into two major and several minor groups. Accounting for about 80 percent of the total estimated Iraqi population of 10 million, the Arabs form a dominant ethnic and linguistic majority. The Kurds account for about 15 percent of the population. Most Kurds are Sunnites, but their religious practices differ in some respects from those of Sunni Arabs. Most of the Iraqi Kurds live in the north and northeast areas of the country, a region contiguous with the Kurdish zones of Turkey and Iran. Since the end of World War I, Kurdish nationalism has manifested in the form of demands and struggle for local autonomy and outright independence. Just as Arab nationalism developed partly as a reaction to Turkish nationalism, so Kurdish nationalism, after World War II, became a more significant movement, in part as a reaction to Arab nationalism and pan-Arabism that the Kurds perceived as a threat to their identity and status in Iraq.[2]

Kurdish nationalism in Iraq has led to brief periods of Kurdish unity, but intertribal rivalries and conflicts between modern and traditional Kurds often have created problems in negotiating terms of agreements with the Arabs. Although most, if not all, Kurds agree that Kurdish identity must be preserved and that some of the wealth from the Kurdish lands (especially the oil revenues from the Kirkuk oil fields) ought to be used for development projects in the Kurdish region, there is little else that could be construed as a common demand. In their official demands, the Iraqi Kurds have not sought independence from Baghdad, nor have they shown much sustained interest in the idea of a Kurdish state to be carved out of Iraq, Turkey, and Iran.

For the Iraqi government, the Kurdish problem has been a continuous source of strife, political instability, and a serious drain on the country's economic, military, and human resources. Until March 1975, the Kurdish problem was a source of bitter tension between Baghdad and Teheran because, for a variety of political and strategic reasons, Iran was using the Kurds to apply pressure on the Ba'athist regime in Baghdad. (The Kurdish problem will be discussed in more detail in a later section.)

In addition to the Arabs and the Kurds, who make up about 95 percent of the Iraqi population, other ethnic groups in the country are the Turkomans (2–3 percent), the Persians, the Lurs, the Armenians, and the Jews (2 percent). Although these groups are active in agriculture and trade, they play practically no role in the decision-making process of the country.

But the divisions within the population of Iraq do not end with religious and ethnic groups. Other divisions arise due to linguistic, regional, educational, and ideological differences. For example, although Arabic is the official language of the country, at least 20 percent of the population speaks Kurdish, Turkoman, or Farsi. Kurdish was accepted as the primary language of education for the Kurds in their region. The March 11, 1970 agreement, which temporarily halted the war between the Kurds and the Iraqi government forces, stipulated, *inter alia,* that although Kurdish would be taught to Kurdish students in schools in the Kurdish region, Arabic would remain compulsory for all children in Iraqi schools. This provision, while satisfying the cultural needs of the Kurds, would, it was hoped, create a linguistic link between the Arab majority and the Kurdish minority. It is interesting to note, however, that no similar requirement was imposed on the Arabs living in the Kurdish areas—that is, they are not required to learn Kurdish.[3]

Regional differences are another source of social friction in Iraq. In the absence of strong integrative forces, the traditional rivalry between the urban, the rural, and the Bedouin populations has not been substantially reduced. Each manifesting an attitude of superiority toward the other, these groups have remained practically isolated from each other. In part, this attitude is reflected in the educational policies of the Iraqi government, which, being controlled by a small group of urban elites from Baghdad, Mosul, and provincial towns, has not followed a consistent policy of equal education for all Iraqis.[4] Although educational facilities have expanded at a rapid rate since 1958, they have benefited urban rather than rural areas of the country. Iraq does not lack the means to build schools, laboratories, and other educational facilities or to pay teachers and instructors. Nor do Iraqi parents and children lack the desire for education. The problem is with staffing small-town and village schools, because most young men refuse to work in rural areas after receiving their diplomas. The same problem arises in the health field; it is virtually impossible to entice physicians and nurses to work outside the main urban centers. Thus, the rural population, which accounts for 70 percent of the total population, does not have adequate educational facilities and sufficient health services.[5]

Because of the uneven distribution of educational facilities in the country as a whole, the role of education as an integrative force has not been impressive. Traditional attitudes, values, and prejudices still play a significant role in the daily lives of the masses, especially of those living in the provincial towns and rural areas. Although education and the mass media have popularized the concepts of territorial nationalism and pan-Arabism among the urbanites, these concepts are still of marginal importance in the daily lives of a significant portion of the masses. Furthermore, these concepts have not eliminated factionalism, confessionalism, and other negative social attitudes that have prevented the social and political integration of the country.

In the context of domestic politics, the average Iraqi might still identify himself as a Baghdadi, a Nejefi, a Takriti, a Kurd, an Arab, a Shiite, or a Sunnite. Political alliances often are based on such identifications and affiliations, a factor that makes it difficult for Iraq to play a significant role in the Arab movement toward unity. This factionalism has been a major source of instability and weakness in Iraqi's domestic and foreign policies. Domestically it has caused civil strife and has taxed the country's scarce human and nonhuman resources, while internationally it has been responsible for causing military confrontations, recently with Iran and earlier with Turkey, both of which have sizable Kurdish populations on their borders with Iraq.

Being acutely aware of these domestic schisms and political aspirations of the major factions—Shiites, Sunnites, Kurds, Arabs—Iraqi governments have endeavored to reconcile the Sunni Arab demands for union with other Arab states with the Shia Arab and Kurdish demands for maintaining Iraq's separate identity, not to mention the Kurdish demands for regional autonomy.

To satisfy the unity sentiments of Iraqi Sunnites, the government entered into a series of political and military agreements, ostensibly to achieve unity with several Arab states. Baghdad, however, being cognizant of the Kurdish and Shiite opposition to such a union, was unable to pursue an active unionist policy. This should not be construed to mean that all Iraqi Sunnites favor an Arab union that would destroy Iraqi identity. This point has been a bone of contention among Sunnite elites and masses alike. Pro-union groups have often achieved power in Baghdad, but they have never been able to effect a union with Egypt or Syria, the two most promising partners. Both internal dissension and external circumstances have contributed to frustration of the unionists' political goals.[6]

Structure of the Government

Iraq is ruled by a strong presidential government (see Figure 3). In addition to being the chief executive of the government, Hassan al-Bakr is commander in chief of the armed forces, prime minister, minister of defense, and president of the Revolutionary Command Council (RCC), the highest legislative body in Iraq. The president of the republic has the authority to appoint ministers to the Cabinet, to transfer them, and to dismiss them at his discretion. Theoretically, all ministers are answerable to the prime minister-cum-president, but in reality the ministers who concurrently hold membership in the RCC are not as subservient to him as those technocrats who hold no privileged position in the Ba'ath party hierarchy. The president also has the authority to dismiss the vice-presidents of the republic. The president is elected by a two-thirds' majority of the RCC and is responsible to the RCC.

Although in 1973 some powers were removed from RCC jurisdiction, that group remains the most powerful decision-making body in the country. As discussed below, its membership had shrunk from 15 in 1969 to 6 at the end of 1975.[7] The provisional constitution states that the RCC is the highest legislative body and that it will continue to make law until a popularly elected National Assembly comes into existence. Because the Ba'ath party is not a popular organization, the Ba'athists in power have not made any serious effort to hold elections for the National Assembly. When, after the March 1970 declaration, the Kurds demanded an election, as provided for in the autonomy plan, the government said that conditions were not conducive to holding an election.

The provisional constitution of Iraq provides for several vice-presidents to be elected by the RCC. For a while, Hardan Takriti and Salih Mehdi

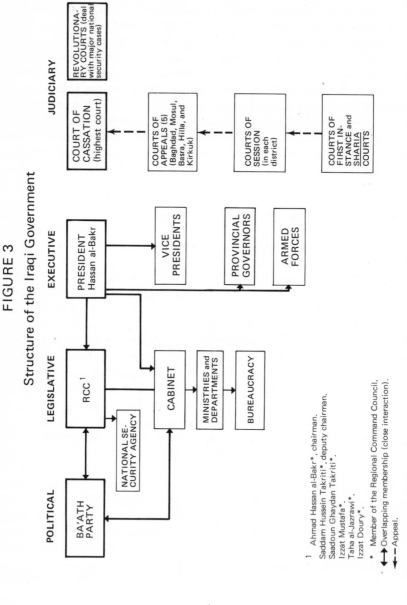

FIGURE 3

Structure of the Iraqi Government

POLITICAL   LEGISLATIVE   EXECUTIVE   JUDICIARY

BA'ATH PARTY

NATIONAL SE-CURITY AGENCY

RCC [1]

PRESIDENT Hassan al-Bakr

CABINET

VICE PRESIDENTS

MINISTRIES and DEPARTMENTS

PROVINCIAL GOVERNORS

BUREAUCRACY

ARMED FORCES

COURT OF CASSATION (highest court)

REVOLUTIONA-RY COURTS (deal with major national security cases)

COURTS OF APPEALS (5) (Baghdad, Mosul, Basra, Hilla, and Kirkuk)

COURTS OF SESSION (in each district)

COURTS OF FIRST IN-STANCE and SHARIA COURTS

1   Ahmad Hassan al-Bakr*, chairman.
Saddam Hussein Takriti*, deputy chairman.
Saadoun Ghaydan Takriti*.
Izzat Mustafa*.
Taha al-Jazrawi*.
Izzat Doury*.

*   Member of the Regional Command Council.
↕ Overlapping membership (close interaction).
-‑- Appeal.

Source: Europa, *The Middle East and North Africa 1974–75* (London: Europa Publications, 1974), p. 384.

Ammash were serving as vice-presidents in addition to being members of the RCC. By September 24, 1971, both had been removed from all official positions; they were replaced by Saddam Hussein Takriti as vice-president.

Although under the March 11, 1970 accord with the Kurds, the RCC had agreed to appoint a Kurdish vice-president, this was not done until 1974, when Taha Muhyi ad-Din Maaruf assumed the position. Since then, Saddam Hussein seems to have abandoned his vice-presidential role. It should be noted that since the Ba'ath assumed power in July 1968, Maaruf is the first vice-president not to hold membership in the RCC. He also does not possess the same powers as his predecessors. Prior to his appointment, only the RCC could dismiss a vice-president. After the aborted coup of July 1973, the powers of dismissal were given to the president. Under the present laws, the vice-president performs ceremonial functions only; he has little substantive power. Previously, especially under Saddam Hussein, the vice-president would have assumed presidential power if the president were incapacitated or if he died. Since July 1973, this provision is no longer applicable; under the current provisions, the RCC must elect a new president if the incumbent is unable to perform his duties. Thus the Kurdish vice-president stands no chance of succeeding Bakr.

The Cabinet is appointed by the president, in consultation with the RCC and the Ba'ath Party Regional Command. With the exception of four RCC members (Saadoun Ghaydan Takriti, Izzat Mustafa, Taha al-Jazrawi and Izzat Doury), four Regional Command members (Naim Haddad, Mohammed Mahjub, Ghanim Abdel Jalil, Taha Abdul Karim), and one reserve member of the Regional Command, Tariq Aziz—most other Cabinet ministers are technocrats and bureaucrats who are responsible only for the implementation of the policy formulated by the RCC and the Regional Command. The input of the technocrats and bureaucrats at the highest level of the decision-making process seems almost negligible.

One of the most notable aspects of the Iraqi governmental structure is the overlapping membership of the country's three most influential political institutions. Since the provisional constitution provides that the members of the RCC must be elected from among the Ba'ath party's regional leadership, it automatically places the Regional Command Council in a key position of influence in the decision-making process. With the sole exception of Saadoun Ghaydan Takriti all five members of the RCC are currently members of the Regional Command of the Ba'ath. Similarly, all members of the RCC, with the sole exception of Saddam Hussein Takriti, hold key portfolios in the current Cabinet under the premiership of Bakr. This overlapping membership does not end at the RCC-regional-Cabinet level. It continues on to the party bureaus, many of whose chairmen and vice-chairmen hold dual or even triple memberships in the RCC, the Regional Command, and the Cabinet.

Although this mechanism has enabled the regime to maintain firm control over the country, it has caused serious rifts between Ba'ath and other competing political groups, such as the Kurds and the Communists, who demand membership in the RCC and more responsibility in the Cabinet. Unless the Ba'ath party begins to admit non-Ba'athists to the RCC, the "opposition" parties will continue to express dissatisfaction with the workings of the government. Although the Communists, the Kurds, the Independent Nationalists, the Progressive Democrats, and the National Leaguers are all represented in the Cabinet, none of these groups seems satisfied with the role assigned to it. Apparently the Communists, more than any other group, are seeking a wider role in the country's decision-making process. It has been reported that the Iraqi Ba'athists were concerned about the changes taking place in the Iraqi Communist party, which, recognizing the Ba'ath's unwillingness to share power, was showing signs of detachment from the ruling party.[8]

Below the national level of governmental structure, the Kurdish autonomy plan has been implemented since March 1974. Since this issue has been one of the most crucial factors in Iraqi domestic and foreign policies, a brief discussion of it is in order. While giving the Kurds a modicum of self-rule in the northern part of Iraq, with the city of Erbil as the administrative center of the autonomous region, the Baghdad government maintains strong control over the administrative affairs of the region. Article 10 of the autonomy plan provides for an elected legislative council in the region and defines its powers of legislation and the procedural aspects of its meetings. Among the powers given to the council are legislative authority to make decisions "to develop the region and promote its social, cultural, constructional and economic utilities within the bounds of the state's general policy"; to suggest a budget for the region; and to cast or withhold votes of confidence in the Executive Committee or in one or more of its members. "Anyone in [sic] whom confidence is withheld shall be relieved of his duty."[9]

The Kurdish autonomy law further provides for an Executive Council to administer the region; it consists of a chairman, a deputy chairman, and 10–12 members. The president of the republic appoints the chairman from among the elected members of the Legislative Council; the appointed chairman chooses his team from among the members of the Legislative Council. The president of the republic has the authority to dismiss the chairman of the Executive Council and, in such a case, the entire Executive Council is dissolved.

In the administration of the region, the Executive Council is provided with assistance from the national planning bureaus. The personnel of these bureaus and the Executive Council coordinate their developmental activities, and they jointly supervise the activities of the regional departments (see Figure 4). Each member of the Executive Council is responsible for a regional department, and in this capacity the supervising member is known as the secretary-general.

Under this plan, the central government retains its power to issue directives to the regional administrative departments. Through the ministers of

FIGURE 4

Structure of the Kurdish Autonomy Plan

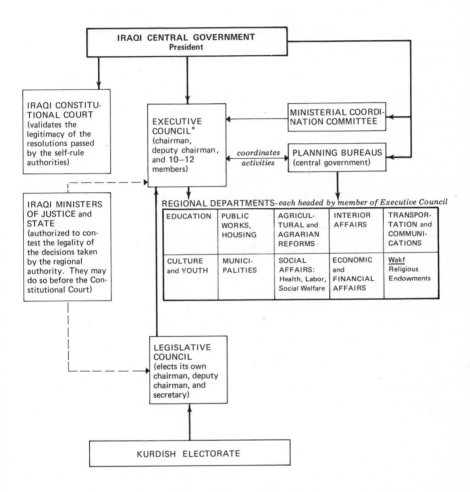

*Chairman is appointed by the president of the republic from among the members of the Legislative Council. The chairman in turn chooses members for the Executive Committee from among the Legislative Council. The chairman and members of the Executive Council hold the rank of minister. The president has the power to dismiss the chairman; in such a case, the Executive Committee is dissolved.

Source: Compiled by the authors.

justice and state, it may contest the legality of the decisions taken by the regional authorities. Such a challenge must be made before the Iraqi Constitutional Court within 30 days of the passage of a resolution. The court must reach a decision within 30 days, and its decisions are irreversible.[10]

From this brief treatment of the Kurdish autonomy plan, it should be evident that although the Kurds have been granted some powers, the financial, executive, and judicial powers are still very much in the hands of the Ba'athist regime in Baghdad.

OPERATION OF THE IRAQI POLITICAL SYSTEM: INTEREST GROUPS

The preceding analysis of the Iraqi decision-making environment focused entirely on the religious, ethnic, and other factions whose political and economic aspirations and goals are often competing, if not in contradiction, with each other. With the sole exception of the Kurds, whose separate identity has been recognized by the provisional constitution of Iraq and whose interests are being articulated primarily by the Kurdistan Democratic party (KDP), no other group or faction discussed above is officially recognized as an interest group entitled to conduct political activities in the country.[11] There are, however, interest groups that carry out political activities either across all religious, ethnic, and other lines in the country or confine themselves to professional, labor, and students' associations. Although the provisional constitution places no serious restrictions on forming political parties, currently only three function in the country: the Ba'ath, which controls effective political power; the Communist party (pro-Soviet), which holds two Cabinet posts but has little real power in the decision-making bodies, such as the RCC; and the Kurdistan Democratic party, which speaks on behalf of the autonomy-minded Barzani group of the Kurds in Iraq.

The Arab Socialist Resurrection Movement: The Ba'ath

In Iraq, the *Ba'ath al-arabi al-ishtiraki* movement came into existence in the summer of 1952 when a Shiite student, Fuad al-Rikabi, who had just graduated from the Baghdad Engineering College, began to create secret cells of members and sympathizers in the country.[12] Gradually, the Ba'ath began to attract adherents from a variety of social, economic, and professional groups, including the armed forces. Realizing the significant role the armed forces could play in capturing power, the Ba'ath proselytized a number of army officers, who, along with other "nationalist" and "progressive" officers, took part in the anti-monarchist coup of July 1958. (See Figure 5 for the basic organization of the Ba'ath party.)

FIGURE 5

Iraqi Ba'ath Party Organizational Chart

THE REGIONAL COMMAND COUNCIL

Ahmad Hassan al-Bakr,* PM secretary-general; Saddam Hussein Takriti,* assistant secretary-general; Izzat Mustafa,* MC Taha al-Jazrawi, Izzat Doury,MC Naim Haddad,MC Taha Abdul Karim, Adnan al-Hamadani,OA Mohammed Mahjub,MC Ghanim Abdel Jalil,MC Tahir al-Ani, Abdel Fath al-Yassin, Hassan al-Amari[1]

PARTY BUREAUS

| ARAB AFFAIRS Chairman: Taha Abdul Karim | ECONOMIC Chairman: Dr. Fakhri Khadduri | PUBLIC RELATIONS Chairman: Syed Ali Ghannam; deputy chairman: Tariq Aziz, editor Al-Thawra [2] | NORTHERN AFFAIRS Chairman: Saadoun Ghaydan Takriti* [3] | KURDISH AFFAIRS Chairman: Murtada al-Hadithi [4] | POLITICAL AFFAIRS Chairman: Naim Haddad [5] | POPULAR ORGANIZA-TION AFFAIRS Chairman: [6] | LEGAL AFFAIRS Chairman: [7] | VICE PRESI-DENTIAL AFFAIRS Chairman: Ghanim Abdel Jalil [8] |

REGIONAL UNITS

DISTRICT UNITS

PARTY CELLS (Basic Units)

* Member of the RCC.

1 There are five reserve members: Tariq Aziz, Jafaar Qassem Hammoudi, Zuhair Yahya, Saadoun Bakr, and Shafik al-Kamali.

2 Reserve member of the Regional Command Council and minister of information (since November 1974).

3 Minister of interior until 1974, now minister of communications. We are not certain whether he retains chairmanship of this bureau.

4 Held this job until June 1974, when he was appointed envoy to Moscow.

5 Member of the Regional Command, secretary-general of the Progressive National Front, assistant secretary-general of the Arab Front Participating in the Palestinian Revolution, and minister of youth.

6 Until July 1973, Abdel Khalek al-Samarrai was chairman of this bureau; present occupant unknown.

7 Unknown.

8 After the appointment of Maaruf as vice-president in 1974, this bureau may have undergone changes.

PM = prime minister.
MC = member of cabinet.
OA = secretary-general of the Follow-up Committee in Chargi of Oil Affairs and Agreements.

Source: Compiled by the authors.

117

After the coup, ideological and personality conflicts within the Ba'ath and the party's struggle with President Abdul Karim al-Qassem, who began to monopolize power, made the Ba'ath-Qassem break inevitable. As the Qassem regime became more tolerant of Communist activities, the Ba'ath became less friendly. Having failed to outmaneuver him through internal and external intrigues, the Ba'ath attempted to kill him in October 1959.[13] After this incident, many known Ba'athists had to live in exile until the party returned to power in 1963. Before this, however, it had to enlarge its contacts with both military and nonmilitary groups. In 1961, the Ba'ath resumed its covert activities under Ali Salih al-Saadi, who was entrusted with the leadership of the party. During the next two years, the Ba'ath again endeavored to win adherents among military officers. In February 1963, a group of Ba'athist and Nasserite officers overthrew the Qassem regime and established a coalition government under Abdul Salam Aref. A highly devout Muslim and a pragmatist, Aref could not continue his relations with an ideologically oriented party whose leadership was disunited and ill-prepared for making day-to-day decisions. On its part, the Ba'ath was making preparations to oust Aref, whom they distrusted because of his religious and political views.

During this period, the Ba'ath leaders were divided into three groups. The right-wing group consisted of Talib Shabib; Hazim Jawad, minister of state; Hardan Takriti, commander of the air force; Tahir Yahya, chief of the General Staff; and Abd al-Sattar Abd al-Latif, minister of communications. This group advocated cooperation with other nationalist elements, especially those in the army. They also favored postponing the implementation of radical reforms, especially the imposition of socialism in the country. On this point, at least, this group could support its opposition to socialism by referring to Michel Aflaq's statement that declared the Ba'ath should not try to carry out socialism until Arab union was achieved. In other words, the principle of "socialism in one country" was not to be pursued.

The left-wing group was composed of Ali Salih al-Saadi, deputy premier and minister of interior (later minister of guidance), Muhsin al-Shaykh Radi, Hamdi Abd al-Majid, Hami al-Fukayki, and Abu Talib al-Hashimi. This group, composed mainly of civilians, was vehement in its insistence on socialism. They argued that socialism would accelerate the process of distributing wealth to the masses, whose firm support was essential for maintaining political control of the country. The leftist group was opposed to cooperation with the nationalist (Nasserite) army officers, especially those who rejected Ba'athist ideology.

Between these two extremes was a moderate group led by Ahmad Hassan al-Bakr, prime minister and later vice-president, and Salih Mehdi Ammash, minister of defense. Ammash tried to reconcile the differences between the two extreme groups but failed.

This internal rift in the Ba'ath provided an opening for Aref to weaken the opposition to his regime. Aref, conservative in his political and economic outlook, favored the moderate and the rightist wings of the Ba'ath, though he himself never joined the party. At a crucial time in November 1963, he supported these two groups in their effort to oust al-Saadi from the party leadership. After his ouster, al-Saadi was arrested and exiled to Spain. At this point, the Iraqi Ba'ath made an important change in the traditional ratio of military to civilian members of its Regional Command. Instead of keeping the civilians in the majority, the November 1963 session of the Ba'ath elected an equal number of civilian and military members to the Regional Command.[14]

In the meantime, the March 1963 coup in Damascus brought the Ba'ath to power in Syria. There, the military wing of the party consolidated its power at the expense of the civilian group. As a result, the Iraqi moderate and rightist factions did not receive any support from the Syrian Ba'athists, who disagreed with Bakr and Ammash on cooperating with the nationalist army officers. The Syrian Ba'athists believed in an "ideological army" that would defend not only the country's territorial integrity but also the political and social values imposed by the party. Because of the disagreements between the Syrian and Iraqi Ba'athists, the position of the Iraqi Ba'athists, vis-à-vis the nationalist officers, was further weakened. Consequently, Aref was able to expel the Ba'athists without any serious challenge to his authority.[15]

After nearly five years, the Ba'ath reemerged as the dominant political force in Iraq. During this period, it analyzed and reflected on the causes of its failure to maintain power in the country. It seems that the Ba'ath learned at least two important lessons from its experiences in Syria and in Iraq. First, the Iraqi Ba'ath came to realize that sharing power with any group or political party is not conducive to its political interests. Second, it seems to have learned that the military should not be allowed to dominate the party, whose civilian leadership must maintain strict control over the armed forces and the party apparatus.

That these two cardinal principles have heavily influenced its decisions can be seen from the policies the Ba'ath has followed since it recaptured power in July 1968. Although it has appointed Communists and non-Ba'athist Kurds to the Cabinet and to the vice-presidency (the incumbent vice-president, Taha Muhyi ad-Din Maaruf, is a Kurd), the Ba'ath has been unwilling to share power at the highest level of the decision-making process. Despite pressure from its Communist allies and from the pro-government faction of the Kurds, as well as the nationalists and other groups, the Ba'ath has persistently refused to appoint any non-Ba'athist to the RCC, the highest decision-making body in the country. Similarly, the Ba'ath has monopolized the political activities in the armed forces. The Ba'athists are adamant in their refusal to allow any other organization or group to engage in any form of political activity within the armed forces, which are the mainstay of the Ba'athist control of the country.[16] As a result, the Ba'athists have been successful not only in providing stability and continuity to the regime but also in surviving as a ruling elite, despite internal dissension between the military and civilian wings of the party hierarchy.

These two wings have disagreed on several issues facing Iraq: the Kurdish-Arab conflict, relations with Arab states, economic development, relations with Iran and the superpowers, and problems related to Palestine. Since July 1968, this rift has caused a number of political casualties within the RCC and its auxiliary governing bodies, such as the Cabinet and the Regional Command. In this process of elimination, the civilian wing of the party, under Saddam Hussein Takriti, has emerged as the strongest faction in the ruling institutions. This is a moderate center group that has removed, by a variety of legal and extra-legal means, the opposition posed by the right-wing and left-wing extremists. This does not mean, however, that this group has foresaken Ba'athist ideology, goals, and aims. What it does mean is that this moderate group is pragmatic in its relations with most foreign powers, the possible exception being Syria, with which the Iraqi Ba'ath is engaged in an ideological battle.

To obtain a better understanding of the emergent leadership of the Iraqi Ba'ath, it is essential that we discuss briefly the stages through which the RCC has passed since its establishment in 1968. Although the Aref regime[17] was overthrown essentially by two non-Ba'athist officers—Col. Abdul Razak Nayef, deputy intelligence chief and a Nasserite, and Col. Ibrahim Daoud, commander of the Republican Guard—the Ba'ath party had prepared the ground for a coup by spreading dissatisfaction among the army officers. The old party stalwarts, such as Ahmad Hassan Bakr, Saleh Mehdi Ammash, and Hardan Takriti and their followers, extended full cooperation to the conspirators—and were awarded key positions in the new government. Bakr became president, Ammash was made minister of interior, and Hardan Takriti was appointed army chief of staff and acting commander of the air force.[18] The day after the coup, the Middle East News Agency (MENA, the semiofficial Egyptian news agency) reported that the military junta had established a five-member Revolutionary Command Council that consisted of four known Ba'athists—Ahmad Hassan Bakr, Saleh Mehdi Ammash, Hardan Takriti, Maj. Saadoun Ghaydan Takriti—and a rather unknown figure, Lt. Col. Kamel Jamil Abbud.

Soon after the report appeared, MENA withdrew it and replaced it with a list of six names from the RCC. Not only was the RCC enlarged by one member, but the membership announced was completely new, the only exception being Bakr. It was obvious that an internal struggle for power was being waged between the Ba'athists led by Bakr, on the one hand, and the extreme Nasserites represented by Col. Abdul Razak Nayef, and moderate Nasserites, represented by Maj. Gen. Naji Talib, on the other.[19] The second MENA report named the following as members of the RCC: Rajab Abd al-Majid, former deputy premier; Abd al-Aziz al-Uqayli, former defense minister; Brig. Gen. Said Salibi, commander of the Baghdad garrison, then out of the country for medical treatment; Colonel Nayef; Col. Ibrahim Daoud; and Hassan Bakr. It is not clear whether these conflicting reports merely reflected a state of instability and uncertainty in Baghdad after the coup or whether they were a deliberate attempt by competing interest groups to spread rumors, in the hope of eliciting support from the undecided military and other factions in the country. In any case, it was not until July 23, a week after the revolution, that Baghdad Radio broadcast the names of the RCC, which, the broadcast said, was composed of six members, all military officers. Four—Bakr, Ammash, Hardan Takriti, and Hammad Shehab Takriti—were Ba'athists, and the remaining two were "nationalist" (Nayef was a Nasserite and Daoud was a pan-Arabist with strong Islamic and Arab ideals).[20]

Of the 26-member Cabinet appointed on July 18 and headed by Nayef, six were military officers (three of whom were Ba'athists: Khalid Makki al-Hashimi, Diyab al-Alqawi, and Anwar Abd al-Qadir al-Hadithi); four were civilian Ba'athists; four were Kurds; and the remaining were nationalists, technocrats, and bureaucrats.[21]

From the distribution of Cabinet portfolios and membership in the RCC, it was evident that the Ba'athists were in a much stronger position than the nationalists or the Nasserites, who seemed to have had no political experience and hardly any support from an organized popular group. The Ba'ath-Nasserite coalition was created for sheer expediency, and could not survive the pressures created by mutual suspicions and lack of common goals and ideals. Within two weeks of the July 17 coup, the Ba'athists outmaneuvered the two non-Ba'athist officers—Nayef and Daoud—and expelled them from the RCC and the Cabinet.

Although the November 1963 special session of the Iraqi Ba'ath had established a parity[22] between the civilian and military members of the Regional Command Council, the civilian group stayed in the background during the two weeks of postrevolution (1968) struggle between the Ba'athists and the non-Ba'athist members in the junta. However, no sooner did the Ba'ath succeed in monopolizing power than the civilian-military rift within the party began to manifest itself in the form of demands for the expansion of the RCC; purges of the rival factions; intensified ideological debate (the civilian faction's weapon against the military); and statements on strategic politics (the military faction's weapon against the civilians).

In the initial stages of the July 1968 coup, the military faction of the Ba'ath monopolized the RCC and held key positions in the Nayef and Bakr Cabinets. However, since the military faction did not control the party apparatus, it was evident that the civilian faction would demand an equal, if not dominant, role in the power hierarchy. In addition, the Ba'ath National Command expressed apprehension about the dominant role the military faction was playing in the Iraqi government. After initially approving of the Ba'athist coup in Iraq, the National Command began to warn its adherents against allowing the military faction to dominate the highest decision-making bodies in the country.

As a result of these internal and external pressures, the Iraqi Ba'ath adopted a three-point program designed to reduce the civil-military rift and to consolidate the Ba'athist control of the country. The civil force behind the adoption of this program was Saddam Hussein Takriti, assistant secretary-general of the Ba'ath. The program, which had been enunciated by Michel Aflaq long before the Ba'athists came to power in 1968, called for a national, democratic settlement of the Kurdish problem; a formula for cooperation between the Communists and the Ba'ath internally as well as between the government and the socialist states abroad; and the avoidance of military control of the party, with the creation of a balance between military and civilian groups.[23] Since ethnic and ideological schisms were two major factors in Iraqi disunity, it is not surprising that the Ba'ath party chief decided that healing them would be among the three major goals to be achieved.

Focusing again on the civilian-military conflict within the Ba'ath party hierarchy, it should be noted that not all the changes that took place within the RCC were induced by the civilian-military struggle. Members were added and dropped for a variety of ideological, personality, political, and other reasons. Occasionally, the reason for the expulsion of a member of the RCC was not even announced, unless it signified the member's disgrace and removal from the party. In such cases, elaborate accusatory statements were published in the press.

After further consolidating his hold on the party, Saddam Hussein Takriti, with the help of the Regional Command Council and the moderate faction of the RCC, expanded the membership of the RCC to 15.[24] In addition to Saddam Hussein Takriti, who was elected vice-president of the RCC, the new members were: Dr. Abdul Karim al-Shaikhaly (foreign minister), Shafik al-Kamali (minister of youth affairs), Dr. Izzat Mustafa (minister of health), Abdul Saloum al-Samarrai, Abdel Khalek al-Samarrai, Saleh Omer Ali, Izzat Doury, Murtada al-Hadithi, and Capt. Taha al-Jazrawi.[25] By enlarging the RCC with mainly nonmilitary members, the civilians in the Ba'ath took an important step toward subordinating the military faction of the party. As it was constituted in the fall of 1969, it could not count for support on more than six or seven members of the 15-member RCC. At least in form, the military faction was reduced to a minority. We say "at least in form" because the key military commanders, in case of serious ideological or strategic differences between the civilian and military groups, could always try to impose the military's will on the civilian faction. This would not, however, be an easy task because of lack of unity among the military officers and because of their dependence on the party for "popular" support. Only the civilian faction of the Ba'ath could provide this support, because the military faction had practically no contact with the public.

Despite this advantage, the civilian faction for awhile did not manifest complete confidence in its ability to subordinate the military to the party. During the early months of the revolution, both the National Command and Regional Command of the Ba'ath expressed public concern that the military might regain control of the country. Their apprehensions were based on the fact that only a handful of officers could be counted on as "true believers" who were ideologically committed to the Ba'ath. The rest were either opportunists or young Unionists (Nasserites) who were waiting for an appropriate occasion to oust the Ba'ath from the government. That is why the Nasserites had refused to join the Ba'athist-sponsored national front, despite Bakr's efforts to seek cooperation with all segments of the society. A serious difficulty in convincing the non-Ba'athists to join the front lay in the Ba'ath's refusal to share effective power with its competitors, whose cooperation it sought only in the implementation of the party's policies. The non-Ba'athists were given no opportunity to participate in the formulation of these policies.

Although the enlargement of the RCC placed the military faction in a minority, this arrangement did not reduce either the civilian-military tension or the disagreements among the civilian members. Consequently, these divisions provided Saddam Hussein Takriti with a number of opportunities to manipulate the RCC so as to concentrate power in his own hands. By using the method of "divide and rule," he eliminated all major contenders for power in the RCC. From November 1969 to November 1975, the membership of the RCC was reduced to its original size of six. Some members were removed because of personality clashes and disagreements over tactics; others were "voted out" because of ideological conflicts; and still others were offered as scapegoats for collective decisions that became ideologically embarrassing to the party.[26] Of the remaining six members, three are military—Bakr and Taha al-Jazrawi are retired officers and Saadoun Ghaydan Takriti is still an active officer—and three civilian—Saddam Hussein Takriti, Izzat Mustafa, and Izzat Doury.

One of the earliest casualties of the internal strife in the RCC was Saleh Omer Ali, whose dismissal from the RCC and the Cabinet (he was minister of culture and information) was announced on July 2, 1970. Although no official explanation was given, it is safe to assume that his dismissal did not reflect a serious power struggle within the RCC. The date of his dismissal, however, suggests one plausible explanation. Prior to his dismissal, the Iraqi government had come under severe criticism in the foreign press for executing a number of spies allegedly working for Israel and the United States. It is possible that Ali was accused of failure to counter the foreign press attacks against the regime.[27]

If Ali's removal from the RCC did not cause a political storm in the country, the dismissal of Gen. Hardan Takriti did rekindle the fear of military intervention and a take-over of the government. It was in recognition of his strength and support in the armed forces that the decision to dismiss him was taken while the general was in Spain, en route to the United Nations General Assembly. Furthermore, the announcement was kept secret until the regime could take precautionary measures against any possible counteraction by pro-Takriti officers.[28] There are several explanations for his dismissal from the RCC, the Cabinet, and the party. One hypothesis is that because of his role in ousting the Ba'ath from the Aref regime in 1963, Hardan Takriti had been suspect in the eyes of the civilian faction of the Ba'ath. This suspicion seems to have turned into a certainty as a result of Takriti's efforts to consolidate his control over the armed forces through transfers and promotions of his trusted friends to key positions.[29] Thus, it is postulated that his dismissal was no surprise and that the Ba'ath hierarchy had simply been waiting for an appropriate "cause" and opportunity to remove the general, who was considered a potential threat to the civilian group.

This opportunity was provided by the Palestinian-Jordanian conflict that exploded in September 1970. During this period, Hardan Takriti was on an inspection tour of the Iraqi forces stationed in Jordan. Although the Iraqi government had declared that it would order its 12,000 troops in Jordan to support the guerrillas against the Jordanian troops, the Iraqi forces remained neutral in the Jordanian civil war. This neutrality, it was reported, was imposed by Hardan Takriti, who remained at the Iraqi base in Mafraq to ensure the implementations of his orders.[30]

The Iraqi failure to intervene intensified the civilian-military rift in the Ba'ath. The National Command of the party, led by Michel Aflaq, expressed a "deep concern" about the lack of ideological conviction among the leaders of the Iraqi Ba'ath, which claimed to have based its policies on the Ba'athist principles of revolution, unity, and socialism. Aflaq informed Saddam Hussein Takriti that unless the Iraqi Ba'ath purged itself of party deviants, especially of Hardan Takriti, Saleh Mehdi Ammash, and Hammad Shehab Takriti, who were opposed to the Iraqi military intervention in the Jordanian civil war, the National Command would be forced to take disciplinary action against it. Under this pressure, criticism from the Palestinians, and Hardan Takriti's previous record of anti-Ba'athist activities under the Aref regime, the RCC had no choice but to expel him from the government and party apparatus.[31]

Another hypothesis of the Takriti affair posits that Hardan Abdul Ghaffar was singled out as a scapegoat for the RCC, which probably made a unanimous decision against intervention in the Jordanian-Palestinian conflict. According to a knowledgeable source, the Iraqi forces could not have intervened even if they wanted to do so, because they had been sent to Jordan as "political exiles" and without any ammunition. The commander of the Iraqi force in Jordan, Col. Hassan Naqib, told members of the Palestine Resistance Central Committee that the Iraqi forces were exiled "because the loyalty of the officers to the Ba'ath regime" in Iraq was uncertain.[32] It is interesting that neither the RCC nor the Regional Command of the Iraqi Ba'ath ever publicly accused Hardan Takriti of disobeying orders of the RCC, which had "promised" military help to the Palestinians. Therefore, it is our conclusion that the Iraqi government, while paying lip service to the Palestinian cause and inciting Palestinians to fight against the Jordanian forces, was in reality unwilling to provide material aid to the Palestinian guerrillas in Jordan. We further conclude that Saddam Hussein Takriti used this occasion to strengthen the civilian faction by removing one of the most forceful leaders of the military faction of the Ba'ath from the RCC and the Cabinet.[33] After the removal of Hardan Takriti, Saddam Hussein had to contend with only two more "heirs apparent" to Bakr—Saleh Mehdi Ammash and Hammad Shehab Takriti.[34]

Saddam Hussein was not alone in his efforts to eliminate Ammash and Shehab Takriti from the RCC and the Cabinet. He was supported in this by Michel Aflaq, who had let it be known that he wanted these two officers removed from responsible positions before he would "resume normal relations" with the Baghdad regime. For Aflaq, the dismissal of Hardan Takriti was merely a gesture to placate the Ba'ath National Command, whose support the Baghdad regime had sought as a means of acquiring legitimacy and acceptance by the "revolutionary" or "radical" regimes in the Arab world.

One of the three Aflaqian principles had called for finding a formula for cooperation between the Communists and the Ba'ath internally as well as between the Iraqi government and the socialist states abroad. Internally, and as early as December 31, 1969, the Ba'athists succeeded in obtaining support of the Iraqi Communist party (the pro-Soviet faction, known as the Central Committee), which agreed to join the Cabinet as a sign of Communist-Ba'athist cooperation.[35]

Externally, however, the Ba'athist regime in Iraq was finding it difficult to reconcile its differences on the issue of the Rogers Peace Plan, which Iraq had rejected but which had been supported by the Soviet Union. The Iraqi opposition was based on the argument that the U.S. plan did not deal with the heart of the Arab-Israeli problem—the Palestinians. The Iraqi rejection of the plan caused Iraqi-Soviet tension and an Iraqi-Egyptian estrangement. It was within the context of the Iraqi-Soviet tension that Gen. Saleh Mehdi Ammash, vice-president and a member of the RCC, was removed from his party and government positions. Dismissed with him was Abdul Karim al-Shaikhaly, foreign minister and a member of the RCC.

Reporting the governmental changes in Iraq, John Cooley pointed out that the removal of Ammash and al-Shaikhaly had some bearing on Iraqi-

Soviet relations, which were not as close as the June 17 protocol, April 8 trade agreement, or August 19 oil agreement would indicate.[36] However, neither Cooley nor any other writer has explained the link between these dismissals and Iraqi-Soviet relations. From the little information we have on Ammash, we surmise that the Iraqi vice-president lost out on two counts: first, he was known for his anti-Communist sentiments and, second, he and a number of civilian and military leaders favored Egyptian acceptance of the Rogers Peace Plan. This placed him against the pro-Soviet faction and against the "rejection group" within the RCC.

Since the Iraqi efforts at this stage were directed toward improving relations with the Soviet Union, Ammash's anti-Communist views were used to eliminate him from the power hierarchy. Of course, Aflaq's opposition to Ammash was also a contributing factor to his dismissal from the RCC and the vice-presidency.[37] The removal of al-Shaikhaly was not connected as much with Iraqi foreign policy as it was with the internal dissension in the RCC. Shaikhaly, considered to be a close ally of Saddam Hussein Takriti, reportedly was removed from the RCC and the Cabinet as a quid pro quo for the removal of Ammash.

In mid-1972, two more members of the RCC were dropped. Shafik al-Kamali and Abdul Saloum al-Samarrai were "demoted" from their positions. Kamali, a member of the RCC and minister of information, was appointed a member of the Educational Affairs Bureau at the RCC; and Samarrai, after a short jobless period, became minister of state in the Cabinet appointed after the July 1973 abortive coup. In January 1974, the Eighth National Congress of the Iraqi Ba'ath elected Kamali as one of the five reserve members of the (Iraqi) Regional Command Council, which provides members for the RCC.[38] Murtada al-Hadithi, who succeeded al-Shaikhaly as foreign minister, did not nominate himself for election to the Regional Command Council. Six months later, in June 1974, he was removed from the RCC and the Cabinet, and appointed envoy to Moscow.[39]

The latest casualties of the power struggle within the Ba'ath hierarchy were Gen. Hammad Shehab Takriti, minister of defense and a senior member of the RCC, and Abdel Khalek al-Samarrai, reputed to be the party's chief ideologist. In an attempted coup led by the director of security, Nazem Kazzar, and Mohammed Fadel, also of the Security Bureau, Hammad Shehab was captured and killed by the conspirators. During the investigations that followed, it was discovered that Abdel Khalek al-Samarrai, although not an active participant in the abortive coup, had nevertheless been informed of the impending coup by the conspirators.[40] In view of the close relationship that had existed between Saddam Hussein Takriti and the conspirators, it was contended that the abortive coup had been directed against the remnants of the military faction in the RCC and that if the coup had succeeded, "it would have been a logical conclusion of Hussein's drive toward party supremacy and isolationism."[41]

Although the conspirators killed Gen. Hammad Shehab Takriti and wounded Gen. Saadoun Ghaydan Takriti, both members of the RCC, it is difficult to accept *An-Nahar*'s unifactorial analysis of the event, especially when we are told by the same periodical that Kazzar was opposed to the government's policy of appeasing the Kurds and to a closer relationship with the Soviet Union.[42] If this interpretation of Kazzar's motives is valid, then he should have directed his efforts against Saddam Hussein, at least as far as ties with the Soviet Union were concerned. It is Saddam Hussein who, perhaps more than any other Ba'ath leader, has effected a rapprochement with the Soviet Union.

So far as the Kurdish question is concerned, the military faction is as divided as its civilian counterpart. It would be inaccurate to identify the military faction with "appeasement" of the Kurds and the civilian with "inflexibility," or vice versa. As Dana Adams Schmidt, a veteran observer of the Iraqi scene, points out, while certain segments of the Iraqi military have been expressing "revulsion against the war" in Kurdistan, the Iraqi government is making a two-pronged political and economic effort to win the support of the Kurdish people.[43] A report in *An-Nahar* indicates that the Iraqi military blames the civilian faction for not providing enough matériel to crush the Kurdish rebellion. In addition, *An-Nahar* reports that the military faction wants to reestablish closer ties with Egypt and Jordan.[44] Although these reports appeared after the attempted coup, they do not invalidate our argument that the Kazzar effort could not have been directed primarily against the military faction because he, of all people, should have known about the existence of a split between the military "hardliners" and the military "appeasers," and between the civilian "hardliners" and civilian "appeasers" who wished to reconcile the Kurdish-Arab differences. Our assessment of the event is that Kazzar most probably acted for personal gains, with ideology and territorial nationalism playing a minor role in inspiring him to act against the government.[45]

Although Saddam Hussein Takriti seems to have maintained his ascendancy in the RCC and the Regional Command of the Ba'ath, a number of significant powers that were previously held by the Ba'ath "collective leadership" were, after the abortive coup attempt in July 1973, given to President Bakr, who might exercise these powers either directly or through the Cabinet. The July 1970 amendment to the provisional constitution had provided for a strong president who could exercise his powers either directly or through a deputy, an arrangement that favored Saddam Hussein's position. A post-July 1973 amendment to the constitution "disallowed the delegation of authority to a deputy (thus implicitly downgrading Hussein's position)" and permitted the president "to bypass the RCC to rule either directly or through a council of ministers provided for by the amendment."[46]

Notwithstanding the new powers conferred on Bakr, who is a pragmatist and represents the military faction of the Ba'ath, the civilian faction, especially its "hardliners"—Ghanim Abdel Jalil, member of the Regional Command Council, chairman of the Bureau of Vice-Presidential Affairs of the Regional Command, and minister of higher education and scientific research; Syed Ali Ghannam, member of the Ba'ath Party National (Pan-Arab) Command and chairman of the Bureau of Public Relations in the Regional Command; and Tariq Aziz, chief ideologist of the Iraqi Ba'ath, reserve member of the Regional Command Council, deputy chairman of the Public Relations Bureau, and minister of information—have become more influential in the decision-making process than was the case prior to the July 1973 events. Saddam Hussein, though the most influential leader of the civil faction, is not in full agreement with the civilian "hardliners" on such issues as relations with Arab states, reconciliation with the Kurds, and acceptance of the Palestine Liberation Organization (PLO) as the sole legitimate representative of the Palestine people (with its related issues, such as whether or not to support the "rejection front").[47]

Realizing that Iraq has been isolated in the region because of political, ideological, or territorial differences with all of its neighbors except Turkey, Saddam Hussein has endeavored to effect a rapprochement with Egypt, whose strong ties with Iran and Saudi Arabia seem to worry the policy makers in Baghdad. Iraq and Egypt have exchanged a number of high-level visits by ministers, military officers, and party officials, with a view to forging closer ties at all levels of the bureaucracies and the political parties. In these efforts, the Ba'ath party's civilian "hardliners" are reputedly opposed to Saddam Hussein, who, at least in this area, is being supported by the military faction that is anxious to reassert Iraq's role in Arab affairs. An instance of this cooperation came to light in 1974, when, at the initiative of the military faction, the Iraqi government agreed to lend $700 million to Egypt. The civilian "hardliners" reportedly were strongly opposed to the move, and Saddam Hussein "was forced to throw his weight behind the military."[48]

Similarly, Saddam Hussein Takriti has endeavored to dissociate himself from the supporters of the "rejection front" in Iraq. During a 1974 meeting with Khaled Fahoum, president of the Palestine National Assembly, Saddam Hussein criticized the stance taken by the leaders of the "rejection front," and promised the PLO leadership that Iraq's policies toward the Palestinian guerrilla organizations would change, presumably in favor of the PLO. He informed the PLO that Iraq would no longer oppose the creation of a Palestinian state in the territory that might be evacuated by Israel and that Baghdad would raise no objections to the PLO's participation in the proposed Geneva peace talks.[49] If Saddam Hussein's view was reported accurately, the events that followed suggest that he was unable to convince his colleagues in Baghdad to adopt his recommendations on the Palestinian issue.[50]

It is evident that despite Saddam Hussein's great prestige and immense influence in the RCC and the Regional Command, he faced a serious challenge from within the decision-making bodies. It is interesting to note that while he was reportedly reassuring the PLO of the Iraqi regime's support, Baghdad Radio was announcing the arrival and activities of the rejection groups in the country. (Tariq Aziz, minister of information, under whose jurisdiction the broadcasting facilities fall, may have played up the event in order to embarrass Saddam Hussein.) During the five-day visit (October 6–10) of these dissident Palestinian groups, Baghdad Radio did not broadcast any report of any meeting between the Palestinians and Saddam Hussein, although their meetings with Hassan Bakr, Syed Ali Ghannam, Dr. Abd al-Majid ar-Rafi, Dr. Abd al-Wahhab al-Kayyali, and other national and regional leaders were promptly broadcast. From this, we may plausibly assume that Saddam Hussein did not meet with the Palestinian leaders who came to Iraq at the invitation of the Ba'ath National Command.[51] That the invitation was issued by the National Command alone is an indication of a rift between the National Command and the Regional Command, at least on the topic under discussion.

The Ba'ath National Command, under the leadership of Michel Aflaq, has consistently refused to accept the idea of setting up a Palestinian state on the West Bank and the Gaza Strip. As early as April 1974, Aflaq expressed his views on the subject in an article published in *Arab Revolutionary,* the organ of the Iraqi-backed Palestinian organization, the Arab Liberation Front. In this article, Aflaq rejected the idea of a Palestinian state as part of the proposed peace settlement; opposed King Hussein's claim to the West Bank and opposed its return to the Hashemite king; urged all Arab states to attempt to scuttle the peace efforts in Egypt and Syria; and stated that the Arabs must prepare for war, because only through force could the occupied lands be liberated.[52]

Although Saddam Hussein is reputed to be an Aflaqite in ideology, his political decisions and statements are not always motivated by this body of ideas. As a responsible leader of a country beset by enormous political, ethnic, and technological problems that require compromises with adversaries and cooperation with neighbors and regional powers, he cannot afford the luxury of ideological pronouncements that may prove counterproductive in achieving the country's goals.

For Michel Aflaq, it is a different story. As a philosopher and ideologist, he must look at the situation from a different perspective than that of Saddam Hussein. Aflaq has no day-to-day responsibilities for running a complex state, as Hussein does. Saddam Hussein sees Iraq caught between two regional powers—Saudi Arabia and Iran—both of which are in the process of developing closer relations with Egypt and both of which see Iraq as a threat to their conservative monarchies. In order to break out of this isolation, Saddam Hussein and his supporters are seeking better ties with Egypt, whose national prestige has reemerged after the October War. So far, Saddam Hussein has been a brilliant player on the political chessboard of Iraq, and through intrigue, political acumen, and the ruthless use of the National Security Agency, he has been able to eliminate most of his opponents from positions of power. Will he be able to remain at the top and survive the intrigues of a younger generation? We offer no prognosis on the chances of his survival. For the time being, he is firmly in control of the country.

It is assumed that unless a more moderate group begins to emerge in the Ba'ath hierarchy, the civilian "hardliners" will make it difficult for Bakr and Saddam Hussein (both are moderates in their approaches to Iraq's problems and opportunities) to resolve the Kurdish-Arab dispute or to accept Egypt's leadership in resolving the Arab-Israeli conflict.[53] Currently, Saddam Hussein seems to be playing the role of the conciliator between the civilian "hardliners" and the military, in the hope that the regime, faced with external opposition, will be spared the trials of an internal split that could weaken, if not destroy, the Ba'ath regime in Iraq.

The Kurds

In addition to the Ba'ath, two other clearly recognizable major interest groups are engaged in political activities in Iraq: the Kurds and the Iraqi Communist party (ICP).[54]

Before World War I, the Kurdish population lived under two Middle East governments: the Ottoman Empire and the Qajar Dynasty of Iran. The fall of the Ottoman Empire brought into independent existence a number of Arab states, two of which—Iraq and Syria—inherited a significant portion of the Kurdish population. Of the two, Iraq acquired by far the larger number of the Kurds, who by this time had been stirred by the Western concept of nationalism. To the Kurds, like so many other ethnic and linguistic groups, the Wilsonian principle of self-determination made good sense, if the multinational empires were to be broken up in the "interest of world peace."

As a result of their cordial relations with the victorious European powers (especially the British, who used the Kurds and other Ottoman ethnic minorties to break up the empire), the Kurds were promised, under the Treaty of Sevrès, an autonomous Kurdistan and, "if they should show that they wanted it, the right to independence."[55] Although the area promised to the Kurds was for the most part in eastern Turkey, the Kurdish aspirations clearly went beyond this artificial line that separated the Kurds in eastern Anatolia from their ethnic kinsmen in Iran, Iraq, and Syria. These aspirations pitted the Kurds against the nationalist Turks, the Iranians, and the British as the holders of the mandate in Iraq. The Kurdish "revolt" or "war of independence" in Anatolia was waged intermittently for about 12 years and was crushed by the Turkish military in 1947.[56]

While the Kurds in Turkey were being suppressed, the Iraqi Kurds began to demand autonomy from the British. Soon, they discovered that the British were in no mood to accept the principle of self-determination in an area strategically and economically (oil) important to them. Having failed to convince the British to grant them autonomy, the Kurds, under Mullah Mustafa Barzani, began fighting against the Iraqi government and the British in 1931–32. During the 1930s and the 1940s, the Kurds engaged the government forces in intermittent guerrilla warfare that brought them no nearer their goal of autonomy at the end of two decades than they had been at the end of World War I.

During most of this period, the Kurds could not find strong foreign allies willing to support their cause against the British and its client, the Iraqi government. This situation, however, took a rather dramatic turn in the mid-1940s when the Soviet Union, availing itself of an opportunity provided by the presence in northern Iran of Russian troops (1941–46), began to encourage the Azerbaijani Turks and Kurds in Iran to declare independence under the protection offered by Moscow.[57] In January 1946, the Kurds in Iran declared their independence as the Republic of Mahabad.[58] Since the territory of the new republic was contiguous to the Kurdish area in Iraq, the Iraqi Kurds were greatly encouraged. Moreover, because of the Soviet role in the creation of the republic, Mullah Mustafa Barzani became "convinced" that Moscow would continue to support the Kurds, despite clear indications that neither the regional powers (Turkey, Iraq, and Iran) nor the United States and Britain would be willing to recognize a Soviet-dominated Kurdish state in the heart of a strategic area. As a result of this "conviction," Barzani moved several thousand of his tribal troops from Iraq into the Republic of Mahabad, where he fought against the Iranian army.

In the meantime, the Soviet Union and Iran reached an understanding that would allow the Soviet Union to prospect for oil in northern Iran, in return for the withdrawal of Soviet troops from Iran and for the discontinuation of support to the Kurds and Azerbaijanis.[59] With the termination of Soviet help, the new republic came to a sudden end. For the Barzani forces the only prudent choice was to seek asylum in the Soviet Union, in which they had put an unduly high trust for their continuous survival as an autonomous people. In mid-June 1947, Mustafa Barzani and a remnant of his army (about 500–800 soldiers) crossed over to the Soviet Union, where he would stay until being allowed to return to Iraq on October 6, 1959.[60]

Between 1945 and 1959, there were no major disturbances in the Kurdish area of Iraq, despite daily "provocation" in the Kurdish-language broadcasts by a Soviet-sponsored clandestine radio operated by the Kurdish expatriates in the Russian Caucasus.[61] One reason for this apparent Kurdish docility was that the Kurds had again been hemmed in by the cooperation of the three

Middle East governments most directly concerned with them—Turkey, Iran, and Iraq. Under the Baghdad Pact, these governments had agreed to cooperate in strengthening and protecting the territorial integrity of the member states. Under such an arrangement, there was hardly any possibility for a foreign power to provide large-scale military aid to the Kurds without creating a serious international dispute that would involve not only the three Middle East powers but possibly Britain and the United States. With the overthrow of the Hashemite monarchy in Iraq and the installation in Baghdad of a "revolutionary" regime in July 1958, this international cooperation began to weaken, thus destroying the *cordon sanitaire* that had prevented foreign powers from interfering in the domestic affairs of these countries.

Soon after his return from the Soviet Union, Mullah Mustafa Barzani, with the cooperation of the former members of the outlawed Kurdish Nationalist party (Heva) and the Freedom Group, founded the Kurdistan Democratic party (KDP) with a leftist program aimed at radical land reform and coordination of Iraq's foreign and economic policies with those of the Soviet Union and other socialist states.[62] The KDP and the Iraqi Communist party (ICP) became two major links between the Qassem regime and the Soviet Union. Domestically, Qassem used the Kurds against the regime's opponents —from the big landlords and the monarchists to the Nasserite and Unionist officers. The Qassem regime generously armed the Kurds and often used them against "rebellious" tribes or military officers who did not agree with Qassem's policies.

On at least one crucial occasion in March 1959, the Kurds and the Communists (some of whom were also Kurds) saved the Qassem regime by containing the Shawaf revolt in Mosul and by preventing the pro-Nasser Arabs of the Shammar tribe from joining the rebellious military units.[63] This is not to suggest that the Kurds were merely pawns in the hands of Qassem, who could move them as he wished. It had become evident to the Kurds that their and the regime's interests had temporarily converged in the form of a common opposition to the pan-Arab sentiments in the country. In addition to this opposition, two other common factors brought the Kurds closer to Qassem: opposition to the Baghdad Pact and friendship with the Soviet Union and the Communists. With time, the perceptions of the Kurds and the Baghdad regime of these "common factors" began to diverge, causing misunderstanding and mutual suspicion of each other's motives; in the spring of 1961, the Kurds again revolted against the Iraqi regime. The Quassem-Barzani "honeymoon" was over.

Before we proceed further, we should mention some of the constitutional gains achieved by the Kurds during a period of cooperation between them and Baghdad. Even before Barzani returned to Iraq, the Qassem regime had promulgated a new provisional constitution for the country. Declaring that Iraq is an integral part of the Arab nation (article 2), the constitution stated that the Arabs and Kurds are "considered partners in this fatherland, and their national rights within the unity of Iraq are acknowledged by this Constitution" (article 3).[64] In return for the support of the Kurdish nationalists, Qassem recognized the claims of the KDP and freed hundreds of Kurdish prisoners who had been detained by the previous regime. Despite these gestures of goodwill, however, Kurdish relations with Qassem did not improve beyond the limits achieved during the Mosul collaboration.

As Qassem's loyal allies during the Mosul rebellion, the Kurds expected to see a great many material and political changes in Kurdistan: administrative autonomy, a Kurdish university and schools, and economic development of the region. None of these changes, however, would be forthcoming, because Qassem's relations with the Communists had begun to deteriorate and "he was not interested in encouraging any element considered pro-Communist."[65] (At that time, the Kurds were considered allies of the Communists.) Furthermore, the Kurds themselves were so disunited that for almost two years, neither the KDP nor any other group was strong enough to speak on behalf of the Kurds —this although the Qassem regime had already recognized the KDP as a representative body of the Kurds! In fact, not until July 1961 were the KDP and Mullah Mustafa Barzani able to draw up a memorandum outlining the Kurdish demands in Iraq. For the first time, this petition officially asked for wide Kurdish autonomy in Iraq and presented the following other demands to the government: that Kurdish be declared the principal official language in Kurdistan; that the police and army units in the region be composed entirely of Kurds; that educational facilities in the region be placed under the Kurdish provincial government; that a substantial share of the oil revenues be spent in Kurdistan; that the vice-premier, assistant chief of staff, and assistant ministers of all ministries be Kurds; and that outside Kurdistan, the deployment of Kurdish army units be made only with the consent of the Kurdish leaders, except in the case of an external threat.[66]

The rejection of these demands by the Qassem regime precipitated the Kurdish revolt that continued until April-May 1975. In intensity and scope, that Kurdish revolt was more serious and threatening to regional peace than any of their previous uprisings had been. This was primarily because of an Iraqi-Iranian struggle for influence in the Persian Gulf, which caused the two competitors to encourage the centrifugal forces across each other's national boundaries. (Iraq supported the Baluchis and the Arab tribes in Iran, and Iran aided the Kurds in Iraq. The Shiites of Iraq, who have strong sympathies with Iran, were not encouraged by Iran to create problems for the Baghdad regime.) The Kurdish rebellion of 1961 continued intermittently, with temporary cease-fires, armistices, and extended negotiations, during the 1960s. The first attempt at a cease-fire took place soon after the Ba'athist coup of February 1963: that March the military junta reaffirmed the government's recognition of the "natural rights" of the Kurds, based on the concept of "administrative decentralization." Neither this declaration nor the negotiations that followed, however, produced a mutually acceptable solution to the conflict. Once again the fighting resumed, followed by another cease-fire and more negotiations without agreement.

In 1963, the Kurds presented another set of demands that, however, did not differ significantly from their 1961 proposals.[67] While negotiations between the Kurds and the Baghdad government were in progress, a Ba'ath coup in Syria raised the hopes of the pan-Arabists for a union of Egypt, Iraq, and Syria. That the Kurds did not share the Arab enthusiasm for a union was reflected in a memorandum presented by the Kurds to the Iraqi delegation that was going to Cairo for the Arab unity talks. In it, the Kurds said that they would be willing to accept "decentralization," as proposed in the March proclamation of the Iraqi government, provided Iraq remained as presently constituted. If, however, Iraq joined other Arab states in a federation, the Kurds would demand autonomy "in the widest meaning of the term." And, finally, if Iraq became part of an Arab unitary state, the Kurds would demand a "separate region within that state."[68]

After another period of extended hostilities, the Kurds and the Iraqi government under Premier Abdur Rahman al-Bazzaz reached an agreement in June 1966. Under this agreement, the Kurds were promised wider political, cultural, and economic rights. Although they were not fully satisfied with the provisions of this agreement, it was the most they could get from the government, which was under constant counter pressure from the anti-Kurdish "hardliners."

Soon after this agreement was reached, the interim constitution of Iraq was amended to reflect the Kurdish-Arab understanding of their respective roles and obligations in the state.[69] The new agreement provided, inter alia, that the "Kurdish nationality" would be recognized in the permanent constitution; that wider administrative powers would be given to locally elected councils; that in Kurdistan, the Kurdish language would be used for administrative and educational purposes; that parliamentary elections would be held at an early date and would give the Kurds a proportional representation in the National Assembly and in all branches of the public service; that generous government grants would be given to Kurdish students for study abroad; that a faculty of Kurdish studies would be established at Baghdad University; that Kurdish officials would be appointed in Kurdistan; that permission would be granted for political association and for literary and political publications; that a general amnesty would be granted to political prisoners "when violence ended"; that a special ministry would be established to supervise reconstruction and to coordinate administration in the various Kurdish districts; and that the evicted Kurds either would be resettled in their previous homes or would be compensated for their property losses.[70]

Whether or not the government intended to implement the agreement in full, the provisions of the June agreement in themselves were a clear victory for the Kurds, who, it seems, had negotiated with the government from a position of strength. Whatever its strengths and weaknesses, this agreement did maintain a tense truce between the government and the Kurds for almost two years.

In the meantime, the Kurds began to express dissatisfaction with the slowness with which the provisions of the June agreement were being implemented. The long-promised elections were continuously postponed, with the excuse that the situation in the country did not encourage the proper carrying out of general elections. After nearly a year of the agreement, not all Kurdish political prisoners had been released; and those who had been let go were released on probation of four months to one year. By April 1967, the Kurds were able to start a Kurdish newspaper, *Al-Taahi,* which had been authorized by the government in the June 1966 agreement. It was primarily through this medium that they informed the public of their grievances and demands.

In the first issue of *Al-Taahi* (April 29, 1967), Barzani expressed his disappointment at the government's inability to implement a large part of the program promised under the previous year's agreement. He was pointedly critical of Aref's reluctance to hold general elections and to release Kurdish political prisoners.

Within a week of its first appearance, *Al-Taahi* was suspended for 30 days on the ground that it had published statements "prejudicial to national unity." This action by the government caused the two Kurdish ministers to resign from the cabinet, thus creating further tension between the Kurds and the government.[71]

The next serious effort to resolve the Kurdish problem was made soon after the Ba'ath regained power in July 1968. On August 3, 1968, speaking on behalf of the RCC, President Bakr said that the new government would abide by the June 1966 agreement and that it would negotiate with the Kurds on the basis of that agreement. Although there was a temporary respite in the hostilities, the Kurdish problem remained of major concern to the government. It should be recalled that one of the three Aflaqian principles adopted by the Iraqi Ba'ath had called for an equitable settlement of the Kurdish problem as a means of strengthening national unity, which was considered a prerequisite for an effective Iraqi role in the Arab revolution and the Arab movement toward unity. The new Ba'ath regime, especially Saddam Hussein Takriti, apparently was determined to achieve an amicable resolution of the Kurdish problem, which had been a major source of domestic friction and a cause of coups by dissatisfied military officers.

The Kurdish problem was so complex that no amount of "goodwill" and "sincerity" on the part of a small group of decision makers could change, within a brief period, the mutually hostile attitudes and perceptions of the Kurdish and Arab masses. As mentioned earlier, the Kurdish problem was no longer a domestic issue. The covert involvement of Iran, and reputedly of Israel, made the resolution of the dispute even less likely, although for the same reasons the need for resolution became more urgent than before. Furthermore, the generous military aid provided by Iran made the Kurds less flexible in their demands for regional autonomy and for sharing the oil revenues from Kurdistan oil fields. In the minds of some Iraqis, the Kurdish dispute became closely associated with the shah's "megalomania," manifested by his use of force in "occupying" three islands at the head of the Strait of Oman and by his declared policy of making Iran the dominant military and economic power in the area.[72]

If the Iranian involvement was not bad enough, the rumored presence of Israeli instructors among the Kurdish guerrillas made the situation even more complex and difficult to solve peacefully. The Iraqis seem to believe that the Kurds under Barzani (not all Kurds, of course) had become a tool of Iranian imperialism and of Zionism. Under these circumstances, it was extremely difficult for Saddam Hussein to make any new major concessions to the Kurds. Although he seems to have been intellectually and philosophically committed to resolving the Kurdish problem, political and practical difficulties created considerable pressure against doing so.

Nevertheless, after nearly two years of negotiations and armed hostilities, the Baghdad government announced a 15-point program for ending the Kurdish dispute. This program (known as the March 1970 agreement) promised the Kurds a number of new political and cultural incentives for ending the long and intermittent civil war. Under the 1970 plan, the government promised to take the following measures:

recognition of the existence of the Kurdish nationality in the new provisional
    constitution;
establishment of a university in Sulaimaniya and a Kurdish educational
    academy;
teaching of Kurdish in all schools, institutes, universities, teachers' schools, the
    military college, and the police academy;
establishment of a Kurdish printing house that would publish cultural and
    scientific papers and books by Kurdish men of letters and scientists;
declaration of *nowruz* (the Kurdish new year) as a national holiday;
creation of a new governorate of Dohuk (Dihok), to be separated from the
    liwa of Mosul, near the Turkish border;
decentralization of the local government;
granting of a general amnesty to all civilians and soldiers involved in the
    Kurdish war.[73]

Immediately following this statement, the RCC announced that it had approved the 15-point program for the Kurdish peace settlement.[74] This declaration, while granting wider autonomy to the Kurds, did not make any specific commitments about the sharing of oil revenues or the inclusion of Kurdish representatives in the RCC. Furthermore, only vague and noncommital references were made to ending job discrimination against the Kurds. Although five Kurds were appointed to the Cabinet soon after the March 1970 agreement, a Kurdish vice-president, provided for in this agreement, was not appointed until April 21, 1974. Despite the early enthusiasm and mutual praise expressed by the Kurdish and the Ba'athist leaders, there were reasons to believe that this agreement did not plug all the loopholes that had caused the failure of earlier declarations and agreements.[75]

According to an unconfirmed report from Beirut, a "secret appendix" to the March agreement contained clauses concerning the disposition of the anti-Barzani Kurdish militia, known as "the forces of Saladin"; the dissolution of a dissident Kurdish party led by Barzani's archenemy, Jalal Talabani, a Kurd who had been fighting against the Barzani forces since 1966; and the maintenance of a Kurdish force of 10,000 as national border guards.[76]

If this report is correct, it shows that Barzani was able to retain control over a fairly large armed force and, at the same time, to alienate his opponent from the government, which had been the primary source of matériel and economic aid to the anti-Barzani forces. At least for a while, Barzani became the undisputed Kurdish leader in Iraq.

No sooner had the accord been announced than there were reports that the agreement reached between the Iraqi government and the Kurds was faltering. Once again Barzani stated that the Kurds were dissatisfied with the way the government was implementing its side of the agreement. Specifically, he accused the Baghdad regime of equivocating on the appointment of Kurdish governors for Erbil, Mosul, Sulaimaniya, and Kirkuk provinces. Barzani said that unless the RCC appointed Kurdish governors of these districts, he would not name a Kurdish vice-president for the republic.[77] In addition, he again rejected the notion (stated in the Iraqi constitution) that Iraq was part of the Arab world. This has been a constant irritant between the Kurds and the Arabs at least since the promulgation of the 1958 constitution. As early as 1960, the Kurdish newspaper *Khabat,* then the organ of the KDP, categorically rejected this idea, on the ground that historically Kurdistan was never considered part of the Arab lands.

> Throughout history, it sometimes happened that Kurdistan either wholly or in part found itself in an Islamic state, as was the case with respect to many Muslim countries. Nevertheless, Kurdistan was not considered a part of the Arab lands. . . . It is enough to consider the historical facts and concrete reality which clearly show that the eternal Iraqi Republic consists of a part of the Kurdish nation, whose country is Kurdistan, and a part of the Arab nation, whose country is the great Arab homeland. . . . [78]

In August 1970, Barzani raised the same issue, which was a signal for the resumption of the rhetorical and military battles.[79]

For four more years, between March 1970 and March 1974, the Kurds and the Iraqi government endeavored to resolve their differences and to alleviate their mutual suspicion. While the Kurdish guerrilla activities continued throughout most of this period, the two sides kept their lines of communication open for consultations. Finally, just a day or so before the expiration of a deadline set in March 1970, the Iraqi government proclaimed local self-rule for the Kurdish people. The terms, however, fell far short of the Kurdish demands and expectations. Briefly, the government declaration reiterated the fact that Kurdish was one of the two official languages of the country, set up a special regional budget, and provided for the election of a Legislative Council and an Executive Council for the Kurdish region. However, the president of the republic retained strong executive power over the Kurdish institutions, which could be dissolved at his discretion. To discourage any thought of the government's weakening power over Kurdish affairs, the declaration emphasized that the Kurdish region was an integral part of Iraq.

In their negotiations with the government, the Kurds had demanded "all but veto power over legislation in Baghdad pertaining" to the Kurdish region. They also had asked the government to define clearly the boundaries of the autonomous region. The Kurds wanted to be assured that the oil-rich district of Kirkuk would be an integral part of the region. However, none of these demands proved acceptable to the government. The Baghdad regime did, nonetheless, promise to define the region's boundaries in accordance with a census that would be conducted within the framework of an earlier one taken in 1957. These conditions were immediately rejected by the Kurds, who, two days after the government announcement of autonomy, resumed hostilities against Iraqi forces in the northern region.[80]

The resumption of hostilities created an open rift among the Kurds—between those who accepted the autonomy plan and those who rejected it, the latter being led by Barzani and the former by a number of anti-Barzani Kurds, including his son Obeidullah Mustafa Barzani, minister of state; Taha Muhi ad-Din Maaruf, the vice-president of Iraq; Ismail Mulla Aziz; Hashem Akrawi, president of the Executive Council of the Kurdish region; Aziz Akrawi; and a number of others.[81] This group calls itself the Kurdistan Revolutionary party and is led by Abdel Sattar Sharif.

Between March 1974 and March-April 1975, the Kurds and Iraqi military units fought several pitched battles. They were armed with sophisticated modern weapons supplied by their external patrons—Iran equipped and trained the Kurds, and the Soviet Union provided military supplies to the Iraqi forces. Since entering into a treaty of friendship with Iraq in 1972, Moscow has stopped expressing its sympathies with the anti-government Kurds. Occasionally, Moscow "urged" the two disputants to resolve their differences in the spirit of "socialist brotherhood," but the Soviet Union did not put sufficiently effective pressure on either side to move toward a peaceful goal. Moscow, of course, did not have much, if any, leverage over the Kurds, especially Barzani, who does not recall his sojourn in Russia with fond memories.[82]

The Iraqi government was determined to follow through with its autonomy plan and to conclude the Kurdish-Arab conflict. In this respect, several subsystemic and systemic factors proved helpful to its efforts. Perhaps the two most significant were the phenomenal increase in oil prices that provided Iraq with the means to meet the economic demands of the Kurds without sacrificing the Arab interests in the country, and Iran's policy of rapprochement with the Arabs, especially with Egypt, which proved beneficial and helpful to the Iraqi government; with the help of the Algerian and Egyptian presidents, it managed to settle its lingering dispute with Iran. As a consequence of this détente between Iraq and Iran, the shah's government ceased its financial and military help to the Kurds, whose revolt did not last two weeks after the Iraqi- Iranian agreement was announced in Algiers on March 6, 1975.

In their struggle for autonomy, the Kurds have sought aid from any source willing to help them; they have not allowed ideological, religious, or ethnic considerations to influence their decisions on the sources of matériel and financial aid. The Kurds' goal has always been national, not ideological. In the past, fighting both against Iran and Iraq, they willingly accepted aid from the Soviet Union. Recently, they were aligned with Iran against the Ba'athist regime in Iraq. As had happened in the case of the Republic of Mahabad, the Kurds were "abandoned" by their foreign patron Iran for its "larger self-interest" in Iraq and the Arab world. Again, the three regional powers most directly concerned with the Kurds have managed to create a *cordon sanitaire* around them.

The Communist Party of Iraq

The Iraqi Communist party (ICP), the third interest group to be considered here, was founded as a clandestine organization in 1934. During the next quarter of a century, the Iraqi Communists remained underground and generally functioned from neighboring countries, such as Lebanon. The violent overthrow of the monarchy in July 1958 and the subsequent split between Qassem and the pan-Arabist officers (also called the Nasserites) led by Abdul Salam Aref provided the Iraqi Communists with an opportunity to function more openly. In his struggle to consolidate power against the enemies of his regime, Qassem relied on the Communists (and others) for support. During the Shawaf revolt, Qassem armed the Communists and the Kurds to fight against the rebellious military unit and against the Shammar tribe that supported the Nasserite officers. Realizing that Qassem had moved too close to the Communists, the Ba'athists withdrew their support of the regime. This action reopened the Ba'ath-Communist "ideological" rift that went back to the early days of the establishment of the Ba'ath.

Although Qassem had received Communist support against the pan-Arab opponents of his regime, he was unwilling to allow the Communists to broaden their base of activities. Without permitting them to seize political initiative and to become a serious threat to his own position, he exploited the Communists as a force against his enemies. Taking advantage of the traditional split in the Iraqi Communist movement, Qassem prevented the strengthening of the ICP by recognizing a less representative Communist group led by Doud al-Saigh, while the "genuine" party, Itihad al-Shaab ("unity of the people"), was declared illegal. Although the Communist press was banned in 1959 and many front organizations also came under attack, the ICP members were not seriously harassed at the official level for some time. The banning of the Communist press, however, was a portent of the relentless persecution of the Communists that began in early 1961.

During this period, hundreds of Communists were tried for their alleged role in the Kirkuk disturbances and other riots in 1959. The violent overthrow of the Qassem regime in February 1963 caused the suspension of Communist activities in Iraq. Between February and November 1963, the Ba'athists, who came to power in Baghdad, carried out a policy of persecution and of vengeance against their erstwhile allies.[83]

During the regimes of the Aref brothers (November 1963-July 1968), the Communists did not fare too badly, considering that the Arefs reputedly were "fiercely" anti-Communist. Although they were not allowed to function openly, the Communists were not hunted down by the state police. There seemed to be a cautious truce between the military regimes and the Communists during this period. Perhaps one reason was Abdul Salam Aref's efforts to improve relations with the Soviet Union. Another reason could be that there was a real desire on the part of the government to unite the Iraqi people, regardless of their ethnic and ideological orientations.

The second Ba'ath government, which came to power in July 1968, manifested much more tolerance toward the Communists. From the beginning, it endeavored to form a united front of the various political factions in the country. The initial effort, however, was unsuccessful because the Ba'athists were unwilling to share power with the non-Ba'athist groups. Consequently, until December 1969, the ICP remained outside the power structure. However, by the end of the year, the Ba'ath and the ICP had reached a compromise under which the government agreed to appoint Aziz Sharif, a prominent leftist, as minister of justice.[84] In return, the Communist party agreed to support the regime's efforts to establish a united front in the country.

In addition to the mutual distrust between the ICP and the Ba'ath caused by the traditional conflict, two other major factors precluded a rapprochement. One factor was related to the traditional support that the Communist party had extended to the Kurds in their fight for autonomy. The other was the attitude of the ICP toward the Palestine issue. On the latter, the ICP generally had followed the Moscow line and had called for a peaceful solution of the conflict. In 1970, when the Ba'ath government of Iraq rejected the Rogers Peace Plan, the pro-Soviet faction of the ICP called for a peaceful solution of the Israeli-Arab conflict. Since the signing of the Iraqi-Soviet treaty in April 1972, the Iraqi Communists generally have supported the Iraqi government's statements on the Middle East conflict; like the Soviet Union, they are calling for an international conference at Geneva to resolve the dispute. On the Kurdish question, the ICP has declared its support for the government's autonomy plan that was implemented in 1974.

As a result of closer collaboration between the Ba'athists and the Communists in Iraq, the Baghdad government in August 1973 permitted the ICP to publish its own newspaper, *Tariq al-Shaab* ("The People's Way"). In addition, Mukkaram al-Talabani (a Communist Kurd) and Amir Abdullah (a Communist Arab) were added to the Cabinet in 1972. Talabani was given the portfolio of irrigation and Abdullah that of minister of state without portfolio. In a later reshuffle of the cabinet, Aziz Sharif was moved from justice to minister of state without portfolio, perhaps a demotion for the leader of the Progressive Democrats.

ISSUE AREAS

Until March 1975, when Baghdad reached an understanding with Teheran on the Kurds and the Shatt al-Arab River, Iraq's most serious territorial dispute was with Iran. After years of negotiations and confrontations, the two states resolved the dispute in a comprehensive treaty that was signed in Baghdad on June 13, 1975. In the treaty, Iraq accepted the Iranian proposal that the Shatt al-Arab waterway border be drawn down the center of the estuary, dividing it equally. The two signatories also agreed to delineate 670 disputed positions along the land border, and to prevent infiltration from either side through cooperative security measures.[85]

Although the Shatt al-Arab dispute is no longer an Iraqi foreign policy issue, it is interesting to recall that this territorial dispute evoked perhaps the strongest reaction from Iraqi leaders because it had become a test of wills of two "ideologically" diverse neighbors who were engaged in an arms race and competition for influence in the Persian Gulf. From the Iraqi perspective, the Shatt al-Arab dispute, the Kurdish revolt supported by Teheran, the Iranian occupation of the three Arab islands in the Persian Gulf, and the massive buildup of the Iranian forces with sophisticated weapons acquired from the United States were orchestrated steps toward the imposition of a Pax Iranica on the region.

Iran, on the other hand, saw the Iraqi Ba'athist regime as a source of subversion and a threat to the traditional political systems in the Persian Gulf. Being the strongest state of the region, Iran considered it its sacred duty to counter the Ba'athist regime's activities by creating and supporting domestic and international problems for Iraq.

The Shatt al-Arab Issue

The origin of the Shatt al-Arab dispute goes back to the Ottoman Empire, which prior to World War I controlled both sides of the river.[86] As a successor state to the Ottoman Empire, Iraq claimed the same rights after it became independent in 1932. After several years of negotiations in which the British reputedly urged Iran to concede the Iraqi demand, in 1937 Teheran and Baghdad signed a treaty that confirmed Iraqi sovereignty over that 100-mile stretch of Shatt al-Arab (the estuary of the Tigris and Euphrates rivers) that divides the two neighbors before emptying into the Persian Gulf. Unlike most other international river treaties, this one gave Iraq exclusive navigational rights up to the low-water mark on the Iranian side, rather than to the midstream point of the river. Excepted were the anchorage areas at the Iranian ports of Abadan, Khorramshahr, and Khosrowabad, about ten miles below Abadan, where the border is moved to the center of the river.[87]

Relations between the Hashemite dynasty in Iraq and the Pahlavi dynasty in Iran remained friendly until 1958, when, after the Qassem coup in Baghdad, the Iranian-Iraqi ties began to deteriorate. In December 1959, the Iraqi government questioned the validity of the 1937 treaty and asked Iran to return to Iraq all the roadsteads outside the Iranian ports of Abadan, Khorramshahr, and Khosrowabad on the Shatt al-Arab. Following minor border skirmishes, the Iranian government issued a statement in January 1960, in which Teheran charged Iraq with violating the treaty by refusing to respond to repeated proposals for a joint committee to negotiate a settlement of the Shatt al-Arab; by using fees collected by the Basra Port Authority for purposes other than river development; and by inciting the Iraqi people against Iran. On the basis of these alleged violations of the treaty, the Iranian government declared that henceforth the Iraqi-Iranian border would be marked by the midway line at the deepest point of the navigable channel of the Shatt al-Arab.[88]

During the next few years, Iraqi-Iranian relations remained tense, except the period when President Abdul Salam Aref (November 1963-April 1966) endeavored to settle the dispute by negotiations. After the July 1968 coup in

Iraq, Hardan Takriti and President Bakr took diplomatic initiatives to reestablish cordial relations with Iran, which responded favorably. A number of high-level visits were exchanged, and there were references in the media to the Iranian-Iraqi "honeymoon" in the making. These expectations, however, proved premature.[89]

After months of fruitless talks, Iran, alleging that Iraq had been in violation of the treaty for many years, denounced the 1937 agreement on April 19, 1969. The Iranian announcement further declared that Iranian ships plying the Shatt al-Arab would no longer pay Iraqi tolls and would not fly the Iraqi flag, as required by Iraqi laws. In turn, the Iraqi government described Iran's abrogation of the treaty as a "unilateral action contravening the principles of international law." Baghdad reiterated its claim to the entire Shatt al-Arab.[90] Furthermore, Iraq warned that ships not complying with Iraqi regulations would be prevented from entering Shatt al-Arab. To assert its claim on part of the Shatt, the Iranian government dispatched a cargo ship, with naval and air escort, through the estuary to the Persian Gulf. The ship arrived unmolested by the Iraqis, who took no action despite their previous threats. For the next six years, the Shatt al-Arab dispute remained frozen. During this time several states, including Turkey, Algeria, Egypt, and the Soviet Union, endeavored to resolve the issue amicably. Although initially unsuccessful, their efforts finally bore fruit in March 1975, when the two disputants reached a settlement of this and other issues.

The Kuwait Issue

The Iraqi claim on Kuwait has been responsible for tension between Baghdad and Kuwait. The genesis of this dispute is based on Baghdad's claim that Kuwait was an integral part of Iraq under the Ottoman Empire and that, as a successor to this empire, Iraq should inherit the oil-rich sheikhdom that became independent of British rule in 1961. Announcement of the impending independence of Kuwait prompted Prime Minister Qassem to claim Iraqi sovereignty on June 25, 1961, only six days after the sheikhdom and Britain signed an agreement terminating the Anglo-Kuwait agreement of 1899 that had recognized British hegemony over Kuwait. Qassem justified his claim on two counts: that Kuwait was part of the province of Basra in the Ottoman Empire, and that this fact had been recognized by Britain in the treaty of 1899.[91] This Iraqi claim was firmly rejected by Kuwait and Britain, as well as by all the Arab states, which immediately and unanimously admitted Kuwait to the League of Arab States, thus recognizing its sovereignty and independence.[92] Furthermore, on receiving a Kuwaiti request for military aid against the Iraqi threats, a number of Arab states provided military contingents that replaced the British expeditionary force that had landed soon after Qassem proclaimed Iraqi sovereignty.[93]

Realizing that no Arab or non-Arab state had supported Iraq's claim to Kuwait, Qassem turned to the Soviet Union to block Kuwait's admission to the United Nations. The resolution for Kuwait's membership, sponsored jointly by Britain and Egypt, was vetoed by the Soviet Union on the ground that the sheikhdom was still under the "tutelage" of Britain and thus did not qualify as an independent state.[94] The unanimous Arab opposition and a 50-million dinar Kuwaiti loan to Iraq helped defuse the conflict, which remained dormant until December 11, 1972, when a road-building crew, under the protection of an Iraqi military brigade, crossed the border and began to build a road leading to the Persian Gulf on Kuwaiti territory. This time, Iraq justified the "troop concentrations" (it did not admit a violation of Kuwaiti sovereignty) at the Kuwaiti border on the ground of "national defense" against a possible military threat from Iran. Again, the leaders of the Arab states put pressure on Baghdad and urged it to withdraw from any planned confrontation with the Kuwaitis.

Hardly three months after the road-building incident, a contingent of Iraqi troops occupied a Kuwaiti police station near the Iraqi-Kuwaiti border at Samitah. During this incident, two Kuwaiti policemen were killed and four injured. It was the most violent confrontation between the two disputants since Kuwait became independent in 1961.

These incidents raise a number of questions about the Iraqi motives in creating an additional diplomatic headache when Baghdad was already isolated in the region. Were these incidents staged for economic reasons? Were they staged for diplomatic reasons? Or were they staged for strategic reasons? We believe that the road-building incident and the occupation of the police station at Samitah were related to Iraq's financial difficulties and to its desire to expand its narrow coastline at the expense of Kuwait. Since the nationalization of the Iraqi Petroleum Company in June 1972, the country had been faced with serious economic problems. In November of that year, Iraq tried to obtain loans and grants from the Arab states, whose foreign and defense ministers were meeting in Kuwait. However, in the face of Saudi opposition, Baghdad's efforts were not successful. Although Kuwait provided a 5-million dinar loan, Iraq was evidently piqued by the treatment it received at the conference. Perhaps it was in the hope of creating pressure on Saudi Arabia and Kuwait to loosen their purse strings that Iraq created tension on the border with Kuwait. This episode also helped Iraq to focus Arab attention on Baghdad, to which a number of Arab diplomats rushed to ease the tension between Iraq and Kuwait.

In addition to the meager financial assistance it received from Kuwait and the expanded diplomatic contacts with other Arab states, Iraq seemed to have gained a Kuwaiti acquiescence to the use of Kuwait territory for Iraq's strategic needs. Reportedly, Iraq wanted to acquire a strip of Kuwaiti territory along the coast, including the two Kuwaiti islands of Warba and Bubiyan. The purpose of this was to provide better protection for the new Iraqi deep-sea port of Um Qasr, where the Soviets are building a large naval base, and to protect the coast opposite Warba, the only deep channel in the area.[95] Realizing the strategic importance to Iraq of the two islands and the Iraqi-built road, the Kuwaiti government reportedly was prepared to lease the territory around Samitah and the two islands to Iraq, provided Baghdad recognized Kuwaiti sovereignty over these parcels of land. Despite high-level discussions between Iraq and Kuwait, a permanent solution to the border problems has not been found.

Palestine

On the pan-Arab level, the most important territorial issue for Iraq is that of Palestine and the lands under Israeli occupation since June 1967. Iraq has persistently and unequivocally demanded a just solution to the Palestine problem. As a member of the Eastern Front, it participated in the June and October Arab-Israeli wars. In addition, after the June War, Iraq maintained a sizable force in Jordan as an indication of Iraqi commitment to the Arab-Israeli conflict.

Despite its support of the Palestinians at the international level, however, Iraq's relations with Palestinian representative bodies have not always been friendly. Both the internal conflicts in Iraq and Baghdad's isolation in the Arab world contributed to the creation of tension between the Palestinian commando groups and the Iraqi government. Internally, the Ba'ath government was engaged in a military conflict with the Kurds, and its relations with the ICP had yet not improved. Externally, Iraq's relations with Syria and Egypt were not cordial; and the Baghdad regime felt extremely insecure in its dealings with the Palestinian command organizations because of their contacts with the regime's internal and external enemies.

Prior to 1972, the only commando organization favored by the Baghdad regime was the Arab Liberation Front (ALF), founded in April 1969 by the Ba'athists. The motive behind the creation of the ALF was to have an Iraqi counterpart to the Syrian-sponsored Sa'iqa. Although a number of other commando organizations welcomed the formation of the ALF, the latter's policy of not confining its membership to Palestinians caused serious disagreements between it and other commando organizations. The ALF believed that only through general Arab participation and mobilization would the Palestinians be able to achieve their political goals. In contrast, the other commando organizations rejected the principle of general Arab participation in their activities, on the ground that it would bring the resistance movement under the tutelage of Arab regimes.[96] As a result of this policy, the ALF has more non-Palestinians than Palestinians among its rank and file. Consequently, it has less influence in the resistance movement than does its main competitor, the Sa'iqa.

Iraqi-Palestinian relations plummeted to a new low in September 1970, when the Iraqi army units stationed in Jordan refused to aid the commandos, despite their urgent appeals for help. (For a discussion of this episode as it related to the struggle for power in the RCC, see the section on the Ba'ath in this chapter.) For the next 18 months, Iraqi-Palestinian relations remained tense. The Iraqi government proceeded to impose further restrictions on the activities of the commandos and refused to pay the salaries of the Palestinian Qaddissiyah Brigade stationed in Iraq.

After mending its fences with the Iraqi Communists and the Kurds, the Ba'athist regime moved to effect a rapprochement with the Palestinians. With this aim in mind, the RCC announced that Iraqi citizens employed by public and private institutions would be allowed to join the resistance without losing their rights and salaries as employees. Moreover, Palestinians would be given equal treatment in employment, and Palestinian students would enjoy equal opportunities for scholarships.[97] These and other changes announced by the RCC created a better feeling between Iraq and the resistance movement. The nationalization of the Iraq Petroleum Company in June 1972 raised the Ba'athist status with the commandos, who "regarded the takeover as a revolutionary act to be supported without reservation."[98]

This wholehearted support did not last beyond the end of the October War. Iraq's rejection of the U.S.-sponsored peace initiatives again caused a split between Baghdad and the commandos' largest representative organization, the Fatah. This time, Iraq was supported by the PFLP and the PFLP General Command, which opposed the formation of a Palestinian state only in Gaza and the West Bank.

On other pan-Arab territorial issues, Iraq's support has been mostly verbal. In certain cases, however, it has provided financial assistance to the Arab claimants of land still under foreign occupation. This category includes such groups as the Eritrean Liberation Front.[99]

Economic Development

Prior to the discovery of oil in the late 1920s, Iraq was an agricultural country. Although agriculture continues to contribute a substantial portion of the gross national product, Iraqi agricultural exports earn a limited amount of foreign exchange. The main source of Iraqi industrial development has been its oil revenues, which account for four-fifths of the country's foreign exchange receipts, two-thirds of the government's revenue, and one-fifth of the gross national product. Because of its heavy reliance on oil revenues for development, Iraq's industrialization programs have fluctuated with the international oil market. In the early 1960s, while Iraqi oil revenues were stagnant, the country's industrialization plans were kept at a level far below the country's developmental needs.[100] To be sure, the lack of availability of capital was only one of the problems Iraq faced in industrializing. Another important factor was, and still is, the shortage of trained personnel: technicians, engineers, and the like. Additionally, the attitudes of most Iraqi governments "toward successful industrialists have been ambivalent." They have, on the one hand, "favored industry for reasons of prestige; on the other, they have been suspicious of anyone who has made a profit."[101]

Since its assumption of power in 1968, the Ba'ath government has endeavored to increase the rate of industrial and economic growth in the country. Although the 1970–74 national development plan did not achieve all its goals, it did enlarge the industrial base on which to construct future developmental projects. There were five major reasons for the plan's failure to meet its goals:

lack of skilled labor and managerial personnel;
absence of entrepreneurial initiative;
a limited domestic market;
lack of export marketing channels for nonoil products;
lack of diversification of manufactured goods.[102]

A sharp increase in oil revenues has enabled Iraq to invest more in the industrial and agricultural sectors of the economy. This was reflected in the 1975–76 investment program. The appropriation for this program is 1.5 billion dinars (100 Iraqi dinars = U.S. $337.78). Of this amount, 709 million dinars were allocated for the industrial and 268 million for the agricultural sectors. This is almost five times more than the appropriation of 310 million dinars for 1973–74. In March 1974, a new five-year development plan, with a projected investment of about $7.5 billion, was launched. This amount probably will be revised upward as Iraq receives higher revenues from oil sales than had been expected. Of this amount, 225 million dinars were slated to be invested in industry and 178 million dinars in agriculture.[103]

Although the Ba'ath party professes to be a socialist organization, it has not gone as far in enacting socialist decrees as its neighbor, Syria, or its traditional rival, Egypt. Despite its militant rhetoric against capitalism, the Iraqi Ba'ath has been encouraging private national and foreign investments in the country. All fields of investment, other than strategic and heavy industries, are open to the private sector.[104]

However, since there is no tradition of private investment in industry, the Iraqis have not shown willingness to invest in anything that involves risk. Most of the people who have savings prefer to acquire tangible assets that entail minimum risk. Therefore, most Iraqis with capital invest in agriculture and real estate.[105] In view of Iraq's considerable agricultural potential, the government is investing large sums of money and effort to develop the agricultural sector of the economy. Its aim is to produce an agricultural surplus for export by reducing dependence on weather conditions and by solving the salinity problems that affect irrigated land.

Oil has played a significant role not only in the industrial development of the country but also in Iraq's relations with major foreign powers. Traditionally, Iraqi public sentiments have been against foreign oil concessions in the country. From the earliest days of its development, Iraqi "nationalism" focused its attention on the foreign oil concessions that had been awarded by the British to the Iraq Petroleum Company (IPC) in 1925. Although the anti-concession sentiments were high among both the general public and the Free officers,* the Qassem regime rejected nationalization as impractical. The new regime, however, pressed for higher shares of oil profits. For a while relations between the oil companies and the revolutionary regime continued to be friendly, but in 1961 their ties began to show serious strains because of their inability to reach a settlement on the issue of oil royalties. Consequently, the Iraqi government expropriated all IPC concessionary areas not yet under production. This action deprived the IPC and its affiliates of 99.5 percent of the area over which the oil conglomerate held prospecting rights under the agreements signed in the 1930s.[106]

The crisis engendered by the rift between the IPC and the government seemed to polarize Iraqi public opinion on how to settle the oil dispute. While one group called for a negotiated settlement, the other insisted on confronting the oil companies with a fait accompli by nationalizing their assets in the country.[107] Caught between the nationalists and the technical and financial realities of oil politics, the Iraqi government enacted a law that, it believed, would satisfy the two "extreme groups" in the country. The new law authorized the state-owned Iraqi National Oil Company (INOC) to exploit all resources throughout the country, except in the areas already being exploited by the IPC and its associates.[108] This law broke the near-monopoly of the IPC and opened the country to other foreign oil companies.

Despite the IPC efforts to discourage other companies from entering the Iraqi market, several oil companies expressed willingness to invest capital in prospecting for oil in Iraq. One of the first new oil concession holders was the French state-owned group of companies Entreprise de Recherches et d'Activités Pétrolières (ERAP). This agreement did not give the French organization co-ownership rights over future oil discoveries. ERAP became a contractor under INOC, which held all proprietary rights pertaining to oil and installations to be constructed in Iraq. However, the agreement provided that the

---

*Those Iraqi officers who conspired against the monarchy and supported Qassem after the coup.

French agency would receive from INOC 50 percent of the oil discovered in commercial quantities.[109]

Soon thereafter, the Soviet Union expressed its willingness to enter into an agreement with INOC for oil prospecting and exploitation. On December 24, 1967, it agreed to aid INOC in the exploitation, transportation, and marketing of oil. Through mutual consultations and negotiations, Moscow and Baghdad agreed to focus their attention on the oil-rich Rumeila field in southern Iraq. This understanding, however, did not materialize because INOC decided to exclude both the French and the Russians from Rumeila. Instead, INOC acquired Soviet loans totaling $72 million to develop the North Rumeila fields. In addition to the Russian loans, Iraq received promises from the Soviet Union and its East European allies for technical cooperation in drilling oil wells, constructing pipelines, and building port facilities for oil tankers in the Persian Gulf.[110]

Although by April 1972 the North Rumeila field had started to produce oil in commercial quantities, the Iraqi government still received a major portion of its oil income from the Western oil companies operating in the country. In early 1972, either for purely commercial reasons (as the IPC and its affiliates claimed) or to put financial pressure on the government (as the Iraqi regime perceived), the Western oil companies began to reduce oil production in Iraq. This action caused an irreparable rift between them and the Ba'athist regime, which on June 1, 1972 announced the nationalization of all IPC assets in Iraq.[111]

The nationalization of IPC was one of the major achievements of the Ba'athist government since its coming to power in 1968. It was a major achievement because several previous governments had not been able to establish a viable relationship with the foreign oil companies, whose monopolistic control of the oil industry could not prudently be broken under the existing circumstances. Furthermore, the oil transportation and distribution systems were owned and operated by the oil companies, which could conveniently defeat Iraqi efforts to sell oil independently if Iraq had tried to nationalize the oil industry. In addition, Iraq did not have adequate manpower to administer the oil industry, although it possessed one of the largest pools of trained oil technicians in the Arab world.

However, by mid-1972, both domestic and international factors had begun to change in Iraq's favor. First, the Arab world had become more conscious of its strategic importance to the industrialized world and the Arabs had realized that existing world conditions would not permit any single bloc of powers to establish hegemony over the region. Therefore, the Arab governments were able to take bolder political decisions than were thought possible in the 1950s or early 1960s.

Second, despite the internal dissension among the Arab states, they had begun occasional cooperation at the international level. This cooperation was especially significant in oil negotiations with the foreign corporations and in providing financial aid to the needy members of the League of Arab States. It was manifested in the oil nationalization decision of 1972, when Iraq was unanimously supported by the Arab states; and Kuwait, despite the Iraqi-Kuwaiti border rift, offered to provide financial aid to Baghdad so as to keep the Ba'athist regime from cracking under pressure from the oil companies.[112]

Third, prior to the nationalization decision, the Ba'ath regime had succeeded in training larger numbers of technicians and managerial personnel, and it had made arrangements to sell oil directly to a number of European, Asian, and African states. Even the previously crucial factor of oil tankers was no longer a serious consideration in making the nationalization decision: the Soviet Union had agreed to lease tankers to INOC, and Spain had earlier agreed to build seven 35,000-ton tankers.[113]

The IPC nationalization crisis had hardly subsided when the October War broke out. Accusing the United States of collaboration with Israel, the Iraqi government nationalized the assets of Exxon and Mobil, the two U.S. companies that had held a joint 23.75 percent share in the Basrah Petroleum Company. The Iraqi nationalization decree, issued on the second day of the war, said that the Iraqi action was being taken "in conformity with an undertaking to use oil as a political weapon to face the escalation of the Zionist and U.S. imperialist aggression against the Arab nation."[114] Two weeks later, on October 21, the RCC nationalized all Dutch interests in the Basrah Oil Company. On this occasion, the Iraqi government said that the nationalization was designed to "punish Holland 'for its hostile attitude to the Arab nation and to the struggle of our people.' "[115]

While Iraq claimed that its nationalization was in accord with an "undertaking to use oil as a political weapon," Baghdad not only did not accept a unanimous Arab decision to reduce oil production, it actually raised it. In this action, the Iraqi government apparently found no logical contradiction. Dr. Saadoun Hammadi, minister of oil and minerals, defended the nation's action by pointing out that as a political weapon oil should be used only against the enemy, and that the countries that had always stood by the Arabs should not be punished along with the enemies of the Arabs. Chiding the Arab critics of Iraqi oil policy, Hammadi challenged the Arab oil producers to match Iraq's performance by nationalizing U.S. oil interests, by withdrawing deposits from American banks, and by breaking diplomatic relations with Washington.[116]

Despite the stated Iraqi reasons for not joining the oil boycott, it is noted that the Iraqis had no choice but to continue to produce and sell oil to meet the heavy foreign-exchange needs of their development projects. In addition, INOC had signed agreements with a number of foreign states; and as a new oil producer anxious to establish credibility, it did not want to default on its commitments to buyers.

In conclusion, it may be stated that although oil will continue to be the financial source of Iraq's industrialization, it has been, and will be, used to achieve political as well as economic goals. This means that in signing long-term agreements for oil, a commodity that is becoming scarce, Iraq will not expect just the financial returns due it, but will insist on additional benefits, either political or technological. In other words, future oil negotiations between Iraq and industrialized states will most probably deal as much with oil prices and oil quantities as with Iraq's industrial and development needs. Those industrialized states that cannot or will not offer a political quid pro quo for guaranteed oil supplies must be prepared to offer Iraq the technology and manpower it urgently needs to expand the country's industrial base. Iraq's minister of oil and minerals, Saadoun Hammadi, has succinctly stated his country's policy: "Iraq, a developing and oil-rich country, is not interested only in money, but also in know-how (expertise and technological assistance) which would increase the rate of development."[117]

Unlike Egypt, where the university and high school students have occasionally participated in anti-government riots and in ideological discussions and demonstrations, the Iraqi regime has not faced student challenges to its educational or training policies. This apparent docility of the Iraqi students may be attributed to the firm control the Ba'ath party maintains on the country's campuses or to the lack of ethnic and religious cohesion, which prevents the students from forming a "united front" against the authorities. Our assumption is that the Iraqi students associate themselves more with ethnic or ideological groups than with purely student organizations. Those who are active in the latter groups probably are not keenly interested in the political and ideological questions being discussed in the country. Those active in ethnic or ideological organizations manifest their opinion through the KDP, and KRP, the Ba'ath, or the Communist party of Iraq.

Similarly, the question of military training has not caused any serious disagreements among the Iraqi decision makers, although press rumors have indicated that a group of unnamed officers opposed Iraq's total dependence on the Soviet Union for training and matériel. Again a contrast with the Egyptian situation is revealing; unlike the Egyptian military officer corps, the Iraqi officer corps (under the Ba'athist regime) does not seem to have formed anti-Soviet or pro-Soviet pressure groups. In fact, ever since Saadam Hussein Takriti "succeeded in subordinating" the military to civilian control, the Iraqi officers have not publicly expressed opinions on matters relating to Iraq's relations with the great powers.[118]

Foreign Relations

Before the Persian Gulf became one of the most important strategic areas in the world, Iraqi regional policies were concerned with issues related to Palestine and relations with Syria and Egypt. Now, however, the Iraqi focus has shifted to its south and southeastern borders, toward the Persian Gulf.[119]

The Iraqis perceive their role as the strongest Arab rival of Iran for influence in the Persian Gulf. Although it has the smallest coastline on the Gulf, Iraq's claim to leadership is based on its population of more than 10 million, its agricultural potential, and its very substantial oil reserves.[120] This change in Iraq's foreign policy focus has caused consternation in Kuwait, with which Baghdad has a border dispute, and in Saudi Arabia, which is apprehensive about the Ba'athist rhetoric against the monarchist regimes.

Although Iraq has signed border agreements with both Iran and Saudi Arabia, with whom its bilateral relations have become cordial, there are some regional and systemic issues over which disagreements still exist. For example, Iran views Iraq as a Soviet strategic base in the Persian Gulf, from which Teheran is endeavoring to keep the rival superpowers and great powers. Iraq, being heavily dependent on the Soviet Union for sophisticated weapons and technological aid, is obliged to provide port facilities to the Soviet naval ships visiting the Persian Gulf. The Iraqi-Iranian competition for influence does not end in the Persian Gulf; their rivalry has been manifested in the Omani civil war, in which the shah of Iran is supporting the legitimate government of the country and the Iraqi government allegedly is aiding the rebels.

Within the Persian Gulf area, Iraq has improved relations with the United Arab Emirates and Bahrain, whose students are being offered scholarships to study in Iraq. In addition, Iraq is participating in several multilateral regional organizations and was a founder member of the Gulf News Agency.

IRAQI OBJECTIVES AND POLICIES

Since its independence, Iraq has had a series of monarchist and revolutionary governments whose domestic and foreign policy goals have not differed radically. Since all these governments were confronted by practically the same set of problems, the goals they pursued did not differ substantially; only in the formulation and implementation of their policies might they be considered different. Since the July 1958 revolution, Iraq has pursued the following major goals:

to maintain its political independence and territorial integrity;
to develop a sense of national unity among the diverse ethnic, religious, regional, and other groups;
to participate in Arab unity efforts;
to maintain cordial relations with regional powers, especially Turkey;
to accelerate the country's economic and industrial development;
to maintain good relations with at least one superpower;
to assert Iraq's leadership in the eastern Arab world.

Political Policies

Since the political aspect of Iraqi policy has already been covered in the section "Policy Environment," which dealt with the ethnic, religious, and ideological conflicts in the country, there is no need to repeat the substance of that discussion. However, we should like to recapitulate the highlights of our previous analysis.

Although Iraq's domestic political goals have not altered significantly since the revolution of 1958, the present Ba'ath regime's policies, in respect to such issues as oil and the Kurds, have changed perceptibly. This government, though still plagued by the Barzani faction, has granted wider autonomy to the Kurds than any previous Iraqi government has. For the first time a Kurd has been appointed vice-president of the republic, a ceremonial office that is considered "prestigious" by the Iraqi masses.

In addition, the Iraqi regime has followed a policy of reconciliation with the Communists, who, only a few years ago, were thought to be the worst enemies of the Ba'ath party. This policy has been encouraged by the Soviet Union, which seems to have found in Iraq a countervailing force against Egypt and a willing ally in the strategic Persian Gulf.

As a result of a settlement with the Kurds and a reconciliation with the Communists and other amenable forces in the country, the Iraqi government has succeeded in forming a long-sought united front that purports to project a spirit of national unity among the diverse ethnic and ideological groups.

On the regional level, Iraqi policies have not been very successful in extending the country's political influence. With the exception of a rapprochement between Baghdad and Cairo, and the continued cordial relations with Turkey, Iraq has been unable to break out of the isolation that the country's policies have created. These policies have failed because they seem to be in direct conflict with general political trends in the area. For example, most Arabs, following an Egyptian decision to seek a peaceful settlement of the Arab-Israeli dispute, are supporting the current U.S. efforts toward this goal. Iraq, on the contrary, has rejected this approach and is now practically the only state in the region that supports the "rejection front," formed by a coalition of the Palestinian commando groups. Since Iraq has usually found itself competing with Egypt for political influence, it is natural that it should go against the tide; this is perhaps the only way for Baghdad to assert itself as a leader of the Arab world.

At the systemic level, Iraqi policies have achieved a number of significant objectives. Perhaps the most important is the nationalization of the IPC and a number of other oil companies. This was done with the cooperation of the Soviet Union, France, Turkey, Japan, India, and several other European, Asian, and African states. The cooperation was manifested in the form of technical and financial aid from the Soviet Union and its East European allies;

technical and financial support from France; and political support from a number of states that showed willingness to purchase oil from the nationalized, but still disputed, fields. Other significant achievements at this level concerned military hardware and military training programs. Although the Soviet Union has supplied a substantial amount of sophisticated weapons to Iraq, it is by no means the sole source of Iraqi armaments. Since 1968, Iraq has been diversifying its sources of weapons and has purchased small quantities of armored cars, helicopters, small arms, and ammunition from France.[121]

During this period no significant changes occurred in Iraqi-U.S. relations; diplomatic ties, which were broken at the beginning of hostilities between the Arabs and the Israelis in June 1967, remain severed at the time of this writing (October 1976). After the diplomatic ties were severed, Iraq maintained a team of diplomats in the Indian embassy in Washington. The United States, however, chose not to exercise this option until July 1972, when two American diplomats were sent to Baghdad to look after U.S. interests in Iraq.[122]

Despite the strained diplomatic relations between Washington and Baghdad, Iraq recently expanded its business contacts with several U.S. corporations that are building port facilities and irrigation projects in the country.[123]

Military Policies

First as an ally of Britain and later as a member of the Baghdad Pact, Iraq received sufficient amounts of military hardware from Western sources; and all Iraqi military personnel were trained by either British or American instructors. The July 1958 revolution, however, changed this relationship radically. Because of its departure from the Baghdad Pact, Iraq could no longer qualify to receive arms from its traditional sources. This Western reluctance to continue supplying arms to Iraq forced the Qassem regime to enter into an arms agreement with the Soviet Union. The first consignment of Soviet weapons arrived on November 27, 1958. The Soviet-Iraqi agreement provided for provision of matériel and training of Iraqi personnel by Soviet instructors. The first Soviet shipment included MIG-17s, YAK-11s, and IL-28s, motorboats, and light and heavy tanks. Two Soviet advisory teams were stationed in Baghdad and 40 Iraqi military cadets were sent for training in the Soviet Union.[124]

In 1960 Soviet-Iraqi relations were strained because of Qassem's rift with the Iraqi Communists, who tried to expand their activities against the wishes of the regime. Although this rift did not cause the termination of Soviet military supplies, it did lead Qassem to buy new weapons from Britain. Realizing that a complete cutoff of weapons would almost certainly force Iraq to reestablish military relations with the West, the Soviet Union continued to supply the Qassem regime, which was engaged not only in anti-Communist activities but also in fighting the Kurds, who traditionally had been supported by Moscow. (For details, see the section on the Kurds above.)

After the overthrow of the Qassem regime, the new junta under Bakr and Aref became militantly anti-Communist and began to change its military orientation from the Soviet Union to the West. Two months after it came to power in February 1963, the new Iraqi regime signed a military agreement with Britain, under which London agreed to sell a number of Saracen armored personnel carriers and a quantity of medium artillery ammunition. The Soviet Union suspended its aid program and withdrew Soviet technicians from Iraq. Iraq withdrew the 69 air force cadets who were being trained in the Soviet Union, and sent most of them to Britain.

The dismissal of the Ba'athists from the Iraqi government in November 1963 improved Iraqi-Soviet relations and caused Moscow to resume arms supplies to Iraq. Baghdad also continued to purchase planes, tanks, and other matériel from Britain, which in 1964 shipped a number of Hunters and Jet Provosts to Iraq. In the same year, Iraq and the Soviet Union entered into a new military aid agreement that provided for the supply of jet fighters and trainers, heavy and light tanks, automatic weapons, ammunition, spare parts, and five arms and ammunition factories. Supplies of Soviet equipment were temporarily halted in early 1967 because an Iraqi pilot had defected to Israel in a MIG-21.[125]

After the June War, in which it lost more than 20 aircraft on the ground, Iraq expressed interest in acquiring the French Mirage. In 1968, the French government, which was anxious to acquire oil exploitation rights in the North Rumeila fields, expressed willingness to sell 54 Mirages to the Aref regime. This agreement, however, was not consummated because, after the overthrow of the Aref regime in July 1968, the new Iraqi government decided not to allow foreign participation in the exploitation of the Rumeila fields. Nevertheless, Iraq did buy a number of French armored cars and Alouette helicopters.

Although the new government was dominated by the Ba'athists, its relations with the Soviet Union began on the basis of cordiality and understanding. Consequently, Baghdad's military programs again benefited from expanded Soviet military aid for the Iraqi armed forces. In May 1969, the Iraqi and Soviet governments signed a new military aid agreement under which 15 MIGs and 20 SU-7s were immediately delivered to Iraq. In addition, 10 more SU-7 all-weather fighter-bombers and 150 T-54/55 tanks were received from the Soviet Union during the next year. During 1971–72, Iraq received more than 200 more T-54/55 heavy tanks, one TU-16 medium bomber, 2 IL-28 light bombers, and 25 MID-21 interceptors. In addition, the Iraqi armed forces increased their personnel by 10,000, bringing the total to a new high of 105,000.

Soviet-Iraqi military cooperation was further increased after the two countries signed a 15-year treaty of friendship and cooperation on April 9, 1972. Since then, the Iraqi government has received large quantities of Soviet weapons, including an undisclosed number of T-62 tanks with 115-mm. guns and night-vision equipment; 10 MIG-21s; and the Frog surface-to-surface missile.[126]

An analysis of the Iraqi defense budgets between 1963 and 1973 shows that Baghdad has steadily increased its budget. However, with the exception of three significant jumps in 1968, 1971, and 1973, Iraq has not increased its defense budget as rapidly as Iran has. The primary reasons for these exceptional increases were the June War of 1967 and the rapid expansion of the Iranian military forces, which are acquiring large quantities of weapons from a variety of Western sources.

In terms of the total defense expenditure during these three years, Iraq increased its 1968 defense budget from $235.2 million* to $310.8 million, a jump of $75.6 million. Out of the total defense budget for 1968, $133.0 million was spent on importing new weapons. Since the import figures are high in proportion to the total defense budget, we assume that they include expenditure from the development (capital) budget, which usually is not reflected in the ordinary budget. In 1971, there was another increase of $88.2 million in the defense budget, from $403.25 million (in 1970) to $491.43 million. This time, however, only $35.0 million was spent on weapons acquisition. Perhaps the main reason for this decrease in weapons imports was Iraq's stagnant economy, caused by the reduction of oil production by the IPC.

The third large increase occurred in 1973, when Iraq allocated $558.1 million ($83.8 million more than the previous year) for defense. During the same year, Baghdad imported weapons systems worth $306 million, the highest amount ever spent by Iraq on arms. This increase is reflected in the figures given for Iraq in *The Military Balance 1974–1975*. It should be noted that Iraq had committed this large amount for weapons before the sudden increase in oil prices in early 1974.

This analysis further indicates that between 1963 and 1973, Iraq spent a total of $874 million on importing weapons from a variety of sources. Of this amount, $742 million went to the Soviet Union, $77 million to Czechoslovakia, $18 million to the United States, $15 million to the United Kingdom, $7 million to France, $5 million to West Germany, $3 million to Poland, and $7 million to all other countries.[127]

Economic Objectives and Policies

As indicated earlier, Iraq's development plans have depended almost exclusively on oil revenues, which, since the end of World War II, expanded gradually until 1972, when, after the nationalization of IPC, the country's oil

---

*The conversions are in 1975 dollars.

income nearly doubled. Iraq's oil revenue has jumped from $600 million in 1972 to an estimated total of $7.6 billion.[128] Cognizant of the finiteness of this natural asset, the Iraqi government has been endeavoring to invest the oil income in enterprises that will yield continuing profits beyond the end of the oil era. This has been the explicit policy of all Iraqi governments since the 1940s.[129]

Since 1951, successive Iraqi governments have formulated a series of economic development plans, none of which has accomplished the goals established for it. Albert Badre points out that on the average, none of the Iraqi five-year development plans survived more than two years. The reason for this low average was not financial, but political and technical. Political instability and lack of trained manpower have been the primary causes of the past failures.

Not to be deterred by these failures, the new Ba'ath government launched yet another five-year plan (1970/71 to fiscal 1974/75) that would cost 973 million dinars by the end of the plan. Of this sum, 690 million dinars would be invested by the public sector and 283 million dinars by the private sector. The breakdown of total outlays by the public sector shows that agriculture would receive 41 percent; industry, 35 percent; transportation and communication, 12 percent; and construction and housing, 12 percent. Recognizing the importance of agriculture and industry to the country, the new plan allocated 16 percent more money to agriculture (it had received 25 percent in the 1965–70 plan, the total cost of which was 820 million dinars) and 7 percent more to industry. Housing and construction, as well as transportation and communication, were downgraded in the 1970–75 plan; the housing and construction sector, which in the previous plan had been allocated 20 percent, received only 12 percent in the new plan; similarly, the transportation and communications sector received 4 percent less money than in the previous plan. This clearly shows the direction in which the new government wished to move the country economically and socially.

Despite housing shortages and an inadequate transportation and communication systems, the new regime preferred to invest more in agriculture and industry. Of course, the agricultural sector is extremely important to Iraq, not just because it produces food but also because a very large proportion of Iraq's population depends directly on the land for its livelihood. Most of the investment allocations for agriculture were for irrigation, drainage, land reclamation, storage, and fertilizers. Most of the outlays for industry were directed, at least in the initial stages of the plan, to completion of projects already begun and to upgrading the efficiency of industrial management.[130]

In April 1976, the Iraqi government announced the country's annual budget, which, at 5.45 billion dinars was five times as large as the 1973 budget. Besides being impressive in its magnitude, the new budget announced several new plans that would be of immediate benefit to the Iraqi people.[131]

Both the annual budget and the 1974–79 development plan reflect the government's heavy emphasis on industry. Although agriculture continues to receive a significant portion of the allocations, industrial development clearly has become the number-one priority of the Baghdad regime. In the 1973–74 budget year, the industrial sector had received only 45 million dinars.[132] In the 1976 budget, agriculture received 268 million dinars, 90 million dinars more that it was allocated in the 1974–79 plan. Other key sectors of the economy also were provided with larger sums than they had received in any previous plan or annual budget. In 1976 alone, Iraq intended to spend 242.5 million dinars on transportation (35 million dinars in 1973) and 213.2 million dinars on construction and services (35 million dinars in 1973).

Realizing that the previous plans had failed primarily because of a short-age of trained personnel (as well as political instability), the Iraqi government has passed a law designed to attract expatriate Iraqis. This law, issued in November 1974, offers attractive terms to both Iraqis and Arab nationals who may wish to work in Iraq. Among the incentives being presented to educated, skilled, and trained prospective employees are paid travel for them and their families, the right to bring duty-free cars with them; a loan equal to six months' salary, to be repaid in five years; the option to buy land at a reduced rate and another option on a 4,000 dinar loan for that purpose; and exemption from military service. In pursuit of this policy, the Iraqi government has sent abroad several high-level delegates to encourage qualified Iraqis and Arab nationals to return to Iraq and to participate in its development. In addition, to stem the Iraqi "brain drain," the RCC passed a law that guarantees a job to any and all high school and university graduates who wish to work for the govern-ment.[133]

Although the Soviet Union continues to be a major trade partner of Iraq, the Baghdad government has been endeavoring to diversify its commercial and trade ties. Since about 1974, and more specifically since the signing of the Algiers agreement in March 1975, the Iraqi government has taken several steps to broaden its commercial and technical relations with the Western states and Japan. France is fast becoming a major supplier of nuclear technology to Iraq, from which Paris has secured oil supplies for several years. Similarly, Japan has agreed to transfer oil and other technology to the Iraqis in return for an assured supply of oil. This means that, for economic development and supply and weapons, Iraq is not as dependent on one source—the Soviet Union—as Egypt was between June 1967 and 1973.

NOTES

1. Although under the Hashemites, Shiites occasionally achieved Cabinet rank, only one prime minister, Fadhil Jamali, belonged to this community. A similar pattern is evident in the cabinets and revolutionary councils since 1958. While it is difficult to identify the religious

affiliation of today's ruling elite in Iraq, it is certain that no more than two or three members of the 13-member Ba'ath Regional Command are Shiites, and that none of the present 6-member Revolutionary Command Council, the highest ruling authority in the country, is a Shiite. In the Cabinet appointed after the Aref-Bakr coup of 1963, there were five Shiites and three Kurdish ministers. Majid Khadduri, *Republican Iraq: A Study in Iraqi Politics Since 1958* (London: Oxford University Press, 1969), p. 198.

2. David Adamson, *The Kurdish War* (London: George Allen and Unwin, 1964); Hasan Arfa, *The Kurds: An Historical and Political Study* (London: Oxford University Press, 1966); Cecil J. Edmonds, *Kurds, Turks and Arabs: Politics, Travel and Research in North-Eastern Iraq* (London: Oxford University Press, 1957); Dana Adams Schmidt, *Journey Among Brave Men* (Boston: Little, Brown, 1964).

3. The Iraqi Kurds are subdivided into three groups: the Badinan, the Suran, and the Baban. The Surans and the Babans speak the Kurdi dialect; the Badinans speak Kemanji. Each of these groups is further divided into tribes and clans. Harvey H. Smith et al., *Area Handbook for Iraq* (Washington, D.C.: U.S. Government Printing Office, 1971), pp. 61–62.

4. For an excellent analysis of the social, regional, and educational background of Iraqi leadership, see Phebe Marr, "Iraq's Leadership Dilemma: A Study in Leadership Trends, 1948–1968," *Middle East Journal* 24, no. 3 (Summer 1970): 283–301; and "The Political Elite in Iraq," in George Lenczowski, ed., *Political Elites in the Middle East* (Washington, D.C.: American Enterprise Institute, 1975), pp. 109–49.

5. Smith et al., *Area Handbook for Iraq*, pp. 115–30.

6. For an excellent analysis of Iraqi domestic politics, see Khadduri, *Republican Iraq*; and for an equally penetrating analysis of intra-Arab rivalries, see Malcolm Kerr, *The Arab Cold War, 1958–1967: A Study of Ideology in Politics*, 3rd ed. (London: Oxford University Press, 1972).

7. Although Europa, *The Middle East and North Africa 1974–1975* (London: Europa Publications, 1974), p. 382, states that there are 12 members of the RCC, to the best of our knowledge this is not the case. Europa provides only eight names; one, Murtada al-Hadithi, was dropped in June 1974; and Col. Shafiq Hammadi al-Daraji is listed as secretary- general. The latter probably holds an administrative job, because his name does not appear in any other source. Furthermore, he is not a member of the Regional Command, which provides all members of the RCC, with the sole exception of General Saadoun Ghaydan Takriti; the other six names are those given by us. (Also see the organizational chart.)

8. *An-Nahar Arab Report* 5, no. 46 (November 18, 1974): 4. For a different view, see Ghazi al-Ayyash's comments in *Al-Anwar* (Beirut), November 13, 1974, as reported in FBIS, November 15, 1974, p. E-1.

9. Art. 10, 11, and 12, as reported in FBIS, March 12, 1974, pp. C-14 to C-15.

10. Ibid., pp. C-16 to C-17, art. 16, 18, and 19.

11. The KDP is not recognized as the sole representative of the Kurdish people in Iraq, despite its claim to the contrary. A large number of Communists are Kurds who express their political views through the Iraqi Communist party (ICP), which, along with the Ba'ath and independents, is a partner in the government-sponsored National Progressive Front. Despite the government's efforts, the KDP refused to join the Front until the March 1970 agreements were implemented. Mukarram al-Talabani, a member of the Central Committee of the ICP and one of two ministers representing the Communist party in the Iraqi Cabinet, is a Kurd (*The Arab World*, November 20, 1973, p. 12). Talabani (irrigation) and Amir Abdullah (minister of state without portfolio) were added to the Cabinet after Soviet Prime Minister Aleksei Kosygin's first visit to Iraq in April 1972, when a 15-year treaty of friendship and cooperation was signed between Moscow and Baghdad (*An-Nahar Arab Report* 4, no. 21 [May 21, 1973]: 2). After the autonomy plan of 1974, the KDP split into pro-Barzani and anti-Barzani groups; the latter, which called itself the Kurdistan Revolution Party (KRP), accepted the terms of the autonomy.

12. Khadduri, *Republican Iraq,* p. 115. After the July 1958 coup, Fuad al-Rikabi was appointed minister of development by the Ba'ath National Command (all-Arab); Rikabi's participation in the Qassem government was considered to be "strictly personal." Although at the time Rikabi was secretary-general of the Regional Command, there were serious differences of opinion between him and the National Command. One of them revolved around the conflict between the Ba'athists and the nationalist officers. Rikabi believed that the Ba'ath should not discriminate against the nationalist officers, because fundamentally there were hardly any political differences between them and the Ba'athists. He pointed out that as nationalist officers, their credentials were far superior to those of the Communists, with whom the Ba'ath had previously cooperated. Furthermore, Rikabi believed that regardless of differences between Nasser and the party on the issue of liberty, for example, the Ba'ath should not insist on a separate existence if unity served the cause of Arab union. In addition, Rikabi differed from the majority of his party on the use of violence in resolving political differences. It is alleged that he participated, without permission from, or knowledge of, the Regional Command and National Command, in the assassination attempt on Qassem in September 1959. Because of these differences, Rikabi was expelled from the party in August 1961. (Kamel S. Abu Jaber, *The Arab Ba'th Socialist Party* [Syracuse: Syracuse University Press, 1966], pp. 54–55). On May 20, 1969, the Ba'athist regime ordered the arrest of Rikabi and confiscation of his property; scores of other Iraqi citizens, former ministers, bureaucrats, and businessmen also were affected. He was sentenced to three years' imprisonment; and while serving the last two weeks of his incarceration he was stabbed to death by an "unknown" assailant. (FBIS, December 16, 1971, p. C-2; Eliezer Beeri, *Army Officers in Arab Politics and Society* [New York: Praeger, 1970], p. 177).

13. Beeri, *Army Officers,* p. 188; Phebe Marr, "How Ba'athists Keep Lid on Turbulence in Iraq," *Christian Science Monitor,* June 8, 1971, p. 5, states that Saddam Hussein Takriti participated in the attempted assassination of Qassem; also see *An-Nahar Arab Report* 5, no. 44 (November 4, 1974), and Lorenzo Kent Kimball, *The Changing Pattern of Political Power in Iraq, 1958 to 1971* (New York: Robert Speller, 1972), p. 98.

14. Beeri, *Army Officers,* pp. 198–200; Khadduri, *Republican Iraq,* pp. 202, 209–10.

15. While the al-Saadi group was being weakened by a coalition of the moderate and rightist groups of the Ba'ath in Iraq, the Sixth National (all-Arab) Congress of the Ba'ath met in Damascus from September 5 to September 23 and approved the resolutions and plans introduced by the extreme wing of the party. Beeri, *Army Officers,* p. 199.

16. The provisional constitution provided that the RCC, the highest authority in the state, consisted of not more than 12 persons chosen from the members of the Iraqi leadership of the Ba'ath party—from the Regional Command (*Who's Who in the Arab World 1974–1975* [Beirut: Publitec Publications, n.d.], p. 433). In July 1973, an amendment to the constitution gave more powers to Ahmad Hassan Bakr but did not materially change the central role of the RCC and the Ba'ath monopoly over the council. It was not until November 21, 1971 that the RCC officially banned all political activity and organizations, except the Ba'ath party, within the Iraqi armed forces. (FBIS, November 22, 1971, p. C-1.)

17. Abdul al-Rahman, brother of Abdul Salam Aref. After Abdul Salam's death in a helicopter crash in April 1966, his older brother, Abdul al-Rahman, became president of the republic.

18. The Nasserite coconspirator, Abdul Razak Nayef, headed the government as premier and his colleague, Col. Ibrahim Daoud, headed the ministry of defense. Daoud also was appointed deputy commander in chief of the armed forces. In addition to Saleh Mehdi Ammash, there were seven Ba'athists in the Cabinet: Dr. Ahmad Abd as-Sattar al-Juwari, who since 1968 has been minister of education; Anwar Abd al-Qadir al-Hadithi, who still holds the portfolio of labor and social affairs; and Dr. Izzat Mustafa, who, in addition to being minister of health since 1968, has become a member of the RCC and the Regional Command Council. Other Ba'athist ministers

were Khalid Makki al-Hashimi, industry; Dr. Ghaile Mawlud Mukhlis, municipal and village affairs; Diyab al-Alqawi, youth care; and Kazim Mualla, minister of state without portfolio. FBIS, July 19, 1968, p. C-1; *Who's Who in the Arab World 1971–1972* (Beirut: Publitec Publications, n.d.), pp. 384–85; Europa, *The Middle East and North Africa 1968–69* through *1974–1975,* FBIS, July 22, 1968, pp. C-2 to C-7.

19. FBIS, July 19, 1968 (quoting *Al-Hayah,*), p. C-8. Lt. Col. Saadoun Ghaydan Takriti was promoted to brigadier and was appointed commander of the Republican Guard, replacing Lt. Col. Ibrahim Daoud, who was promoted to lieutenant general and appointed deputy commander in chief of the armed forces. It should be noted that because of the Republican Guard's location in Baghdad and its role in the protection of the Presidential Palace, the position of commander of the Republican Guard is considered more important than deputy commander in chief. This shows that from the beginning the Ba'athists were systematically seizing power and eliminating the non-Ba'athists from the government.

20. FBIS, July 24, 1968, p. C-1; and July 22, 1968, p. C-5. *Keesing's Contemporary Archives* 16 (August 17–24, 1968): 22869, states that the RCC was composed of seven members, the additional member being Col. Saadoun Ghaydan Takriti. In view of the official broadcast and of proclamation no. 23 (both dated July 23, 1968), *Keesing's* statement seems inaccurate. Saadoun Ghaydan, commander of the Baghdad garrison, was added after Nayef and Daoud were expelled. This addition kept total membership at five until November 1969, when the RCC membership was tripled.

21. FBIS, July 22, 1968, pp. C-2 to C-7. For names of these ministers, see note 18.

22. While no further mention of this parity's continuous existence has come to our attention, it is assumed that the Ba'ath Regional Command did not change it between 1963 and 1968. This assumption is based on the premise that since the Ba'ath needed the military to seize power, it would have avoided conflict on this issue.

23. *An-Nahar Arab Report* 1, no. 20 (July 20, 1970): 1–2.

24. This expansion, announced on November 10, 1969, was preceded by a meeting of the Regional Command Council in Baghdad. See *Keesing's* 17 (February 14–21, 1970): 23823. In our study of the Iraqi Ba'ath, we have been puzzled by the fact that no effort seems to have been made to keep this strength constant. Between 1969 and 1974, eight members of the RCC were fired and one was killed. None of these vacancies was filled. The membership strength of the council progressively decreased, and at the end of 1975 it stood at six.

25. *Keesing's* 17 (February 14–21, 1970): 23828. This source gives Captain al-Jazrawi's name as Taher. Based on our information from a variety of other sources, we have given his name as Taha Yasin. See Europa, *The Middle East and North Africa 1970–71,* p. 319.

26. Khadduri, *Republican Iraq,* pp. 207–08. Khadduri maintains that the "lack of a deeper understanding of basic principles (of socialism), especially their relevance to Iraq, was one of the important causes of disagreement" among the Ba'athist leadership.

27. The Ba'athist regime carried out mass arrests of its opponents and alleged spies in the later months of 1968 and in 1969. The first wave of arrests occurred in October 1968, when more than 80 officers were arrested following an attempted military coup led by Gen. Abdul Hadi al-Rawi. In mid-1969, further announcements of alleged plots and espionage caused the arrests of hundreds more officers, former ministers, and other political opponents. During that year 98 persons were executed for conspiracy or espionage. *Keesing's* 17 (February 14–21, 1970): 23827–30.

28. The RCC reportedly made the dismissal decision sometime in early October, but it was not announced until October 15, 1970.

29. Even though he had been a "suspect," Hardan Takriti was reinstated in the party because his support was considered essential for a successful coup against the Aref (Abdul Rahman) regime in July 1968. Between November 1963 and March 1964, Takriti held the posts

of minister of defense and deputy commander in chief of the armed forces. After his dismissal from the government, he underwent "confession and self-criticism," which restored him to the Ba'ath hierarchy. *An-Nahar Arab Report* 1, no. 33 (October 19, 1970): 2

30. *Keesing's* 17 (November 14–21, 1970): 24292.

31. *An-Nahar Arab Report* 1, nos. 33, 34 (October 19 and 26, 1970): 1–2 and 2, respectively. While in Kuwait in March 1971, Hardan Takriti was assassinated by two "unknown" gunmen. Unsubstantiated stories suggested three possible causes of his murder: that he was involved in a countercoup against Saddam Hussein, who had him murdered; that he was assassinated by members of a Palestinian guerrilla group for his role in the Jordanian civil war; that his murder was carried out by the followers of an exiled Iranian general, Teymour Bakhtiyar, in whose assassination Hardan Takriti allegedly was involved. Ibid. 2, nos. 15 and 41 (April 12 and October 11, 1971): 3 and 1–2, respectively. Also see Phebe Marr, "How Ba'athists Keep Lid on Turbulence in Iraq," *Christian Science Monitor,* June 8, 1971, p. 5.

32. *An-Nahar Arab Report* 1, no. 34 (October 26, 1970): 2–3.

33. Saddam Hussein was reported to have made the following charges against his distant cousin Hardan Takriti: that the general was responsible for the execution of 26 young officers recalled from Jordan, where they had been stationed with the Iraqi force (no reasons for the executions were given); that Hardan Takriti had contacted the Nasserite officers, with a view to using them against the Ba'athist regime (one source suggested that Hardan Takriti was expelled from the RCC and the Cabinet because of his anti-Egyptian attitude! Smith et al., *Area Handbook for Iraq,* p. XVI); and that the general had received commissions from oil companies operating in the country. *An-Nahar Arab Report* 1, no. 34 (October 26, 1970): 2–3.

34. Ibid. 2, no. 5 (February 1, 1971): 1, reports that Bakr had written a will in which he appointed Saddam Hussein his successor in case of his (Bakr's) death.

35. Aziz Sharif was appointed minister of justice, a post he held for less than two years; thereafter he was named a minister of state; at the end of July 1974, he was still in this position. *Keesing's* 17 (February 14–21, 1970): 23828; and Europa, *The Middle East 1970–71* through *1974–75.*

36. The announcement of their dismissal was broadcast by Baghdad Radio on September 28, 1971. See Washington *Post,* September 29, 1971, p. A-16, and *Christian Science Monitor,* October 2, 1971, p. 14. Ammash was assigned to the Ministry of Foreign Affairs and Shaikhaly was sent to New York as Iraq's ambassador to the United Nations. FBIS, September 29, 1971, p. C-1. MENA reported that the dismissal of Ammash and Shaikhaly was preceded by a sharp critical attack by Saddam Hussein on their attitude toward the Kurdish issue. FBIS, October 13, 1974, p. C-1.

37. *An-Nahar Arab Report* 1, no. 24 (August 17, 1970): 2–3; John K. Cooley, "Leadership Shuffle in Iraq Signals New Internal Ferment," *Christian Science Monitor,* October 2, 1971, p. 14; on Ammash being an anti-Communist, see *An-Nahar Arab Report* 4, no. 28 (July 9, 1973): 2–3.

38. *The Arab World,* January 14, 1974, p. 5.

39. Murtada al-Hadithi was relieved of his duties on June 23, 1974. The same day, he was appointed ambassador to the Soviet Union. He was succeeded as foreign minister by Shazel Jasem Taqa. Taqa is not a member of the RCC (*An-Nahar Arab Report* 5, no. 26 [July 1, 1974]: n.p.). Commenting on Hadithi's dismissal from the RCC, *An-Nahar Arab Report* 5, no. 27 (July 8, 1974): 3–4, said that the removal of the foreign minister indicated that Iraq was perhaps seeking openings in certain completely new directions: Reconciliation with the Arab world and an opening on the international plane might be behind the replacement of the foreign minister by a career diplomat, even though internal intrigue had certainly played a part in the foreign minister's fall.

40. Ibid. 4, no. 30 (July 23, 1973): 2–3. Both Nazem Kazzar and Mohammed Fadel were executed; Abdel Khalek al-Samarrai's death sentence was commuted at the request of Michel Aflaq.

41. "The Iraqi Ba'ath Party—I," ibid. 5, no. 44 (November 4, 1974). A year before the coup, *An-Nahar Arab Report* noted the existence of a close relationship between Saddam Hussein Takriti and Mohammed Fadel, who at the time was a member of the Public Relations Office in the Regional Command Council of the Ba'ath party. It further pointed out that Saddam Hussein, with the help of the National Security Agency, which he headed, had succeeded in liquidating all opposition in the Ba'ath and the army. However, the attempted coup of July 1973; the large-scale transfers and appointments within the army in August; the civil disturbances in Baghdad in October, which led the government to impose a curfew in the capital; and a mutiny in September 1974 in which the air force commander, Brig. Husain Hayawi Takriti, and commanders of the 8th Division and the Republican Guard participated, show that opposition to the regime has by no means ended. Ibid. 3, no. 28 (July 10, 1972); ibid. 4, no. 41 (October 8, 1974); and FBIS, (October 10, 1974), p. E-1.

42. *An-Nahar Arab Report* 4, no. 30 (July 23, 1973): 2–3. For an official account of the Kazzar attempt, see FBIS, July 2, 1973, pp. C-1, C-4; and July 9, 1973, pp. C-1, C-3.

43. *Christian Science Monitor,* December 12, 1974, p. 4.

44. *An-Nahar Arab Report* 5, no. 40 (October 7, 1974): 3.

45. An official spokesman of the Iraqi regime claimed that the coup attempt was directed against President Bakr and Saddam Hussein. FBIS, July 9, 1973, p. C-1

46. "The Iraqi Ba'ath Party—II," *An-Nahar Arab Report* 5, no. 45 (November 11, 1974): n.p.; under this amendment, Bakr assumed the post of defense minister that had previously been held by Hammad Shehab Takriti, a relative of Bakr, who was killed during this abortive coup attempt. FBIS, July 27, 1973, p. C-1; and *Christian Science Monitor,* July 16, 1973, p. 3.

47. *An-Nahar Arab Report* 5, no. 46 (November 18, 1974): 3. This report excluded Tariq Aziz from the list of civilian "hardliners," instead naming Abu Jabbar as one of the trio.

48. Ibid. Earlier in February 1974, the Syrain Ba'ath party had attacked the Iraqi Ba'ath for its failure to fulfill its pan-Arab commitments, which called for mutual help and consultations. Because of this failure, the Iraqi Ba'ath could not be "allowed to return to the Arab revolutionary fold . . . ," commented the Syrian party's organ *Al-Ba'ath* in its issue of February 24. Coincidentally, on the same day the *Al-Ba'ath* article appeared, the Iraqi Ba'ath's main organ, *Al-Thawra,* reported the RCC decision to grant $50 million to Syria for the reconstruction of economically important installations destroyed during the October War. *The Arab World,* February 27 and 28, 1974, pp. 6 and 8, respectively.

49. *An-Nahar Arab Report* 5, no. 40 (October 7, 1974): 3; and no. 46 (November 18, 1974): 3.

50. In early October 1974, the Iraqi regime agreed to support the formation of an anti-PLO front that would work against the establishment of a Palestinian state on the West Bank and against similar proposed solutions to the Arab-Israel conflict. The Baghdad government supported the following groups: the Popular Front for the Liberation of Palestine (PFLP), the Popular Front for the Liberation of Palestine-General Command (PFLP-GC), the Arab Liberation Front (ALF), and the Popular Struggle Front (PSF).

51. We must confess that our assumption is based on extremely tenuous grounds. During part of this period, Sheikh Mujibur Rahman, prime minister of Bangladesh, was paying an official visit to Iraq; and it is possible that Saddam Hussein's schedule did not allow him to meet with the Palestinians. FBIS, October 8, 1974, pp. E-5 to E-6.

52. *The Arab World,* April 17, 1974, p. 11.

53. In view of Bakr's role in the suppression of the Kurdish revolt in 1963, a significant number of Kurds probably would disagree with our classification of Bakr as a moderate. Despite their understandable objection, most observers of the Iraqi scene today consider Bakr as a moderate and pragmatic leader.

54. This does not mean that no other interest groups are politically active. Groups such as the Nasserites and the Qaddafites are difficult to identity, although occasional references are made to them in the Arab press.

55. Schmidt, *Journey Among Brave Men,* p. 53.

56. See Edmonds, *Kurds, Turks and Arabs.*

57. For an account of Soviet involvement with the Iranian Kurds and the Azerbaijanis, see George Lenczowski, *Russia and the West in Iran, 1918–1948* (Ithaca, N.Y.: Cornell University Press, 1949); and Sepehr Zabih, *The Communist Movement in Iran* (Berkeley: University of California Press, 1966).

58. For a comprehensive treatment of the short-lived Republic of Mahabad, see William Eagleton, Jr., *The Kurdish Republic of 1946* (London: Oxford University Press, 1963).

59. Ibid., p. 76.

60. Eagleton observes that at that time "very few Azerbaijanis and virtually no Kurds realized that the Soviet Union, in exchange for the Prospect of an oil concession, had decided their fate in a sense contrary to the private assurances of the preceding year." Ibid., p. 73.

61. Ibid., p. 128; Beeri, *Army Officers,* p. 189.

62. Arfa, *The Kurds,* pp. 73, 106, 120–26, 129–30.

63. Col. Abd al-Wahhab Shawaf, commander of the 5th Brigade of the 2nd Division, was stationed at Mosul in the spring of 1959. A son of the grand mufti of Baghdad, he was an advocate of Arab unity. There seems to be some disagreement among scholars as to the role the Shammar tribe played in the Shawaf revolt. Arfa contends that the Kurds prevented their arrival from the outskirts of the Syrian desert (p. 132); Beeri, *Army Officers* (pp. 183–84), says that the Shammar tribe participated in what their leader reportedly called a war against "the Kurds and infidels." To us, the significance of this event is that it clearly reflects the Kurdish-Arab antagonism to which we referred earlier.

64. Text of the provisional constitution in Muhammad Khahil, *The Arab States and the Arab League,* I (Khayyats, 1962), pp. 30–32.

65. Beeri, *Army Officers,* p. 190.

66. Arfa, *The Kurds,* p. 134.

67. For a summary of their demands see Khadduri, *Republican Iraq,* pp. 270–71.

68. Ibid., p. 272.

69. After the overthrow of Qassem, the new military junta annulled the provisional constitution and replaced it by an interim constitution. Unlike the provisional constitution, which had declared the Kurds as partners, the interim constitution made no such specific reference. In this respect, it merely stated that "all Iraqis are equal by law" and that "all Iraqis including both Arabs and Kurds shall cooperate to safeguard their homeland." Europa, *Middle East 1965–66,* p. 243.

70. Kimball, *The Changing Pattern,* pp. 141–42.

71. Ibid., p. 143.

72. It should be noted that despite the Iranian support and sympathy for the Iraqi Kurds, the Iranians probably do not want to see an autonomous Kurdish region established in the territory contiguous to the area where Iranian Kurds live. The establishment of such a region would encourage the Iranian Kurds to demand similar rights from Teheran.

73. FBIS, March 12, 1970, pp. C-3 to C-4.

74. Text of the 15-point program as broadcast by Radio Baghdad is in FBIS, March 12, 1970, pp. C-4 to C-6.

75. Expressions of joy and satisfaction were broadcast by Baghdad Radio; FBIS, March 12, 1970, pp. C-4 to C-6.

76. *Daily Star* (Beirut), March 13, 1970, as quoted in FBIS, March 18, 1970, p. C-1; *Christian Science Monitor,* October 5, 1971, p. 2.

77. Dana Adams Schmidt, "Iraq-Kurd Accord Is Said to Falter," New York *Times,* August 17, 1970, p. 7.

78. Beeri, *Army Officers,* pp. 190–91.

79. See John K. Cooley, "New Attack Breaches Iraqi-Kurdish Accord," *Christian Science Monitor,* October 5, 1971, p. 2. "Attack" in this context refers to the assassination attempt on

Mullah Mustafa Barzani by nine religious sheikhs who came to visit the Kurdish leader in his stronghold at Nawbirdan. For a detailed account of this event, see David Hirst, "Ba'ath-Kurdish Pact Breached in Iraq," Washington *Post*, December 2, 1971, p. F-1. In this story, Hirst predicted that hostilities between the Kurds and the Iraqi forces would break out in the spring of 1972.

80. Text of President Bakr's speech giving details of the autonomy framework is in FBIS, March 12, 1974, pp. C-11 to C-18; also see *The Arab World,* February 8, 1974, pp. 7–8; Raymond Anderson, "Limited Local Autonomy Granted to Kurds in Iraq." New York *Times,* March 12, 1974, p. 5; Joseph Fitchett, "Kurds Take to Hills, Rejecting Iraqi Plan," Washington *Post*, March 16, 1974, p. A–12; "It's Those Kurds Again," *The Economist,* March 23, 1974, p. 38. Commenting on the Kurdish demand that Kirkuk Province be included in the autonomous region, Saddam Hussein pointed out that this province was populated by a number of ethnic groups, including the Kurds, the Turkomen, and the Arabs, and therefore it would not be right to include it in the region. He said that the RCC had suggested a joint administration for the province but that this proposal was rejected by the Kurds, who demanded either an outright inclusion of the province in the region or, if that was not acceptable to the government, a joint administration for Kirkuk and attachment of it to the self-rule region. Both ideas were rejected by the government. FBIS, March 15, 1974, pp. C-1 to C-4.

81. "Split Reported Within Kurdish Democratic Party: Barzani Accused of Dictatorship," *The Arab World,* February 12, 1974, p. 7; the Akrawis and Obeidullah Barzani defended their defection from the Barzani faction on the ground that Mullah Mustafa had become totally "beholden" to the imperialists—Iran and Israel.

82. In March 1974, *Pravda* reportedly attacked the Kurds for their refusal to accept the autonomy plan. Joseph Fitchett, "Kurds Seize Area Along Iraq Border," Washington *Post,* March 19, 1974, p. 1; "Kurds Seek U.S. Aid for Anti-Soviet Stand," *Christian Science Monitor,* March 20, 1974, p. 2.

83. We have discussed the role of the Communists in Iraq in more detail in another study. See R. D. McLaurin and M. Mughisuddin, *The Soviet Union and the Middle East* (Washington, D.C.: American Institutes for Research, 1974), pp. 275–314.

84. *An-Nahar Arab Report* 1, no. 9 (May 4, 1970): n. p. Aziz Sharif is a member of the Presidium of the World Council of Peace and a recipient of the Lenin Peace Prize. Although he was closely associated with the ICP, he was never a member. His brother, Abdul Rahman, who was a member of the ICP Central Committee, was executed following the Ba'athist coup in 1963.

85. *Middle East Monitor* 5, no. 11 (June 1, 1975): 4.

86. Under a 1913 treaty between the Ottoman Empire and Persia, the latter country recognized Turkish sovereignty over the estuary up to the low-water mark on the Persian shore. *Keesing's* 12 (April 9–16, 1960): 17357.

87. Smith et al., *Area Handbook for Iraq,* p. 213.

88. *Keesing's* 12 (April 9–16, 1960): 17357.

89. *Kayhan International,* December 9, 1968, as in FBIS, December 18, 1968, pp. C-1 to C-2.

90. *Keesing's* 17 (August 30-September 6, 1969): 23544.

91. *Keesing's* 13 (July 8–15, 1961): 18187.

92. The vote was recorded as unanimous because the Iraqi delegation had walked out of the League meeting held in Cairo on July 20, 1961. *Keesing's* 13 (July 15–22, 1961): 18221.

93. On August 12, 1961, the ruler of Kuwait and the secretary-general of the Arab League signed an agreement that bound the League (Iraq alone dissenting) "to preserve Kuwaiti territorial integrity and independence under its present regime; to regard any aggression against the Sheikhdom as aggression against the League's members and, in the event of any such aggression, to render Kuwait immediate assistance and, if necessary, repel it with armed force." *Keesing's* 13 (October 7–14, 1961): 18355.

94. *Keesing's* 13 (December 2–9, 1961): 18462. The Soviet veto was cast as much to express Moscow's support of Iraq as it was to manifest the Kremlin's displeasure with Nasser, with whom Khrushchev was not cordial during this episode. See McLaurin and Mughisuddin, *Soviet Union and the Middle East,* pp. 275–314.

95. *An-Nahar Arab Report* 4, no. 13 (March 26, 1973): 1–2; no. 14 (April 2, 1973): 2–4; and no. 35 (August 27, 1973): 2–3.

96. Riad N. el-Rayyes and Dunia Nahas, eds., *Guerrillas for Palestine* (Beirut: An-Nahar Press Services S. A. R. L., 1974), pp. 55–56.

97. Ibid., p. 105

98. Ibid., p. 106

99. Although ethnically the Eritreans are not Arabs, they have been "adopted" as such by most Arab states. Iraq, Syria, Kuwait, and Saudi Arabia, among others, have expressed their firm support for the Front. See newspaper stories on the issue since the ELF escalated its activities on January 31, 1975.

100. Europa, *Middle East 1974–75,* p. 368.

101. Riggan er-Rumi, "Iraq," in Michael Adams, ed., *The Middle East: A Handbook* (New York: Praeger, 1971), p. 210.

102. *The Arab Economist* 6, no. 60 (January 1974): 39.

103. FBIS, April 20, 1976, p. E-1; Europa, *Middle East 1974–75,* p. 376.

104. Foreign capital can participate only in a joint venture with domestic capital holding at least 60 percent of the total.

105. "Industrial Development and Legislation in Iraq," *The Arab Economist* 6, no. 60 (January 1974): 33.

106. Kimball, *The Changing Pattern,* p. 130.

107. Khadduri, *Republican Iraq,* p. 292.

108. Kimball, *The Changing Pattern,* pp. 134–35. This new law was passed on August 6, 1967.

109. Ibid., p. 137

110. John K. Cooley, "Kosygin Visit Linked to Cloudy Iraqi Scene," *Christian Science Monitor,* April 7, 1972, p. 2.

111. In 1970, the joint production of crude by the IPC, Basrah Petroleum, and Mosul Petroleum was 75,241,000 long tons; in 1971, they produced 82,500,000 long tons; and in 1972, the production dropped to 69,000,880 long tons. In 1973, after nationalization, Iraqi oil production jumped to 92 million tons. This total included 10 million tons from the North Rumeila field (Europa, *Middle East 1974–75,* pp. 371–78). On April 7, 1974, Saadoun Hammadi inaugurated the second stage of the Rumeila oil field. On this occasion, the Iraqi minister for oil said that the production capacity of this field would be increased to 40 million tons annually, during the third stage of the project. He did not say when the third stage would begin or end. FBIS, April 5, 1974, pp. A-1 to A-2.

112. Phebe Marr, "Iraq Puts Oil Politics on Trial," *Christian Science Monitor,* July 10, 1972, p. 14; according to *An-Nahar Arab Report* 5, no. 45 (November 11, 1974), Iraq was given a £53 million loan during the nationalization crisis that lasted until February 1973, when the oil company accepted a negotiated settlement of its claims. Under the settlement, the IPC was given 15 million tons of crude to be loaded at eastern Mediterranean ports, free of all charges. On its part, the IPC conceded the loss of its Kirkuk oil fields, waived its objections to the 1961 seizure of the Rumeila fields, and agreed to pay the Iraqi government £141 million as settlement of all Iraqi claims on the corporation. Europa, *Middle East 1974–75,* p. 373.

113. *An-Nahar Arab Report* 3, no. 2 (January 10, 1972): n. p. Prior to the nationalization of the IPC, Iraq had made arrangements with Yugoslavia, Hungary, and Czechoslovakia to deliver 17 million tons of crude annually. At the time, Yugoslavia had agreed to build a 250-mile pipeline

from the Adriatic coast to Hungary and Czechoslovakia. Iraq announced that it would partially finance the pipeline, which was scheduled to be finished by the end of 1975. The text of the Iraqi-IPC agreement is in ibid. 4, no. 12 (March 19, 1973): n. p.

114. Ibid. no. 43 (October 22, 1973): n.p.

115. Ibid. no. 45 (November 5, 1973): n.p.

116. Ibid. no. 53 (December 31, 1973): n.p. Iraq boycotted the meeting of the Arab oil ministers in Kuwait to consider sanctions against the United States and other friends of Israel. While this conference was being held, Dr. Rashid Rifai, the Iraqi minister of communications and acting minister of defense, reiterated his country's opposition to reducing oil production. Repeating the points made earlier by Hammadi, Rifai urged other Arab oil producers to nationalize U.S. oil assets, to withdraw deposits from American banks, and to sever relations. *The Arab World,* December 28, 1973, p. 10.

117. Ibid., December 18, 1973, p. 5.

118. This statement is based on our perusal of such reliable sources as *An-Nahar Arab Report, The Arab World, Keesing's,* and newspaper and journals emanating from the Middle East.

119. Dana Adams Schmidt, *Armageddon in the Middle East* (New York: John Day, 1974), p. 86.

120. Total arable land in Iraq is more than 14 million acres; in Egypt it is 6 million acres; in Iran, 48 million acres; and in Syria, 17 million acres.

121. Because of France's interest in Iraqi oil and sulfur, Paris lifted the arms embargo on Iraq on December 6, 1967. In April 1968, negotiations for the Iraqi purchase of 54 Mirages were completed; but the agreement was never consummated because the Iraqis decided to exclude all foreign interests from the North Rumeila oil field, in which both France and the Soviet Union had expressed a keen interest. Stockholm International Peace Research Institute (SIPRI), *The Arms Trade with the Third World* (Stockholm: Almqvist and Wiksell, 1971), p. 588.

122. Marilyn Berger, "U.S. Is Sending Diplomats to Iraq, First Since 1967," Washington *Post,* July 28, 1972, p. A-28.

123. *The Arab World,* October 12, 1973, p. 9.

124. SIPRI, *Arms Trade,* pp. 555–56.

125. Ibid., p. 557

126. According to International Institute for Stratetic Studies (IISS), *The Military Balance 1971-1972* (London: IISS, 1971), p. 28, the Iraqi army had 800 T-54/55 tanks in 1970–71; the same source (1974–75) says that by the end of 1974, Iraq's tank strength had increased to 1,300 —this total included T-62, T-54/55, and 90 T-34 medium and PT-76 light tanks. This means that the main increase was in the numbers of heavy tanks: T-62, T-54, and T-55.

127. The statistical information given above was gathered from a number of sources, including IISS, *The Military Balance;* and U.S. Arms Control and Disarmament Agency, *World Military Expenditures and Arms Trade 1963-1973* (Washington, D.C.: U.S. Government Printing Office, 1975).

128. John K. Cooley, "Iraq to Double Oil Income," *Christian Science Monitor,* June 24, 1971, p. 8; *Time,* January 6, 1975, p. 26.

129. Albert Y. Badre, "Economic Development of Iraq," in Charles A. Cooper and Sidney S. Alexander, eds., *Economic Development and Population Growth in the Middle East* (New York: American Elsevier, 1972), p. 284.

130. Smith et al., *Area Handbook for Iraq,* p. xxiv. In 1965, 42 percent of the total labor force in Iraq was employed in the agricultural sector; in 1970, 47 percent was so engaged. In 1965, agriculture contributed 19 percent to the gross domestic product; in 1969, its share was 18 percent. *Middle East Journal* 28, no. 4 (Autumn 1974): 392.

131. FBIS, April 20, 1976, p. E-1.

132. The figures for the 1974–79 plan are from Europa, *Middle East 1974–75,* p. 376; and

the figures for the Iraqi 1974 budget are from *An-Nahar Arab Report* 5, no. 15, (April 15, 1974): n.p. The plan figures are low, perhaps because the plan was prepared before oil price increase came into effect.

133. *An-Nahar Arab Report* 6, no. 7 (February 17, 1975): n.p. This law was passed in early February 1975. It should be noted that Iraq faces a shortage not only of skilled and trained workers but also of unskilled manual labor.

5

ISRAELI FOREIGN POLICY

Fundamental to the analysis of Israeli foreign policy is an understanding of the policy-making process and the impact that key groups within Israel have on the formulation of the nation's foreign policy. As a parliamentary democracy, and possibly the most democratic of the Middle Eastern states, Israel (and its policy makers) have been particularly sensitive to influence from a wide range of interest groups. The Israeli political system provides a series of formal and informal mechanisms through which these groups are able to influence and limit the nation's foreign policy and ultimate approach to questions of security and settlement.

As is the case with other states in the Middle East and elsewhere, foreign policy depends on the interrelated elements of governmental structure, operation of the political system, and impact of key interest groups within that system. These elements serve to define the environment within which the nation's decision makers operate. An understanding of these elements and their evolution is, therefore, crucial to the analysis of Israeli perceptions of vital foreign-policy issue areas, as well as of the objectives and policies ultimately formulated.

ISRAELI POLICY ENVIRONMENT

Structure of the Government

The government that emerged as the state of Israel in 1948 drew on two major sources: the Yishuv—the prestate Jewish community and quasi government that gave Israel its parties, personalities, and many of its institutions—and the British mandate government—which gave Israel much of its governmental structure, common law, bureaucratic organization, and civil administration.

Israel is a parliamentary democracy with lawmaking power vested in its Knesset, or parliament, of 120 seats. Elections must be held at least every four years, with the current government having the option of calling new elections prior to the expiration of the four-year term, much as in the British system. Each party (or group registered as a party) that makes a required deposit of I£ 1,000 becomes eligible to put forward a list of 120 names, with voters selecting a single preferred list. Seats in the Knesset are apportioned to the parties in a ratio to the votes received by each list, with each party taking the names from its list in order to fill the seats allotted. A party receiving 10 percent of the total vote, for example, would be allotted 12 seats, which would go to the first 12 individuals on its list.

The Israeli party system has remained remarkably stable since 1948, with the proportion of votes going to the major parties changing little in the eight Knesset elections that have been held since the inception of the state.[1] To a major extent, Israel's parties reflect the factions that emerged in the prestate Jewish Agency. David Ben-Gurion's Mapai (Labor) party, which took control of the Jewish Agency in 1933 and of the state of Israel in 1948, remains in power, having controlled every coalition in Israel's history. Today the Mapai-dominated Labor Alignment (Ma'arach) continues to control the socialist-Zionist middle ground. To the left of the Ma'arach are Israel's various Communist parties and leftist splinter factions. To the right of the Ma'arach is the Likud (Unity) bloc, composed of the Herut (Freedom) party, formed from the prestate Irgun terrorist organization, and the Liberal party, composed of the old General Zionist and Progressive parties. Somewhat removed from the left-right ideological spectrum are the National Religious Party (NRP) and the various Arab parties that receive minor but consistent support and have been traditional coalition members.

In addition to the Knesset and political parties, there are significant elements of the executive area of the Israeli governmental organization that are essential to foreign policy making.

The President

The president of the state of Israel is elected by the Knesset for a five-year term, and may be reelected once. He serves as the official head of state, but has minor executive powers and limited influence in foreign policy and security affairs.

The Prime Minister

Central to all policy making are the prime minister and the Cabinet, which perform the usual functions of the executive branch of government. The government must obtain the Knesset's vote of confidence before it can function; a subsequent vote of no confidence substantially weakens any government and generally is cause for new elections. The prime minister must be a Knesset member; Cabinet members need not be, although they usually are.

The Defense and Foreign Ministers

Besides the prime minister, the defense and foreign ministers are central to the foreign-policy system. Under David Ben-Gurion, Israel's first prime minister, the Office of the Prime Minister and Defense Ministry were consolidated under one individual. Under the present political arrangement, the portfolios have been split, with both ministers playing central and often competitive roles in the policy-making process. As in other states, the foreign minister plays a significant role in the formulation of policy as well as in its execution and implementation, with the extent of influence being determined by interpersonal relationships rather than by organizational structure.

Operation of the Israeli Political System

Although the structure of the Israeli government is a fundamental part of the environment in which foreign policy is made, it is at best only a rough skeleton of the policy-making process. Of at least equal import in the policy-making environment are the way in which the foreign-policy system has evolved since Israel's establishment; the institutions and processes that constitute this system; and the personalities who have been an integral part of the system since its inception.[2] All of these factors can be considered as forming the operational aspect of the Israeli foreign-policy system.

Since the establishment of Israel as a state in 1948, the events surrounding that nation's birth and the ongoing Arab-Israeli conflict have had a major influence on the way in which the political system has developed, as well as on the policy decisions made. The deep hostility toward Israel on the part of the surrounding Arab population, a distrust of the major powers (based on historical factors), and divisions and tensions within Israeli society have resulted in a foreign-policy system oriented toward self-reliance, and a foreign policy oriented toward force and active deterrence.

Although the Israeli governmental structure, institutions, and, to a major extent, the personalities involved have remained mostly unchanged for more than two decades, the manner in which the foreign policy system operates has undergone a number of significant changes. An understanding of these changes, and the nature of the system as it currently exists is essential to understanding the present set of policy issues and the decisions that come from the system. Quite clearly, the process has been under considerable internal pressure since May 1967, and was at the center of major political crises both in May 1967 and following the October War.[3]

Considering first how Israeli policy is formulated, it can be seen that the decision-making process has undergone a considerable amount of analysis and revision in the course of Israel's history. Although the evolution of this decision process prior to 1973 has been explored at length elsewhere,[4] it is worthwhile to review briefly a number of significant changes to illustrate the problems that have emerged in the contemporary context and Israel's attempts to meet them.

The Role of the Cabinet

From 1948 through the end of 1953, policy making in the defense, security, and foreign policy areas was concentrated in the hands of David Ben-Gurion, who was both prime minister and minister of defense, with limited authority delegated to Foreign Minister Moshe Sharett. During this period, the Cabinet generally acquiesced to Ben-Gurion, and few lines of influence existed for any key public holding views different from his.

From 1954 to mid-1956, the Cabinet became increasingly influential because of Ben-Gurion's "semi-retirement" and Sharett's practice of bringing all policy questions before it. Some key publics began to exert influence, particularly in the making of foreign policy. Sharp domestic divisions emerged in 1957, following Ben-Gurion's decision to withdraw from Sinai and Gaza, although the influence of dissenting opinions was insufficient to bring about any genuine consideration of policy alternatives. Ben-Gurion reasserted his total dominance in 1956 and maintained control until his last resignation in June 1963. Although he held absolute control over policy making, a number of individuals did come to play important roles in the shaping of high-level decisions. This group included Levi Eshkol and Pinhas Sapir in the economic area; Golda Meir in the political/diplomatic realm; Moshe Dayan, Shimon Peres, and Yigal Allon in military matters; and Abba Eban in foreign affairs.

Evolution of the Ministerial Committee on Security and Defense

From 1964 through May 1967, under Prime Minister Levi Eshkol, the Ministerial Committee on Security and Defense (MCSD), actually a subset of the full Cabinet, emerged as the principal decision-making body, with Eshkol serving as "first among equals." During this period the MCSD formulated government policy, with actual decisions being ratified by majority vote of the full Cabinet. Under Eshkol the MCSD was informed at the "highest levels" and served as a genuine decision-making mechanism. Prior to May 1967 the

MCSD and Cabinet enjoyed broad-based national support, and there was limited cause for the key publics to press for alternative policies.

The crisis of May 1967, which culminated in the outbreak of the Six-Day War, brought extreme dissatisfaction with Eshkol's policy, as well as with his apparent failure to reach a decision that an increasing number of key publics thought necessary for the survival of the state: the launching of a preemptive strike on Egypt and Syria. It was the intense feeling of several key publics, utilizing the Knesset, Cabinet, and press as modes of influence, that brought about changes in the government, the MCSD, and the defense policy. Coincident with the decision to go to war in 1967 was the enlargement of the Cabinet and MCSD to include the opposition parties and the formation of a National Unity government that lasted until 1970.

The opportunity for members of the MCSD, as representatives of various key publics, to influence policy making was now far greater than at any previous time. In the words of opposition member Menachem Begin:

> it [the MCSD] actually made decisions. Every member could express opinions and they were taken seriously. If he desired, each member could bring his motion to a vote in the full Cabinet.[5]

Even with this broadening of the government in 1967, it is important to note that from 1948 through the outbreak of war in October 1973, the making of strategic-level decisions was concentrated in the hands of a relatively homogeneous group of 18 persons. Most had arrived in Palestine before the British mandate and had been predominant throughout the first 20 years of independence, sharing a common perception often referred to as "the Second Aliya [the 1904–14 wave of Jewish immigration] mentality." Only four of these were native-born sabras—Allon, Dayan, Rabin, and Ahron Yadlin. Thus, if there was influence during this time, it was limited to those key publics that shared the background and views of the entrenched political and military leadership.

Following Eshkol's death in 1969 and the accession of Golda Meir to the prime ministry, policy making again became highly concentrated. As former foreign minister, Mrs. Meir took a more personal and decisive role in foreign affairs than Eshkol had. Trusting only a few of her closest colleagues and staff, she relegated the MCSD to a nominal role. By 1970 membership of the MCSD included almost the entire Cabinet, and by 1973 it had ceased to be the mechanism of policy making.

Mrs. Meir's Kitchen Cabinet

Central to decision making under Mrs. Meir was a small, informal group consisting of the prime minister and a few of her closest colleagues. While unfixed, this group usually included Golda Meir (prime minister), Yisrael Galili (minister without portfolio), Moshe Dayan (minister of defense), and Yigal Allon (deputy prime minister and minister of education). From time to time other individuals, such as Gen. David Elazar (Israel Defense Forces [IDF] chief of staff) and Abba Eban (foreign minister), participated. To the extent that the various key publics were represented in this small group, they were able to exert direct influence over policy formulation.

The last decisions taken by the "kitchen cabinet" were those surrounding the outbreak of war on October 6, 1973. Meir, Galili, and Dayan, advised by Chief of Staff Elazar and IDF Intelligence Chief Eliahu Zeira, took the fundamental decisions not to mobilize additional IDF units on October 5–6, and not to strike preemptively on October 6. This latter decision was taken unilaterally by Mrs. Meir, against the advice of Elazar.

Viewed in Israel as a disaster or failing (the Hebrew term used is *michdal,* meaning omission), the outbreak of war and initial Israeli setbacks severely damaged the ability of the "kitchen cabinet" to function as an exclusive policy-making body. During the October War, the full Cabinet and General Staff played an increasing role in policy formulation. In the months following the cessation of hostilities, Meir and her colleagues Galili and Dayan, as well as Elazar, came under increasing criticism from a broad range of groups within the Israeli public over prewar decisions, conduct of the war, and subsequent actions.

In the national turmoil that characterized Israel during the months following the October War—including official investigations, national elections, and Mrs. Meir's almost continual illness—few formal changes were implemented in the policy-making process. Indeed, decision making took on an ad hoc character, being done on a day-to-day basis, much of it by key staff members such as Mordechai Gazit (director general of the Prime Minister's Bureau), with virtually no long-range policy planning at all.

Immediate priority was given to rebuilding the IDF to meet the possibility of renewed full-scale fighting and to securing a disengagement of forces on the Egyptian and Syrian fronts. To the extent that settlement policies of an interim nature were required for these ends, they were formulated by the established political and military leadership. With regard to the general decision-making environment following the October War, it is possible to conclude the following:

the full Cabinet and Knesset were no longer willing to tolerate a small, exclusive decision-making body immune to influence on key defense, security, and settlement issues;

the public at large, and particularly key groups, were no longer willing to permit policy making on an exclusive basis;

a wide range of key publics modified their own policy positions to ones differing from both their own prewar positions and established government positions;

key publics sought and established increasing influence over policy making.

Thus, it is possible to say that, as a result of the October War and its aftermath, there is a set of motivated key publics seeking to influence the making of Israeli defense, security, and settlement policies. The relationship of these groups to actual policy making is, however, still amorphous and their groups' efficacy is unclear. On the basis of the 1973 elections, the resignation of the Meir government, the formation of the Rabin government, disengagement talks, and other evidence, however, it is possible to assume that influence by such key groups will be significant for the foreseeable future.

OPERATION OF THE ISRAELI POLITICAL SYSTEM: INTEREST GROUPS

Although Israel is a relatively small and new nation with a society composed of cohesive and seemingly homogeneous groups, it is clear that a number of segments within the society and the groups that represent them exert significant influence over the policy-making process. As a practical matter, identifying these groups and analyzing their influence over policy making is most readily accomplished by considering the set of groups that have emerged as effective policy advocates and by analyzing those interest groups that are perceived as being influential by the nation's political and military leadership.

The first step in this process considers the range of regional, religious, cultural, political, economic, educational, and other groups that have emerged over the years.[6] It is possible to narrow the list to those groups that have been able to gain national recognition or are for other reasons perceived by the national leadership as being influential.[7]

Central subpopulations are Israel's Jewish, Arab, and Christian communities, although both Israeli Arabs and Christians lack significant influence in the political system, as such, and Israel's Orthodox Jewry is more directly represented through the NRP.

The principal cultural division is between Israel's Jews of European origin (Ashkenazim) and those of Eastern or Oriental origin (Sephardim). While the former are best considered in terms of the other publics to which they belong, the Sephardim have acquired the status of being Israel's major minority group and have begun to seek recognition and influence as such.[8] With the possible exception of Israel's short-lived Black Panther party, this group has thus far failed to establish itself as an effective interest group in foreign-policy making.

While such a vacuum of influence for this group exists at present, it is important to note the enormous potential for influence in the future. As one analysis points out:

> It is significant that the government officials most intimately seized with the problem and most knowledgeable about it are the ones most worried about the malign potential of the Orientals. . . . Equally, they are the ones most concerned lest unawareness among the Europeans of the Oriental resentment could inhibit the fundamental changes in priorities. . . .
>
> Surprisingly, in view of the fertile field that would seem to exist, there has been very little demographic imbalance for electoral purposes. . . . But its absence so far is no guarantee for the future.[9]

For the most part, economic divisions within Israeli society are coincident with other common factors. To the extent that it represents Israel's workers, the Histadrut (General Federation of Labor) could be examined separately; but it generally is viewed as an associational group rather than an economic one.

One highly effective segment of the public that does have an economic base is the members of Israel's *kibbutzim* (collective farms). Since the beginning of the state, *kibbutz* members have formed a vital part of the IDF and have held a disproportionately large share of top military and political posts.[10] Since many *kibbutzim* are border settlements and have provided Israel's first line of defense, the interests of this public are vitally linked with Israel's defense, security, and settlement policies.

The three basic institutional groups are the military and the defense establishment, civil servants in key Israeli ministries (Foreign Ministry and Defense Ministry), and the world Jewish community. By any set of criteria, the first two are major interest groups and are included in the analysis. The third presents a more difficult problem.

Among the civil service and bureaucracies, the senior staffs of the Foreign Ministry and Defense Ministry have been influential in the implementation of policy, if not in its formulation. In this process, there has been a certain amount of interest group advocacy on issues such as recognition of South Africa, relations with the People's Republic of China in 1954–55, and Israel's decision to vote against a U.S.-sponsored resolution on Arab refugees at the United Nations in 1965.

Selecting from the myriad associational groups that do, or may, exert influence over strategic policy making is no small task. Major groups, such as the Histadrut, the Israel Manufacturers' Association, and the *kibbutz* organizations, are well-established and obvious candidates. Of these, only the Histadrut and *kibbutz* organizations have been selected for more detailed analysis.

A different problem is posed by a public led by a number of academics and intellectuals who have been persistent advocates of accommodation-centered policy and alternative approaches to the Arab states. From time to time marginal political parties have been formed, often through the cooperation of concerned academics and dissatisfied political figures, in an attempt to provide alternatives to the traditional opinion leadership of the two major parties. In the period following the October War, the pressure generated by such groups contributed significantly to the downfall of the Meir government. In general, however, such efforts have been short-lived and have had only marginal success.

As the ranks of this accommodation-centered public have swelled in the aftermath of the October War, this group has become a more potent force, although no single interest group or political party has yet emerged to fully utilize its thrust. It remains one of the major centrifugal forces within Israeli society today. The traditionally leftist political parties, which would be expected to represent such sentiment, have failed to do so. With the continued inability of the government to bring about a political settlement, the probability increases that this latent force will ultimately assert itself in some form.

In lieu of specific interest groups to represent the academic-intellectual community, the latter will be included in the analysis of a "nonassociational" group. Another group that could be considered here is Israel's journalists and commentators (the media), who generally reflect the positions of specific parties and other organizations. (See Table 3.)

Religious Groups

The role of Israel's Orthodox Jews in the formulation of foreign policy has often been misunderstood, both within and outside Israel. Here an initial problem stems from an old division that existed in the Orthodox community over the use of force, and the refusal of some Orthodox Jews to fight in the IDF. Convinced that Zion could be established only by divine action, the Agudah faction opposed all force-centered policies for many years.

A second problem arises from the apparent approval of all foreign and security policies that were promulgated by the government up to May 1967. The interpretation given this acquiescence was that the foreign-affairs issues simply were not salient to this group; and that as long as they were allowed to influence domestic policy in religious and related areas, their support for established foreign policy could be taken for granted. Such an interpretation is inaccurate, as subsequent events have demonstrated.

From 1948 through May 1967, the religious community placed its trust essentially in one man—David Ben-Gurion—and believed that his policies were the best for the state. From Ben-Gurion's semi-retirement in 1963 to May

TABLE 3

Israeli Interest Groups and the Formulation of Policies

Effective (Key) Publics (population)	Institutional Groups (representation)	Explicit Policy Makers	Defense/ Security Policies	Contingent Outcomes
Israeli military	IDF leadership	IDF Gen. Staff	Defense/ security policy	Interaction with other concerned actors
Organized labor	Histadrut	Histadrut sec.-gen.		
Voters	Political parties	Prime minister; other ministers; Cabinet/MCSD	Foreign policy	
Orthodox Jewry	NRP; orthodox rabbinate	Minister of religious affairs	Settlement policy	
World Jewry (outside Israel)	KKL, UJA, AJC, WZO,* Hadassah			
Academics and intellectuals	Media; political parties; academic associations			
Israeli Arabs (pre–1967)	Arab political parties	Arab coalition members		

Keren Kayemet Leyisrael (Jewish National Fund); United Jewish Appeal; American Jewish Committee; World Zionist Organization.

Source: Compiled by the authors.

1967, in the absence of imminent war, this attitude continued and became institutionalized in support of the Eshkol government. When the crisis of May 1967 arose, however, Eshkol lost Ben-Gurion's support over the initial decision to go to war.

Since 1967, the religious groups represented by the NRP have advocated defense and security policies more force-centered than those favored by the Labor Alignment (Ma'arach) parties.

Victory in the 1967 war, particularly the recapture of Jerusalem's holy places and the West Bank territories from Jordan, strengthened the demands of Israel's religious Jews. The group's policy now included a refusal to return or even negotiate over Jerusalem's holy places, and an insistence that Israel retain the West Bank areas of Judea and Samaria, which the NRP regards as part of the biblical Eretz Yisrael (Land of Israel).

The policy interests of Orthodox Jews as a group have been most directly reflected in Israel's religious parties. Originally represented by two pairs of parties (split on socialist/nonsocialist and earlier force/no-force issues), they are now represented by the NRP and the smaller Agudat Yisrael (Religious Front) party. As a member of every government since 1948,[11] the NRP has had direct influence on policy making both in the Cabinet and on the MCSD

Economic Groups

Since the major ideological divisions are represented in the political parties, and since it was the hope of Israel's founders to create an economically homogeneous society, the economic interest groups that usually emerge as important in smaller nations are absent here, with two notable exceptions.

The more important of these groups is organized labor, represented by the Histadrut, Israel's semi-official General Federation of Labor. In addition to its representational function as a union, the Histadrut serves a variety of other functions, including administering the national health service (Kupat Cholim), assisting with immigration problems, and organizing world Jewry through its international affiliates. More important, it forms the broad power base of the ruling Mapai (Israel Labor party).

It is through this relationship that organized labor is able to influence policy making, and in turn the Histadrut is used by the government for the promulgation of its policies. In 1956 and 1967, for example, the Histadrut rallied its trade unions in support of free passage for Israeli ships and cargo through the Suez Canal.

The major thrust of the Histadrut's efforts, however, is in the area of domestic economic policy. To the extent that the group holds views on foreign-policy issues, it is fairly well represented in the Mapai. Thus, its primary functions are implementation and communication of Israeli policy to other nations of the Western world. It has long been the opinion of Israel's labor/socialist leadership that the state must seek support from and solidarity with other socialist nations; and it has utilized the Histadrut to this end, although with only qualified success.

Far smaller than the Histadrut, but still important in the formulation of policy, is the key public composed of Israel's *kibbutz* members. This group embraces the dual ideals of nationalism and socialism, and lives in a situation that places many of them, settled on the frontier, at the crux of the defense, security, and settlement problems. Despite this pivotal position, the *kibbutz* movement generally has sought to exert influence through established political parties, Ahdut Ha'avodah and Mapai.

Institutional Groups

The role of the IDF in the foreign-policy process has been a matter of considerable concern in Israel for a number of years. A fundamental precept of the state is that the military be the instrument of foreign, strategic, and security policy, not its maker. The situation becomes critical in Israel, where foreign affairs are so closely linked to defense and settlement policy, and play such a critical role in the day-to-day life of the nation.

The distinction is further blurred because the political leadership must rely heavily on the military for vital intelligence, critical assessments, and ultimate policy implementation. Further, most of Israel's political leadership shares experiences and close personal associations with the military leadership. For example, Mrs. Meir's decisions prior to the October War document that military decisions are ultimately political; but other cases, such as Eshkol's change of policy in the May 1967 crisis, demonstrate the ability of the military to exert sufficient influence to change policy. Similarly, the decisions of the Rabin government with respect to the Sinai II accords in 1974 were heavily influenced by the IDF.

Obtaining hard data on the extent to which the IDF and its top leadership are effective in influencing foreign-policy making is difficult because of the secrecy surrounding the IDF and the fundamental postulate of "civilian" rule in Israel. Indeed, many authorities have consistently denied the status of interest group to the IDF, relegating it to a subordinate role in the policy-making process.[12]

As late as 1965 Gen. Yehoshafat Harkabi, one of the leading authorities on strategic matters in Israel, denied such influence existed, although he has since revised his views.[13] At the time he noted that officers belonged to different political parties, that policy divisions appeared among many of the staff, and that there existed a lack of "clearly defined views" on major foreign-policy questions. Overriding all of this, however, has been the belief, generally shared in the IDF, that Israel's security position is of paramount importance and that all other foreign-policy decisions must be evaluated in this light.

Influence is exerted by the military through formal channels and a number of alternative modes. Given its institutional position, it is required to make a continuous input into the foreign-policy decision-making process. Since requisite inputs in the areas of intelligence, analysis, and assessment necessarily include both subjective and objective elements, this process can be considered influence.

The formal channel of policy advocacy has been the weekly meetings of the General Staff (more often, when the situation requires), which usually are attended by the defense minister. He, in turn, is able to present the views of the military to the Cabinet. It has been the design of Israel's political and military leadership to make the line of communication between military and decision makers simple and direct. Since 1948, the demands of Israeli security have required such a relationship; and for the most part, this system has served Israel well.

Questions concerning this system have arisen in light of the October War experience. In this context, it is necessary to examine two aspects of the situation: communication within the IDF itself and the formal (and informal) channels between the military and government policy makers. At this point we may note that, within the military, internal failures of intelligence analysis prevented it from reaching the decision that mobilization and interceptive war were required.[14] Thus, in contrast with May 1967, the meeting of the General Staff of October 5, 1973 failed to conclude that it must press the prime minister and others in the "kitchen cabinet" for immediate action. In short, the proposal of an interceptive strike made by Chief of Staff Elazar to Defense Minister Dayan at 0600 on October 6, 1973 cannot be considered as having the full weight of the military behind it.

As far as its relationship with the government is concerned, the military was unable to exert full influence on Mrs. Meir and her associates. To the extent that the military had a consensual opinion, there was no breakdown in its communication to Mrs. Meir. Indeed, the General Staff meeting of October 5 was ultimately moved to, and concluded in, Mrs. Meir's Tel Aviv office (located within the Defense Ministry complex). On the following day Elazar's recommendation of an interceptive strike was taken directly to Mrs. Meir by Dayan; she flatly rejected it on political grounds.

Since October 1973, steps have been taken to avoid recurrence of these failures. On an informal basis, additional channels are open for the communication of views. For example, frequent ad hoc discussions and meetings between the military and political leadership augment the formal channels and provide for a continuous and direct mode of policy influence. Even under Mrs. Meir, Elazar often participated in the informal discussions that constituted "kitchen cabinet" meetings. Under Yitzhak Rabin, a former IDF chief of staff, close personal and working relationships with Chief of Staff Motta Gur provide informal access and influence.

Evaluating the extent of IDF influence presents a more difficult problem. Since the precise nature of policy advocacy is secret, only rough estimates are possible. In the field of defense policy, pressure from the military to acquire more and higher-quality weapons has been constant. Here the government has made all possible efforts, within the realm of political and economic possibility, to respond.[15] In addition, recommendations of the military on troop levels and other strategic matters generally have been followed.

One example has been the advocacy by General Moshe Dayan, since 1955, of a force-centered policy of retaliation. Backed by the General Staff, this policy was advocated by Dayan (then chief of staff) and was made official by Ben-Gurion. Here we have a clear link between IDF advocacy, formulation by the government, and implementation vis-à-vis the Arab states.

Similar examples are the November 1956 decision to withdraw from Sinai and Gaza, which the IDF was unable to prevent, and, more important, the events of May 1967, when alarmed members of the General Staff (led by Chief of Staff Rabin) demanded the immediate adoption and implementation of a force-centered policy and the launching of a preemptive strike against Egypt and Syria.[16]

In general, the military has been described by one authority as "a permanent arms lobby" promoting the acquisition of weapons for Israel's security over all other considerations.[17] On this basis the IDF encouraged an alliance with France in 1954–55 and closer ties with the United States following the 1967 and 1973 wars.

The basic foreign-policy position of the IDF can be viewed as force-centered, seeking to provide for the security of the state through an adequate supply of arms and the utilization of force to best advantage, given the perceived numerical imbalance in the strategic situation. In the past, this policy has included retaliation in force and the use of "interceptive" or preemptive warfare against the Arab states.

In the 1956 and 1967 wars, the IDF sought to establish a policy of "decisive victories," a policy the IDF feels was not followed in the 1973 war, when the military's recommendation to reject the Soviet cease-fire ultimatum was voted down by the Cabinet.

Israel's decisions with respect to the Sinai I and Sinai II accords in 1974 and 1975, as well as the 1974 disengagement agreement with Syria in the Golan Heights, were greatly influenced by the IDF leadership. Only after extended negotiations and assurances from the IDF did Israel sign these accords, in the belief that fundamental security would not be compromised.

In any future conflicts it is unlikely that IDF advocacy of preemption and decisive termination will be taken lightly. Given the military background of Israel's present political leadership, it can be expected that the military will exert influence in the making of any future strategic and settlement policy.

The Nonmilitary Bureaucracies

On a subjective basis, the only ministries with possible influence over foreign and defense policy are the Defense Ministry and Foreign Ministry.[18] Other bureaucracies have no formal influence over policy making, although an occasional minister may—for reasons unrelated to the ministry he heads.[19]

Within the Foreign Ministry there is no formal organization equivalent to the military's General Staff, although there has been a key group of senior staff referred to as the Hanhalah (Directorate).[20] Regular meetings of this group with the foreign minister provide a mechanism for communication and influence, and the membership of the foreign minister in the Cabinet and top policy-making elite seemingly would provide the same formal channels. The only apparent limitation here is that the Defense Ministry is directly concerned with defense and strategic policy, whereas it is the role of the Foreign Ministry to advise on the diplomatic implications of policy options and to explain Israeli policy throughout the world. Actually, considerable overlap exists, and the area of greatest commonality and influence for the Foreign Ministry comes on the settlement issue.

In general, the policy positions of senior civil servants in Israel's Foreign Ministry have been more accommodation-centered than those of their counterparts in the Ministry of Defense or of official government policy. Over the years the Foreign Ministry staff has, for example, pressed for the recognition of South Africa and establishment of diplomatic relations with the People's Republic of China (1954–55). The limits of this accommodation can be seen in the staff's support for Israel's vote against a U.S.-sponsored resolution on Arab refugees at the 1965 General Assembly, preferring an overall agreement among the states concerned. There is some evidence, however, that this decision was heavily colored by Foreign Minister Meir's personal feelings on the matter.

Under Foreign Minister Eban, who believed in accommodation-centered modes of action, the senior staff moved further in this direction. Since this group implements the official government policy, it is difficult to find evidence of the policy positions and beliefs that it advocates to policy makers. However, it is possible to outline elements of a basic policy:

accommodation and conciliation toward the Arab states, based on withdrawal
    of Israeli forces (possibly to the June 4, 1967, lines);
direct negotiation with all of the Arab states involved in the conflict;
modification of established government policy with respect to "occupied"
    territories: following an Israeli withdrawal, the future of these areas is an
    internal Arab matter, not to be settled by Israel (that is, de facto recognition of a Palestinian entity).

Here the plan recently offered by Israeli Foreign Minister Yigal Allon closely follows the views of his civilian staff.[21] It is likely that the latter strongly supports this plan, which has yet to be adopted as government policy.

The obvious mode of influence for this group is through its own minister, although such direct influence has not been so clear in recent years. Although Eban held accommodation-centered views of his own, there is evidence to suggest that he refused to consider the views and positions of his senior staff. Before the 1973 war, for example, their efforts to influence him on strategic and settlement matters were fruitless.

On another level, Eban had almost no influence over the making of policy before the 1973 war. His accommodation-centered views were not in keeping with those of Mrs. Meir and her associates, and Eban generally was not included in the "kitchen cabinet." After the 1973 war, Eban did assume more of a decision-making role. However, we are left with the situation that the senior staff of Israel's Foreign Ministry had little influence over this minister, and he in turn had little impact on policy making.

The situation has changed to some extent with the new foreign minister, Yigal Allon. Although from a military background (unlike Eban), Allon has expressed views more accommodation-oriented than those of his associates in the Cabinet; they reflect many of his staff's views, although it is still unclear that the staff of the ministry is able to exert much more influence over Allon than over Eban.

The World Jewish Community

An interest group unique to Israel, and one not formally a subgroup of Israel's domestic population, is the world Jewish community. It is included in the analysis because of the leverage and influence exerted on Israel's foreign-policy system.

First, world Jewry acts as both a positive pressure on Israel's leaders and as a restraint on foreign policy. Second, in the implementation of policy, it has much the same role as that of the Histadrut, bringing Israel's message to other nations and mobilizing international support for Israeli policy. Further, the group provides funds for military and development purposes and has been able to bring some pressure on major powers, such as the United States and France, to supply Israel with needed weapons.[22]

From prestate times through 1956, the American Jewish community pressed Israel for an accommodation-centered policy of greater conciliation and cooperation with the Arab states. It supported Foreign Minister Moshe Sharett's soft line, and sought to achieve permanent settlement through the United Nations, an organization Prime Minister Ben-Gurion viewed with considerable disdain.[23]

Another element of policy advocated by American Jewry stems from a dislike of Israel's reprisal policy. Beginning with the Kibya raid in October 1953, the Lake Kinneret raid in 1955, and throughout the 1960s, the group has continually pressed the Israeli leadership for caution and a limitation of raids, which were seen as undermining Israel's position as a legitimate and peace-seeking power. These exhortations fell on deaf ears, as a luxury that could be afforded by Jews thousands of miles from Arab guns but not by an Israel struggling for survival.

Likewise, dissent arose from America over Israel's Sinai conquest of 1956. In addition to pressure from President Dwight Eisenhower and Secretary of State John Foster Dulles, this urging by Nahum Goldmann led to Ben-Gurion's acceptance, in principle, of Israeli withdrawal on November 8, 1956:

> Goldmann informed Ben-Gurion that American Jewry had been most happy about the Sinai victory but would not stand behind Israel if she persisted in keeping the conquered territory. He added that collections to the national Jewish funds might be forbidden.[24]

A similar position was advocated following the 1967 war, although in a far more subdued tone. American Jews urged Israeli concessions and entry into indirect talks with the Arab states. The foreign policy advocated by the American Jewish community appears to contain two basic elements:

the view that the United States has an obligation to supply Israel with vital weapons systems to defend itself from the Arabs;

a belief in accommodation rather than force vis-à-vis settlement issues, reflecting a growing feeling that additional wars are pointless and that a settlement can be accomplished only through conciliation.

The mechanism through which the world Jewish community attempts to exert influence is the World Zionist Organization (WZO) and several institutional adjuncts. As important is the American Jewish Committee (AJC). Founded in 1890 in New York, it began as anti-Zionist, becoming at best ambivalently non-Zionist following World War II. Since 1948, the AJC has supported Israel's basic right to exist, but has consistently pushed for full and equal rights for Israel's Arabs, conciliation toward the Arab states, and the elimination of what it sees as "military government" in Israel.[25]

The WZO and AJC have been able to exercise direct influence in the policy-making process for several reasons, including the following:

a fundamental belief by Israel's founders that links with "Diaspora" (exile) Jewry are essential to the survival and development of the state;

the stream of new immigrants and financial support provided by the American Jewish community, and the implicit "threat" of eliminating such support;

the perceived need (by Israeli leaders) for American Jews to influence the U. S. government to provide military and supporting economic assistance to Israel;

the direct personal influence of American leaders such as Nahum Goldmann and the AJC's Jacob Blaustein over prime ministers Ben-Gurion, Eshkol, Meir, and, to a lesser extent, Rabin.

Nevertheless, Israel has taken an independent stand in many foreign-policy matters, despite dissent from the world Jewish community. This has been clear in such cases as efforts to establish a UN military presence on Israeli territory, in which mitigating efforts by the American Jewish community were fruitless.

Political Parties

Israel's numerous political parties have over the years fairly well reflected the policy divisions and interests that existed within the larger society. To a considerable extent Israel's party-list electoral system, which makes the nation a simple multimember district, and the fact that no party has ever won a clear majority of Knesset seats, supports this view, although parties often have adjusted their positions upon joining the government coalition.

Against this view is the fact that over the years, the population of Israel has undergone an enormous change in size, composition, and policy positions, yet the parties have tended to remain constant in both their proportion of Knesset seats and basic policy positions. Further, for the most part, the same personalities have, to a major extent, dominated the parties since statehood (1948). This latter factor has been the source of a great deal of tension in Israeli society since the October War, and supports the charge that Israel's parties no longer represent the center of opinion of their followers.

In terms of alternative orientations toward major foreign-policy and security issues, the parties fall into several major categories representing the principal divisions within the electorate. Because of the tendency of Israeli parties to split, merge, and change names over time, it is useful to consider the voters and the party system in terms of basic policy orientation.

Mapai

Central to any consideration of Israeli policy is an analysis of the Mapai (Israel Labor party), which has dominated every government and coalition since 1948, and whose policy has been the government policy. During this time it has controlled the key portfolios concerned with foreign affairs, defense, security, and settlement policy (prime minister, foreign minister, and defense minister); and most major policy decisions have originated within it. Since the October War, however, it is not altogether clear that the Mapai still accurately represents the views of those it claims to represent. Nevertheless, Mapai, and especially its Cabinet members, is still the essential group to be influenced.

The ideological center from which other party policies must be evaluated is the Mapai position (actually a range of opinion). Traditionally, major policy positions have been worked out within the Mapai Central Committee rather than in government meetings or other interparty processes. In crisis situations it has been Mapai's members of the Cabinet, holding the key prime minister's, defense minister's, and foreign minister's portfolios, who have made the crucial decisions. Finally, when new leadership was demanded after the October War, the new leaders were selected by vote of the Mapai Central Committee. Thus, this committee is a source of direct influence over policy making in all issue areas.

Over the years the basic position of the Mapai has shifted toward a force-centered policy, reflecting both the personal views of its leadership and pressure from its factions (most importantly the Ahdut Ha'avodah) to increase military preparedness and protect border settlements. A number of the disputes that have separated the Mapai from its coalition partners either are unrelated to foreign affairs, defense, and settlement issues or are no longer points of contention—for example, the debate over alignment with the Soviet Union and relations with India and China.

Thus, Mapai policy has been government policy, with its emphasis on force, strength, security, and pragmatism. Further, the selection of this policy by Mapai's followers and the nation has not been by default. Over the years alternative policies and options have been hotly debated within the party and the electorate as a whole. In the aftermath of the October War, these policy debates erupted anew; and if a shift in policy is to come, it is most likely to come from within the Mapai.

Ahdut Ha'avodah

To the left of Mapai within the Labor Alignment (Ma'arach) is the nationalist-socialist Ahdut Ha'avodah (Unity of Labor party). This group has had a history of merger and splits from both the Mapai and Mapam, for it shares the ideological ground between the two. More important than pure ideological considerations, however, is the key public that this party represents and the leadership it has produced.

The basic policy position of the party stems directly from the hard core of the *kibbutz* movement. Many *kibbutzim* have joined the Ha-Kibbutz Hame'uhad (United Kibbutz) movement, which provides the organizational base and support for Ahdut Ha'avodah. It has no substantial ideological differences with Mapai; rather, it is basically an agrarian-oriented group, while Mapai's base of support has been in Israel's urban areas. The special security problems of agricultural settlements, which often are border outposts, gave rise to differences over defense and security policy. These differences were reflected in the defense organizations that emerged in prestate times and in the military and political leadership the movement has produced.[26] Among the military and political leaders produced by Ahdut Ha'avodah are Yisrael Galili, Moshe Carmel, and, most notably, Yigal Allon.

The policy of Ahdut Ha'avodah has been more force-oriented and impatient than that of either Mapai or Mapam. In the past it has opposed alliance with the United States on the grounds that the latter would not help Israel when necessary, and would endanger control over Jordan River waters. Since October 1973, these considerations have taken on reduced significance.

More important is the divergence between this group and the Mapai over security and settlement issues. Ahdut Ha'avodah has traditionally rejected the concept of a binational state contained in the 1947 UN Partition Resolution, and has dismissed the possibility of territorial concessions to the Arabs. Arab refugees are to be rehabilitated, with international help, on "unused lands" of the Arab states. In defense, the party has stressed the need for a high degree of military preparedness for subsequent wars they see as inevitable. The party has quite successfully exerted influence for the adoption of a force-centered policy of retaliation to stop border incidents.

As a member of the government, the party's line has been largely merged into that of the Mapai. Thus, the public it represents holds more force-centered beliefs than do its representatives. Still, the group represents a relatively small, but highly influential, subpopulation of *kibbutz* members. These are the people who have provided the backbone of the IDF and who live at the center of the conflict, many of them within gunshot of Arab borders. Therefore, any changes in policy will require the support of this key public.

The group's most important representative, Foreign Minister Yigal Allon, has voiced views that are regarded in Israel as dovish or accommodation-centered.[27] Coming from a *kibbutz* and military background, Allon has the respect of both groups. He is in a key position to play a major role in bringing about a shift in Israeli policy toward a more accommodation-oriented posture. With his support, this key public would be more willing to accept and support a modified policy.

Nevertheless, it is important to keep in mind that, despite Allon's present position, he is the weakest of the top three leaders, and does not enjoy widespread respect either in the general public or within the military and political leadership of which he is a member. To some extent his present position is a function of his nonassociation with the "disaster" of the October War and the political necessities of forming a viable government afterward. In speculating on his present and future influence, this qualification must be kept in mind. Since his appointment was more one of political necessity, his subsequent influence on strategic policy must be viewed in this light.

Mapam

To the ideological left of Mapai and Ahdut Ha'avodah is the Mapam, with its core of Russian population and Marxist Leninism. For many years it advocated Israel's alignment with the Soviet Union, although this position has of necessity been moderated since the June War. Further modification of Mapam's views took place when it joined the government coalition with Mapai. Mapam's policy derives from the government, of which it is still a member, and its own position, which has been inconsistent over the years. It has shifted from early support of accommodation and a binational (Jewish/ Palestinian Arab) state to a force-centered policy in the June war, and back to urging a confederation with Jordan. Since the October War, Mapam members have advocated a more accommodation-centered policy than have their Mapai colleagues, and have urged the government to map out its minimal final demands as part of the settlement process.

Communists

The Communist party of Israel (Maki) belongs to the far left ideologically, and represents the bulk of the Marxist-Leninist sentiment and there is little demand for another such party, particularly one that has been consistently hostile to Zionism. In recent years the Communists have split into smaller factions: the New Communists (Rakah), an Arab group with four seats, and Moked, a Jewish Communist group with one seat. Having no influence, these groups confine their activities to verbal accosting of both the government and the opposition in Knesset debate.

Likud

Israel's perennial opposition party of the nationalist right has been the Herut (Freedom) party, the political successor to the prestate Irgun military movement. In recent years it has allied itself with the Liberal party (as Gahal) and, with the further addition of the small Free Center party, formed the Likud (Unity) bloc, which presented a unified party list in the 1973 elections. Likud supporters are a fairly coherent group, ranging from old-time Herut and Irgun supporters to more youthful advocates of free enterprise and a strong, force-oriented military policy.

The major differences that have existed between Likud and Mapai since 1967 are over issues of economics. As a member of the government from 1967 to 1970, the group modified its irredentist position, and few differences on strategic and settlement issues exist. Criticism of government policy since 1967 has been more a function of the group's status as the "opposition" than a fundamental policy disagreement. Following the October War, Likud's criticism of the government intensified, but in no case did it go beyond a point where the Likud could join a new unity government. Recently it has moved toward full support for government policy.

Its fundamental defense policy has always been force-oriented, and disputes in this area usually were more personality clashes between Mapai's Ben-Gurion and Herut's Begin than substantive policy differences. Recently, these differences have been reflected by the Mapai members of the General Staff and Likud military, notably Gen. Ariel ("Arik") Sharon.[28] To the extent that differences do exist, the Likud supports a more active and force-centered policy, stressing yet stronger retaliation and decisive victory in any renewed warfare.

More pronounced are the differences in Likud policy toward settlement issues. Likud's predecessor, Herut, traditionally stressed the following as a basis for any settlement:

Israel must maintain its claim to "Trans-Jordan," lest it be forced to withdraw
from territory captured from Jordan in future wars (this claim anticipated
the capture of the West Bank in the June War);

Israel should not make a formal settlement with Jordan, but accept an interim
accord not compromising the basic claim;

with the exception of Jordan and Gaza, peace treaties with the other Arab
states would be acceptable;

a policy of "hot pursuit" should be adopted whereby "if they [the Arabs] send
marauders across the border, we will pursue them into their own territory
and not come back";[29]

the concept of a binational state is rejected, although Arabs in "acquired"
territories are free to become citizens in Israel.

In short, policy grew out of both defense and security considerations, and
a desire on the part of the Herut to establish Eretz Yisrael roughly along the
Biblical lines.

Not included in original policy statements were consideration of Sinai and
the Golan Heights. Recently such statements have been expanded to resist the
return of Sinai and Golan territory, but they do not stipulate the annexation
of these areas as the basis of a settlement. While the Likud persists in its
demand that the West Bank territories of Judea and Samaria be retained, there
is also evidence of flexibility. Since the formation of Likud, the tone of policy
has continued to be moderate, with references to the historic boundaries of
Eretz Yisrael being dropped and the idea of repatriation of Arab refugees being
rejected.

On a broader level, Likud has long supported alliance with the West,
emphasizing that the state of Israel is part of the free world.[30] This view has
been tempered with a desire for Israeli military self-sufficiency, now viewed as
an impossible goal; concern over the Kissinger missions; and the possibility
that Israeli interests will be compromised in the spirit of détente.

The actual influence of Likud in policy making is limited, since it no
longer is a member of the government coalition, but is important for a number
of reasons. For example, its supporters hold many key military and related
posts. Second, there has been considerable pressure for the formation of a new
unity government, which would bring the Likud back into the policy-making
process. A sharp split of opinion exists within the present government over the
desirability of such unification, with Mapam and some elements of Mapai
vigorously opposing it, and more pragmatic elements, such as the Rafi and
NRP, supporting its inclusion.

More important, if a basic shift in government policy toward accommodation is to take place, it probably will have to be with the acquiescence of the
Likud and its supporters. It will be far easier for the government to secure this
support if it brings Likud into the coalition.

Rafi

Crucial to the formation of any Israeli government, and to the security and settlement issues, is the small but influential Rafi faction. Formed as a splinter of the Mapai in 1965 by David Ben-Gurion, Moshe Dayan, and Shimon Peres, it merged back into the Mapai during the crisis of May 1967 but has retained its identity. Rafi represents the middle ground between Mapai's center, on the one hand, and the Likud and NRP, on the other. With its base in pragmatism rather than ideology, it has strong support in the segment of the public that favors a realistic defense and settlement policy.

As a part of Mapai and the government except for a brief period, Rafi's position is close to Mapai's but has peace and security, rather than the establishment of some historic set of boundaries or a Zionist state based on specific socialist principles, as primary objectives. Given a viable possibility of peace and security through an accommodation-oriented policy, Rafi could be persuaded to modify its stand. Further, it frequently has taken the position that the vital issues of peace and settlement cannot be readily decided without bringing the Likud into the government, and has supported such inclusion since the 1973 elections.

Because of its key position in the political system and the importance and popularity of its leaders, notably Shimon Peres (now minister of defense) and Moshe Dayan, Rafi has direct influence on actual policy making. It can be expected to continue to play a significant role in changes in the government's composition, as well as in future shifts of defense and settlement policy.

Indicative of Rafi's willingness to adopt accommodation-oriented action was Peres' use of the military to prevent various Israeli settlement efforts in the "occupied" West Bank.

National Religious Parties (NRP)

For many years Israel's religious parties and their supporters were considered almost exclusively in terms of their influence over specific aspects of domestic policy. It was assumed by both the government, to which they generally have belonged, and the population in general, that the defense and settlement issues were not overly important to them. Before 1967, this probably was a correct view, since the NRP and its affiliates did not seriously expect the capture of Jerusalem and the West Bank area of Judea and Samaria (places with religious significance).

Pronouncements by the NRP included such vague statements as support of a "realistic" policy, continued efforts to achieve support at the United Nations, consideration for "any reasonable peace plan," and strengthening the IDF.

It was only with the crisis of May 1967 that the NRP attempted to exert influence over the foreign policy-making process, in the face of what it viewed as an impending disaster. Threats by the NRP to quit the coalition in the midst of the May 1967 crisis forced Prime Minister Eshkol to enlarge his government, bringing in the opposition (then Gahal) and Rafi, and making Rafi's Moshe Dayan minister of defense. The NRP's thrust was not toward the capture of territories but toward defensive interception of what they (and most of Israel) perceived as an impending Arab invasion.

After the 1967 victory, the policy of the NRP shifted to include retention of at least Jerusalem's holy places and the areas of Judea and Samaria on the West Bank. Thus, it moved closer to the Likud position on settlement, though it did so more for religious than for defense reasons.

Following the October War, the NRP persisted in its territorial demands and embarked on a program to force the inclusion of Likud in any new government formed after the 1973 elections. Convinced that solution of the grave defense and settlement problems required a broad-based unity government, it posed an ultimatum to Prime Minister Meir. As a necessary coalition partner, it refused to join a new government unless that government agreed either to review the "Law of the Return," covering citizenship for Jewish immigrants, or to include the Likud in a unity government.

Mrs. Meir refused to concede either point, and was forced to form the first minority government in Israeli history. Hence the strategy of the NRP—to use the first condition to force the second—was unsuccessful. For a time it appeared that Rafi would join NRP in forcing the formation of a national unity government, but increased tension on the Syrian front caused Rafi members to return to the government. The NRP itself has returned to the coalition on a tentative basis. However, it is still the belief of the NRP and Rafi that a major policy shift, or implementation of any policy, will require broad-based support that the government does not now enjoy.

To some extent the position of the NRP is complicated by the views of the subgroups that form it, and the lack of a dynamic leader to draw these elements together and represent the party in policy negotiations. Without such leadership, it will be difficult to determine the limits and flexibility of NRP policy toward a more accommodation-centered policy. It is hoped that the NRP would follow the lead of Rafi and the Likud in supporting any settlement reached.

Minor Parties

The minor parties that emerge from time to time are more a function of Israel's electoral system than representatives of major groups in society. Such parties are more often of interest to political scientists than to Israel's political and military leadership, and none is presently in a position to exert significant influence.

One recent attempt to form an accommodation-oriented coalition included elements of the Mapai, under Arieh ("Lova") Eliav, the Civil Rights party, and supporters of previous peace movements. It is possible to conclude that influence of the minor parties on actual foreign-policy making has been marginal at best, and is unlikely to increase substantially in the future.

Knesset

In view of Israel's claim to be a "parliamentary democracy," it is to be expected that the Knesset plays some role in policy making. It may be noted that in the identification of interest groups, the Knesset was not included. This analysis has chosen to consider the parties that constitute the Knesset and the segments of the population they represent rather than the Knesset itself.

The Knesset does, however, provide two modes of influence for parties over the policy-making process. First, and most important, are the Knesset debates on defense and settlement policy, in which direct influence over government members of the Knesset is possible.[31] In actuality, direct access often is limited, since government members attend irregularly and frequently refuse to enter serious debate of security policy when they do. For those parties that are also members of the government coalition, influence is far more direct in coalition meetings and through their Cabinet representatives than in Knesset debate.

What influence the Knesset does have comes from the ability of debate on foreign policy and security issues (frequently televised) to mold public opinion and, thus, indirectly to influence policy making, and from the ultimate necessity of bringing crucial defense, security, and settlement issues to a vote. Hence, while Knesset influence may not be direct, the parameters of what government policy can be passed are of considerable importance. Further, the Knesset has the ability to "bring down" an unpopular government through a vote of "no confidence."

The second mode of influence parties can utilize in the Knesset is through the Committee on Foreign Affairs and Security. Although this committee contains some of the most prestigious Knesset members, who are not members of the government, and debates matters of strategic importance, it has little influence over actual policy making. Although the prime minister and defense minister regularly brief the committee and consult with it, its role is aptly summarized thus:

The consensus of members, observers, officials and ministers is that the Knesset Committee was, for the most part, a consumer of information on foreign and security policy, and only occasionally a decision-making organ.[32]

Another mode of influence often utilized by parties belonging to the government is to press alternative policies within the bloc. Since coalitions are a necessary fact of political life in Israel, keeping the coalition together requires policy makers to pay attention to demands made by coalition partners. The implicit threat here is that a given party could withdraw from the coalition, with the possible result that a majority of the Knesset seats would no longer be controlled by the government. Loss of a majority generally has meant the fall of the government, requiring a new coalition or new elections or both.

In recent years the greatest such threat has come from NRP, with a strong possibility of the Rafi leaving again, as it did in 1965. Under present conditions, loss of NRP and Rafi support would be highly injurious to the coalition. It can be taken for granted that any shift in strategic or settlement policy, particularly toward accommodation with the Arabs, will require the support of a strong coalition. Thus members of the coalition are able to exert considerable influence over the policies adopted through the parameters they place on the policy they will accept.

Direct Public Opinion

A mode of influence employed by virtually all key publics is that of direct public opinion. Efforts to mobilize public opinion are based on the implicit assumption that government policy cannot be adopted or implemented without broad-based public support. Over the years Israeli public opinion has had a significant effect on policy, but not the controlling effect one might assume.

Basic Israeli defense policy has had broad popular support and, with few exceptions, public opinion has seldom been mobilized against the government. Notable exceptions are the changes in the composition of the government and its policy in May 1967 and the loss of support by Mrs. Meir and Dayan after the October War. More often than not, policy makers themselves have sought to mobilize public opinion in support of policies adopted, rather than looking to public opinion for guidance.

The real significance of public opinion lies in the limits it places on policy alternatives. It is obvious that a final settlement cannot be implemented unless it has the wide support of the Israeli public, and the ability of the government to mobilize support for official policy may prove to be as important as the influence of public opinion on policy making.

Associational Groups

The two major associational groups, the Histadrut and the *kibbutzim,* have already been considered in the economic context. What remains is a less well-defined group consisting largely of academics, intellectuals, and political defectors who have consistently advocated accommodation-oriented policies.

This somewhat amorphous group holds a range of views running from abandonment of Israel as a secular Jewish state to accommodation with the Arab states. The main problems in defining the position of this growing public stem from the often differing views of its members and from the fact that no major organization has yet gained widespread support or been recognized as its legitimate representative.

Group members have from time to time become associated with Israeli publications, such as the monthly journal *New Outlook,* although none of these publications appears to have retained either continued support or a broad-based readership.

Despite the growing popularity of accommodation-centered policy since the October War, the impact of this group has not grown. Significantly, a major reason may be the strong leftist ideology associated with *New Outlook* writers and their academic and intellectual colleagues. If anything, the 1973 Knesset elections demonstrated an electoral shift to the right.[33] Thus, while a growing segment of the Israeli population appears willing to support an accommodation-centered security and settlement policy, they are unwilling to use this as a basis for supporting leftist organizations and parties.

Nonassociational Groups

Israel contains a multitude of nonassociational interest groups, each with a small following. The views put forth by such groups on foreign policy and settlement issues range from annexation of all occupied territories to abandonment of the Jewish state. None of these fringe groups has had, or is likely to have, any significant influence on policy making, even though, because of the nature of Israel's electoral system, such groups have from time to time gained a few Knesset seats.

More important here are Israel's academics and members of the media. Although the academics have had virtually no influence as a group, it is not possible to conclude that individual academics have been without influence. Indeed, Israel's university personnel traditionally have been politically active. A number of them have joined in party policy debates, and several have served in the Knesset.[34]

Following the June War, a group of academics expressed its views on the security and settlement issues, taking an accommodation-centered line that is often referred to as the "Buberist" (after Martin Buber) spirit of concessions. They were represented by groups such as the Movement for Peace and Security and the Land of Israel Movement. Their views, critical of official Israeli policy, were expressed in a symposium sponsored in April 1970 by *Newsweek* magazine.[35]

The media in Israel are best viewed as an extension of the multiparty political system. This view is complicated, however, by the special relationships that exist between a number of Israel's leading journalists and members of the military and political leadership. In a number of cases, such as the May 1967 crisis, members of the media have acted as an effective public and served to exert considerable influence on policy makers.[36]

Representing the range of party opinions, as well as several independents, Israel's newspapers have no common position that they advocate. Opinion is most commonly led by Israel's highly respected and influential *Ha'aretz, Ma'ariv,* and, to a lesser extent, *Yediot Ahronot. Ha'aretz* enjoys New York *Times* status and a reputation for high-quality journalism, and both *Ma'ariv* and *Ha'aretz* have exceptional access to policy makers and information.

While none of these papers has individual writers of national stature, a number of the writers have military and political leadership backgrounds and write from an informed position. In turn, they are taken with seriousness by, and share the confidence of, their former colleagues. A number maintain close personal relationships with Israel's leaders as well.

ISSUE AREAS

Given the social and interest groups that shape and limit Israeli foreign policy, it is possible to raise the question of issue areas that are perceived as being most critical and what options are available to the Israeli leadership. It must be noted that, under the present governmental and institutional decision-making scheme, the entire range of options has not always been fully analyzed by the leadership, the political parties, or the other interest groups. As indicated previously, policy making since the October War generally has been ad hoc in character, with only limited consideration given to systematic analysis of alternatives or contingency planning.[37]

The Territorial Issue

The issue of what borders could be accepted by Israel in the framework of an overall settlement accord has received considerable attention from the Israeli leadership and the general public. In a settlement that would include a statement of nonbelligerency by the major Arab powers, virtually all major groups in Israel have expressed a willingness to accept borders similar to those of June 4, 1967.[38]

Sinai and the Gaza Strip

Premier Rabin has repeatedly stated Israel's willingness to return almost all of Sinai "in exchange for a genuine peace."[39] The one condition he has attached is that Israel be allowed to maintain a "presence and control" at Sharm el-Sheikh. This demand has taken the form of a land link to Israel, but probably could be met by granting joint use of the new Eilat-Sharm el-Sheikh road that Israel has constructed. Since the Arab states were able to close off the Israeli port of Eilat at the Straits of Bab al-Mandeb in the October War, it appears that an Israeli presence at Sharm el-Sheikh does not hold the same strategic and economic importance to Israel that it did before 1973.

It is widely felt that upon being returned to Arab sovereignty, the Sinai should be largely demilitarized, or Arab forces limited as under the Sinai II accord, although the present Israeli leadership has not irrevocably committed itself on this question. Further, it would appear to be the Israeli desire that the Gaza Strip be returned to Egyptian sovereignty or autonomous Palestinian control. To the extent that Gaza would be incorporated into a new Palestinian entity, the question is relevant to settlement of the Palestinian problem, which Israelis thus far have not addressed directly.[40]

The West Bank

Israel appears willing to accept return of a major part of the West Bank either to Jordanian administration or to an autonomous West Bank leadership under a federation. The majority of the Israeli leadership and interest groups dismiss the idea of turning any territory over to the PLO as the representative of the Palestinians. Other views on Jewish settlement in the West Bank have been offered by Premier Rabin, who favors restricting such settlement to areas such as Hebron; Moshe Dayan, who does not propose annexation, but a more liberal policy toward settlement; and Shimon Peres, who administers the territories.

Only the NRP actively advocates direct Israeli annexation of any West Bank territories, particularly Judea and Samaria. It is, however, doubtful that it could influence a final settlement in this regard. Defense Minister Peres has suggested three possibilities:

division of the "Biblical" land between Israel and Jordan;
an Israeli-Jordanian federation;
a common market on the European model.[41]

Peres favors a federative or common market approach to the West Bank problem. The other alternatives retain the assumption of Jordanian sovereignty and refuse to recognize an independent Palestinian entity.

The Golan Heights

A more serious problem appears over return of the Golan Heights to Syria. First, Israel has yet to overcome reservations about its ability to maintain the security of its northern territory, given an outright return of the Heights to Syria. Second, Israeli settlements in the Golan since the 1967 occupation present political problems for the government in negotiating its return.

Pressure from such interest groups as the *kibbutzim* (on the left) and the Likud (on the right) severely limit the government's flexibility and ability to negotiate a total withdrawal from the area. Further, given the government's present composition, it is highly unlikely that such a withdrawal could be negotiated and subsequently approved in the Knesset.

Jerusalem

A special problem is raised by the status of Israeli-occupied East Jerusalem, particularly with respect to Jewish, Muslim, and Christian holy places in Jerusalem's Old City. Here the present government, as well as opposition and religious groups, have expressed sincere determination not to return control of Jewish holy places to Arabs.

While options such as internationalization of Jerusalem are discussed abroad, they are not yet actively under consideration in Israel. It can only be assumed that as negotiations proceed toward some final settlement, flexibility on this issue will develop.

The Palestinian Issue

Since the accession of the Rabin government in 1974, there has been only limited change in the established policy of refusing to recognize or negotiate with the PLO as the legitimate representative of the Palestinian people. Evidence of minor change comes from Defense Minister Peres, who has noted a more moderate stance by Yassir Arafat (in form, however, not content):

> As far as the Palestinian people are concerned, two other parties are better equipped to negotiate: the King of Jordan, and the local leaders of the West Bank.[42]

This statement and others have raised the possibility of a West Bank referendum and negotiations with established West Bank leaders and Jordan's King Hussein, as agents of the Palestinian people. The Israeli leadership has devoted extensive effort to developing working relationships with the present West Bank leadership, and has considerable hope that these relationships will be the basis for accommodation.[43]

Recent elections on the West Bank, and the emergence of an independent West Bank leadership not closely associated with the Israeli government, present an opportunity for Israeli-Palestinian accommodation and an alternative to Israeli negotiation with the PLO.

Some support exists within Israel for direct negotiations with the PLO as the only realistic way to approach the Palestinian problem. It comes from the left, elements in the Foreign Ministry, and even from a number of leaders on the right. Such a policy shift has had diminishing support as the Lebanese crisis has progressed and Arab support of the PLO has all but disappeared.

Military and Economic Assistance

Although not an issue in the true sense of the word where specific alternatives exist for Israel, it is clear that Israeli policy will be greatly affected by the continued availability of advanced weapons systems that serve to stabilize the arms balance in the area and to reduce Israeli dependence on territorial buffers for security. To the extent that Israeli security, and the leadership's perception of security needs, can be maintained in any territory-for-technology tradeoff under a peace settlement, Israeli policy flexibility will be increased.

Ultimate return of the occupied territories, and settlement on a modification of the June 4, 1967 borders, will depend on the Israeli conviction that these are defensible frontiers and that it can maintain its strategic posture vis-à-vis the Arab states.[44] In the view of Defense Minister Peres, the belief that "in the foreseeable future Israel would be able to maintain the present military balance of one-to-three with the Arab states" seems to meet this requirement.[45]

In the Israeli view, such a defensive capability is a function of sophisticated conventional forces, training, mobilization capabilities, and the IDF's ability to carry out deep interdictive strikes in Arab territory. To the extent that the advanced weapons systems purchased and requested from the United States, such as Lance missiles, F-15 aircraft, and numerous others, maintain this capability and technical superiority over the Arab forces, Israel's military and political leadership may take a more flexible view of interim concessions as well as of final settlement lines.

At the same time, it does not necessarily follow that simply meeting Israeli requests for military and supporting economic assistance will bring about the posture required to achieve an overall settlement with the Arab states. The question will remain one of maintaining Israel's position in the strategic balance with the Arab states, in addition to any initiatives that might be taken toward an overall settlement accord.

The aspect of the issue that is of increasing importance to Israel stems from the growing burdens being placed on the Israeli economy and social system by the nation's defense posture. Despite the major assistance programs sponsored by the United States, the ongoing costs of maintaining the Israeli defense status in economic and manpower terms present problems of major importance to the Israeli population.

International Guarantees

An issue closely related to Israeli security and settlement prospects is the assurances that can be given by the major powers and through the United Nations. Israel views with extreme skepticism the ability of the United Nations to keep peace in the Middle East, except through the express agreement of the superpowers. In the absence of such superpower guarantees, any UN efforts are likely to be largely discounted.

However, recognition and guarantee of final settlement lines, underwritten by the superpowers, will provide the Israeli leadership with both the confidence they need to accept such lines, and the ability to gain popular and *Knesset* support and approval.

Optimally, the United States and the Soviet Union, as cochairmen of the Geneva conference, would recognize any settlement reached by the parties and guarantee the settlement lines and borders. Offensive action by either side in violation of these lines would then constitute a *causus belli*.

Superpower action in such an event could range from direct action to a cutoff of military supplies to the party in violation. Here it is important to note that, *a priori*, the stronger the commitment of the superpowers to underwriting and enforcing an agreed-upon settlement, the greater the negotiating flexibility of both the Arab states and Israel.

In this regard, it is important to note the high regard given the American monitors manning early-warning stations in the Sinai, which were provided by the United States as part of the 1975 Sinai II accord. Although of limited strategic importance, these monitors create an American presence in the region and provide concrete evidence of the U.S. commitment to Israel and to peace in the region.

Economic and Other Issues

A final issue area includes those elements of a settlement in the economic, social, and cultural areas that could become part of an overall accord and could reduce the uncertainty and hostility between Israelis and Arabs, thus increasing the stability of the area.

The following specific issues and proposals have been mentioned in this regard although this is not an exhaustive list:

an end to the economic boycott of Israel by Egypt and other Arab states and the beginning of a trading relationship—the basis for such a relationship could be present economic ties with the West Bank community, or direct export of Israeli agricultural technology to Egypt, along the model of the United States and the People's Republic of China;

an end to the political boycott of Israel, whereby Egypt accepts some form of political relationship with Israel, such as exchanging "interest sections" in third-country embassies (this possibility is not, however, viewed as likely, or as important as the beginning of economic relationships);

demilitarization, or minimal military presence, in the lands returned to Arab sovereignty;

free Israeli passage through the Suez Canal or agreement that Israeli cargo pass through on third-country ships (implemented under the Sinai II accord);

direct air connections for third-country airlines;

direct mail and telephone communications;

cultural and sports exchange, including an Egyptian willingness to allow Egyptian players and teams to compete against Israel in international events;

reciprocal visits by Israeli and Arab journalists—for instance, permission for an Israeli news representative to return the recent visit of Sana Hassan, an Egyptian, to Israel.

To the extent that any of these achievements are accomplished, they will serve to further reduce both the tension and the uncertainty that exist between the parties to the Middle East conflict, and will broaden the basis for a genuine and lasting peace.

ISRAELI OBJECTIVES AND POLICIES

Political Objectives

One of the major problems facing the Israeli leadership for some years, and particularly since the October War, has been the formulation of a definitive statement that includes the specific goals to be achieved in settlement negotiations with the Arab states.[46] Indeed, Israel's national debate over these goals and the conduct of the negotiations has occupied the center stage in Israeli politics since the October War.[47]

Some limited consensus has emerged on the broad policy goals to be achieved in settlement negotiations, but far less agreement exists with regard to Israel's approach to the negotiations and the concessions that can be made as part of further interim agreements and in the absence of an overall settlement accord. Considered below are some of the basic policy objectives that appear to have consensual support in Israel.

Political and Economic Assurances

One area of Israeli policy goals is the complex realm of the political and economic guarantees that will be necessary to provide Israeli security and to promote stability in the Middle East.[48] Included in this category are the assurances Israel seeks from the Arab states, the United States, and other nations involved in the settlement process.

The specific political agreements Israel demands from the Arab states as a prerequisite to a final settlement accord continue to be the subject of considerable debate within the Israeli political and military leadership. Most recently this leadership has shifted from a demand of formal "nonbelligerency" to a "nonuse of force formula" and "substantive elements of nonbelligerency," a formulation closer to the thinking and language of the major Arab states.[49] At a minimum, any assurance from the Arab states must contain the recognition of Israel's basic right to exist within secure borders, as well as substantive actions taken to reduce tension and lower the probability of renewed warfare.

From the United States, Israel seeks continued political support both in settlement talks with the Arab states and in the international forum. The stress placed on formal security guarantees from the United States stems in part from vivid memories of prior experiences, and in part from a desire to secure long-term assurances from a responsible party that has some expectation of continuity and internal stability.[50]

Of critical concern in Israeli thinking have been the way in which American support (military, economic, and diplomatic) is viewed by decision makers, and the extent to which the latter are willing to rely on United States efforts, assurances, and guarantees. Throughout its history, Israel's relations with the superpowers have been the subject of an intense internal debate.[51] Prior to the October War, major supplies of advanced weapons systems from the United States were elusive; and until recently, the goal of securing them on an ongoing basis seemed doubtful.[52]

The advent of the Nixon administration in 1969 and the massive American support effort in the October War proved to be a watershed in American-

Israeli relations and Israeli perceptions of the U.S. commitments to Israel. Debate continues, however, over the degree to which the United States is truly committed to maintaining Israel's strategic balance with the Arab states, and what political support can be expected in settlement negotiations. Indicative of current thinking is a statement by Moshe Dayan, who described Israel's relations with the United States as "the most positive phenomenon of this generation" and went on to say, "I do not believe that their friendship is shallow, or that they would sell us for the sake of a few dollars less per ton of oil."[53]

A more skeptical view is that of Shimon Peres, who compares U.S. efforts to bankers' credits: "You can get them if you have convinced the bank that you don't need them, nobody wants to run the risk."[54]

Political Support in the World Community

Isolated within the Middle East, and to some extent in the global community, Israel has increasingly been forced to seek support from the United States and a few other major powers. Following their preemptive strike in June 1967, Israeli leaders became sensitive to charges of "aggression," at least until October 1973, when Prime Minister Meir rejected the suggestion of another preemptive strike, primarily because of a perceived inability to gain American and other worldwide support for Israel on such short notice.[55]

Since the October War, Israeli thinking and public opinion have shifted toward the more balanced view that long-run American support is vital, and that any policy must have at least implicit U.S. backing. Short-run security considerations, however, cannot be made conditional on American approval.

Even though UN effectiveness in promoting Middle East settlement has been largely discounted, Israeli decision makers view with particular interest American support and action on related questions in the General Assembly and Security Council. U.S. actions there have been taken in Israel as signs of potential variation in American support.

American Efforts Toward Negotiating a Settlement

The greatest divergence in Israeli perceptions occurs in this highly sensitive area. For the most part these efforts had become personalized in the Kissinger missions and, more recently, the efforts of President Ford. As shown by the constant flow of press reports from Israel, the perceptions of various key groups ran from extreme skepticism and a feeling of U.S. pressure to trust.

The Israeli leadership's most pragmatic view of American efforts and of the concessions that will be required was stated by Defense Minister Peres:

[Israel] cannot escape the fact [that it] is likely to be called upon to pay a
price, so that other forces, including those friendly to her, can maintain their
influence and guarantee their legitimate interests in the Middle East. There
is nothing wrong with that, and there is no point in ignoring a demand of
this sort. . . .[56]

Other groups and leaders do not hold such a pragmatic view. Reservations about U. S. pressure on the Israeli leadership have been expressed within
the leadership by former Information Minister Aharon Yariv and Foreign
Minister Yigal Allon.

Additional evidence of the Israeli leadership's increasing realization of the
limits placed on Israeli policy by the United States came in Prime Minister
Rabin's response to the Likud proposal for a three-year truce with the Arab
states. He dismissed the "Begin plan" as "an unlikely export article which U.S.
politicians would not buy."[57]

American Security Guarantees and Willingness
to Underwrite a Settlement with the Arab States

It follows from fundamental Israeli concerns about security and the Israeli perception of the U.S. role in the Middle East that Israel's policy is linked
to the extent to which the United States is willing to underwrite the nation's
vital military requirements. Thus, a range of opinion exists regarding the
potential American role and Israeli responses to American proposals. In general, the Labor Alignment leadership feels that strong U.S. guarantees of
support, such as a long-term arms agreement or mutual security pact, would
permit Israel a greater degree of flexibility in settlement negotiations and
concessions to the Arab states. To a large extent the opposition Likud supports
this policy goal as well.

Long-Run Survival of Israel

The principal objective of Israeli policy is the long-run existence of the
state of Israel as a Jewish state. This was summed up by one of the architects
of early Israeli policy, and remains a cornerstone of policy making today:

Against this complex background [modern Jewish history] the single objective of Israel's foreign policy can be stated in quite concrete terms. It is to
mobilize all the resources of diplomacy for the protection and preservation
of [Israel] as it is. This is no different, of course, from the basic objective of
the foreign policy of any other State, and although to that extent commonplace it nevertheless well bears repetition as it is so often overlooked. . . . the
State's continued existence and its continued security and prosperity are

equally [essential to] the survival of the Jewish people. Such preoccupation
with national survival—both spiritual and physical—engendered by a sense
of historic mission would impress its stamp on Israel's foreign relations
under all circumstances. It is even more prominent as things are when Israel
found itself from the moment of its inception beset by powerful enemies bent
on its complete physical destruction.[58]

Four specific reasons are offered in support of this position. First, all Jews
who desire to make their home in Israel must be able to do so "in full human
dignity" and with freedom of movement. Second, as a result of the untenable
position in which Jews have found themselves in many European lands, Israel
cannot be indifferent to their plight. Third, Israel must exist as a vital spiritual
and cultural link between itself and the Jewish communities of the world.
Fourth, the state exists to provide for the resettlement of many Diaspora Jews.

Thus, in the view of the Israeli leaders, Israel exists not only as a Jewish
homeland but also as the last hope for millions of the world's Jews who have
no other place to go. In practical terms, this causes the leadership to view Israel
as an end in itself, to be preserved at all costs, and serves to explain the
widespread feeling that Israel must survive as a Jewish state.

Viewed in this context, it is possible to understand the often-repeated
Israeli demand that, as a precondition to any negotiated settlement, it receive
sufficient assurances from the Arab states, as well as guarantees from third
parties, that its right to exist will not be challenged. However, this does not
mean that a consensus exists over the specified geographical boundaries of the
state of Israel. Nevertheless, it should be kept in mind that direct and continued assurances to the Israeli leadership that the integrity of Israel as a Jewish
state will be guaranteed in any settlement will help to maximize flexibility in
other areas.

Short-Run Security Policy Objectives

Of a more problematic nature for policy making than ultimate survival
are a host of short-run, ongoing security considerations. Combining military
elements with technology, geography, and other factors, these goals call for
Israel's maintenance of its security through active deterrence of the Arab
states, external terrorist attacks, and internal dissension.

At a minimum, these objectives include the following:

active deterrence of the Arab states from first strikes on Israeli positions;
Israeli capability to undertake both first-strike and second-strike actions
against the Arab states, as conditions might warrant—including the capability to undertake limited operations against hostile forces;

ability to check or control terrorist incursions—while no leader expects to
    "hermetically seal" the borders, protection of border settlements from
    escalated terrorist strikes has become increasingly important;
maintenance of secure borders, or interim cease-fire lines, in the absence of a
    negotiated settlement;
maintenance of technological superiority in weapons systems.

On all of these objectives, limited consensus exists as to how they are to be
made operational. Considerable debate arises, however, as to how they can be
achieved.

In the area of active deterrence, for example, views range from the hard
view of Shimon Peres that Israel "must be prepared for new challenges" and
must "remain strong, fortified and able to meet any menace" to the more
moderate stand of Moshe Dayan and Chaim Herzog, who look more toward
a modus vivendi acceptable to Israel and Egypt.[59] Still more moderate are the
views of Abba Eban and Nahum Goldmann. Eban has doubted Israel's ability
to secure the present disengagement agreements, while Goldmann has called
for "full peace" as an answer to short-run security problems.[60]

Basically, this set of short-run policy objectives forms a "package" of
goals that any policy must address; but if any flexibility is to be achieved in
this area, it will stem from a change in the conditions that go with these
security problems.

Territorial Settlement Goals

Since 1948 it has been the belief of a majority of the Israeli population
and the groups that represent it that peace can be maintained only on the basis
of secure borders, and the 1949 armistice lines (June 4, 1967 frontiers) constitute a close approximation to such borders.[61] Since these were the borders
granted to Israel by international agreement, at least in the United Nations,
they were seen as the basis of Israel's rightful territorial claim. Since then,
elements within the Israeli political and military leadership have maintained
that in an overall settlement, these are the only secure borders that Israel can,
or ought to, obtain.[62] Consistent with this perception has been a fundamental
belief that the partition plan and subsequent frontiers of the 1949 armistice
provide ample room and resources for Israel to exist, grow, and prosper as a
Jewish state.

One major source of debate in Israel today stems from the popular view
that the 1949 armistice lines (June 4, 1967 borders) are indefensible and do
not provide an adequate security frontier. Short of an overall negotiated settlement with neighboring Arab states, these borders are seen as continuing security problems. Speaking in the mid-1950s, Moshe Dayan summed up Israeli
feeling:

The area of the country is only 8,100 square miles. But owing to the configuration of its territory there are 400 miles of frontier. Three-quarters of the population of Israel lives in the coastal plain. . . . The country's main roads and railways are exposed to swift and easy incursion. Scarcely anywhere in Israel can a man live or work beyond the easy range of enemy fire. . . .

Thus the term frontier security has little meaning in the context of Israel's geography. The entire country is a frontier, and the whole rhythm of national life is affected by any hostile activity from the territory of neighboring states.[63]

Stages short of these borders are still referred to as interim lines, indicating acceptance of the idea that the pre-1967 borders will be the ultimate frontier. Indeed, the stated objectives of the present Israeli government have been in terms of these lines, with modifications made for critical security reasons and related agreements over the demilitarized status of the territories returned to Arab sovereignty.

A second source of debate, arising since the Israeli occupation of the Jordanian West Bank in the June War, is Israeli retention of the areas in Judea and Samaria that are of religious significance, particularly to the Orthodox Jews in Israel. This policy objective is most strongly stressed by the NRP.

Beyond the NRP, some limited support remains for permanent annexation of these areas in a "greater Israel." Some verbal support was temporarily offered for a "greater Israel" by the Likud bloc during the 1973 election campaign, but has been conspicuously dropped:

Mr. Begin is no longer saying "rak kach" ("only thus," the former party slogan that accompanied a drawing of a hand clutching a gun on a map of the whole of the original area of the mandate, including what is now Jordan).

Mr. Begin now proposes a three-year truce during which talks could be held on all issues, including borders. There is nothing wrong with the plan except there are no Arabs, dissident or otherwise, to support it, and there is very little except the phrasing to distinguish it from what the government seeks. It is perhaps a point for the Arab world to ponder that their intransigence has pushed the two major parties in Israel so close together. . . .

The Herut conference has not decided the status of Hebron . . . the only opposition came from the left-wing Jewish groups. If the session proved anything it may have been that, in the long run, Arab-Israeli relationships will prove more important, and difficult than borders.[64]

Recent statements by a range of Labor Alignment leaders confirms this generally held goal of settlement with the pre-June 1967 borders. The late Pinhas Sapir, one of Mapai's key policymakers, stated:

We must make loud and clear that for peace we are prepared to withdraw from all those [occupied] territories not vital to our security . . . so as to prevent another war.[65]

Former Foreign Minister Abba Eban:

> Israel does not have the strength to maintain a state in the borders of the
> present disengagement agreements, against the will of the Arab world, and
> without international support. But we do have the strength to maintain a
> state in the 1967 borders, with the addition of strategic adjustments.[66]

Former Defense Minister Moshe Dayan:

> The line I would like to see in a final settlement between us and Egypt should
> provide us with security, but it shouldn't provoke another war.[67]

Within the context of an overall settlement, most groups and individuals
speak of the 1967 borders with strategic adjustments as a final objective,
although no consensus exists over the exact nature and extent of alterations.
Such final goals are to some degree flexible, but the following modifications
appear common:

retention of Jerusalem and Judaism's holy places either as an Israeli entity or
    as an internationalized area;
annexation of several Israeli settlements on the Golan Heights that have been
    established since the June War;
modification of access routes to Jerusalem, particularly in the Latrun area;
return of the Sinai, Gaza, West Bank, and Golan Heights areas, on the basis
    that they be largely demilitarized.

Policy Objectives of the Major Interest Groups

Although the role of the various interest groups in the Israeli political
system and foreign policy-making process has been considered previously, it
is important to note the range of policy objectives and differences that each
of these groups perceives as being critical. It is this range of objectives and
divergence of views that is central to many of the problems presently facing
Israel in its search for a comprehensive foreign policy and settlement negotiations with the Arab states.

The NRP. Since 1967, and particularly since the 1973 Knesset elections, the
NRP has become one of the pivotal groups in both coalition formation and
policy flexibility. During this period, it is possible to note a strengthening of
the traditional force-centered orientation of NRP, which developed in the
1960s, to a position roughly equivalent to the nationalist right (Likud). Elements of this policy are not specific and include generalizations such as active
retaliation, a strong IDF, more and better arms, and retention of strategic

territorial positions. The NRP would support any use of interceptive warfare advocated by the IDF or Likud. In terms of settlement goals, the NRP demands that accommodation with the Arab states not include the West Bank areas of Judea, Samaria, and Jewish holy places in Jerusalem.

The basic shift of the NRP since the October War has not been so much one of actual policy as one of process. That is, the party's shift to the belief that accommodation with the Arab states can be accomplished only with the broad-based support of itself, Likud, and the left.

Organized Labor. To the extent that Israel's organized labor and its representative, the Histadrut, have goals different from those of Mapai, labor has undergone a basic shift toward an accommodation-centered approach. It has always supported a settlement based on the concept of an overall peace agreement.

In foreign affairs and defense the group still supports government policy, and has not advocated a specific approach different from that recommended by the IDF. Dismay exists among organized labor over the enormous rate of military spending by the government and the increasing impact of the defense burden on the Israeli economy; but no alternative is seen, in view of the pressing demands of security. With respect to the United States, there has been a shift from a desire to remain as independent as possible to a pragmatic recognition that Israel must depend on the United States for major amounts of military and economic assistance, diplomatic support, and mediation with the Arab states.

What concessions labor is willing to make on settlement are unclear. What is evident is that the group is more accommodation-oriented than either the general population or the government coalition.

The Kibbutzim. As always, most *kibbutz* members continue to support a strong force-centered defense policy. As in previous wars, they provided Israel's first line of defense and took the brunt of casualties. Least affected by the increased taxes, they have given full support to obtaining more and better arms, and generally have been critical of the United States for not supplying advanced weapons systems more rapidly and in greater quantities.

Similarly, the *kibbutzim* have been highly critical of any territorial concession that would bring the enemy back to their doorsteps and resume the shelling of the Galilee, which many experienced for some two decades. Working against this has been a fundamental desire to reach some accommodation with the Arabs that will stop the repeated rounds of warfare and terrorist attacks that have taken a disproportionate toll of casualties among the *kibbutzim*. Thus the twin goals of short-run security and the necessity of an overall peace settlement have produced a basic tension in the policy advocacy of the *kibbutzim*.

World Jewish Community. Since the October War, support for U.S. supply of arms to Israel and active diplomacy by the United States to bring about the disengagement of forces, interim agreements, and an overall settlement has been virtually universal. The only criticism of these policy objectives has been that Secretary of State Henry Kissinger has been too accommodation-oriented and that Israeli concessions in advance of an overall peace agreement could jeopardize the nation's security. Such concerns are, however, not widely held. There is also a fear among American Jews that anti-Israel and "oil" interests within the U.S. Defense Department and State Department might serve to interrupt the flow of arms in the future. As far as supplies of military equipment for Israel is concerned, the American Jewish community has become more force-oriented since 1973.

On settlement goals, however, American Jews continue to support concessions by Israel that could lead to an overall settlement. Considerable support exists for Israel's recognition of a Palestinian entity and return to the June 4, 1967 borders. Keeping in mind the fact that most American Jews lack an accurate conception of the strategic situation and hold unspecific views on boundaries, it can be assumed that they will support any settlement acceptable to the Israeli government and underwritten by the major powers.

Civil Servants. In essential defense matters, civil servants still defer to the military and Defense Ministry on actual policy goals. To the extent that this group can exert influence, it has urged a more accommodation-centered policy with limitations on retaliation and, if possible, diplomatic solutions rather than interceptive warfare.

The major shift has come in the field of settlement policy. The perceived time frame within which a settlement can be reached has been drastically reduced as a result of the October War. Although civil servants traditionally have been accommodation-oriented and have favored territorial concessions, the need for immediate concessions to facilitate an agreement is now perceived. It does not, however, appear that such a view is presently reflected by Defense Minister Shimon Peres.[68]

Academics and Intellectuals. As indicated, the October War gave rise to considerable debate within Israel's academic and intellectual community over the entire range of defense and settlement issues. In the area of defense, a split has developed, with one faction moving toward the force-centered approach of the Likud and the other to that of the left-wing academics and intellectuals, that a permanent accommodation must be reached through immediate territorial concessions. While extreme views of accommodation are not widespread, it is clear that a majority supports a wider range of concessions than that presently offered by the government.

Mapai and Mapam (Ma'arach). As a result of what were perceived as failings in political and military leadership during the October War, the weight of public opinion in Israel demanded new leadership from Mapai, particularly following the 1973 elections.[69] Prior to October 1973, the real differences in the policies of the three largest parties (Mapai, Likud, NRP) had virtually dissipated. In Mapai the view that Israel should withdraw from all occupied territories, advanced by Arieh Eliav, the late Pinhas Sapir, and Yitzhak Ben-Aharon, was clearly a minority position. At the time, a majority of Mapai supported the status quo; and party debate was over a compromise "Galili Plan," which was basically a compromise between the positions of Defense Minister Dayan and former Finance Minister Sapir.

Within Mapai, a 14-point plan was adopted that shifted emphasis to an accommodation-oriented goal of "attaining peace and cooperation with the peoples of the area." Although the plan rejected a return to the June 4, 1967 borders, it did recognize the need for compromise and territorial concessions, although without mention of specific boundaries. This plan further toned down references to Israel's role in the "occupied" territories.

Since 1973, a new debate has centered on whether the "Galili Plan" compromise has been repealed by the war. The late Finance Minister Sapir insisted it has been, and demanded a less force-centered policy. Mapam interpreted Sapir's statement as a radical move toward its own position of accommodation based on immediate and total withdrawal from the "occupied" territories, and demanded that the government put forth a map of its minimal final demands as part of the ongoing settlement negotiations. The Rafi faction, led by Dayan, insisted that the "Galili Plan" had not been repealed, and that any new plan "overlay" the previous one. Bitter personal attacks brought the prime minister to the center of the storm, and a vote of confidence (291 to 33) backed Dayan.

A major difference of the Mapam plan concerned the Palestinians. It called for Palestinian self-determination, in contradiction to the prime minister's statement that "there is no such thing as a Palestinian," and suggested that Palestinians seek "self-identity" within Jordan or the "established" West Bank leadership. Mapam went on to propose joining Gaza with the Palestinian entity, but stopped short of advocating an independent Palestinian state.

Despite her rejection of the more accommodation-oriented views within Ma'arach, Mrs. Meir categorically rejected the concept of forming a unity government with Likud, even when faced with Dayan's resignation over the issue. Public demands for new leadership finally caused the resignation of her government.

Policy objectives within the Ma'arach under Rabin have become more divergent as the three key ministers—Rabin, Peres, and Allon—have sought to impose their own perceptions of policy on the government. Rabin's position has been less accommodation-oriented than that of many within the coalition, and reflects a general attitude of inaction in critical settlement issue areas. As one observer commented:

> In Mr. Rabin's Government, it is very clear indeed, that the majority [of the Government] will be far more ready to make concessions than most of those who voted for the Labour Party list headed by Mrs. Meir want.[70]

Clearly the most accommodation-oriented of the key ministers has been Foreign Minister Yigal Allon, whose proposals have come closest to the policy advocated by the Israeli leftists and the demands of the major Arab states.[71] Equally clear, however, has been the government's failure to adopt either the "Allon Plan" or its objectives as official policy.

In the pragmatic middle remains Defense Minister Shimon Peres, whose personal views and policy objectives are oriented toward accommodation based on mutual concessions and substantive elements of nonbelligerency. Although not as precisely defined as Allon's objectives, the Peres approach leaves a considerable amount of room for negotiation with the Arab states. As an internal challenge to the prime minister, the Peres approach offers more in style and process toward settlement than in ultimate policy objectives.

Likud. Following the October War, the opposition Likud failed to exhibit any real shift in position. Besides its involvement in the national debate over the ineptitude and irresponsibility of the military and political leadership during the war, it did not put forth alternative policy. Instead, it has campaigned for a unity government including itself and the Mapai, as well as other parties.

In the December 1973 elections, Likud reiterated its opposition to a "repartition of Eretz Yisrael," but has not been specific on what this means.[72] Further, it has called for "direct negotiation of treaties at a peace conference with the Arab states" and has eliminated its unqualified rejection of withdrawals, shifting its position to a rejection of "withdrawals which would endanger the peace and security of the nation."

In defense policy, Likud has taken a position surprisingly similar to that of the other parties. Even in the October War, Likud's Menachem Begin has said, such a preemptive strike would have been unnecessary "if the Government had placed sufficient forces in Sinai and the Golan Heights after receiving advance information about the Egyptian and Syrian buildup"—and there would have been no war.[73] Here Begin's views probably represent those of a majority of the population.

Other Parties. In the wake of the October War the minor parties have reformulated their goals, with varying degrees of detail about peace plans. For example, the small left-wing factions of Moked (Communists), Meri (Israel Radical party, which holds no Knesset seats), and other ideological factions of the far left have failed to present any unified policy objectives. Since the

October War, these groups have been engaged in personality clashes, and have offered little to the electorate.

Prior to the October War, such groups generally supported an Israeli withdrawal to the June 4, 1967 boundaries; a unified Jerusalem; and Israeli security through demilitarization of the Middle East based on international guarantees of some sort. In addition, they have strongly supported the right of Palestinian self-determination. There is no evidence that they have changed this line.

Military Goals

As a basic policy goal, Israel has long sought to achieve a position of military self-sufficiency in terms of both defense manpower and critical matériel. While the IDF never has, and is unlikely ever to, require supplementary forces, it is equally unlikely that Israel will be able to achieve total self-sufficiency in conventional arms production.[74] Under present economic and technological limitations, the Israeli leadership looks toward a two-pronged goal:

increasing the percentage of critical weapons systems manufactured in Israel to approximately 60 percent;
securing an American guarantee of long-term military assistance to meet perceived vital defense needs.

Moving toward the first of these goals, the Israeli leadership has dramatically augmented its domestic weapons research and development program, and expanded the nation's capability to manufacture a broad range of sophisticated weapons systems.[75] With regard to the second goal, the Israeli leadership has clearly sought a new long-term American-Israeli arms supply relationship based on the Israeli Matmon-B plan, which will insure Israel's ability to obtain those systems it deems vital to its security until the 1980s, a point particularly critical under conditions of substantial territorial withdrawal.

Military Aid and Long-Range Guarantees of Supply

One parameter that the Israeli military leadership has linked directly to settlement concessions has been American assurances of a continued supply of the advanced weapons systems necessary to maintain the present quantitative and qualitative strategic balance vis-à-vis the Arab states. Israel anticipates receiving some $2.5 billion annually in military and supporting economic assistance through the 1980s, including some of the most sophisticated military equipment in the U.S. arsenals. Although considerable concern has been voiced over alleged delays and problems encountered in obtaining certain advanced systems, the Israeli military leadership views with favor statements such as one made by former Secretary of Defense James Schlesinger that "the United States can provide the resources to sustain Israeli fighting should a new war erupt."

Of growing concern, however, has been the increasing supply of American arms to Arab states. Voicing the Israeli government position, one report addressed a recent U.S. sale to Saudi Arabia:

> The supply of American arms in such vast amounts to an Arab country is liable to disrupt the balance of forces throughout the Middle East. Israel cannot accept the notion that such planes and weapons will not be placed at the disposal of another country, in time of war . . . such American competition . . . adds fuel to the flames that the Arab states are fanning around Israel.[76]

While it is clearly an objective of the Israeli military to see American supplies of weapons systems to the Arab states curtailed, there is only limited recognition of the role such sales play in maintaining the strategic balance in the Middle East. Indeed, the potential transfers of modern weapons systems to Arab confrontation states, and nonconfrontation states that could enter into a future Arab-Israeli war, are viewed with considerable concern in Israel. Major efforts are being mounted to limit such transfers.

Geographic Security Considerations

The policy objectives of actual settlement, or final borders that would be acceptable to Israel as security frontiers, are very much a center of policy debate within the leadership. Indeed, the question of whether or not the government of Israel should set such minimal borders as a precondition to negotiation is a major issue.[77] While resisting pressure from both the left and the right to map out final borders in advance of settlement negotiation, Prime Minister Rabin and his principal associates have increasingly reflected a national consensus that substantially all of the occupied territories must be returned. Responding to questions, he stated:

> I am in favor making far-reaching concessions, particularly in the Egyptian sector, in return for peace.

With regard to the Sinai, Rabin continued:

> I have neither an historical attachment, nor any other attachment to Sinai. For me Sinai is mainly a card for bargaining in order to achieve peace, or

in order to achieve a significant move toward peace, and it is worthwhile to yield for the sake of peace.

In the absence of peace, Sinai provides us with strategic depth and the ability to defend ourselves against the largest and strongest of the Arab states.

When asked if this included all of Sinai and the Golan Heights, Rabin stated:

I do not want to enter into details, and I do not want to draw maps. As for the Golan Heights, my view is that even in return for peace, the State of Israel cannot, from a security point of view come down from the Golan Heights.

Finally, with regard to the West Bank territories, Rabin has pledged his government to national elections before any concessions are made:

With regard to Judea and Samaria, there is a government commitment that if we arrive at a situation in which peace will be achieved and in which concessions over parts of Judea and Samaria will be required, elections will be held.

In terms of Israeli security on the West Bank, Rabin concluded:

I am in favor of suitable arrangements, with the Jordan River being the security border of Israel—arrangements that do not necessarily involve territorial changes, or territorial changes that do not affect the security of Israel and allow freedom of access and perhaps also freedom of settlement.

I think that basically, the borders—the peace borders—will be determined also as a result of population problems, but most of all as a result of Israel's overall ability to face the Arab states, the world, and the United States. At the time of decision-making, I do not believe that anyone other than we, for whom this thing has a value, is impressed by the fact that 300 Jews are settling in a certain place close to a place with a quarter of a million Arabs.[78]

With the exception of such extremist groups as the Land of Israel movement, both the left and right in Israel now support the basic concept of an ultimate return to the borders of June 4, 1967, with some border adjustments—as former Foreign Minister Abba Eban has put it—dictated by "considerations of security and topography."[79] The extent to which such adjustments will impede an overall settlement is as yet unclear, but it is highly unlikely that any foreseeable Israeli government would agree to a complete territorial compromise, even under full settlement conditions.

Shifts in Postwar Policy Objectives

The October War marked the first time since 1948 that Israel had come under direct attack by Arab armies, and resulted in the first major loss of public support for an Israeli government in a wartime situation. While charges and countercharges continue to be traded among the various political and military factions, it is possible to identify shifts in the basic perceptions and policy objectives of many of the key interest groups within Israel.

Criticism of the military prior to and during the October War came from within the IDF as well as the public, and has produced an ongoing reassessment of defense policy in light of that experience. At the same time, the Israeli government conducted an official inquiry into IDF conduct, placing primary blame for any errors on Chief of Staff Elazar and Military Intelligence Chief Zeira.[80]

For the first time in recent history, the military leadership split over a number of issues related to the conduct of a war, including the distribution and analysis of intelligence, failure of the chief of staff to press the prime minister to undertake interceptive warfare, failure of the General Staff to commit strategic reserves in Sinai when required, failures of the General Staff to exploit the advance across the Suez Canal to the fullest extent possible, and failure to resist the imposition of a cease-fire under threat of a Soviet ultimatum. The net effect of these charges and countercharges was to produce a sharp rift in the military leadership that has subsided since 1974.

On one side of the conflict was the General Staff, including Chief of Staff Elazar, and on the other side was Gen. Ariel Sharon, supported by a number of less senior officers as well as the *Likud* and NRP political parties. Sharon was able to spark a thorough review of most aspects of military operations and policy. With the departure of General Sharon, Chief of Staff Elazar, and IDF Intelligence Chief Zeira from active duty, the IDF was able to restore a unified policy on basic defense and settlement questions. Although it is still too early to define the precise nature and limits of changes in IDF policy, we can draw some preliminary conclusions.

First, the perceived failure of the IDF to achieve a complete and decisive victory in the October War has led to a policy calling for interceptive warfare in anticipation of any Arab attack. While this is qualitatively the same policy advocated by the IDF in 1967 and 1973, it seems likely that the military will press the political leadership to the greatest extent possible should a similar situation arise again. In short, the military is committed to preventing another disaster.

Second, particularly in light of the October War experience and the revised perceptions of Arab fighting abilities and armaments, the IDF has increased its pressure on the political leadership to obtain a larger supply of more sophisticated weapons systems from the United States. In view of the

American commitment to Israel, a fact previously held in some doubt, the IDF has sought an upgrading of its capabilities in almost all areas, with particular emphasis on the following:

American fighter/bomber aircraft (F-4, A-4, and F-15), along with advanced electronic counter-measures (ECM) and electronic counter-counter-measures (ECCM) equipment;

supply of sophisticated air-to-ground (ATG) ordinance, including electro-optical and laser-guided systems;

transfer of advanced weapons systems technology with the United States under the existing exchange agreement, so Israel would have the capability to construct effective ECM equipment domestically;

increased stocks of antitank systems;

increased supplies of armored personnel carriers.

As evidenced in the IDF approval of the Sinai I and Sinai II accords, the military leadership accepts the concept of continued territorial concessions to Egypt within the process of incremental settlement. Here the IDF places an increasing degree of importance on demilitarization of territories and sophisticated early-warning systems, and less emphasis on the traditional demand for territorial buffers.

On the Syrian front, pressure to maintain strategic control of the Golan Heights and key tactical positions on Mt. Hermon continues. The lack of room for maneuver between Israeli settlements in the Galilee and the Heights has made retention of this land a key goal of IDF strategy. The IDF position does not, however, preclude some alternative security arrangement with respect to the Golan Heights.

Finally, the IDF strongly opposes reintroduction of a major Arab force capability on the critical West Bank.[81] If it is possible to restore Arab (or Palestinian) sovereignty over this area with sufficient guarantees that major weapons systems be kept out, such a policy could be acceptable to the IDF.

In the final analysis, virtually all aspects of Israeli foreign-policy making reduce to political considerations, based on the perceptions of security held by the wide range of personalities and interest groups within the state. Increasingly, it is the difficulty of integrating these competing interests and often divergent views in the policy-making process that causes the problems encountered in formulating an effective Israeli foreign policy and in settlement negotiations with the Arab states.

In many respects Israel's problems in reaching a solution to the Arab-Israeli conflict and an overall settlement accord with the Arab states lie within the internal policy-making process and its inability to provide decisive leadership behind which the nation can unite. To the extent that Israel's leaders can provide a foreign and security policy having broad national support from the existing process and interest group structure, Israel will be better able to meet the challenge of resolving regional conflicts, superpower relations, and its own internal problems.

NOTES

1. See Don Peretz, "The War Elections and Israel's Eighth Knesset," *Middle East Journal* 28 (Spring 1974): 111–25.

2. See Michael Brecher, *The Foreign Policy System of Israel: Setting, Images, Processes* (New Haven: Yale University Press, 1972).

3. See Abraham R. Wagner, *Crisis Decision-Making: Israel's Experience in 1967 and 1973* (New York: Praeger, 1974).

4. See Brecher, *The Foreign Policy System* and Wagner, *Crisis Decision-Making,* for extensive compilations of the literature in this area.

5. Menachem Begin, interview with A. R. Wagner, Tel Aviv, February 1974.

6. See Aaron Antonovsky and Alan Arian, *Hopes and Fears of Israelis: Consensus in a New Society* (Jerusalem: Jerusalem Academic Press, 1972).

7. Abraham R. Wagner, *Israel's Perceptions of American Security Policy,* AAC-4601/76 (Beverly Hills, Calif.: Analytical Assessments Corp., 1976).

8. See, for example, "Israel's Oriental Immigrants and Oriental Druzes," *Minority Rights Group Report No. 12* (London: 1973).

9. Ibid., p. 14.

10. See, for example, Amos Perlmutter, *The Military and Politics in Israel* (London: Cass, 1969).

11. With the exception of several months in 1974.

12. See, for example, Perlmutter, *The Military,* and Nadav Safran, *From War to War: The Arab-Israeli Confrontation 1948–1967 (New York: Pegasus, 1969).*

13. Dr. Harkabi was then in charge of strategic studies in the Ministry of Defense, and is former director of military intelligence. He presently serves as a key adviser to Minister of Defense Shimon Peres and Prime Minister Rabin.

14. For a detailed analysis of these "failings," see Wagner, *Crisis Decision-Making,* and Yeshoyahu Ben-Porat et al., *Ha-Michdal* ("The Omission") (Tel Aviv: Special Edition Publishers, 1973), translated as *Kippur* (Tel Aviv: Special Edition Publishers, 1974).

15. See Shimon Peres, *David's Sling* (London: Weidenfeld and Nicholson, 1970).

16. A detailed analysis of the decision process is found in Wagner, *Crisis Decision-Making.*

17. Brecher, *The Foreign Policy System,* p. 136.

18. An exception may be the Ministry of Transport, which is involved in military logistics. Because of the issue's importance, almost all civil servants in Israel would like to believe that their position is somehow central to the security of the state, and that they are in a position of influence. Interestingly, those closest to actual power are the first to recognize their limitations.

19. A good example here is (Res.) Gen. Chaim Bar-Lev, minister of commerce and industry, who is former chief of staff and a close personal associate of many in the political and military leadership.

20. Namely, the director-general, assistant directors-general, advisers, and relevant department directors, in addition to others invited at the pleasure of the minister on an ad hoc basis.

21. Yigal Allon, "Israel: The Case for Defensible Borders," *Foreign Affairs* 55, no. 1 (October 1976): 38–53.

22. Arms sales from the United States were secured on a limited basis in 1962 from President Kennedy, and on a major scale beginning in 1969 under President Nixon. See Shimon Peres, *David's Sling.*

23. This disdain for the United Nations is shared by Ben-Gurion's younger protégé Shimon Peres, who has toned down his public statements regarding the United Nations since assuming the post of defense minister in 1974.

24. Michael Bar-Zohar, *Ben-Gurion: The Armed Prophet* (Englewood Cliffs, N.J.: Prentice-Hall, 1968), p. 235.

25. See American Jewish Committee, *In Vigilant Brotherhood* (New York: the Committee, 1965).

26. See Yigal Allon, "The Making of Israel's Army: The Development of Military Conceptions of Liberation and Defense," in Michael Howard, ed., *The Theory and Practice of War* (London: Cassell, 1965), pp. 335–71; and Yigal Allon, "Active Defense—Guarantee for Our Existence," *Molad* (Tel Aviv) 212 (July/August 1967): 335–71 (in Hebrew).

27. See Allon, "Active Defense."

28. Central to the discussion here is the ongoing debate in Israel over the politicization of the IDF. The basic charge is that the IDF, which is supposed to be apolitical, has tended to promote Mapai officers and that Likud generals such as Ariel Sharon were passed over for chief of staff in favor of less-qualified Mapai men.

29. The appeal of this novel concept of "fluid" borders seems to be more rhetorical than practical.

30. Instructive here are the private reports of Mr. Nixon's meeting with this group during his 1968 visit to Israel as a private citizen.

31. As in the British system, Cabinet members are generally (although not necessarily, in Israel) Knesset members, and are supposed to respond to questions posed to them in debate. In practical terms, all questions in the security area asked recently have been "referred to committee," effectively terminating any open Knesset discussion.

32. Brecher, *The Foreign Policy System,* p. 427.

33. See Wagner, *Crisis Decision-Making,* and Peretz, "The War Elections."

34. A number of academics, including Emanuel Gutmann, have been active in the Mapai Central Committee. See Emanuel Guttman, "Some Observations on Politics and Parties in Israel," *India Quarterly* 17, no. 1 (January/March 1961): 3–29.

35. See Jerusalem *Post,* April 14, 1970.

36. See Wagner, *Crisis Decision-Making.*

37. Brecher, *The Foreign Policy System,* p. 136.

38. See Col. Merrill A. McPeak, "Israel: Borders and Security," *Foreign Affairs* 54, no. 3 (April 1976): 426–43.

39. See, for example, interview with Y. Cuau, *Le Figaro,* January 9, 1975 (in French).

40. See Harold H. Saunders, "Statement Before the Special Subcommittee on Investigations of the House Committee on International Relations," November 12, 1975.

41. Shimon Peres, interview in *Die Welt* (Bonn), January 25, 1975, p. 2, reprinted (in English) in Jerusalem *Post,* January 26, 1975, p. 1.

42. Interview in *Newsweek,* January 14, 1975, pp. 30–31.

43. See Richard H. Ullman, "After Rabat: Middle East Risks and American Roles," *Foreign Affairs* 53, no. 2 (January 1975): 284–96.

44. See McPeak, "Israel."

45. Quoted in Jerusalem *Post,* January 16, 1975, p. 1.

46. Settlement terms have been a major political issue in Israel at least since the Six-Day War, and were a major topic in the 1973 Knesset elections, even prior to the outbreak of the October War. For a review of the various party platforms, see Peretz, "The War Elections."

47. See Shimon Peres, "Minister Peres Discusses Breakdown in Talks," *Ma'ariv,* April 15, 1975, p. 13 (in Hebrew).

48. Throughout the settlement process, Israel has insisted on linking political goals to geographic and military considerations.

49. Shimon Peres, interview on "Face the Nation," CBS Television, December 14, 1975.

50. See interview of Prime Minister Rabin in *Hazofe,* May 15, 1975, pp. 3, 4 (in Hebrew). The problem of U.S. assurances in the 1967 crisis, which is valid in Israeli thinking, has been further explained in a recent article by (then) Assistant Secretary of State Lucius D. Battle:

> The United States had a commitment, of sorts, to the Israelis with respect to the Straits of Tiran. We had assured Israel that we would continue to consider it an international waterway, use it, and encourage others to do so. In 1967, we were, however, unable to find the record of the meetings and the discussions of the 1956 period. Therefore, the obligations that Mr. Dulles undertook at the earlier time were unclear and unknown. The Israeli records of the period were readily available, full, and proved accurate. American records were, for economic reasons, stored in the Middle West—Cleveland, I believe—and were therefore not available when we needed them.... Despite their vagueness, United States assurances at the time had been accepted by the Israelis as the basis for withdrawal (under intense American pressure) from the conquered territory of the war of 1956. These assurances were weak reeds and meaningless in the face of crisis (*Foreign Policy,* no. 18 [Spring 1974]: 116–17).

This continuity and need for a guarantee from a "stable" power are evident in a concern voiced by Israeli Foreign Minister Allon. See Jerusalem *Post,* April 15, 1975, pp. 5, 7.

51. See Brecher, *The Foreign Policy System.*

52. See Peres, *David's Sling.*

53. Quoted in the Jerusalem *Post,* January 19, 1975, p. 3.

54. See note 41.

55. The statement attributed to Mrs. Meir, in response to Chief of Staff Elazar's request for a preemptive strike, has been reported as follows:

> This time it has to be crystal clear who began, so we won't have to go around the world convincing people that our cause is just (Terrence Smith, "Israeli Errors on Eve of War Emerging," New York *Times,* December 10, 1973, pp. 1, 18).

56. Interview with Terrence Smith, New York *Times,* January 8, 1975, pp. 1, 5.

57. Quoted in Jerusalem *Post,* January 15, 1975, p. 2.

58. Shabtai Rosenne, "Basic Elements of Israel's Foreign Policy," *India Quarterly* 12, no. 4 (October/December 1961): 335.

59. Sara Honig, "Peres: Soviets Still Giving Egypt Weapons." Jerusalem *Post,* January 22, 1975, p. 1.

60. See A. Rabinovich, "Dr. Goldmann: Chances now for Full Peace with the Arabs," Jerusalem *Post,* January 25, 1975, p. 1.

61. Rosenne, "Basic Elements," pp. 356–57; United Nations, General Assembly Resolution 273 (III) of May 11, 1949; resolutions of October 19, November 4, and November 16, 1948; and documents S/1044, S/1070, S/1080, and Resolution 194 (III) of December 11, 1948.

62. See, for example, David Ben-Gurion, "Israel's Position Before and After the (1956) Sinai Campaign," *Israel Government Yearbook, 5720* (Jerusalem: Government Printing Office, 1960), pp. 9–87.

63. Moshe Dayan, "Israel's Border and Security Problems," *Foreign Affairs* 33, no. 2 (January 1955): 250.

64. Jerusalem *Post,* January 15, 1975, p. 8.

65. Interview with G. Lev-Ari, broadcast on Israeli radio January 18, 1975. Reported in FBIS, January 18, 1975, pp. N1–N2.

66. Jerusalem *Post,* January 10, 1975, p. 2.

67. Interview with Terrence Smith, New York *Times,* February 15, 1975, pp. 1, 3.

68. Allon, "Israel: The Case for Defensible Borders."

69. See Peretz, "The War Elections."

70. "The Worst Government," *Israel Economist* 30, no. 5 (May 1974): 84.

71. Allon, "Israel: The Case for Defensible Borders."

72. See Peretz, "The War Elections."

73. Interview with A. R. Wagner, Tel Aviv, February 1974.

74. For Israel, this was one of the truly significant "lessons" of the October War.

75. Even so, Israel continues to depend on the United States for the supply of critical components, such as the General Electric J-79 engines for its new Kafir fighter/bomber. See Herbert J. Coleman "Israel Aircraft Develops New Capabilities," *Aviation Week and Space Technology,* March 31, 1975, pp. 14–18.

76. *Ha'aretz,* January 13, 1975, p. 8 (in Hebrew).

77. In an unusual show of unity in the "map" vs. "no map" debate, both the leftist Mapam and right-wing Likud bloc have urged the government to propose a map of minimal final borders prior to further negotiations.

78. Interview in *Hazofe,* May 15, 1975, pp. 3–4 (in Hebrew). Reported in FBIS, May 16, 1975, p. N1.

79. Abba Eban, "The Failure of Negotiations: What Next?" *Ha'aretz,* March 28, 1975 (in Hebrew), pp. 14, 20. Reported in FBIS, March 31, 1975, pp. N2–N6. Eban has recently referred to such areas for border adjustments as "neuralgic spots," and gives as one example the Latrun salient.

80. See the report of the Agranat Commission, summarized in New York *Times,* April 4, 1974, p. 12. For full text of the public summary, see "Press Release Issued by the Commission of Inquiry: Yom Kippur War Upon Submission of Its Third and Final Report to the Government and the Defense and Foreign Affairs Committee of the Knesset on 30 January 1975," Israel Government Press Office, January 30, 1975.

81. See Dayan, "Israel's Border and Security Problems," pp. 250–67.

6

SYRIAN FOREIGN POLICY

SYRIAN POLICY ENVIRONMENT

Background

Syria is a political term given to a geographical entity. The reality is that this name, which today unites Syrians to some degree, covers a bewildering array of opposing forces and ideas. Syria is characterized by heterogeneity and the schisms to which it has given rise—schisms based on political philosophy and support, on sectional rivalries, on economic philosophy, on economic group, on religion, on the urban-rural dichotomy, and on ethnic background, to name only the most important. Although individual scholars have searched for a unifying theme to explain the differences that rend Syrian society,[1] we believe this unnecessary for our purposes. It suffices to understand that Syria in its present form is a result of (European) colonial boundary making.

In 1946, Syria was scarcely more than a name. The French mandate over Syria and Lebanon was characterized by a determination to fractionate these territories, to maintain French control by encouraging the extant social divisions.[2] Not until the 1950s did a feeling of Syrianism develop, and only during the 1958–61 union with Egypt did the feeling take hold. Since the advent of the Ba'ath regime in 1963, however, rapid progress has been made in the establishment of a Syrian personality.[3]

Syria was composed of nine agro-cities (Aleppo, Dair as Zor, Damascus, Deraa, Hama, Homs, Kuneitrah, Latakia, and Suwayda) that still form the basis of Syrian regionalism. Syrian "political" thought has until recently emphasized Arab nationalism or subnational loyalties rather than (and therefore to a large extent at the expense of) Syrian nationalism. Political groupings before 1970 sought a personal, regional, or class following instead of a broad national one.[4]

The absence of a body of political belief or behavior that might be called "national" and the unavailability of jobs meant that politics took place on two levels—among the powerful families who constituted the traditional political system and among the powerless group of politically interested individuals of middle-class and peasant origins. The political training ground of the latter was the government high school. The career destinations of the products of this training were teaching and the military.[5]

We shall not discuss the stormy political history of postwar Syria before 1966 in any detail, for that has been done elsewhere.[6] It is a story of coup after coup. For the most part the resulting regimes enjoyed no significant popular constituency. As a result, even though much of the energy of the adult male population has been devoted to political thought,

> this energy has typically been employed to oppose whatever government is in power at the time and to criticize other political forces and even other members of one's own political group. . . . [M]ost politically aware individuals have had limited means of expressing opinion. Often frustrated, they have sought the most direct means available: strikes and demonstrations, personal contacts with influential politicians and, at times, removal of an offending individual through assassination.[7]

Despite revolutionary rhetoric, until 1963 none of the military regimes that succeeded either each other or one of the intermittent civilian administrations ever undertook a true revolution or even major social change.[8] Even after 1963, a concerted and broad-based movement toward social change had to await the advent of the neo-Ba'ath in 1966.

The Ba'ath party was founded in Syria and recruited members among ex-peasant, lower-middle class groups. Important elements of Ba'athism included pan-Arabism and secularism (although the special place of Islam as a cultural influence in Arabism was recognized), the latter being particularly attractive to religious minorities such as the Alawis. Indeed, when the Ba'ath began serious recruiting in 1947, one of the first cells was established in the Alawi-populated Latakia region. Both the Ba'ath and the Syrian Social Nationalist party, particularly the latter, were highly successful in recruiting the socially mobilized and downtrodden Alawis.[9]

Soon after the union of Egypt and Syria in 1958, Gamal Abdel Nasser disbanded the Ba'ath party in Syria. In fact, however, the party simply went underground in the Latakia region. In another action to subordinate Syria and preempt any military threat to the union, a number of officers were transferred to Egypt or dismissed from military service. In 1959, several of those officers in Egypt founded a secret Ba'athist military committee. The leadership of this committee consisted of three Alawis and two Ismailis (another Islamic minority group). The leaders included Salah Jadid, Hafez Assad, and Abd al-Karim al-Jundi, all of whom were to become major figures. After the secession of Syria from the United Arab Republic in 1961, many military officers with political ties, including much of the membership of the still-secret military committee, were separated from the army. Meanwhile, the Syrian Ba'athists who had remained organized surfaced as Qutriyin ("regionalists," that is, separatists)[10] after the Ba'ath Fifth National Congress (1962) and established a distinct Ba'ath organization. Neither the Qutriyin Ba'ath nor the old-time Ba'ath (now essentially an Iraqi creature) considered the other to be legal.[11]

On March 8, 1963, a military coup toppled the Syrian civilian government. The Ba'ath party played no real role; indeed, within the military there were very few Ba'athists just before and during the coup. Once the operation was completed, however, Ba'athists were well represented: through careful pre-coup placement of individuals in personnel jobs, Ba'athist officers were called back and put in crucial positions throughout the army. The Ba'athists dominated the army by virtue of their effective organization (based on the military committee founded in 1959) and sectarian loyalties. As a result of the unity of the Ba'athist military participants and followers (contrasted with the disunity of the other groups that took part in the coup), the Ba'ath gained control of the new regime, holding half the Cabinet posts.

There were still two distinct Ba'ath parties, however, and the civilian Ba'athists were unaware of the existence of the secret military committee. Through a variety of maneuvers,[12] the military group infiltrated the civilian organizations while its own committee remained secret. The years following the "Ba'ath" coup of March 1963 and leading up to the seizure of power by Salah Jadid were marked by the consolidation of the position of the secret military committee, which eliminated one group of rivals after another, and by the division of the army along sectarian lines. The latter development was unintentionally hastened by Amin al-Hafez, the Syrian strongman, and directly benefited Salah Jadid, for the minorities (Alawis, Druze, Ismailis) tended to consolidate while the Sunnis did not. During these years, the Ba'ath also witnessed a growing schism between the National Command under Michel Aflaq and Salah Bitar and the Regional Command, which was dominated by the military Ba'athists.

The Syrian army has had a tradition of overrepresentation of the ethnic minorities. There are several reasons for this. First, the French consistently recruited military personnel from the minorities in order to prevent Syrian unity. Second, the Sunnis did not cooperate with the French, refusing to enlist. Third, the rural minorities could not afford the fee required for exemption from military service. Fourth, a military career offered one of the few avenues for social advancement. Fifth, Alawis used the military academy as a means to further their education. Sixth, military life was more attractive to rural villagers than to urban members of the ethnic majority. Seventh, Alawis and Druze recruited among and promoted their friends and relatives. Eighth, the succession of coups in Syria led to the dismissal of many Sunni officers. The result of all these factors was that by December 1965—on the eve of the neo-Ba'ath coup—Alawi and Druze officers were in charge of 70–75 percent of all army units[13] and Sunnis only 25–30 percent. Since Sunnis constitute the vast majority of the population, this pattern of power is remarkable.[14]

Thus, with the army (and the secret Ba'ath military committee) and the Ba'ath Regional Command behind him, Salah Jadid led a coup on February 23, 1966 that removed Amin al-Hafez from the government and party, and the Aflaq-Bitar-led National Command from party leadership.[15] The new Syrian leadership preached a radical doctrine. The novelty was that a serious effort was made to implement the program.

Ba'ath doctrine, radicalized after the Sixth Ba'ath National Congress (1963) as a part of the political process[16] and as a function of minority discontent with the Syrian social status quo, gave rise to more rapid and extensive land reform, nationalization, socialism, and secularism. All economic support was directed to the public sector. The favoritism shown rural districts and the minorities, especially the Alawis, was flagrant under the new regime.

The first challenge to Jadid's authority was an abortive coup, led by Salim Hatum, that probably was based on ethnic grounds. (Hatum was Druze. After the neo-Ba'ath take-over in 1966, the Alawis began consolidating their position and eliminating the other minorities that had been allies.) Although the Hatum coup was foiled, intraparty conflicts began to arise in late 1966. By then, Jadid apparently had recognized Hafez Assad as his major potential rival. Assad's position in the military had been crucial to the success of the Jadid coup.

As the conflict between Jadid and Assad grew more apparent, anti-government (in fact, anti-Alawi) demonstrations erupted and the June War began. These episodes may be seen as interludes in the Jadid-Assad confrontation that lasted for four years (1966–70). It is probable that Assad would have initiated a coup sooner or later. His power was increasing,[17] and power lay with the military. Jadid, in order to overcome this fact, tried to establish new forces in Syria. Setting up and arming Sa'iqa and looking to the militia for additional support, Jadid governed through the party and tried to reduce the military's role in Syria. (Indeed, Jadid maintained control from a relatively obscure position in the Ba'ath, preferring low visibility because of the Alawi-Sunni division.)

In 1967, Jadid sought to blame Assad's military for Syria's poor showing in the June War. Although public opinion placed blame on both the party and the armed forces, the latter was subject to particularly scathing attacks from both ends of the political spectrum. However, in 1968 the militia's arms were withdrawn, and in 1969 the security forces were taken over by the Ministry of Defense. Increasingly, Jadid's supporters in the military were removed or changed their allegiance. By 1968, Assad's ascendancy to power was relatively clear. In 1969, he staged a semi-coup that was inconclusive but continued the trend of improving his position vis-à-vis that of Jadid. Assad, a frequent critic of the Soviet role in Syria—and more specifically of Jadid's agreements with Moscow—continued to move against possible opposition groups while trying to smooth his relations with the Soviet Union.[18] Finally, in September 1970, Jadid and others in the party hierarchy decided to send Syrian tanks to participate in the Jordanian civil war. Hafez Assad and some others in the military hierarchy strongly opposed the commitment; and Assad, commander of the air force, refused to send in support for the Syrian armor, on the ground that greater Syrian participation in the Palestinian-Jordanian conflict would result in Israeli, or perhaps American, involvement. The outcome of the Syrian "invasion" was not in doubt, since the tanks had no protection against Hussein's air strikes. Yet the final outcome was even more significant for Syria—the replacement of Jadid by Assad.

Since March 1969, Syria had been on the verge of civil war, the conflict between the two former military allies, Jadid and Assad, having become open. In the end, the fact that Assad controlled the only armed force in the country proved decisive.[19] Although the Ba'ath party voted to remove Assad and several of his supporters from their positions, the coup that followed that decision resulted in Assad's assumption of unquestioned political supremacy. Jadid and many of his allies were replaced in mid-November 1970.

Despite a number of attempted coups and frequent rumors of unrest within various sectors of the population (the military, Alawis, Sunnis, Damascenes, Ba'ath cadres), Hafez Assad's regime seems to have brought Syria its greatest political stability in many years. This is all the more remarkable when it is recalled that the entire Assad tenure has been accompanied by Israeli occupation of the Golan Heights, and that since 1970 Syria has experienced one major Middle East war, rapidly shifting regional alignments, and open cooperation in military operations against Palestinian forces in Lebanon.

Structure of the Government

The Syrian constitution, revised in 1973, has remained fundamentally unchanged for many years (see Figure 6). The newest revision provides for a very strong executive (with substantial legislative powers as well) directly elected by the populace. The president, however, is nominated by the People's Assembly on recommendation of the Ba'ath Regional Command. Although the judicial system is nominally independent of the executive, the president appoints members of the Supreme (or Higher Constitutional) Court, as well as of the Higher Judicial Council, whose responsibility is to ensure this inde-

FIGURE 6

Structure of the Syrian Government

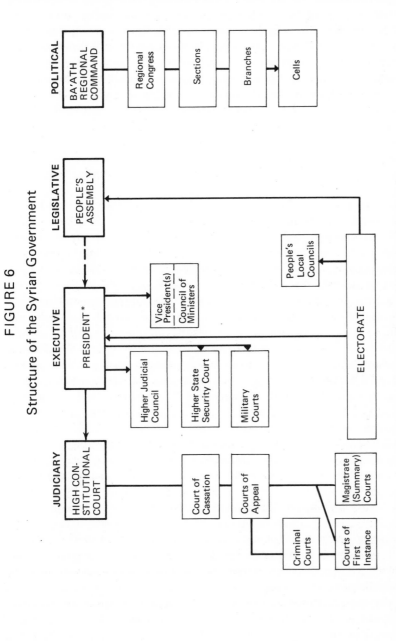

*President nominated by People's Assembly on recommendation of the Ba'ath Regional Command.
Source: Compiled by the authors.

227

pendence. Moreover, the constitution provides for military courts, which have played an important role in Syria by circumventing the civil and criminal court systems.

The arenas in which Syrian politics takes place have changed under the Assad regime. The People's Assembly serves as a national legislature and is directly elected. This body and the local councils effect most of the legislation. The president, however, has important legislative functions, principally between sessions of the People's Assembly but also "in cases of absolute need."[20] Moreover, he can "submit important matters concerning higher national interests" to a popular referendum.[21]

Operation of the Syrian Political System

The Ba'ath party's formal role in governance is indirect but multifaceted: "The vanguard party in the society and state is the Ba'ath Arab Socialist party." To the party falls the responsibility for direction of the National Progressive Front.[22] In addition, the Ba'ath Regional Command proposes one or more presidential nominees to the People's Assembly, which in turn nominates a presidential candidate.[23]

Yet the primary mission of the Ba'ath in the national leadership is more visible at the local level, where its two main functions are penetration and mobilization. Thus, the Ba'ath must ensure communication of local views upward to the national leadership and of national programs and concepts downward from the leadership to the masses. Despite many problems and the shortage of resources necessary to fully implement this model, the Ba'ath party system in Syria adheres rather closely to it.[24] The party extends down to the smallest villages, and its membership has expanded to approximately 100,000.[25]

"The party was afflicted by a leadership with a domineering and maneuvering mentality which used terrorist, twisted methods in no way connected with Ba'th Party ethics; they created suspicion, hatred, and isolation everywhere, and led the party and the country to the brink of an abyss."[26] Thus Hafez Assad described the situation in Syria before his coup. Discounting the propaganda content of his description, there is ample evidence to suggest both that the Syrian populace resented Jadid's controls and that Assad placed a very high priority upon reversing the trend toward ever stricter government control.[27] That he has succeeded in relaxing controls is clear. Assad has been able to maintain order with infrequent (but determined, when used) resort to force and with tight control over communications and intelligence apparatuses.

Symbolic of Assad's approach to governing was his promulgation of provisions leading to direct election of the president. In turn, the Syrian electorate gave Assad a strong vote of confidence in the March 1971 presidential election, when 99 percent of the votes affirmed his nomination and elected him to a seven-year term.[28] After selection by the Ba'ath party and the People's Assembly, election may appear superfluous, yet the principle is crucial: popular election allows the president to maintain a position above the party, the army, the Alawis, or other groups within society.[29]

Similarly, Assad early moved toward the creation of more democratic participation in the Syrian government. Three months after his accession to power, he announced formation of the People's Assembly. Although initially appointed, later People's Assemblies were to be, and have been, elected. Perhaps as important as its election was the composition of the Assembly. In the first (appointed) Assembly, Ba'athists barely outnumbered the sum of other groups represented, which included, besides Syrian Communists and Nasserites, members of traditionally anti-Ba'ath groups.

From May 1971 until the spring of 1972, negotiations over the terms of the National Progressive Front (NPF)—a bloc of parties and popular groups —took place. The NPF institutionalizes non-Ba'ath popular representation in the government and can be viewed as another indication of Assad's determination to broaden the power base (support) of Syrian government. Assad has stated that national unity is the key to Syrian progress. Whether his concern is directed toward national stability or his own regime's stability, he clearly has set out to bring about a greater degree of participation in, identification with, and national unity behind the Syrian government.[30] The NPF includes the Syrian Ba'ath, the Syrian Communist party, the Arab Socialist Union (a Nasserite group), the Socialist Union, and the Arab Socialist party. This is also essentially the makeup of the People's Assembly elected in 1973, with 140 of the 186 seats having been won by NPF parties, 42 by independents, and four by opposition candidates.[31] Similarly, the Syrian Cabinet generally has been composed of 50 percent non-Ba'athists since 1972. Since 1973, both Syrian Communist party factions have been represented, as have the Arab Socialist Union, the Socialist Union, and the Arab Socialist party. Also like the Assembly, the Cabinet has a number of independents.[32] The diverse makeup of the Assembly, the NPF, and the Cabinet can be seen as an effort to broaden Assad's power base.

At the local level, too, the new regime has taken a more relaxed attitude, allowing opponents of the regime to run for election. For example, in 1972, Muslim Brotherhood candidates soundly defeated those of the NPF in Homs,[33] a city of conservative, strong anti-Ba'ath feeling.[34]

The foregoing should not be taken as a suggestion that Assad has less control of Syria than did Jadid or others, nor that the Ba'ath and the military have relinquished their dominance. Assad makes the important decisions in Syria today, but he is careful to see that "key members of the party and army elite" are present at critical points in the decision process.[35] Decisions, once reached, receive unanimous or nearly unanimous backing in the People's

Assembly, the NPF, Ba'ath Party Congress, the media, and elsewhere. The decision-making process might be called participatory consensus—that is, a process by which all parties agree at the outset to support the final decision, in return for which the views of each party will be taken into account by the policy makers. That the participants do not necessarily receive any accommodation or compromise on individual issues distinguishes this process from that of consensus in its more widely accepted form. The benefits of participation are significant—the opportunity to function as a political party at the national level, to recruit, to campaign;[36] the chance to advance views on major issues with the knowledge that these positions, constituting the feeling of an important and representative group, will be seriously considered by the regime; and the possibility of shaping opinions through communication "down" and in the media. The regime also derives benefits of capital significance: more broad-based support, the consequently increased legitimacy, an opportunity to hear a variety of positions (and to deal with public opinion) on crucial issues, greater credibility in domestic communications, and a larger resource base in the communications effort.[37] To some extent, the operations of overt and legal parties are both easier and more difficult to monitor than are those of proscribed groups.

Although policy levels of the Syrian government have been particularly affected by the country's succession of coups and political purges over the years, most of the civil service has provided some continuity. Indeed, before the 1963 coup that led to Ba'ath rule, "the civil service remained generally outside of politics, and appointments were usually based upon professional background, including education and the results of written examinations. . . . [C]ivil service rolls showed little evidence of prejudice against religious or ethnic minorities. . . ."[38] However, after the 1963 coup, the increased emigration of trained personnel adversely affected the civil service. In addition, the new regime and those that followed it politicized civil service recruitment. This was particularly true at higher levels of the bureaucracy. Thus, while the structure of the civil service has been stable, the staffing has not, thus lessening bureaucratic effectiveness. Moreover, the Syrian civil service is hampered by problems facing its counterparts in other developing countries: a shortage of trained personnel, unwillingness to accept or delegate responsibility effectively, and lack of coordination between various parts of the bureaucracy.[39]

As in any regime originating as Assad's did, the difficulty of integrating career civil service and political appointee efforts is considerable. This generic problem has both diminished and increased over time. It has diminished insofar as standard operating procedures and routines of interaction have been established to facilitate the implementation of policy. The relative stability Assad has brought to Syria has meant less extensive and frequent personnel turnover. As in any large organization, individuals tend to look for and work with and through those who have been effective in other interactions. Time aids this selection process. Individual and organizational learning and change over time have produced results.

Several factors are operating to produce less integration of policy levels and career civil service actions. First, despite unwonted regime stability, the presence of Alawis in key decision-making roles has increased. Second, Assad has consistently been concerned to see that no one builds bridges to key constituencies of such strength as to threaten his regime. Third, the administrative requirements of his position atop three bureaucracies (government, party, military), of the determination to shoulder important policy decisions, and of the unwillingness of others to do so have slowly isolated Assad. Time and other constraints limit his extensive contact to other key figures in the regime—Abdel Halim Khaddam (foreign minister), Naji Jamil (air force commander), Mustapha Tlas (defense minister), Adnan Dabbagh, and, of course, the most important individual in the regime after Hafez Assad, his brother Rifaat. Given Assad's determination to isolate potential rivals, his estrangement is reinforced.[40] Finally and paradoxically, the stability of the regime acts as a further hurdle to integration by virtue of the socialization of sectoral organization chiefs to the parochial outlooks and approaches of the groups they manage.[41]

OPERATION OF THE SYRIAN POLITICAL SYSTEM: INTEREST GROUPS

Syria, like other countries, has a number of constituencies whose attitudes decision makers ignore at their peril. Although in Western-style democracies we require that groups of people be organized in order for us to consider them as interest groups,[42] this requirement is unrealistic in countries where such organization is proscribed. It would, however, be quite incorrect to conclude that Syrian groups, because some are not organized, are of no consequence in decision-making councils. Indeed, it is precisely the diversity of constituencies —we shall call them interest groups—to which communications are directed and for which specific policies are chosen that confounds outside attempts to explicate those communications and policies.

In Syria, interest groups must be visualized in proper perspective. The complex of issues and cross-cutting interests precludes the facile assumption that because two individuals may subscribe to differing views in one issue area, they will of necessity oppose each other. No single issue has a salience level so high as to dominate all others.[43] Alliances are extremely fluid: groups coalesce and disperse in different patterns, depending upon the issue. Put another way, groups have overlapping membership; few individuals are allied —or opposed—across all issue areas.

We shall consider four types of interest groups: political, military, socio-economic, and nonstate national.

Political Interest Groups

Political interest groups are of two types, ideological and partisan. In fact, of course, the two overlap considerably. Ideological Communists tend to belong to one or another faction of the Syrian Communist party. Ideological dissent is not the stuff of which political opposition is made in Syria, except in terms of intraparty politics. Thus, this analysis will focus on ideology within the context of partisan politics.

The Ba'ath Party

The Ba'ath party is the umbrella of unity under which continual disagreements take place. It is a party riven by personality, ideological, ethnic, associational, and other schisms—yet determined to stay in power. As we have already seen, the Ba'ath party is less the essence of the regime than is Assad himself. Similarly, rivalries within the Ba'ath often concern personalities. The names most frequently mentioned are Salah Jadid, Mustapha Tlas, Naji Jamil, and Rifaat Assad. Jadid is still considered a threat to Assad's leadership by some, though he remains in jail. He symbolizes—ironically, because he, too, was a military officer, one of the original members of the secret military committee—the civilian party leadership once against military control. Rather than Salah Jadid himself, his followers (some under Iraqi influence) have posed a number of challenges to Assad. The Ba'athist cadres frequently are not as pragmatic as Assad and his immediate coterie of advisers. Mustapha Tlas has on several occasions been rumored to be at odds with Assad. There is, however, some reason to believe Assad has used popular individuals loyal to himself as rallying points for dissidents in order to maintain surveillance and control over the latter.[44]

One of the more enigmatic personalities in Syria is Rifaat Assad, Hafez's youngest brother. Rifaat has been involved in a number of conflicts with a variety of leaders, including Mustapha Tlas, Ali Salah, Ali Haidar, and, most notably, Naji Jamil and Mahmoud Ayyubi.[45] The younger Assad has a reputation for radicalism and is a focal point for leftist thinking and action in the Ba'ath Regional Command, to which he was elected in March 1975. The extent to which this reputation is a facade to enable Assad to legitimize himself as a Ba'athist is unknown, but his written defense of the regime's "corrective movement" and his friendship with Lebanese establishment figures cast doubt on revolutionary sincerity.[46] Rifaat Assad is the commander of the Defense

Companies, an elite unit of the Syrian army with regime, as well as national, defense responsibilities.[47] He has become unquestionably the second most important leader in Syria.

Yet the extent to which the Ba'ath itself may be considered an interest group has been reduced by President Assad's control. To the degree that it may still be distinguished as an interest group different from the administration, the Ba'ath—or elements of it—frequently is influenced by the Iraqi position on various issues.[48] Since many of the early Ba'ath leaders and their followers have been purged from the party, Assad has a much more disciplined and less fractionated party.

The Ba'ath party is therefore employed for communication, administration, and legitimization; its blessing is used to legitimize Assad's regime and decisions. Assad, remembering Jadid's fate, can be expected to retain control of the military, the civilian government, and the party. One of his techniques is to restrict the roles of other individuals to fewer branches of political power. This has the advantage of making it difficult for any single individual to have access to several levers of power, while preserving political havens for Assad. The result may well, however, be increased competition among the party, army, and government.

Within the Ba'ath party, and within the country as a whole, there are various ideological trends. These are never clear-cut, for Ba'athist ideology (especially in Syria) is singularly diffuse. In general, then, one can distinguish certain groupings along a radical-conservative spectrum. However, the positions of these groups are clearer with respect to concrete issues than in terms of ideology, or even ideological justification. Ba'athists have traditionally been pan-Arabists (rather than nationalists), secularists, and, more recently, social reformers. (There has been something of an inverse relationship between dedication to social reform and dedication to pan-Arabism.) Although Arabism is still a major force in Syria, Syrian nationalism has taken the fore. And since a real revolution in social thinking has already taken place under Ba'ath guidance,[49] the ideological question has been lessened to a significant degree. Nevertheless, even since Assad's accession to power, the Ba'ath has been torn between ideologically motivated Ba'athists and the more pragmatic group surrounding the new leader. Soviet support for Assad and the effectiveness of his internal Ba'ath personnel shifts have largely contained this conflict.[50]

Other Political Parties

The other political parties and groups in Syria wield much less political power than the Ba'ath—even the Assad-controlled Ba'ath—but may well represent a larger constituency. Major parties include the Arab Socialist Union, the Syrian Communist party, the Arab Socialist party, and the Socialist Union.

The Arab Socialist Union (ASU) is a Nasserite group participating in the NPF. It has perhaps the largest constituency in Syria. Jamal Atassi, head of the Syrian ASU, claims that 80 percent of the population is at least sympathetic to the group.[51] The ASU supports the creation of a single, mass political party in Syria (along the lines of the Egyptian ASU). Although it has been at odds with the Ba'ath—even dropping out of the NPF—Atassi recognizes the necessity of coexisting with the Ba'ath as one of Assad's chosen tools, particularly in view of the restrictions imposed upon the ASU and the other parties.[52] Pro-Nasser groups also continue to demonstrate a coup capability, even if the threat is much reduced.

The Socialist Union (SU) is also a Nasserite party, but is composed of ex-Ba'athists. The party traces its origins to the breakup of the Egyptian-Syrian union in 1961, when Sami Sufan bolted the Ba'ath party separatist group to create the SU. Its following is smaller than that of the ASU; but taken together, the two major Nasserite parties represent a considerable segment of political opinion in Syria.[53]

A smaller but important party is the Syrian Communist party (SCP). Led for many years by Khalid Bakdash, the party has suffered a serious schism in recent years. The difference embraces several issues, one of the most important of which is the independence of the party from Soviet policy. After a number of attempts at reconciliation were aborted, several leaders of the anti-Bakdash group, including Daniel Neemeh and Zohair Abdel Samad, rejoined the Bakdash group at the end of 1973. However, the split was formalized when the unreconciled anti-Bakdash Communists formed their own party. Some sources believe the second SCP is larger than the Moscow-oriented party. In early January 1974 the new SCP held the Fourth Congress of the Syrian Communist party, electing Riad Turk as first secretary. There has been considerable speculation that the Assad government encouraged the split; but although representatives of both factions were in the Cabinet and the People's Assembly before the formal secession of the Turk group, none of the new secessionists has been so placed. Syrian Communists are not as numerous as Nasserites; and since their traditional recruiting ground (universities and schools) has been denied them, they pose no real threat to the regime. Soviet support, direct or through the party, can, however, be helpful. Syrian Communists have supported Assad against the Tlas group; and they tried to calm near-civil war between the Assad and Jadid factions in 1969, even though Assad criticized Jadid for his concessions to Moscow.[54]

The SCP enjoyed a relatively secure and stable role in the political system under Assad, particularly after its institutionalization in the NPF. However, in late 1975 and in 1976 the SCP position deteriorated markedly. Leading Syrian Communists had been concerned for some time over the improvement of Syrian relations with Jordan, Saudi Arabia, and the United States, as well as with the increasingly prominent Western participation in the Syrian economy. Party meetings and publications openly criticized the regime on some of these points. In late 1975 and 1976 the SCP began to insist on its own "identifiable presence" at international meetings. The Syrian government arrested large numbers of Communists during that period. Uneasy over the cooperation of the SCP with Lebanese leftists and Communists, the Assad regime also tried to disband SCP popular associations. Regime toleration of the new SCP also exacerbated SCP-Ba'ath problems. The decline of Soviet-Syrian relations in 1976 also contributed to the difficulties of the SCP, which had looked to Soviet support in the past.[55] Previously, the SCP had been willing to participate in the NPF. This willingness is likely to continue—despite threats to withdraw from the NPF that inevitably arise during Ba'ath-SCP tensions—because in the NPF, the SCP is a sanctioned party with a legitimate and important role, while outside the NPF the SCP could be but one of several illicit political movements unable to exert influence over decision making.

The last of the official participants in the NPF, the Arab socialists, are Hourani socialists—that is, remnants of Akram Hourani's old Arab Socialist party. While they seek to exploit the popularity of his name and do, in fact, agree with Hourani on virtually everything, Hourani has disavowed the Arab socialists (on the ground of his firm principle not to support the Ba'ath in any way). Hourani, the great reform politician of modern Syria, still commands a considerable following.[56]

The term National Progressive Front should indicate that not all currents are represented. None of the traditionally conservative political trends in Syria, for example, is acceptable to the regime. Nevertheless, such views are still current in the public. The Muslim Brotherhood has long had a following in Syria.[57] It continues a relatively high level of activity, especially in the Homs region, where its candidates easily won election in the spring of 1972. It also is active in Hama and Damascus. Saudi Arabia has sporadically financed Brotherhood activities, thus complicating Saudi-Syrian relations. The Brotherhood also has irritated the Assad regime: though they ran on the NPF ticket in the 1972 local elections, the Brotherhood appealed to Syrians to boycott the May 1973 legislative election. Moreover, the anti-Ba'ath activities of Sheikh Habaka and Sunni religious leaders are thought to have been organized, or at least aided, by the Muslim Brotherhood.[58]

Finally, Syrian politics has always allowed a great role for political independents. This is in some measure a function of the agro-cities discussed earlier —that is, of regional leaders who used no conceptual or ideological appeal, relying instead upon personal status in their region.

Another form of "independent" is the political leader or group linked with foreign interests. The Arab world, particularly in the Levant, is a transnational society—or, at the least, a society of nation-states uniquely subject to regional transnational pressures. Political pressures often are exerted through transnational families or through individuals with personal or (often ephemeral) financial ties to other Arab polities. Because of the relative novelty of Syrian nationalism, these forces are singularly strong in Syrian society. The Assad regime often must prepare itself (and communicate its policies) in the light of expected (or unanticipated but actual) pressures from Iraq, Saudi Arabia (sometimes working through the Muslim Brotherhood), Libya, and Egypt.[59]

The Military

Perhaps the most potentially effective interest group in Syria is the military. Although divided by national issues and trends, the military forces—particularly the officer corps—have been homogenized as a result of social factors already discussed and through the long series of political purges. Internal security (intelligence) functions are devoted to identifying anti-regime movements, trends, and individuals. Alawi solidarity also leads to military unity. This is not to suggest that the armed forces are unified, for they are not. Rather, it suggests that on certain issues—such as budget allocations, disengagement, and other war/peace issues where significant unity does exist—the officer corps is in a uniquely powerful position to influence policy. It also suggests that to the extent that differences surface, they must be cast in the framework of policy options, not regime alternatives.[60] Syrian military interests are wide-ranging because "the army's roots . . . preserve its sense of social mission."[61] Thus, the armed forces often have strong feelings concerning social and economic issues. However, the military has been riven with different views on these issues, and therefore is less effective as a single interest group on socioeconomic matters than on military concerns.

The Syrian armed forces are composed of an army, a navy that is administratively part of the army, and an air force. Although manpower levels vary somewhat, the army is by far the largest service. All are Soviet-equipped and Soviet-trained. Thus, Syrian military training is based on partially modified Russian prenuclear strategic and tactical doctrine.[62] Any doctrinal background imposes some sort of limitations on military forces, and Soviet doctrine's limitations were observable in the October War. Clearly, the army is incapable of mounting a sustained offensive beyond Syrian territory against a well-trained and well-equipped adversary. Syrian military forces are overcentralized and poorly led at senior levels. Junior-level officers are considered vastly improved, and enlisted personnel as good, basic fighters. However, the technical level of military personnel is also a handicap. Syrian armed forces are not well educated and come from an environment in which they have not been exposed to sophisticated technology. Moreover, the high rate of turnover has adversely affected overall capability. On the other hand, the Soviet Union has had adequate time to train a large number of officers and enlisted personnel, who have been exposed to increasingly advanced military equipment. All reports from the October War suggested that the Syrian armed forces demonstrated great improvement over 1967. Syrian military preparedness is high, and the Syrian army represents a significant defensive force. The air and naval forces appear to have made less progress than the ground forces, which acquitted themselves very well in 1973.[63]

The Syrian military demonstrates relative solidarity on issues such as the strategy of confrontation with Israel. Generally, Syrian military personnel are "hawks," favoring greater military action and fewer concessions in the conflict with Israel. Agreements of any sort with the Zionist state are suspect. It can be presumed, too, that the armed forces' leadership lobbies actively for a large share of the Syrian budget. Assad has tried to upgrade the pay, benefits, and prestige of the officer corps.[64] Decisions of a political or economic nature that might undermine military effectiveness—for instance, by threatening sources of supply—would encounter substantial opposition. As in most developing states, the Syrian military is jealous of its position as the most important (and best-funded) armed force. Thus, despite some fractionation on this issue when it applies to the Palestinians, the services actively oppose the establishment or arming of any group at such a level that it may threaten their position.[65]

Internal security in the armed forces consists of pervasive intelligence networks directed by persons trusted by Assad and two types of units, the Defense Companies and the Special Forces, directed by Assad's brother and cousin, respectively. Although Assad has been more tolerant of divergent opinions than the previous regime was, he has not hesitated to use force to maintain his position.[66]

Socioeconomic Interest Groups

Ethnic-Religious Groups

The most important of the many divisions of Syrian society is the ethnic-religious. Although Arabs constitute approximately 90 percent of the population (Kurds, Armenians, Turkomans, Circassians, Assyrians, and Jews amount to 6 percent, 3 percent, 1 percent, 1 percent, and a fraction of 1 percent, respectively), homogeneity does not exist. Syrian Arabs include several important religious minority communities, notably the Alawis. Muslims constitute over 85 percent of the population, but they include Alawis (11–15 percent), Ismailis (1–2 percent), and other Shiite sects (1 percent), as well as the Sunnis (about 85 percent). Christians—including Greek Orthodox (Melkite), Syrian Orthodox, Armenian Orthodox (Gregorian), Maronites, Syrian Catholics, Greek Catholics, Armenian Catholics, Chaldeans, and Nestorians

(Assyrians)—make up about 10 percent of the Syrian population. Remaining religious minorities include the Druzes (3 percent of the population), Yazidis, and Jews.

The Alawis make up between 9 and 13 percent of the Syrian population. They are a Shiite sect similar in some of their beliefs to the Ismailis but with greater Christian and other elements. Most Alawis live in Latakia province, but they are dispersing as the nation becomes more urbanized. Alawis consider themselves Muslims; many Sunnis—but, significantly, not the more conservative—so consider them as well.[67] Traditionally, Alawis have been held in contempt and discriminated against as poor, uneducated peasants by the Sunni landowners and Sunnis in general. The results of this status are visible in the occasional anti-Alawi demonstrations based upon an underlying Sunni resentment of Alawi control.

As a group, Alawis favor the continued progress of their position in Syrian society. They tend to support secularism, but cluster most homogeneously on any issue that affects Alawi advancement. Currently, they believe they would benefit directly from the socioeconomic development of Syria. Previously, such development would only have increased the gap between the Alawi standard of living and that of the majority of Syrians. Now, however, with Syria under Alawi control, disproportionate attention is paid to their welfare. They already have partially closed the development gulf separating them from the Sunnis. Latakia, the most heavily populated Alawi area, has received considerable financial inputs from the regime.[68] Alawis continue to follow military careers in large numbers, and under Assad they hold most key positions in the country. Recognizing the potential explosiveness of concerted Sunni resentment against Alawi domination, Assad has given publicity to military discharges of Alawis who failed to perform satisfactorily in the October War; to the appointment of Sunni and minority, non-Alawi, officers to senior military posts; and to the deemphasis of Ba'ath preferences in the armed forces.[69] Indeed, the army is not atypical: Assad has placed most of the key positions in the country in Alawi hands while distributing high-visibility posts with little real power to non-Alawis.[70] Moreover, he has taken a number of steps to blur the Alawi-Sunni distinction—changing the presidential oath, spotlighting his participation in the activities of the Syrian Islamic community, and encouraging Sunni *ulama* to portray the Alawis as Shi'a Muslims, a highly debatable proposition.

The Sunni majority of Syria has not demonstrated a cohesive determination to rid itself of Alawi domination. Nevertheless, Sunni resentment over Alawi rule is unmistakable. (The religious schism is discussed as an issue area below.) However, it is important to recognize that Sunnis frequently oppose the current regime on nonreligious issues, when, in fact, that opposition is based on their desire to return Syria to Sunni rule. Conservative Sunnis lead the "opposition"; and in the anti-regime demonstrations that have taken place,

Sunni sheikhs and the Muslim Brotherhood, as well as representatives of religious purist regimes such as Saudi Arabia's and Libya's, have played a prominent role.

The Druzes were, with the Alawis, the major beneficiaries of the French "divide and conquer" strategy. Like the Alawis, the Druzes came to have a disproportionate representation in Syria's most important political group, the army. Until 1966, they and the Alawis worked together to improve their position in the army. Since the abortive Salim Hatum coup, however, the Druze role has decreased considerably. As a group, Druzes and other minorities see secularism as in their interest. On such issues, Druzes will align with Alawis.

Syrian Christians are more educated, active, and affluent than their Muslim counterparts. Although they participate in public affairs, Syrian Christians have been noticeable by the secularism of their activities. Collective actions as an interest group have included support for religious equality and opposition to favoritism toward Islam. They have consistently opposed the establishment of an official state religion.

Economic Groups

There are several divisions in Syrian society along economic lines: urban-rural, radical-conservative, and merchant-(middle class) peasant. To some extent, analysts tend to merge these conflicts, often combining the categories with groups previously discussed. Certainly, the fact that Alawis, for example, have been poor, rural, social reformists is significant: it is not chance that led the Alawi-dominated neo-Ba'ath to reforms that aimed at improving the lot of poor, rural Syrian classes. It should be recognized, however, that the coincidence of interests is not complete.

The revolutionaries and reformists composing the "radical" wing of economic thought in Syria are not confined to the Ba'ath party. On the contrary, they cross party lines and are an important force in today's Syria. They support nationalization of industries, more consistent implementation of land reform measures already enacted, and generally a larger role for the public sector (in some cases, to the virtual exclusion of the private). Although the revolutionaries are not numerous in Syria, they do have a strong base within the Ba'ath and Communist parties and, therefore, exert considerable influence.[71]

Before about 1970, Syrian social structure, although not based upon economic classes, could be divided into an upper class of landowning aristocracy (Damascus and Hama) and wealthy industrialists (Aleppo), paralleled by *ulama;* a professional and clerical middle class that had begun to emerge after World War I; and the lower classes of laborers, peasants, and others. Traditionally, the middle class of merchants aspired to the position of the upper class; but the new middle class, composed of some scions of the upper class and, primarily, of those of lower-class backgrounds, resented the old upper class. After some years of Ba'ath-led social revolution in Syria, the position of the old upper class had been materially altered, its influence greatly weakened.

> The rising new political and professional elite looks with suspicion on the members of the old upper group. The old urban commercial middle class, in which religious minorities are heavily represented and which traditionally admired and emulated the upper class, consequently finds itself in a precarious position and is likely to avoid any public acknowledgement of the formerly wealthy and powerful. The *ulama* have . . . made peace with the revolutionary regime. . . .[72]

Prestige now lies in education and management. The new middle class of technicians, professionals, bureaucrats, and some merchants has successfully captured symbolic leadership. However, it does not have a class consciousness or a unified value system. In this respect, at least, the old upper class and the merchants just below it retain greater agreement and collective awareness. There remain upper and middle classes, but much of the membership—and capital—of both fled the country beginning in the mid-1960s. That a return movement is now in progress attests more to the continuity of economic interests than to an affection for the Ba'ath.[73]

The Syrian General Union of Peasants has had limited but important success in organizing and mobilizing Syrian peasants. Although it represents largely the Ba'ath sympathizers among the peasantry—it has scarcely recruited around Hama or in the Jazira because peasants in those areas have had ties to Akram Hourani and the SCP, respectively—a concerted effort has been made to spread regime views through the Union. "Peasant" leadership in the organization is frequently well-to-do. In some areas, the Union is unsuccessful because the regime does not care to alter the social status quo; in others, because local leadership is hostile to the regime. The Syrian General Union of Peasants is one of several "popular organizations" widely and correctly viewed as tools of the Assad regime. Given its role and membership, the Union does not exert any real pressure on the Syrian government.[74]

The General Federation of Trade Unions is the only "popular organization" to antedate the Ba'ath regime. Moreover, unlike other organizations in Syria, it has consistently permitted the continued membership of many non-Ba'athists. Houranists, Communists, and Nasserites are numerous. On the other hand, since 1964, the Federation has been controlled by the regime. All political tendencies are allowed, but Ba'ath predominance is exercised at the national level. About half the industrial labor force is in the General Federation. Labor issues do rise through its pyramidal organization, but union and labor as a whole can scarcely be taken as an autonomous interest group on other matters.[75]

Transnational Interest Groups

A most unusual feature of the Syrian political system is the central role played in it by non-Syrians—Palestinians now living in Syria. Palestinian power in Syria is not the result of military force but, rather, a function of the Syrian political self-image. "Most politically-conscious Syrians have held and continue to hold firmly to the conviction that Syria is the throbbing heart of Arab nationalism."[76]

As a result of Syria's self-conscious role as leader in Arab nationalism, the Palestinian cause is a central question, a test (or proof) of Syria's position. Also, Syrians feel a personal link with Palestine as a part of greater, prepartition Syria. Thus, the Palestinian view is accorded great weight in Syria. Palestinians have pushed Syria to lead the "rejection front"—the resistance to any settlement short of the destruction of Israel and re-creation of Palestine—and do not hesitate to use their moral influence. They also were used to buttress the Jadid regime. Jadid consciously created and armed Sa'iqa to reduce the relative monopoly of power in military hands and to increase his own leverage. Hafez Assad, however, replaced the Sa'iqa leadership with Palestinians loyal to him; Sa'iqa has existed under both regimes and will continue to be a creature of Syrian policy.

Syrian policy vis-à-vis the Palestinian resistance as a whole has varied as a function of immediate Syrian foreign-policy goals and domestic needs. The government has not hesitated to restrict the resistance—or even prohibit it from undertaking operations against Israel—when such restriction aided the realization of other objectives. When Syria needed time to install surface-to-air missile (SAM) air defenses, for example, and did not want Israeli retaliatory air strikes, Palestinian operations from Syrian territory were stopped. Both Sa'iqa, which can be considered a Syrian organization, and the Palestine Liberation Army (PLA) brigade stationed in Syria are completely subject to Syrian control. The army supervises the Yarmouk Brigade; the regime, Sa'iqa. Certain elements in the Syrian armed forces are particularly hostile to Palestinian freedom of action.

On the other hand, Palestinian resistance leaders maintain very close relations with the other political groups in the NPF and with extremist and Jadidist factions of the Ba'ath party.[77] Sympathies throughout Syria are extremely pro-Palestinian, and any important Syrian action regarded as anti-Palestinian engenders significant popular opposition, though minor infringements on Palestinian freedom of action are not likely to do so.[78]

Perhaps the most controversial foreign-policy initiative taken by Assad—certainly far more politically dangerous than the decision to go to war in October 1973 or the more unpopular choice to accept a Golan disengagement agreement with Israel—was his decision to use military force in Lebanon to bring an end to the independence of the Palestine Liberation Organization (PLO). Nevertheless, that the decision was made and that Syria went to the extent of committing its forces (as well as those of Sa'iqa and the PLA) against the PLO-Lebanese leftist alliance gives some indication of the solidity of Assad's power base, at least in his own perception. Despite considerable opposition to Syrian policy and actions in Lebanon in 1976,[79] Assad was never in serious danger of losing power, despite the popularity of the Palestinian cause in Syria.

ISSUE AREAS

The two most important issues in Syria have been the recovery of Syrian territory currently occupied by Israel (the Golan Heights) and the resolution of the Palestinian question. They are much more completely interwoven in Syria than in other Arab countries (even those—except Jordan—whose territory is occupied by Israel). Syrians cannot divorce the Palestinian territorial-political problem from their own for a number of reasons. First, Palestine was part of the greater Syria that is still a more real object of loyalty to many Syrians than the present-day state is. Second, there are many Palestinian refugees living in Syria.[80] Third, Syrians have taken pride in their role as the Arab conscience; they, more than others, have remained loyal to the Palestinian cause to demonstrate this role. Fourth, Syria has laid claim to the title of leader in the fight against Israel, a claim that integrates, or at least has integrated, the Palestinian and Arab (hence, Syrian) conflicts with Israel. Fifth, there are a number of political, economic, and social issues similarly affected by Israeli occupation of Syrian territory and by the Palestine problem. Refugee questions[81] and resultant constraints on the demographic options available to Syria are but two of several such areas.

Occupied Territory and the Arab-Israeli Conflict

Syria's own territorial conflict with Israel is limited to the Golan Heights, occupied in June 1967.[82] The public campaign to liberate the Golan has been unremitting. There is no evidence that a Ba'ath government, humiliated by its poor military showing against Israel in 1967, has tried to soft-pedal the issue. Quite the contrary: Syrians were constantly reminded of the Israeli occupation and of the certainty that the occupied Golan would be retaken by Syria.[83]

Thus, the primary issue with respect to the Golan has never been whether to accept its loss or to seek its return. Instead, issues have concerned the means and the timing of its recovery. Virtually all Syrians have accepted the need for force in the effort. How to use force in victory—rather than in a 1967-like defeat—is the problem.

The current set of issues that confronts Syrians on the Golan and Arab-Israeli questions includes the following: should Syria follow a moderate or a rejectionist line? should Syria engage in talks with Israel? should Syria accept any partial approaches, even if linked to an overall settlement?

Individuals and groups within Syria are deeply divided on the direction the nation's policy should take. Syria's traditional "irreconcilable" status has been abandoned, at least for the present. The debate today centers on the wisdom of this abandonment and on alternative strategies. One group, formerly led by Mahmoud Ayyubi, supports the Golan disengagement agreement negotiated in the spring of 1974 and promotes a compromise overall settlement with Israel. The other group, led by Foreign Minister Khaddam,[84] feels that Syria should accept nothing less than total and immediate withdrawal. In practice, however, Khaddam has been more flexible when faced with concrete issues than his identified stand would suggest.[85]

In favor of a settlement, Ayyubi's supporters point to the military outcome of the last war, when virtually everything was in Syria's favor; the undependability of Egypt; and the limited use of alliance with Iraq. They argue that the Soviet Union, as helpful as it has been, has always backed down to the United States, which will never let Israel be conquered. The conclusion of this group is that there will not be a better time for a settlement, and for the realization of Syrian objectives, than the present. Against a settlement, various Syrians suggest that such a resolution in today's terms (with Saudi prominence) would mean an end to the Arab revolution. They also are concerned about the rise of U.S. prestige in this regard. Some see the outcome of the October War as a sign that Israel is "on the ropes" and can be knocked out eventually, and that the oil weapon will neutralize the United States.[86]

Many of those supporting immediate withdrawal are not prepared to accept any compromise with Israel. Most Syrians probably still oppose negotiations with Israel, and certainly they still fear it.[87] There is a substantial body of opinion in favor of Syria's joining a "rejection front" composed of Iraq, Libya, and certain Palestinian elements.[88] (The latter include the PFLP.)[89] In fact, Assad has used this opinion, sometimes by capitalizing on tactical points of agreement to solidify his position, sometimes to strengthen his bargaining posture vis-à-vis Israel.[90] The disengagement agreement was a focal point of this "hawkish" dissent, and it can be assumed that further agreements with Israel would face similar opposition.[91]

In order to still the dissension caused by the disengagement accord and the newly exhibited moderate tendencies, Assad's regime has insisted that the

initial agreement and talks leading to and following from it have been predi-
cated on the direct and close link between these steps and both total Israeli
withdrawal from occupied Arab territory and reestablishment of the rights of
the Palestinian people. This conceptual connection is particularly important
to Syria for another reason: Israel's greater reluctance to relinquish the Golan
Heights than to leave the Sinai or West Bank. The link between initial steps
and ultimate goals has been supported as well by the United States,[92] in order
to provide the firm ground deemed necessary to Assad's continued ability to
negotiate. The Assad government, in control of all Syrian media, has spared
no effort to communicate to the population the importance of disengagement
as a step toward a Syrian victory. Indeed, the agreement was portrayed as a
Syrian victory, in that the costs were depicted as few and the benefits—
especially Israeli evacuation of some of the territory occupied in 1967,[93] including Kuneitra—great. In addition, Soviet support and Palestinian acquiescence were sought to legitimize the agreement (and to shield it from radical
and Palestinian-based criticism).[94]

Palestine

The Syrian government has considered itself, and generally has been
viewed, as the most consistent supporter of the Palestinian cause. There is also
an indissoluble link between the Palestinian issue and the larger Arab-Israeli
and Syrian-Israeli questions. The questions Damascus has had to face in this
area include the extent to which political support should be furnished to the
Palestinian cause; the ends for which this support should be provided; the
degree of military and logistical assistance to be provided Palestinian resistance
forces and the purposes for which the assistance may be used; and, directly
associated with each of these problems, the specific Palestinian groups to be
supported.

To date, Syria has consistently supported the Palestinian cause, even
rejecting UN Security Council Resolution 242 of November 1967. Assad came
to power, however, over Palestinian resistance and after Sa'iqa and the Syrian-
based PLA had been neutralized by the Syrian armed forces. Although Sa'iqa
has been taken over by the Assad regime, Palestinian wishes retain some
influence. The army continues to jealously safeguard its military role, which
the Palestinians have learned to accept. During periodic crackdowns on guerrilla activity, the Palestinians appeal through Iraqi or other sympathetic channels to Syrian opinion; they do not challenge Syrian authority to impose
whatever restrictions may be promulgated.

Political support for Palestinians is, then, substantial; but it is unlimited
only in the sense that the issue of political goals is scarcely argued. Assad
claims he will not become involved in such a debate. (We shall see, however,

that he hedges his bets.)[95] For now, Syrian political support for the recognition of Palestinian rights is undefined.[96]

Damascus has been much more circumspect in concrete support for the Palestinian cause. Syrian territory has been used intermittently by the Palestinian guerrillas in operations against Israel and has been open to Palestinian military support of Syrian military operations. However, such activities have been infrequent, determined by strategic considerations of the Syrian-Israeli relationship or, occasionally, by domestic factors. Syria has not fought for the Palestinians since 1947. The pressure that exists within Syria to fight for the Palestinians can be, and has been, eased by political support and by the mélange of Syrian-Palestinian justifications the government has used as a rationale for essentially national-interest actions. In 1976, Syrian armed forces were used in military operations in Lebanon that were justified as support for the Palestinian cause. In fact, the army, the PLA, and Sa'iqa all operated against a coalition of PLO and Lebanese leftist forces. Substantial Syrian opposition was encountered—predictably—but largely overcome by Assad in this instance. As is discussed below, Syrian military operations in 1976 answer the second of the four questions posed by the Palestinian issue, and in such a way as to respond as well to the other three.

A central problem in Syria is sectarianism. Virtually since the inception of Ba'ath power—even under the Sunni Amin al-Hafez from 1963 to 1966—Sunnis have been concerned over favoritism shown Alawis and Alawi-populated areas. In May 1967, serious sectarian demonstrations took place. They followed from an atheistic (but typically Ba'ath) article in an army magazine. The crisis preceding the June War overshadowed the demonstrations; and the "setback," as Syria and other Arab regimes referred to the outcome of the conflict, created sufficient shock and discontinuity that the sectarian issue was forgotten for a while. In the spring of 1972, unrest surfaced over a radio commentator's minor error in reporting a religious celebration. During the following year there were several months of sporadic sectarian demonstrations, some resulting in violence. These activities began in January with the circulation of a new draft constitution that did not identify Islam as the state religion.[97] Riots occurred in late February, when the People's Assembly ratified the constitution, and again around the Prophet's birthday in April.

The sectarian problem surfaced again in Syria's role in Lebanon during 1976: Syrian and Syrian-sponsored troops supported the Christian-Phalangist forces against the Palestinians and Lebanese leftists (most of whom were Sunni Muslims). The magnitude of the carnage in the Lebanese civil war highlighted the sectarian aspect—an Alawi regime siding with Christians and others against Sunnis. (The sectarian considerations of Syria's role in Lebanon put an even greater value on the Syrian alliance with [Sunni] King Hussein of Jordan.) Despite general domestic dissent concerning the Syrian venture, actual religious protest (in the form of civil violence) was minimal during the period.

In sectarian matters, Alawis receive tacit support from the sizable Christian and Druze communities in Syria. To a large extent, moreover, religious issues are merely the surface rationale for unrest. Conservatives have tended to use the religious issue to mobilize anti-Ba'ath and anti-Alawi sentiment. For this reason, sectarian issues often lead to the mobilization of Communist and Ba'ath supporters of the regime who are anxious to prevent conservative gains.[98]

Foreign Relations

The Syrian relationship with the world outside the Middle East has been limited in recent years. After the Ba'ath, and particularly the neo-Ba'ath, came to power, Syria became increasingly isolated, with ties of growing strength and number to the Soviet Union and its East European allies. Following the June War, disagreement over the role of the Soviet Union and the degree of reliance on it continued as a major issue. Ba'ath ideologues, Communists, and some other groups favored greater alliance with Moscow and the severance of Syrian relations with regional "reactionaries." Some nationalists, however, with tacit support from conservative elements and groups within the military, argued in favor of cooperating more with all Arab countries rather than with the socialist commonwealth, and of placing more traditional limits on Syrian reliance on non-Arab supporters. Assad, for example, opposed the terms of some economic agreements with the Soviet Union, on the ground that they were overly favorable to Moscow.[99]

Prior to his final coup, Hafez Assad had sided rather consistently with the nationalists against overreliance on, and excessive concessions to, the Soviet Union. He had attacked the Jadid regime for improper contacts with the Soviet embassy, undue economic concessions to Moscow, and collusion with Syrian Communists. The army had acted openly against Syrian Communists and pro-Soviet elements throughout much of 1970. Nevertheless, the Soviets did not hesitate to support Assad once his dominance became clear.

Since his accession to power, Assad has been placed in the position of supporting the Soviet Union against anti-Soviet elements, particularly in the military, where Mustapha Tlas and Naji Jamil have served as focal points of agitation against Moscow.[100] Following the July 1972 expulsion of Soviet advisers and other military personnel from Egypt, a debate ensued in Syria over the future of the Soviet personnel in that country. Despite some problems that had arisen from time to time, however, Soviet-Syrian military relations never reached the level of animosity characterizing Soviet-Egyptian problems. Assad did more than strongly support the retention of Soviet personnel: he tried to serve as intermediary to bridge the Moscow-Cairo gap, and undertook new and substantially expanded military agreements with the Soviet Union, under the terms of which some important Soviet strategic needs (unrelated to the Arab-Israeli conflict) previously met by Egypt would be filled by Syria.

Since the October War, Syrian-Soviet relations have been complicated by the entry of the United States into the Syrian political scene. (We shall discuss current policy below.) Renewal of U.S.-Syrian relations has not been the result of Syrian frustration with Russia. Indeed, while there have been intermittent problems of military supply, Assad believes, and has consistently indicated, that maintenance of strong ties between Moscow and Damascus is crucial to the realization of Syrian objectives. Thus, with the exception of the Tlas anti-Soviet group in the military, Syrian-Soviet relations are not a major issue. Virtually all Syrians view the Soviet Union as the only dependable nonregional friend, the only country willing to supply the economic and military aid Syria requires in sufficient quantity and with relatively few (visible) strings. Insofar as Middle East issues are concerned, the Soviet Union is viewed as a tool that is useful and necessary for Syria. This role is more important than bilateral considerations, so that when Soviet support is forthcoming on the Arab-Israeli issue, there is no argument. When there is a difference on this key issue, both sides have concentrated on the points of agreement rather than those of discord.[101] That improving U.S.-Syrian relations have affected Damascus' ties to the Soviet Union is clear, however. The stagnation of Soviet-Syrian relations was evident first in the economic sphere, where the Assad initiatives to attract Western capital investments and technological transfer began to enjoy success —some at the expense of Soviet-Syrian economic cooperation—in 1975.[102] Partly because the opening of doors to the West was perceived in Moscow as a threat to the Soviet position throughout the Middle East, and partly because Syria, like Egypt, has been a principal regional bulwark of the Soviet presence in the Middle East, Russian concern grew in 1974 and then rapidly during 1976, as the coincidence of American objectives and Syria's actions in Lebanon became manifest.[103]

The thaw in relations with the United States has been less uncontroversial than recent dealings with the Soviet Union. Despite a reservoir of good feeling toward the United States and Americans (in general, Syrians can more easily identify with Americans than with Russians), U.S. relations with and support of Israel, suspicions about the trustworthiness of the United States and the reality of its new evenhanded policy, ideological preferences, and the recognition of the need for continued economic and military backing of the Soviet Union have led diverse groups to oppose the warming trend in Syrian-American relations.[104]

For centuries, historians have observed a pattern in which Egypt and Iraq compete for Syria. This pattern bears a striking resemblance to contemporary Syrian politics. (Indeed, the principal error of viewing Egypt as the conservative or moderating force, and Iraq as the revolutionary, is that these positions have been much less stable than the rivalry itself.) Since the Assad regime came to power in Damascus, the roles of Cairo and Baghdad have represented moderation (flexibility) and radicalism (rigidity and isolation), respectively. Even before the definitive ouster of Jadid, however, Assad was Cairo's choice.[105]

Syria's relationship with Egypt has been a major issue, the importance of which is underscored by Syria's inability to fight Israel alone—which means, in practice, Syria's need for a military alliance with Egypt at the time of full-scale hostilities and of threat of force. Egypt's relatively moderate role since Sadat has come to power and the fluctuation of Egypt's relations with the Soviet Union during that same period have been troublesome for Syria, whose role as the "irreconcilable" and whose close ties to Moscow were both prejudiced, thus leading to domestic debates over the wisdom of following Egypt. At the same time, it should be pointed out that when Damascus did not follow Cairo—as in the 1972 expulsion of Soviet advisers—the debate was no less strident.[106] For approximately a year in 1972–73, Egypt and Syria were at odds; but sometime in the spring of 1973, when Assad and Sadat apparently took their decision to use war to prevent further solidification of the status quo, Syria's relations with Egypt—and others—were repaired, bringing about the familiar debate over dealing with "reactionary" Arab regimes. However, the debate was made moot by the second-stage Sinai withdrawal accord. After the Sinai II agreement, Damascus concluded that Egypt was no longer a major actor in the confrontation with Israel. We believe that the tenor of Egyptian-Syrian relations will continue to vary, and that Iraq will continue to be a primary factor in these relations.

Following the October War, which significantly improved Assad's domestic position, the debate was reopened. Assad was careful not to follow Sadat's virtual about-face in his relations with the superpowers; but the Syrian policy trend toward close coordination with Cairo and greatly improved relations with the United States was (and is) the subject of intense debate, mitigated only by the gradualness of the new policy toward the United States and the maintenance of close and cooperative ties to the Soviet Union. Bilateral negotiations and agreements between Egypt and Israel aroused Syrian suspicion and resentment. Generally, the same faction that supports negotiation with Israel, disengagement, and a U.S. role in the settlement has favored coordination with Egypt. Some, on the other hand, feel that Syria has already gone too far in pursuing Sadat-like policies. Syrian Communists, too, are alarmed by the drift toward cooperation with countries like Saudi Arabia and Egypt, even while recognizing the key role these states play in exerting indirect or direct pressure on Israel. Most of the leftist thought in Syria accepts some cooperation as necessary, but there is substantial attention paid to the Soviet view.[107]

For the most part, Iraq's appeal is to those in Syria who oppose Egyptian policy and Syrian cooperation with Egypt. Despite certain sectoral economic cooperation, military cooperation against Israel, Iraqi economic aid to Syria, Syrian political support for Iraq in its dispute with Iran, and strong pro-Iraqi interest groups in Syria, relations between the two Ba'ath regimes never have been very good and often have been bitter. After the neo-Ba'ath took power in Syria, Assad's faction often proposed reconciliation with Iraq; but since Assad has gained power, relations have not improved. The Soviet Union frequently has pressed for a Syrian-Iraqi-Palestinian alliance as a force for the furtherance of Soviet policy, and Soviet supporters in Syria frequently have been linked to pro-Iraqi factions. Iraq is the most potent anti-settlement factor in Syrian politics, now that the PLO has moved toward a compromise with Israel. Thus, Iraq and Libya, with the PFLP (and other Palestine groups), have tried to wean (or force) Syria to join them in a "rejection front." Translated into Syrian political terms, pro-Iraqi and irreconcilable Palestinian elements dissent from—and impede—the current Assad strategy.[108] Of course, it cannot be overlooked in Syria that Iraq's military power can be helpful, and would be necessary in undertaking hostilities against Israel without Egypt.

The countries most important to Syria after Egypt and Iraq are Jordan and Lebanon. Syria's ties to Lebanon are ancient, the latter having formed part of traditional Syria. Many of the customs and much of the commercial philosophy of the two countries have been similar in the past, and personal and family ties are transnational. Lebanon and Syria have, however, had very different postwar histories. Lebanon's military role in the region is minimal, although its commercial role, and in some respects its political situation, are of some importance. The transnational issue regarding Lebanon that has arisen in Syria concerns the plight of the Palestinians. The Syrian government, which generally gave verbal backing to the Palestinians in their complaints against the Lebanese government and occasionally resorted to economic measures to demonstrate support for the Palestinians,[109] conducted "peacekeeping" operations in Lebanon in 1976 that were a facade for military actions against an alliance of Palestinians and Lebanese leftists. Syria, historically the greatest supporter of the Palestinian cause, clearly had made some decisions that constituted a key turning point in Syrian-Palestinian relations.

Jordan has had a less fraternal relationship with Syria than Lebanon has. The two have a long-standing territorial conflict (although that dispute has been of little import for over two decades). The Hashemite kingdom was a consistent target of Syrian rhetoric from the advent of the Ba'ath regime until the 1970s. Long-standing tension between Palestinians, on the one hand, and the Jordanian government, on the other, resulted in a civil war in September 1970[110] ("Black September" to Palestinian guerrillas), in which Syrian armored units participated without air cover. The Syrian operations in Jordan led to the final Assad coup in November 1970. Assad later sent the regime's second most powerful leader, Mustapha Tlas, to meet with the Jordanians. Tlas is a conservative Sunni with personal ties to both Jordan and Saudi

Arabia.[111] Each attempt to improve relations with Jordan was at first low-keyed; nevertheless, they encountered substantial opposition, especially among younger Ba'ath military officers. Thus, Syria did not hesitate to use economic sanctions or allow the Palestinians to "punish" Jordan, even though relations between the Hashemite monarchy and the Alawi regime were in fact relatively good from the outset of Assad's rule.[112]

With the development of a new Syrian foreign policy in 1975–76, Jordanian-Syrian relations improved dramatically. Despite internal resistance to this change at first, the regime imposed its views. Considering the emerging rift with Egypt and the gulf between Iraq and Syria, and in the face of the Israeli problem, the rapprochement with Jordan declined as a rallying point of dissension.

The new power in the Middle East is Saudi Arabia, which has been flexing its muscles in Syria for some time. With a population base to work from, conservative Muslim elements such as the Muslim Brotherhood, supported directly by Saudi Arabia, have actively opposed the Syrian Ba'ath regime. The Saudis also have some good contacts within the Syrian military, including General Tlas, the minister of defense. Assad has made a consistent and concerted effort to win and maintain Saudi support, an effort unpopular among young military officers, the ideological left, the Ba'ath ideologues, and many Alawis.[113]

SYRIAN OBJECTIVES AND POLICIES

Objectives

In the highly heterogenous society that is Syria, consensus on national objectives—or even whether national Syrian (as opposed to national Arab) objectives should exist—cannot be expected. The following constitute objectives of the current Syrian regime:

recovery of Syrian territory presently occupied by Israel (Golan Heights);
maintenance of the current regime and, associated with that goal, development
    of popular support for the regime and government;
resolution of the Palestinian issue;
economic development of Syria and, in support of that policy, the attraction
    of private and foreign government investment;
maintenance and improvement of relations with Arab countries;
improvement of economic, political, and social relations with the West;
acceptable termination of the conflict with Israel.

Policies

Political Programs

Under the rubric of "political programs" we shall consider both domestic and foreign policies of the Assad government. Separation of domestic from foreign policies is arbitrary and misleading, in that foreign issues frequently are of domestic significance. Nevertheless, we shall first discuss questions of internal Syrian politics.

Hafez Assad's primary domestic objective has been to preserve his regime and to establish its legitimacy. To this end, the president has endeavored to build a constitutional foundation in the "permanent constitution" promulgated in 1973. Moreover, added legitimacy is sought in the direct election of the president by universal suffrage.[114] In order to build broad, popular support for his regime, Assad has introduced democratic reforms, undertaken new economic policies more in line with majority Syrian wishes and values, and opened the legislative and public political arenas to parties other than the Ba'ath. Democratic reforms include the popularly elected People's Council and local councils, greater political freedom, and more honesty in government.[115] Assad refers to his 1970 coup as a "corrective movement," thereby suggesting the continuity of Ba'athism. However, from the time of the coup to the present, the president has placed heavy emphasis on the relaxation of internal security measures and the reduction of the government's isolation from the people.[116] The visibility and importance of the secret police have been reduced,[117] as have the stridency of public discussion and the extreme secularism of the Ba'ath party.[118] Indeed, the role of the Ba'ath itself has decreased, partly because of the history of the Assad-Jadid conflict[119] and partly because Assad recognizes and wishes to reduce his vulnerability that derives from the conservative Sunni suspicions of the "Godless Ba'ath."

The inclusion of non-Ba'ath parties in the People's Council and NPF was only part of Assad's attempt to broaden the base—that is, to increase the representativeness—of his regime. Equally important, anti-Ba'ath groups have not been overlooked in Cabinets: Assad has made a real effort to secure popular unity behind his government, to make it "a government of the people."[120]

The reduction of domestic revolutionary rhetoric has carried over to domestic coverage of foreign affairs. Assad has curtailed much of the polemic in the public media. His effort to develop better relations with all his Arab neighbors has been attended by a noticeable decline in the temperature of public political discourse on foreign affairs.

To date, Hafez Assad's approach to governance of Syria has shown positive results. Clearly the most popular regime in the country for many years, his government also has been characterized by a stability remarkable by

Syrian standards. None of the major figures in the regime has been removed. The Ba'ath Regional Command in power in May 1971, after Assad became president, included five generals—Assad, Mustafa Tlas, Abdul Rahman Khleifawi, Naji Jamil, and Abdul Ghani Ibrahim. All of these remain key figures in the present Syrian administration.

While we do not propose to discuss foreign-policy considerations in the context of domestic political programs, a significant policy change under Assad has been the approach taken to the conflict with Israel. Whereas previous governments had insisted on military confrontation and on the unacceptability of a peaceful solution, Assad softened this stand virtually from the time he assumed direction of the government. Often assailed by Jadid for his desire to concentrate on the development of the armed forces before undertaking hostilities with Israel, Assad all but formally accepted Resolution 242 of the Security Council after his coup. And following the October War, Assad accepted Resolution 338. Later, his government entered into negotiations with Israel that culminated in a disengagement agreement. This approach is a radical departure. Domestically, Assad's policy is characterized by a totally different perspective in the media. The Syrians have secured Soviet support and now accuse Israel of wanting war, suggesting that recurrent hostilities between Israel and her Arab neighbors benefit Israel through Zionist expansion. Thus, "we Arabs must put an end to the chain of wars."[121]

Syria's primary concern in its confrontation with Israel is the recovery of the Golan Heights, occupied by Israel in 1967. There are major differences of opinion among the Syrian population on various issues between the two countries. With respect to Golan, however, there is no difference. All Syrians want, demand, and expect return of the Golan to Syrian control. Cession of any part of it, even on the basis of a long-term lease, is unacceptable to virtually any Syrian. Syrian sovereignty and the termination of Israeli control over the Heights are a sine qua non of any settlement. The incessant public insistence by Syrian leaders on return of the Golan is sincere; no agreement is possible for less.[122]

The straightforward Golan issue explains much of Syrian policy. It explains Syria's rejection of the negotiation concept after 1967, for Syrians were convinced that Israel would never agree to return the Golan. Thus, negotiation was refused because it would reduce Arab support for Syria (as others' needs were met). This also explains Syria's insistence on rejection of the concept of "minor adjustments" to the pre-June 5 borders, since Golan (it was felt) would be one such sacrifice.[123]

Given the determination to reacquire the Golan, one can understand the importance the Syrians have placed on blocking any solidification of the status quo. Syrian spokesmen have attacked Israel's demand for secure borders, probably not so much from lack of understanding as from thorough understanding of the logical conclusion—that much of the Israeli-occupied Golan would be claimed by Israel as necessary to security.[124] This, too, is the basis for Syria's demand that disengagement be explicitly tied to a peace settlement requiring withdrawal to pre-June 5 boundaries.[125] Although the disengagement accord was so linked, to the satisfaction of the Syrians,[126] later problems in negotiations have reinforced Syrian doubts concerning the likelihood of a peaceful settlement including restoration of the Golan. Thus, Syrian Golan refugees have not resettled to any extent in that portion of the Golan returned through the 1974 disengagement accord. There are several reasons for their retaining refugee status,[127] but the continued depopulation of the Golan effectively underscores the proximity of war and the readiness of the Syrian government[128] to accept it as a means of regaining control—or ending Israeli occupation—of Syrian territory.

Recognizing the balance of forces, Syria has from the outset insisted upon an Israeli guarantee of total withdrawal before entering "negotiations." Since such a guarantee is unlikely, Syria will continue to demand it.[129]

We have already described the fundamental change in Syrian policy toward Israel. Before the Assad regime, Syria led the opposition to peaceful settlement, rejecting Security Council Resolution 242.[130] From its inception, the Assad regime has looked upon peaceful settlement as the preferable approach,[131] if Israel would relinquish territory occupied in 1967 and recognize the rights of the Palestinians.[132] Moderation was no more successful than the extremist policy Syria had followed, however; and when Egypt's attempt to secure American backing for progress failed, Assad was prepared to consider war. Indeed, the new Syrian position facilitated war planning, for agreement on objectives was easy—war aims were limited, and the destruction of Israel was not even considered.[133] Nor has Syrian policy reverted to its pre-Assad "irreconcilable" image. Since the October War, the Syrians have consistently and publicly favored peace talks. (This implicitly means the acceptance of Israel's existence.)[134] As we have seen, today Syria suggests it is Israel that favors war, while "we are above all for a political solution."[135] It is Israel's unwillingness to return the occupied territories and recognize Palestinian rights, the Assad regime maintains, that makes the use of force inevitable.

That Assad's change in Syrian policy on a peaceful settlement rests on values fundamentally different from Jadid's must be clear. Jadid's Syria was isolated in the Arab world (except for the Palestinians). The Syrian leadership feared Egypt or Jordan might reach a separate accord with Israel. Since Israel was less concerned about Sinai and the West Bank than about the Golan, either Egypt or Jordan or both might settle; but nothing short of war could bring back the Heights. No one even seriously tried to persuade Syria to accept a peaceful solution.[136] The new leadership placed a high priority on Arab cooperation. Recognizing strategic threat (potentially effective use of force) as the key factor likely to persuade Israel to negotiate withdrawal from the occupied territories, Syria initially depended upon cooperation with Egypt to compose that threat. Thus, as it became clear that Egypt would remove itself from the combined strategic threat to Israel, the Syrian leadership seized upon the remaining alternative—an eastern front. The Egyptian agreement—Sinai II—has been opposed and condemned in order to increase the costs of such an option. (Indeed, although preferring a peaceful resolution, Assad has never hesitated to disrupt Egyptian attempts at single-front settlements.)[137]

When Egypt, Jordan, and, to a lesser extent, other actual or potential Arab allies seem to be approaching a position that will remove them from their possible role as a Syrian bargaining resource, they can expect Syrian attacks.[138] Syria's strategy is to actively enlist the aid and cooperation of all who can apply pressure on Israel directly or indirectly—Egypt, Jordan, the oil-producing states of the Persian Gulf, the PLO.[139] Needing Egyptian support and maximum Arab unity to achieve recovery of the Golan and a peaceful settlement sometimes forces Syria to make greater sacrifices than its leadership would like in order to maintain Arab solidarity.[140] On the other hand, recognizing that Israeli strategy places a premium upon the breaking up of the Arab coalition, and particularly on dividing Egypt and Syria, the latter nations sometimes have found that the only way to maintain unity and support is to threaten war.[141]

Another major element in Syrian policy toward Israel is Soviet support. Such backing is necessary not only because Syria's military forces depend upon Soviet matériel, training, and support, but also because of the exigencies of domestic Syrian politics.[142] Thus, while Syria does not subordinate its own policies toward Israel to those of its superpower provider, Damascus' position certainly are strongly influenced by Moscow's. In the past, Syria has not been able to mount either war or peace policies seriously or effectively without Soviet support.

Currently, Soviet policy views the Geneva conference, under the joint chairmanship of the United States and the Soviet Union, as the best vehicle for a settlement in accordance with Moscow's interests. Soviet superpower status would thereby be underscored, and the Soviet Union might be able to exert considerable influence on the outcome. This policy is very much in line with Syrian interests as well, for a multilateral framework brings the Arab alliance (and solidarity) into Syria's bargaining hand, ensures that Egypt is not proceeding too far toward a separate accord, and—if Palestinian presence were effected—would reduce Assad's vulnerability to the Palestinians and to his countrymen.

Whatever the forum of settlement, Syrian policy stresses the importance of the threat or use of force as the talks proceed. The clearest example of this policy was in the extended hostilities around Mt. Hermon preceding the conclusion of the disengagement agreement in the spring of 1974. "Fighting while talking" confers several benefits: it reduces the strength of domestic groups opposing settlement and favoring resumption of hostilities; it adds to the pressure on Israel; it maintains readiness; it forces Israel to absorb higher costs in continued occupation; and it demonstrates the unacceptability of the status quo.[143]

To what could the status quo give way? Syria's views of the shape of an acceptable settlement are ambiguous. Given the bitterness of the policy debate, it is unlikely that Syria will take the initiative. Rather, Syrian leaders will respond to Israeli initiatives, trying to refine proposals that hold out the possibility of success. Generally, Assad will accept a demilitarized Golan or even one occupied by international forces. He is prepared to end the state of belligerency with Israel, to recognize that nation, and perhaps even to establish diplomatic and commercial relations, although he would prefer to broach these separately. Israeli forces must withdraw totally from occupied Golan, possibly in stages but not over an unduly extended period. Although Syrians have pointed out that neither demilitarization nor continued occupation is of avail in preventing violence in an age of missiles, Assad has already given indications of his willingness to accept international forces in the Golan. Syria will not take a firm position on the Sinai front or on Jerusalem. With respect to the Palestinian question, it defers to the PLO and other Palestinian sentiment.[144] It is likely that Assad will continue to search for means to disarm his perceived potential opponents. Certainly he can be expected to require Soviet approval at each step, as well as some sort of Palestinian "blessing." Moreover, he will give substantial weight to the opinions of his brother, Rifaat, minister of defense, Mustapha Tlas, and Foreign Minister Abdel Halim Khaddam.[145]

Rather than align Syria with a "rejectionist front" or take the lead among the moderates on the Arab-Israeli (and occupied territories) issue, Assad probably will continue to attack those who move far ahead of him in coming to terms with Israel; deny any credit to Israel for the outcome of agreements Syria may reach; claim a Syrian victory (a victorious zero-sum game) for any such agreements; confront Israel militarily, politically, and economically in every possible way during the negotiations; and take few initiatives and make very few initial compromises, opting instead to deal on others' terms and his own often-stated basic objectives. This approach facilitates defense of ongoing bargaining, and has been used to defend past negotiations. In view of its relatively weak bargaining position vis-à-vis Israel, Syria would much prefer to deal from the strength of a united Arab front that includes Egypt and Jordan, the two other Arab belligerents bordering on Israel; Saudi Arabia, as the financial backbone and the country with leverage on Israel's primary external supporter; and the Palestinians. Such a strategy has encountered important obstacles:

Egypt, traditionally the most powerful Arab country but also the confrontation state most insulated from Levantine currents, could—and did—

reach separate agreements largely detracting from Syria's bargaining power.

Saudi Arabia could not be counted on to "deliver" an embargo against the United States in many circumstances.

The PLO would—and did—react like Syria to any negotiations to which it was not a party and that might remove an Arab belligerent; also, with substantial independence of action in Lebanon and as a transnational force throughout the Middle East, it could obstruct settlement initiatives Syria considered viable—thus threatening Syrian independence of action.

Finally, the Syrians too have noted the Soviet pattern of behavior delineated in Chapter 2.

The solution to these problems was a united eastern front with elements weaker than (and therefore dependent on) Syria.[146] Such a front necessarily consisted of Jordan, the PLO, and Lebanon.

Jordan's troubled relations with the Palestinian movement [147] have complicated the Syrian-Jordanian relationship. The Palestinian cause is important in Syria, where support for it is a matter of deepest faith; and the bitter Palestinian feelings resulting from the September 1970 Jordanian civil war placed a strain on Syrian policies toward Jordan. In 1970, Syrian armor intervened in Jordan;[148] but the ambivalent and ill-coordinated (or uncoordinated) thrust was aborted largely because of the opposition of Assad, who within three months took over the leadership of Syria. Assad's orientation and policies regarding Jordan were almost diametrically opposed to Jadid's.

Ever conscious of the power of the Syrian Palestinian constituency, and therefore offering nominal support to the Palestinians, Assad sought to improve relations with Jordan immediately after he came to power. Nor has Syria significantly challenged the regime in Amman since. Although Syria closed its borders with Jordan during the July 1971 Jordanian mop-up of the civil war, and left them closed for about a year and a half, this action should not be allowed to overshadow the fact that the Syrian government made considerable efforts to improve both its own relations and those of the resistance with Jordan.[149] All evidence suggests that Assad was enormously relieved to be able to reopen the borders on December 1, 1972, with widespread Arab support for the action. The justification employed by Damascus for reopening the borders —even though Palestinian guerrillas continued to view Hussein's government with almost more bitterness and fury than was directed at Israel—was unity against Israel.[150] Since the lifting of the border measures, relations between these Arab neighbors have been good. Although Jordan was a reluctant and minor participant in the October War, Jordanian soldiers saw action on the Golan front.

Jordan and Syria began to interact openly on a major scale in early 1975, as it became apparent that the Syrian-Palestinian unified command was inadequate to the task of creating a credible strategic threat to Israel. In mid-1975, Assad visited Jordan, and the Arab world soon heard rumors about agreements on Syrian-Jordanian military coordination. These plans, as well as rapid political and economic cooperation, matured over the next few months. As the Sinai II accord was signed, the Syrian-Jordanian alliance was sealed. Jordan's redeployments also reflected the new policy. Although the program of coordination presented a concrete approach to specific areas and types of political, economic, and military cooperation, the broad strategic meaning was clear— Syria and Jordan were thenceforth to constitute a single front. The new eastern front would stretch from Ras an-Naqoura on the Lebanese coast to the Gulf of Aqaba.[151]

Extension of a united front into Lebanon, however, would create a new peril: Israel might hold Syria responsible for Palestinian attacks launched from southern Lebanon. Indeed, from almost any perspective, the Palestinians and Lebanon constituted two major complexes of problems.

We have already reviewed the importance of the Palestinian issue in Syrian politics. The signal role accorded the Palestine question has required the many Syrian governments to adopt strong positions. Before 1967, Syria had supported a group called the Palestine Liberation Front (PLF). Following the June War, however, the PLF, Youth for Revenge, and Heroes of the Return[152] merged to form the Popular Front for the Liberation of Palestine (PFLP), under the leadership of George Habbash.[153] Just before the war, the Syrian Ba'ath had established the (Ba'athist) Vanguards of the Popular War of Liberation Organization. The military element of the Vanguards was known as Sa'iqa. Originally formed from Palestinian elements in, and linked to, the Syrian army, Sa'iqa was later joined to the Ba'ath party apparatus.

From 1967 to 1970, Sa'iqa was perhaps the most active of the guerrilla organizations and therefore rapidly attracted a large number of adherents. It played a major role in Syrian politics, but it also attracted support from other Palestinian organizations as a major alternative to Fatah. Sa'iqa even attempted a coup in Jordan and was a major irritant in Lebanon, where it enjoyed a large following and played a key role in bringing about the Lebanese-Palestinian clashes in April and October 1969.[154]

Syria has not limited its involvement to Sa'iqa. In addition to the PLF and Sa'iqa, it has supported the Popular Revolutionary Front for the Liberation of Palestine (PRFLP), the Popular Front for the Liberation of Palestine-General Command (PFLP-GC), the Palestine Liberation Army (PLA), and Fatah. Other groups also have been permitted to operate on Syrian territory, but Habbash has frequently been in conflict with authorities in Damascus.[155]

Jadid backed the Palestinians because he desired Palestinian support in inter-Arab disputes. Sa'iqa worked to overthrow Hussein. In Lebanon, the Ba'ath was strong among Lebanese and among Palestinian refugees in the Bekaa and South Lebanon. Sa'iqa therefore was a powerful force in this area.

However, Syria supported the Palestinians not only with Sa'iqa: PLA units were dispatched from Syria in October 1969 to reinforce the guerrillas in combat against the Lebanese.[156] A similar but more ambiguous set of events took place in September 1970 in Jordan.

Assad's coup led to a change in Syrian policy toward the resistance. First, over a period of six months, Sa'iqa was purged of Jadid elements. Assad was attempting to repair relations with regimes alienated from his predecessor, and a major concern was Jordan. For this reason, a large shipment of tanks, troop carriers, light weapons, and ammunition—sent by China (via Algeria) to Fatah —was intercepted and confiscated by the Syrians.[157] This action complicated relations with Algeria; and because wide-scale Jordanian-Palestinian fighting erupted in Jordan soon after the seizure, the Assad regime received considerable criticism from the Palestinians. Assad closed the borders with Jordan, but sent the Syrian chief of staff, General Tlas, to mediate.

Soon after July 1971, Syria began to restrict the Palestinians. The number and severity of the restrictions varied, but generally the guerrillas' political activities in Syria were proscribed and operations against Israel had to be approved by the army command. Syria exercises strict supervision over the PLA and over the Yarmouk Brigade (formed primarily by Jordanian defectors from the 1970 civil war).

The new regime, then, has been very circumspect about supporting the Palestinians against other Arab regimes. In the July 1971 fighting, for example, Jordan tried to pressure the Palestinians to accept the settlement proposals advanced in Jidda. The closing of Syria's Jordanian border was a minimum act of solidarity, largely for appearances. However, in 1973, Syria clearly supported the guerrillas against Lebanon. After the initial cease-fire collapsed, Syria closed its borders with Lebanon, and PLA and Yarmouk Brigade units crossed the frontier.[158] It is likely that Lebanon simply paid a double price for objectives unrelated to it. In late 1972 and early 1973, Syria had begun to exert even greater control over the Palestinians in the country. Almost unprecedented restrictions came into play.[159] In this perspective, Assad needed a stage on which to dramatize his continued support for the Palestinian cause. Also, he was determined "to convince the peace-makers in Cairo that any agreement with Israel which does not take the Golan into account will be bound to fail. . . ."[160]

As the planning for the October War reached its final state, Syrian relations with the Palestinian movement neared a nadir. The Assad government seemed to take issue with the quasi-governmental status of the PLO and objected to the PLO claim to be the only legitimate representative of the Palestinian people. New restrictions were placed on the commandos, and Syria refused to allow the transfer of some PLA units to Iraq.[161] Clearly, these initiatives were part of the war preparations. Some were related to political ends and were designed to help shore up the eastern front against Israel. Others were related to Syrian military preparedness.

Since the October War, Syria has tried to reinforce the most moderate Palestinian leadership, whose views are largely in accord with Assad's. Although Sa'iqa has waged a long struggle to wrest the leadership of the Palestinian movement from Fatah, in recent years Sa'iqa's main role has been to represent Syrian views. Fatah's Yassir Arafat was not immediately liked by Assad, and other Arab leaders have had similar reactions. Nevertheless, Syria's decision makers concluded that Arafat represented the best hope for a resolution to the Palestinian issue. As a moderate leader of the largest Palestinian group, he was influential. Syrian leaders apparently also concluded that most of the Palestinians could and would follow Arafat when the proper situation arose. In July 1972, Syria first agreed to allow Arafat to control all of the guerrilla groups in southern Lebanon.[162] From then until 1976, Sai'qa usually supported Fatah. (We shall consider the later Syrian-Palestinian problems after reviewing Syrian-Lebanese relations.) Syria's current policy on the Palestinian issue must be understood: Syria will accept what "the Palestinians" agree to. Likewise, Damascus will oppose what the Palestinians oppose. A Syrian Foreign Ministry official said:

Syria . . . cannot sign any agreement unless the Palestinians agree to it. If they do not agree . . . Syria could not acknowledge any "organization" or "group" . . . called "Israel." Syria . . . was a third party and could no more legitimize Israel than could a third party legitimize one individual's usurpation of another's house. Without Palestinian acquiescence the recognition of Israel by Syria or any other Arab state would be legally invalid and politically without value.[163]

Lebanese-Syrian relations are something of an anomaly. Although there is a strong kindred feeling between the peoples of the two countries, and traditions and customs carry over from one people to the other without any clear distinction based upon arbitrary political demarcations, the recent histories of Syria and Lebanon have been so divergent that a number of disputes have arisen. The relatively open political forum in Lebanon has been a particular source of problems at times, as have the vagaries of Palestinian-Lebanese relations. Syrian political refugees have joined the numerous middle-class émigrés in Lebanon, and their feelings about the Damascus regimes often have not been muffled. Despite some isolated individual problems of this sort, Assad generally has followed a policy of improving relations with Lebanon. The principal difficulty, as with his Jordanian rapprochement, has been the Palestinians. In cases of Palestinian-Lebanese conflict, Assad—at least publicly—has supported the Palestinians. Moreover, the closure of the Jordanian-Syrian border, also undertaken for the Palestinian movement, exacted a heavy economic toll from Lebanon.

Lebanon has long been viewed as the most Western-oriented country in the Middle East, and therefore has perhaps been given disproportionate atten-

tion outside the region. Syrians have perceived their role as growing in importance and that of Lebanon as declining. Indeed, there was a widespread feeling
in Syria after the October War that Lebanon might disintegrate over the
succeeding years while Syria consolidated.[164] It is in the context of this perception that Syrian policy toward the Lebanon conflict must be considered.

After the June War, and particularly after "Black September," the Palestinian leadership increasingly concentrated its political and military activities
in Lebanon. Commando operations brought Israeli shelling to southern Lebanon; the influx of mostly Muslim Palestinians threatened the Lebanese religious political system; internal and international migrations, some caused by
the shellings in the south, altered the social structure of the country; Palestinians and private militias imported large quantities of firearms. By 1975, the
authority of the central government was minimal, and that of traditional
leaders of society was threatened. Lebanon remained at the edge of anarchy,
and only a small incident was needed to push it over the brink. That incident
was a protest by fishermen in Sidon in February 1975. From March to September 1975, an intermittent civil war fought between a complex coalition of forces
arrayed along religious, political, socioeconomic, and other dimensions raged
through Lebanon. Although the various participants received some outside
support, the conflict was primarily internal, concerning domestic issues and
problems.[165]

The renewal of fighting in Lebanon in September 1975 ushered in a new,
international stage of the civil war. Syria had participated in helping to settle
the initial phase, and Syrian good offices led to a compromise resolution, under
the terms of which greater representation was to be accorded certain Muslim
elements of the population, while overall leadership was returned to the hands
of the traditional Lebanese leaders. Syrian support for traditional Lebanese
leaders—the Christian and Sunni "establishment"—was designed to safeguard
stability in the country while rearranging the political system to allow for the
rise of a few younger leaders.

The renewed conflict in September 1975 seriously threatened the territorial integrity of Lebanon. Syria was concerned for two reasons. First, the
mountains in southern Lebanon form a natural defensive frontier. Properly
armed, they could tie down substantial numbers of Israeli troops. If Israel were
to annex southern Lebanon, however, the defense of Syria would be jeopard-
ized. A second concern centered on the appearance of sectarian secession—
Damascus feared the outbreak of sectarian dissidence against the minority
Alawi government in Syria. Thus, after several unsuccessful attempts at mediating the conflict, Assad resorted to the dispatch of Sa'iqa, PLA, and finally
Syrian army units into Lebanon.[166] Although these troops purported to be
"keeping the peace," in fact they began almost immediately to coordinate with
the Phalangists in offensive operations against the Palestinians and Lebanese
leftists.[167]

The Syrian political strategy by 1976, then, had changed to an eastern front strategy combining Syria, Jordan, Lebanon (under Syrian influence), and the Palestinians—against Israel. The Palestinian leadership would be restructured to accommodate Syrian policy; and Syria was to emerge as a dominant factor in a Middle East settlement, able to "deliver" Syrian, Jordanian, Lebanese, and Palestinian blessing to a settlement that, presumably, would see Israeli withdrawal from, and the establishment of international forces and early-warning devices in, the Golan; the construction of a Palestinian entity in the West Bank and Gaza acceptable to the PLO and Jordan (and probably linked to the latter); recognition of and the signing of treaties with Israel; and other such provisions.

Iraq presents a very different problem. Rather than being the object of Syrian intervention, it has had substantial influence on, and attraction for, a large constituency within Syria. The two Ba'ath regimes have shown little interest in a reconciliation. Each bestows more criticism than praise on the other. However, their consistent verbal animosity gains greater attention than their cooperation. Iraq has provided economic assistance to Syria, and each provides firm diplomatic support for the other against its major military threat —Israel in Syria's case, Iran in Iraq's case. The change in Iraq's government, from al-Bakr to Saddam Hussein, a slow revolution (described in Chapter 4), has been attended by a shift to moderation and pragmatism consonant with Assad's approach. Iraq made a major military contribution on the Golan front in 1973; and since the war it has sent very substantial economic aid to Syria in recognition of the devastation the war brought Syria. Moreover, playing the 1967 Syrian role, Iraq disapproved of the cease-fire in late October 1973 and withdrew its forces from the Syrian front. Iraq and Syria have not agreed on disengagement, either.[168] Yet in the absence of the Kurdish conflict, Iraqi forces would surely return in the event of renewed hostilities. Iraq's "rejection front" represents a policy option that increases Assad's leverage on Egypt. It is an option to which Syria would rather not turn at this time, however. Yet should the prospects of a war become even greater, Assad probably will expect Iraq's help.[169]

Relations between the rival Ba'ath regimes seriously worsened in 1975, when a dispute erupted over the waters of the Euphrates River. The erection of the Tabqa dam on the Euphrates has been the principal economic development project in Syria. However, the merits of the dispute seem to play a relatively minor role in its evolution. Rather, the central element in Iraqi-Syrian relations is the competition of the two regimes for subregional leadership. Jordanian fears of Iraq directly contributed to the establishment of the Syrian-Jordanian entente, which assures its members a role greater than any Iraq can reasonably aspire to.

Besides the Euphrates dispute, the two regimes came into conflict over the Kurdish rebellion, in which Syria provided aid to Iraqi Kurds; the Lebanese crisis, in which Iraq and the Iraqi-supported Arab Liberation Front took a militant stand in support of the PLO and the Lebanese leftist (so-called "nationalist") forces. When Sa'iqa and the PLA entered the Lebanon fray, one of their first targets was the editorial staff and offices of the Iraq- and ALF-oriented newspaper, *Al-Moharrer*. Syria and Jordan answered in kind when Iraq redeployed its forces toward the Syrian border following the intervention of the Syrian army in Lebanon in June 1976. In response to Syrian demands for higher transit fees on oil moved through pipelines running from Iraq across Syria and Lebanon, Iraq cut off the oil in the spring of 1976. Because Syria took its fees as oil, the Damascus regime became dependent upon the Saudis to make up for the Iraqi embargo.

The last regional object of Syrian attention is the Arabian Peninsula. As in the other environments we have considered, Assad's approach to the oil-producing countries of the Persian Gulf has differed markedly from the policies pursued by his predecessor, Salah Jadid. In May 1970, ARAMCO's pipeline through Syria was ruptured. Although the break was accidental, the Jadid regime demanded higher transit fees as a prerequisite to repairs. The pipeline lay severed for months. Soon after Assad assumed power, however, the pipeline was repaired (and the fees were increased). Assad terminated the restrictions on trade with Saudi Arabia as well as the prohibition against Saudi overflights. The "Voice of the Arabian Peninsula," a revolutionary broadcast aired over Damascus Radio, also ceased. Similarly, good relations have been established with the Union of Arab Emirates. Assad has sought to improve Syria's relationship with these regimes for two reasons. First, a principal objective of his regime has been the reversal of the isolation in which Syria found itself at the time of his accession to power. Consequently, given the inability of their economies to productively absorb the vast funds accruing to them, these countries represent important potential (and now actual) contributors to the Syrian economy, which has badly needed capital investment and hard currencies, and to the Syrian military.[170] After the war, Assad recognized that King Faisal was not only a Syrian financial benefactor but was also in a unique position to bring American pressure to bear on Israel, and thus to assist Syria in the realization of its political goals. For this reason, Syria will continue to pursue close cooperation with Saudi Arabia, even though policy differences may arise on matters of tactics.[171]

Syria's most important nonregional ties are with the Soviet Union. Beginning in the late 1940s, Syrian governments moved increasingly close to the Soviet Union. The Jadid government pursued a policy of particularly close cooperation with Moscow; indeed, Assad criticized his predecessor for some of his regime's actions in this connection. However, once in power, Assad abandoned his role as critic and generally continued Syria's good relations with the Russians. When the Russians were forced to leave Egypt, they increased their presence in Syria.

The Syrian rejection of Security Council Resolution 242 was a major point of disagreement between Moscow and Damascus; but although the Soviet media attacked Syria's position, there is no evidence to suggest that the Syrian view seriously disturbed the Soviets. Eventually, Assad indicated more flexibility on the question of peaceful settlement, eliminating the most serious point of contention between the two countries.[172] The Cairo-Moscow rift in the summer of 1972 discomfited Syria. Faced with the prospect of his two most important allies (in the effort to recover Golan) taking separate routes, Assad played an active role in trying to reconcile the two.[173] At the time, Syria's relations with Moscow were excellent: a Soviet squadron had visited Latakia in the winter, and a new shipping line was instituted between Latakia and Ilyichevsk.[174] Soviet economic assistance was very considerable (the bulk of foreign aid to Syria); and even if foreign trade was not oriented significantly toward Moscow, the Soviet Union and Eastern Europe were the backbone of the development program.[175] Moreover, Soviet aid in the petroleum industry was beginning to make a substantial payoff.

In the fall of 1972, then, Syria, still trying to repair Egyptian-Soviet relations, was endeavoring to get additional military assistance from the Soviet Union and yet to maintain a safe distance from Iraq, toward which it was being pushed by Moscow.[176] The somewhat uneasy situation between Syrian military personnel and Soviet advisers never reached the crisis stage that in Egypt precipitated the advisers' expulsion.[177] Syria's loyalty was rewarded: the Soviet Union and Syria reached an agreement under the terms of which Syria would receive an advanced, integrated air defense system similar to Egypt's; Russia would have the right to use several airfields for strategic purposes related to the U.S. Sixth Fleet; and the Soviet Union would receive extensive privileges in Latakia and Tartus.[178]

For four years, from late 1972 until 1976, President Assad maintained his cooperation with the Soviet Union rather easily.[179] The post-October War environment brought a new policy toward the United States; but unlike his counterpart in Egypt, Assad took care to maintain the usually close Syrian-Soviet cooperation. Indeed, in his own interest, Assad has seen fit to give Moscow as high a profile as possible in disengagement and the peace talks. Although Syrians have occasionally objected to what they have seen as undue Soviet restraint in providing arms and applying pressure on the Middle East issue,[180] Assad recognizes that the Syrian military forces depend on Soviet matériel and training, and that there is no near-term prospect of replacing that Soviet function. Moreover, certain domestic constituencies preclude such a turning from Moscow. Finally, Soviet support can provide the greater bargaining latitude vis-à-vis domestic critics (as well as Israel) that is essential to a settlement. Thus, however Assad may try to improve Syria's relations with the West, he will not replace Soviet ties—at least not until the Israel problem is resolved.

Syria, needing Soviet support, will likely continue to press for the preferred Soviet approach to a Middle East peace: the Geneva conference. Besides the advantages already identified, Syria can thus be assured of Soviet support. In return, Syria will continue to be a Soviet mouthpiece, insisting on the importance of Soviet participation, and will provide Moscow the high visibility at the conference and in any separate agreements (as in the disengagement talks).[181] Similarly, it can be anticipated that when the Soviets take a more cautious policy toward peace—by opposing the personal diplomacy of Kissinger, by demanding an overall approach to settlement, or because they fear American inroads—Syria will not publicly go beyond the most conservative Soviet position. (Indeed, sometimes Assad will intentionally remain far to the rear of Soviet policy on settlement—at least publicly—in order to secure political, economic, or military concessions.)

Recognizing that he has an increasing number of cards to play, Assad has disregarded Soviet criticism of his Lebanon policy. Since Syrian forces would ultimately defeat the Palestinian-Lebanese leftist groups, Damascus realized the Soviet Union would not go too far in supporting the loser over the winner, especially since the latter represented their largest regional investment (after Egypt).

As we have indicated elsewhere,[182] close Syrian-Soviet relations have not been without controversy in Syria, particularly among the military. The 1976 conflict between Damascus and Moscow also exacerbated existing disenchantment with Soviet weapons systems and resentment against the Lebanese Communist party for its criticism of the Assad regime.[183] The Ba'ath regime must, however, preserve at least the appearance of good relations with the Soviet Union for some time in the future.

Syrian policies toward the United States are more ambiguous. While President Assad is known to wish better relations with the West than Syria has had in recent years—or in 15 to 20 years—he also recognizes the costs and benefits. In this context the cost of a clear-cut and ambitious all-out rapprochement with the United States before a Middle East settlement is reached would be severe: loss of Soviet backing at a crucial time in Arab-Israeli relations, a time when Syrian leaders believe Syria must, and can, deal from a position of strength. Recognizing that they cannot expect untrammeled support from Washington in return, there is no persuasive reason to go too far toward rapprochement. No one can fill the Soviet role in military supply; and Washington would not, even if its production capacity allowed such a policy.

Yet there are benefits in a slight rapprochement. Besides increasing potential pressure on Israel, improving Syrian-American relations increases the potential resources that may be expended for national development. Over time, and after a settlement, better ties with Washington will assist in reducing Syrian dependence on the Soviet Union. A major advantage of improving relations with the United States is the moderate and responsive image thereby given to Syria in Saudi eyes. Finally, a substantial body of opinion in Syria, as elsewhere in the Arab world, looks with favor on Americans and, to some degree, the United States. American technology in particular is highly respected.

Assad, recognizing the benefits of a better relationship with the United States, has made an effort in this direction virtually from the moment he assumed power. He facilitated tourist entry, invited U.S. sports teams, and made other cautious overtures.[184] Although political negotiations in the aftermath of the October War sped up the rapprochement, Assad has made it clear that he does not presently plan to go as far or as fast as Sadat in this connection.[185] Nevertheless, the official position of the Syrian government, like that of Egypt, is that the U.S. attitude has changed.[186]

In the last half of 1975, when Syria began to take an active role in the Lebanese conflict, the United States attempted to keep both Syria and Israel from undertaking actions that might lead to the outbreak of another Middle East war. However, as the Syrian mission became evident and gained acceptance in Israel and the United States, additional leeway was given. The Syrian military operations in Lebanon clearly helped to re-form the image of Syria held by Americans and even by Israelis. Ultimately, the Syrian role in the civil war and alignment with Jordan contributed to a low-profile, but marked, improvement in U.S.-Syrian relations and cooperation.

Military Programs

Until Assad took over, the objective of Ba'ath policy in the military was the creation of an "indoctrinated army." That goal was never achieved, except at the higher ranks, which were subject to political purges and control.[187] Assad has been less concerned with party loyalty than with regime loyalty. With fewer and less consequential challenges than Jadid had to meet, and with much greater popular support, he also has been able to work toward the improvement of the army's military capabilities.

The foregoing notwithstanding, the Syrian Army remains the guarantor of the Assad regime. We have indicated the pervasive presence of Alawis throughout the armed forces. They occupy key positions in every major element of the army, and constitute the true command and control network, bypassing (when necessary) the official unit commanders. Although the army is infrequently used for domestic purposes, it retains a primary capability for regime security.

From June 1967 until October 1973, Syria placed primary emphasis on upgrading its defense, particularly its air defense. The extent to which this stress devolved from Russian doctrine or to which it grew from Syrian military calculus is not clear. The results of the Syrian development of defensive capability were evident in October 1973, when the Syrian army held the Israeli ground forces in a stubborn defensive battle less than 20 miles from Damascus and Syrian surface-to-air missiles (SAMs) exacted a high toll of Israeli aircraft.

Like Egypt, Syria has suffered from the dearth of trained manpower. The impact of this shortage has been particularly acute in the air force, where modern aircraft and air combat demand increasing sophistication on the part of command, combat, and maintenance personnel. Indeed, although Arab air forces possess a combined numerical superiority over Israel, the Israeli air force—at least until the October War—had a distinct advantage over Egypt, Jordan, and Syria in the most important air combat areas: initial ordnance delivery capability, range, turnaround time, and number of qualified pilots.[188]

In an attempt to redress the military imbalance after 1967, Jadid and Assad sought to acquire matériel and training from the Soviet Union, which used its sole supplier status for leverage against Syria's policy of rejecting negotiation. By 1969 the Syrian leadership was dissatisfied with the Soviet response, and tried to use the Sino-Soviet rivalry to bring about more responsiveness from Moscow. Even the signing of a major arms agreement in July 1969 did not materially change the troubled Syrian-Soviet relationship, which improved only after the Assad coup in 1970.[189]

The departure of the Soviet forces and advisers from Egypt in July 1972 led to a rapid improvement of Syria's military position. In May, the two countries had concluded military assistance agreements envisaging Soviet assistance to the Syrian army and air force in exchange for a Soviet naval and air presence in Syria. In addition, Syria sought advanced Soviet aircraft, electronic countermeasures (ECM), and surface-to-air missiles.[190] In the aftermath of the July 1972 Soviet expulsion from Egypt, Moscow wasted little time in demonstrating its willingness to shift emphasis from Egypt to Syria by staging a very unsubtle but prestige-building airlift of matériel to Syria.[191] As a result of further military assistance agreements with the Soviet Union, concluded in the autumn of 1972, some Syrian objectives were realized. Syria received more MIG-21s and an integrated air defense system based on radar-controlled antiaircraft fire and several types of SAM missiles. The Soviet Union would help develop—and use—Latakia and Tartus.[192] In December 1972, the Assad government suspended fighting on the Israeli-Syrian border so that the SAMs (SAM-3 and SAM-6) could be installed by Soviet personnel.[193] However, it is quite possible that the relatively high level of fighting on the border in 1972 and 1973 was part of a policy to increase the training and experience of Syrian personnel[194] and to accustom Israel to a high activity level. Syrians did not fire the newly emplaced SAMs at Israeli reconnaissance aircraft, but only because Soviet operators balked at the idea. Later, SAM technicians from East Asia were secured to operate the SAMs.[195]

The most important military decision Syria has taken in many years was the determination to go to war in October 1973. Although the reason for this decision was political—the apparent impossibility of securing any movement toward the return of the Golan Heights—it is unclear precisely how much Assad really believed Syrian forces could accomplish. Syrian forces carried out an aggressive attack on the Golan at the outset of the war, but command, control, and other aspects of coordination (except withdrawal) seem not to have improved sufficiently. The SAM air defense system, and the Syrian defense line east of Sassa, consisting of concrete emplacements linked by trenches (and mine- and wire-screened), held relatively well, although Israeli aircraft had control of the skies in several sectors by the war's end.[196]

For months after the cease-fire, Assad maintained a policy of keeping the Mt. Hermon front active. Although this was not a serious military action (Syrian artillery fired sporadically and without any apparent effort to inflict damage), the policy at least partially met the demands of the pro-war constituency in Syria and also continued some economic pressure on Israel. Throughout the period of Assad-Kissinger negotiations on disengagement, the fighting continued.[197] The Syrian leadership understands and uses the interaction of political and military action:

> Political action . . . as we understand it, is an inevitable necessity. It should aim at achieving a solution, but not just any solution. It must be an honorable and dignified solution, a solution that straightens out matters, a solution that achieves justice and nothing else. We understand political action this way, and on this basis we shall continue political action. It is also as such and for the sake of this aim that we understand military action. For the sake of this aim we will continue military action.[198]

Soviet policy before the October War was to provide equipment that was, at best, one generation behind Israel's. Since 1973, however, Syria has received MIG-23s, some of the performance characteristics of which exceed those of the F-4. Syrian forces have a much higher proportion of modern equipment today than in October 1973. They also have SCUD surface-to-surface missiles (reportedly controlled by the Soviet Union). MIG-23 pilots may be from the Soviet Union, North Korea, or Cuba, for the most part; but Syrian pilots are being trained. There are approximately 3,000 Soviet advisers in Syria, and some of them are reported to have taken an active role in the October fighting.

The Syrian armed forces have grown in size as well as equipment since October 1973. Air defenses have been built up even more, and the experience gained in ECM and electronic counter-counter-measures (ECCM) in the war will have been useful in training. The defensive strategy will continue unchanged, although greater Arab use of ECM and ECCM can be anticipated. Similarly, aware that little progress has been made in reducing the relative effectiveness differential between Syrian and Israeli pilots in air combat, surface-to-surface missiles are more attractive both for deterrence and for offensive operations. In addition, some air-to-surface stand-off weapons will be sought by Syria to begin to bridge the Arab-Israeli gap in stand-off systems that exists in surface-to-surface and air-to-surface weapons.[199]

Nevertheless, Syrian forces probably have only a marginal offensive capability against Israel. Certainly, they cannot undertake a sustained offensive role. Because of the effectiveness of their defenses, however, and the consequent toll they could exact on limited Israeli resources, Syrian forces are a crucial component of the Arab military threat.

To what extent will Syria be willing to resort to force again for the return of Golan? Without question, if Egypt decided to resort to the ultimate recourse —war—Syria would join in the effort. It is virtually inconceivable that Syria would take on Israel alone or, in effect, without Egypt. One reason the Syrians fear Egyptian negotiations with Israel is the possibility that Egypt may gain enough to insulate itself against other Arab opinion (and thus immunize itself against Syrian pressure). Assad will not go to war with Israel over the Palestinian issue. Recovery of the Golan is a higher priority, however. In the event no further movement is made on the Golan, war is far from impossible as long as Egyptian cooperation can be achieved.

We shall not address Soviet policy in this study. It is, however, clear that Syria cannot go to war without a high level of Soviet support in the creation of an arms inventory, the development of a trained manpower base, and the availability of spares, ammunition, and maintenance. As in October 1973, a war may be launched without complete foreknowledge of the limits to be placed on Soviet support. Clearly, sole supplier status confers immense potential Soviet leverage over Syrian policy. Why, then, does Assad not attempt to diversify Syrian military supply? Will he? Syria has already attempted to purchase some British arms, only to be rebuffed.[200] Thus, at least until a settlement is achieved, Syria must accept Moscow's role as its sole major supplier. No other country has military hardware in sufficient quantities that are immediately available and the airlift and sealift capability (and lack of domestic pressure) to resupply Syria even during hostilities with Israel. Few countries possess aircraft and armor of the level of sophistication now available to Syria from the Russians.[201] Few of the potential Syrian suppliers can provide equivalent training or advisers. And any substantial purchases from the West entail the danger of reducing Soviet support. In addition, the Soviets are required to continue the training they provide for what is already an impressive arsenal in Syria. Thus, until a settlement frees Syria from near-term military requirements, the luxury of substantial diversification of supply is beyond its reach.

NOTES

1. For instance, Michael H. Van Dusen, "Political Integration and Regionalism in Syria," *Middle East Journal* 26, no. 2 (Spring 1972): 123–36.

2. One of the concrete results of this policy was the overrepresentation of minorities in the Syrian military. This development is discussed later in the text.

3. Moshe Ma'oz, "Attempts at Creating a Political Community in Modern Syria," *Middle East Journal* 26, no. 4 (Autumn 1972): 398.

4. Van Dusen, "Political Integration," pp. 123–28; Richard F. Nyrop et al., *Area Handbook for Syria* (Washington, D.C.: Foreign Area Studies Division, American University, 1971), p. 163.

5. See especially Van Dusen, "Political Integration," pp. 126–27.

6. Gordon H. Torrey, *Syrian Politics and the Military, 1945–1958* (Columbus: Ohio State University Press, 1964); Patrick Seale, *The Struggle for Syria* (New York: Oxford University Press, 1965); Itamar Rabinovich, *Syria Under the Ba'th 1963–1966: The Army-Party Symbiosis* (Jerusalem: Israel Universities Press; New York: Halsted Press, 1972).

7. Nyrop et al., *Area Handbook,* p. 163.

8. P. J. Vatikiotis, "The Politics of the Fertile Crescent," in Paul Y. Hammond and Sidney S. Alexander, eds., *Political Dynamics in the Middle East* (New York: American Elsevier, 1971), p. 237.

9. Ma'oz, "Attempts," pp. 399–402; Van Dusen, "Political Integration," pp. 132–33.

10. It should not, however, be inferred that the Qutriyin were alike. They represented a heterogeneous group of Ba'athists united mainly by opposition to the established Ba'athists.

11. Nikolaos Van Dam, "The Struggle for Power in Syria and the Ba'th Party (1958–1966)," *Orient* 14, no. 1 (March 1972): 10–11; Rabinovich, *Syria,* pp. 24–39.

12. These are described in detail in Van Dam, "The Struggle for Power," passim.

13. However, only 75–80 percent of these could be viewed as supporters of Jadid; the remainder followed Mohammed Umran.

14. See Van Dam, "The Struggle," pp. 16–17; Van Dusen, "Political Integration," p. 145; Rabinovich, *Syria;* Eliezer Beeri, *Army Officers in Arab Politics and Society* (New York: Praeger, 1969), pp. 336–38; William Hazen and Peter Gubser, *Selected Minority Groups of the Middle East: The Alawis, Berbers, Druze and Kurds* (Kensington, Md.: American Institutes for Research, 1973), pp. 81–82, 97–98; Martin Seymour, "The Dynamics of Power in Syria Since the Break with Egypt," *Middle Eastern Studies* 6, no. 1 (January 1970): 40; George Haddad, *Revolutions and Military Rule in the Middle East: The Arab States* vol. 2 (New York: Robert Speller, 1971), p. 45; Gad Soffer, "The Role of the Officer Class in Syrian Politics and Society" (Ph.D. dissertation, American University, 1968), p. 26.

15. The Syrian experience proved the validity of what Ba'athists should have learned from the Aref coup of November 1963 in Iraq—the impossibility of maintaining civilian party control over the military. As Michel Aflaq said, "We wish to alter the army's role by precluding the formation of a bloc of military officers within the party's leadership. When the party chooses as a leader someone from the military, he should not retain his military position. Rather, he should devote himself to civilian leadership." *Al-Hayat,* February 25, 1966, pp. 7–8. Also see A. I. Dawisha, "The Transnational Party in Regional Politics: The Arab Ba'th Party," *Asian Affairs,* 61, no. 1 (February 1974): 23–31.

16. Although the change in Ba'ath outlook began to be confirmed as early as 1963, old-line Ba'athists attacked it most vehemently immediately after the neo-Ba'ath coup of 1966, when Aflaq, for example, accused the new Syrian Ba'ath of deviationism, of subverting true Ba'athism. He accused the Syrian leadership of slavishness, comparing them to Arab Communists. *Al-Hayat,* February 25, 1966, pp. 7–8.

17. We shall not chronicle the progressive stages of Assad's control. It should only be noted here that his move in November 1970 was the last step of a multiple-stage change of power.

18. Rabinovich, *Syria,* pp. 215–17; Tabitha Petran, *Syria* (New York: Praeger, 1972), p. 240; Avigdor Levy, "The Syrian Communists and the Ba'th Power Struggle, 1966–1970," in Michael Confino and Shimon Shamir, eds., *The U.S.S.R. and the Middle East* (Jerusalem: Israel Universities Press, 1973), pp. 407–08; Aryeh Yodfat, "The End of Syria's Isolation?" *The World Today* 27, no. 8 (August 1971): 332–34.

19. See *Al-Nahar, As-Sayyad, Al-Anwar* from March 1969 through November 30, 1970. Also see "The Civilians Win," *An-Nahar Arab Report* 1, no. 37 (November 16, 1970): 1–2; "The Loser Wins," ibid. no. 38 (November 23, 1970): 1–2; Yodfat, "The End," p. 335.

20. Syrian constitution, Art. III.

21. Ibid., Art. 112.

22. Both provisions are in Art. 8.

23. Ibid., Art. 71, 84.

24. See Raymond A. Hinnebusch, "Local Politics in Syria: Organization and Mobilization in Four Village Cases," *Middle East Journal* 30, no. 1 (Winter 1976): 1–24.

25. Ibid., p. 6. *Al-Hayat*, the second largest Beirut newspaper, estimated party membership at 20,000 (Muhammed 'Anan, "Syria and the New Strategy for the Battle of Destiny," December 7, 1971, p. 10), but we feel the Hinnebusch estimate to be somewhat closer, if a bit high.

26. Hafez Assad, as quoted by David Holmstrom, "Syria—Unity, Liberty, and Socialism," *Middle East International,* no. 22 (April 1973): 11.

27. Ibid., "Assad's Syria," *The Daily Star* (Beirut), March 18, 1971, p. 6; Petran, *Syria,* pp. 251–52; Rabinovich, *Syria,* p. 217. Mohammad Khleifawi's considerable popularity was testament to the Syrian desire for appreciation of liberalization. Much of his popularity derived from his rescinding of suppressive measures while minister of the interior.

28. "It is true that 99 percent may draw snickers in certain circles, but it must be remembered that the Syrians were very enthusiastic in their support of the new regime." ("Assad Opens New Paths"). "The masses said yes . . . to Hafez Assad because he disagreed with the Ba'ath . . . He also said that 'the party will no longer be that of a special group because the cornerstone is individual freedom. . . .' " (*Al-Hayat* [Beirut], March 15, 1971, p. 3.)

29. See Paul Balta's articles in *Le Monde,* March 23–26, 1971 ("La Syrie baasiste, An VIII": I. "Détente, ouverture, réalisme," March 23, pp. 1, 15; II: "L'armée, source du pouvoir," March 24, p. 5; III: "Un vaste chantier," March 25, p. 6; IV: "L'épine dorsale," March 26, p. 5); Holmstrom, "Syria," p. 12.

30. See Art. 8 of the Syrian constitution; Holmstrom, "Syria," p. 11; Balta, "La Syrie baasiste," *Le Monde,* March 23, 1971, pp. 1, 15; Petran, *Syria,* p. 251; Mahmoud al-Ayyubi, "Syrian Government Policy Statement," FBIS, February 28, 1973, Supp. 6, pp. 1–2; Dawisha, "The Transnational Party," p. 27; Malcolm H. Kerr, "Hafiz Asad and the Changing Patterns of Syrian Politics," *International Journal* 28, no. 4 (Autumn 1973): 702–03.

31. Detailed reporting on the elections is in *al-Ba'ath,* May 3, 6–9, 20, 26–30, 1973; and *L'Orient le jour,* May 9, 14, 21, 28, 1973. *An-Nahar Arab Report* 4, no. 19 (May 7, 1973): 1, no. 4; and 4, no. 23 (June 4, 1973): 1; Europa, *The Middle East and North Africa, 1973–74* (London: Europa Publications, 1973), p. 627.

32. "The New Cabinet," *An-Nahar Arab Report* 4, no. 1 (January 1, 1973): 4; Europa, *The Middle East,* p. 626.

33. In Homs and Hama, traditional Ba'ath opposition and the Muslim Brotherhood attempted to persuade the Syrians to boycott the spring 1973 legislative elections.

34. "The New Cabinet"; Rabinovich, *Syria,* p. 217.

35. Alain Cass, "Cool Head in Damascus," *Middle East International,* no. 60 (June 1976): 7.

36. Only Ba'ath recruitment may take place in the army or among students, however.

37. The Ba'ath party exerts itself to ensure that information flows "down"to the people and up to the hierarchy. Such a communications system is subject to problems in human behavior, however. Thus, assistance from the other parties and "popular organizations" is very useful.

38. Nyrop et al., *Area Handbook,* p. 140.

39. Ibid.; Petran, *Syria,* p. 236.

40. "Waiting for War," *An-Nahar Arab Report* 5, no. 41 (October 14, 1974): 2–3.

41. See Graham Allison, *Essence of Decision: Explaining the Cuban Missile Crisis* (Boston: Little, Brown, 1971), passim.

42. Joseph Dunner, ed., *Dictionary of Political Science* (New York: Philosophical Library, 1964), p. 261.

43. It is incorrect to assume that the Arab-Israeli conflict is an exception. If this were the case, the Syrian government, the position of which has been relatively consistent on this subject, would have enjoyed much greater stability.

44. Riad N. el-Rayyes and Dunia Nahas, eds., *The October War: Documents, Personalities, Analyses and Maps* (Beirut: An-Nahar Press Services S.A.R.L., 1974), pp. 178–80; "Waiting for War"; "Syria: Two Years Under President Assad (1)," *An-Nahar Arab Report* 3, no. 39 (September 25, 1972): "Backgrounder"; "Jordan: Unwelcome Hand," ibid. no. 26 (June 26, 1972): 3; "Syrian Front: Tense but Calm," ibid. no. 51 (December 18, 1972): 2–3.

45. "Domestic Unrest," *An-Nahar Arab Report* 3, no. 23 (June 5, 1972): 1; "Mounting Tension," ibid. no. 25 (June 19, 1972): 2; "Internal Troubles," ibid. 2, no. 29 (July 19, 1971): 4; "Waiting for War."

46. "Rifaat Ali Suleiman Assad," *An-Nahar Arab Report* 6, no. 32 (August 11, 1975): "Profile." Also see Rifaat Assad's dissertation, "Economic, Social, and Political Evolution in the Syrian Arab Region from the National to the Class Revolution, 1946–1963" (Soviet Academy of Sciences, 1974). Some key excerpts appear in "Rifaat Ali Suleiman Assad."

47. The Defense Companies were established during the Jadid-Assad conflict. Personnel have been carefully selected for loyalty; equipment is the most up-to-date.

48. "Syria: The Ball Starts Rolling," *An-Nahar Arab Report* 5, no. 9 (March 4, 1974): 1.

49. Michael H. Van Dusen, "Syria: Downfall of a Traditional Elite," in Frank Tachau, ed., *Political Elites and Political Development in the Middle East* (Cambridge, Mass.: Schenkman, 1975), ch. 3, is the best portrait of the social revolution that has taken place in Syria over the last decade so far as it affects elite values.

50. See "Syria: Two Years Under President Assad (2)," *An-Nahar Arab Report* 3, no. 40 (October 2, 1972): "Backgrounder"; "Potential Trouble," ibid. 2, no. 15 (April 12, 1971): 1–2; "Stress on Stability," ibid. 6, no. 32 (August 11, 1975): 2–3; Douglas Watson, "Assad Seen Planning Cabinet Shift in Syria," Washington *Post*, June 5, 1976, p. 17.

51. Balta, "La Syrie baasiste," *Le Monde*, March 23, 1971, pp. 1, 15.

52. Ibid.; "Potential Trouble"; "The National Front," *An-Nahar Arab Report* 3, no. 18 (May 1, 1972): 2–3; "Military Moves," ibid. 4, no. 20 (May 14, 1973): 1; "Syria-USSR: Crisis Is Brewing," ibid. no. 30 (July 23, 1973): 2; "Domestic Fears," ibid. no. 39 (September 24, 1973): 2.

53. See Petran, *Syria*, p. 151; Rabi' Matar, "Socialist Union of Ba'ath and Nasserites Under the Leadership of Assad," *Al-Hawadith*, March 19, 1971, pp. 16–18.

54. Balta, "La Syrie baasiste," *Le Monde*, March 23, 1971, pp. 1, 15; R. D. McLaurin and Mohammed Mughisuddin, *The Soviet Union and the Middle East* (Washington, D.C.: American Institutes for Research, 1974), pp. 248–49; Aryeh Yodfat, "The U.S.S.R., Jordan and Syria," *Mizan* 11, no. 2 (April 1969): 87; "The Ba'th: Allergic to Advice," *An-Nahar Arab Report* 1, no. 27 (September 7, 1970): 4; "The National Front," ibid. 3, no. 18 (May 1, 1972): 2–3; "Cautious Approach," ibid. no. 32 (August 7, 1972): 2; "Domestic Fears"; "SCP: Titoist Trends," ibid. 5, no. 5 (February 4, 1974): 3–4; Levy, "The Syrian Communists," pp. 404–06; FBIS, December 15, 1974, p. 143; Joe Alex Morris, Jr., "Syria's Ties with Russ Show Signs of Cooling Off," Los Angeles *Times*, March 16, 1976, pt. I, pp. 1, 10.

55. "Ba'ath-SCP Tensions," *An-Nahar Arab Report* 7, no. 1 (January 5, 1976): 1–2; "Dispute Calls for Action," ibid. no. 35 (August 30, 1976): 2–3; Morris, "Syria's Ties."

56. Petran, *Syria*, pp. 150, 155, 203, 230, 243, 250.

57. Syrian Interior Minister Ali Zaza responded to a question on whether anti-regime groups were still active in Syria as follows: "Which groups? Do you mean groups such as the Muslim

Brotherhood or others? None of them has any grassroots now, for the [Assad] regime reached the popularity spirit. . . ." Interview, *Al-Bayraq,* March 30, 1974, p. 7. This vision is far removed from Syrian political realities, however.

58. *L'Orient le jour,* May 9, 14, 21, 28 1973; "Syrian Front: Tense But Calm," *An-Nahar Arab Report* 3, no. 51 (December 18, 1972): 2–3; "Sunnis' Urge to Rule," ibid. 4, no. 12 (March 19, 1973): 1.

59. An unusual feature of these transnational pressures is their visibility: The Beirut press provides a guide to the current views and inclinations of each major Arab state with a political following inside Syria.

60. Vatikiotis, "The Politics of the Fertile Crescent," pp. 227–37.

61. Petran, *Syria,* p. 234.

62. Amnon Sella, "Soviet Military Doctrine in the October War," unpublished ms, 1974; Sella, "Soviet Training and Arab Performance," Jerusalem *Post* Magazine, February 8, 1974, pp. 6–7.

63. R. D. McLaurin and Mohammed Mughisuddin, *Cooperation and Conflict: Egyptian, Iraqi, and Syrian Objectives and U.S. Policy* (Washington, D.C.: American Institutes for Research, 1975), pp. 195–96; Roger F. Pajak, "Soviet Military Aid to Iraq and Syria," *Strategic Review* 4, no. 1 (1976): 57; D. K. Palit, *Return to Sinai: The Arab Offensive, October 1973* (New Delhi: Palit and Palit, 1974), passim; Charles Wakebridge, "The Syrian Side of the Hill," *Military Review* 56, no. 2 (February 1976): 27; *U.S. News and World Report,* March 17, 1975, p. 14.

64. Moshe Ma'oz, "Syria Under Hafiz al-Asad: New Domestic and Foreign Policies," *Jerusalem Papers on Peace Problems* no. 15 (1975): 7.

65. Riad N. el-Rayyes and Dunia Nahas, eds., *Guerrillas for Palestine: A Study of the Palestinian Commando Organizations* (Beirut: An-Nahar Press Services S.A.R.L., 1974), p. 143; *The Arab World* 21, no. 5166 (March 28, 1974): 11–12; "Syria: Ball Starts Rolling."

66. *Svenska Dagbladet,* August 9, 1974, p. 3.

67. The best recent source on the Alawis is Hazen and Gubser, *Selected Minority Groups,* ch. 1.

68. See Eric Pace, "Northern Syria Finds New Prosperity, Thanks to Help from Its Neighbors," The New York *Times,* November 17, 1975, p. 10.

69. Ma'oz, "Syria Under Hafiz al-Asad," pp. 6–7; Ma'oz, "Alawi Military Officers in Syrian Politics," in H. Z. Schiffrin, *The Military and State in Modern Asia* (Jerusalem: Academic Press, 1976), pp. 285–86.

70. Abbas Kelidar, "Religion and State in Syria," *Asian Affairs* 61, no. 1 (February 1974): 19.

71. Andrew Bordwiec, "Syria Opening Doors Despite War Threat," Washington *Star-News,* November 17, 1974, p. A-6.

72. Nyrop et al., *Area Handbook,* pp. 66–67.

73. See Nyrop et al., *Area Handbook;* Petran, *Syria;* "Syrian Front: Tense but Calm"; "The Military in the Arab World: Syria," *An-Nahar Arab Report* 2, nos. 28 and 29 (July 12 and 19, 1971): "Backgrounder"; Vatikiotis, "The Politics of the Fertile Crescent," pp. 226–27.

74. Petran, *Syria,* pp. 228–30; Hinnebusch, "Local Politics," passim.

75. Petran, *Syria,* pp. 230–32.

76. Nadav Safran, "Arab Politics, Peace and War," *Orbis* 18, no. 2 (Summer 1974): 394.

77. By contrast, Tlas is considered anti-Palestinian.

78. Safran, "Arab Politics," p. 399; el-Rayyes and Nahas, ed., *Guerrillas for Palestine,* p. 143; "Disengagement Accord: Syrian Precautions," *An-Nahar Arab Report* 5, no. 22 (June 3, 1974): 1; "Syrian Front: Tense but Calm," pp. 2–3; "Taking Sides," *An-Nahar Arab Report* 1, no. 25 (August 24, 1974): 3–4; "Syria and the Palestinians," ibid. 4, no. 23 (June 4, 1973): "Backgrounder"; "Jordan: Hussein's Peace Efforts," ibid. 5, no. 6 (February 5, 1974): 3; "The Commandos: Plan for Action," ibid. 4, no. 7 (February 12, 1973): p. 4; Petran, *Syria,* pp. 253–54.

79. At the same time, it must be recalled that Syrian policies in this instance were justified on the basis of their contribution to the Palestinian cause. (See Hafez Assad's major speech on the issue, reprinted in full in FBIS, July 21, 1976, pp. H-1 to H-23). The Assad position is most likely not incredible to Syrians, for it is true that the Palestinians could achieve major benefits from a consolidated eastern front that led to a negotiated settlement including some form of Palestinian entity.

80. There are approximately 250,000 Palestinian refugees in Syria.

81. Syria has over 100,000 Syrian refugees from the conflicts of 1967 and 1973, as well as 250,000 Palestinian refugees.

82. Additional territory occupied by Israel in October 1973 and some of the Golan land taken in 1967 have been relinquished to Syria.

83. John Cooley, "Syria Opens Windows to the Outside World," *Christian Science Monitor,* December 27, 1971, p. 5.

84. This group includes Major General Ibrahim.

85. John Cooley, "Syria-Israel Disengagement: Soviets Take Part This Time," *Christian Science Monitor,* February 1, 1974, p. 1; FBIS, January 31, 1974, p. F-1. Also see "Syrian Ba'ath Party Congress Begins Today: Internal Troubles Reported," *Arab World* 21, no. 5215 (June 7, 1974): 5.

86. Safran, "Arab Politics," pp. 396–98.

87. "Is It a War of Attrition on the Golan?" *Arab World* 21, no. 5166 (March 28, 1974): 11–12.

88. See Joseph Kraft, "The Divided Arab World," Washington *Post,* April 16, 1974, p. A-17.

89. Ironically, Syria and the PFLP have had a very tumultuous relationship.

90. See "Syria: A Waiting Game," *An-Nahar Arab Report* 5, no. 13 (April 1, 1974): 1–2.

91. The dissent was centered in the armed forces and some factions of the Ba'ath. Both the negotiation of an agreement per se and the terms were debated before and after the fact. Marilyn Berger, "Mideast Signing Today," Washington *Post,* May 31, 1974, p. A-1; Berger, "Syria Seems Ready to Free POWs," ibid., May 2, 1974, p. A-1; Bernard Gwertzman, "Kissinger Is Given Syrian Proposals on Opening Talks," New York *Times,* January 21, 1974, pp. 1, 6; "Syrian Ba'th Congress: Assad Criticized," *An-Nahar Arab Report* 5, no. 24 (June 17, 1974): 3; "Disengagement Accord: Syrian Precaution," p. 1; "Syria: The Ball Starts Rolling"; *Arab World* 21, no. 5123 (January 28, 1974): 7.

92. This is not to say that the United States has formally committed itself to or supported total withdrawal. Rather, the link is viewed by the United States as being to the implementation of UN resolutions, the meaning of which is at best ambiguous.

93. Liberation of the 1967 territory was crucial to the agreement, since recovery of part of the occupied lands is symbolic of disengagement as a step toward total withdrawal.

94. "Disengagement Accord: Syrian Precautions"; "Syrian Ba'ath Congress: Assad Criticized"; "Syria's Crucial Position in Mideast Situation," *Arab World* 21, no. 5129 (February 5, 1974): 11–12; "Syria-Israel: Where They Disagree," *An-Nahar Arab Report* 5, no. 21 (May 27, 1974): 1; Jim Hoagland, "Kissinger Plan Key to Syrian Shift on Talks," Washington *Post,* March 3, 1974, p. A-25; Jason Morris, "Kissinger Breaks Syria Stalemate," *Christian Science Monitor,* February 28, 1974, p. 1. Iraq and Libya led opposition to the disengagement agreement.

95. See the "Objectives and Policies" section.

96. Safran, "Arab Politics," pp. 394–96; Levy, "The Syrian Communists," p. 399; "Syria-Jordan: A Much-Needed Detente," *An-Nahar Arab Report* 3, no. 50 (December 11, 1972): 2–3.

97. Past constitutions had not done so either.

98. Levy, "The Syrian Communists," p. 399; Rabinovich, *Syria,* p. 216; "Syria: Sunnis' Urge to Rule"; Petran, *Syria,* p. 236; Kerr, "Hafiz Asad," pp. 703, 704; "Syria: Mounting Tension";

"Syrian-Libyan Relations: In the Doldrums?," *An-Nahar Arab Report* 4, no. 10 (March 5, 1973): 1–3.

99. Levy, "The Syrian Communists," pp. 401–06, 408–09; McLaurin and Mughisuddin, *The Soviet Union,* pp. 248–49; Yodfat, "The U.S.S.R., Jordan and Syria," pp. 83–89.

100. "Syria: Cautious Approach," *An-Nahar Arab Report* 3, no. 32 (August 7, 1972): 2; "Syria: New Policy Lines," ibid. no. 35 (August 28, 1972): 1; "Syria-U.S.S.R.: Crisis Is Brewing," ibid. 4, 30 (July 30, 1973): 2; el-Rayyes and Nahas, eds., *The October War,* pp. 178–80; "Syria: Two Years Under President Assad (1)."

101. *Svenska Dagbladet,* August 9, 1974, p. 3; *Arab World* 21, no. 5180 (April 18, 1974): 11–12; *An-Nahar,* March 1, 1974, p. 1; *Al-Muharrer,* January 9, 1974; Jim Hoagland, "Kissinger Plan Key to Syrian Shift on Talks," Washington *Post,* March 3, 1974, p. A-25; "Soviet Experts: Another Eviction?" *An-Nahar Arab Report* 4, no. 40 (October 1, 1973): 1; "The Arab States: New Alignments," ibid. no. 48 (November 26, 1973): 3; Mclaurin and Mughisuddin, *The Soviet Union,* pp. 247–53.

102. See note 55. Also see Economist Intelligence Unit, *QER: Syria, Lebanon, Cyprus,* nos. 1–4 (1975) and nos. 1–2 (1976); and the 1975 and 1976 issues of *Middle East Economic Digest.*

103. R. D. McLaurin and James M. Price, *Soviet Middle East Policy Since the October War* (Alexandria, Va.: Abbott Associates, 1976), ch. 6.

104. U.S. Congress, "The Middle East Between War and Peace," staff report for subcommittee on Near Eastern Affairs, 93rd Cong., 2nd Sess. (March 5, 1974), p. 6.

105. "Egypt's New Ally," *An-Nahar Arab Report* 1, no. 39 (November 30, 1970): 2–3.

106. In that case, the sides were also chosen on the basis of consequent benefits and costs to Syria: agreements reached soon after the Soviet departure provided more and better Soviet military matériel, especially in return for Soviet use of Syrian airfields for strategic purposes, special naval facilities at Latakia and Tartus (replacing Mersa Matruh in Egypt), and an increased presence and freedom of action in coordinating Syrian air defense. "Syrian-Libyan Relations," pp. 2–3; "Syria: Two Years Under President Assad (1)"; "Syria: New Policy Lines," *An-Nahar Arab Report* 3, no. 35 (August 28, 1972): 1.

107. "Assad Meets with Party Leaders," *Arab World* 21, no. 5122 (January 25, 1974), p. 3; "Syria: Domestic Fears"; Safran, "Arab Politics," pp. 398–99; el-Rayyes and Nahas, eds., *Guerrillas for Palestine,* p. 296; Salim al-Lawzi, "The Disengagement as Understood by Kissinger Means Bargaining on Damascus," *Al-Hawadith,* February 22, 1974, pp. 20–22; "Syria: A Waiting Game"; "Disengagement Accord: Syrian Precautions," *An-Nahar Arab Report* 5, no. 22 (June 3, 1974): 1; "Syrian Ba'ath Congress: Assad Criticized"; *Svenska Dagbladet,* August 9, 1974, p. 3.

108. Indeed, the Syrian regime devotes considerable effort to defusing the potentially explosive Iraqi propaganda offensive. Levy, "The Syrian Communists," p. 402; "Syria: Mounting Tension"; "Syria: New Policy Lines"; "Syrian Front: Tense but Calm"; el-Rayyes and Nahas, eds., *Guerrillas for Palestine,* p. 296; "Syria's Crucial Position"; Jason Morris, "Kissinger Breaks Syria Stalemate," *Christian Science Monitor,* February 28, 1974, p. 1; Kraft, "The Divided Arab World"; "Disengagement Accord: Syrian Precautions"; "Syrian Ba'ath Congress: Assad Criticized"; "Bakr in Moscow: A Reply to Sadat," *An-Nahar Arab Report* 3, no. 38 (September 18, 1972): 2–3; John K. Cooley, "Syria-Israel Disengagement: Soviets Take Part This Time," *Christian Science Monitor,* February 1, 1974, p. 1.

109. Kerr, "Hafiz Asad," p. 705; *An-Nahar,* issues of Spring 1973; "Lebanon-Commandos: New Formula Sought," *An-Nahar Arab Report* 3, no. 27 (July 3, 1972): 3–4.

110. See William E. Hazen and Paul A. Jureidini, *The Palestinian Movement in Politics* (Lexington, Mass.: D. C. Heath, 1976); Paul A. Jureidini and William E. Hazen, *Six Clashes: An Analysis of the Relationship Between the Palestinian Guerrilla Movement and the Governments of Jordan and Lebanon* (Kensington, Md.: American Institutes for Research, 1971); John K. Cooley, *Green March, Black September* (London: Frank Cass, 1973); William B. Quandt, Fuad Jabber,

and Ann Mosely Lesch, *The Politics of Palestinian Nationalism* (Berkeley: University of California Press, 1973).

111. Anti-Soviet activities and Jordanian and Saudi intelligence collaborators have been linked to Tlas. "Syria: Two Years Under President Assad (1)."

112. El-Rayyes and Nahas, eds., *The October War,* pp. 178–80; "Soviet Experts: Another Eviction?"; "Syria: Domestic Fears"; "Syria: Two Years Under President Assad (1)"; "Potential Trouble"; "Syria-Jordan: A Much Needed Detente," *An-Nahar Arab Report* 3, no. 50 (December 11, 1972): 2–3; Kerr, "Hafiz Asad," pp. 702, 705; John K. Cooley, "Syrian Move Brings Praise —and Apprehension," *Christian Science Monitor,* December 4, 1972, p. 4; Jim Hoagland, "Syrian Leaders Call on Hussein to Join Battle Against Israel," Washington *Post,* December 6, 1972, p. A-19.

113. "Syria: Two Years Under President Assad (1)"; "Syria-Jordan: A Much Needed Detente"; "Syrian-Libyan Relations"; "Syrian Front: Tense but Calm"; "Syria: Domestic Fears"; el-Rayyes and Nahas, eds., *The October War,* pp. 178–80; Petran, *Syria,* pp. 253–54.

114. A Syrian political "first." Balta, "La Syrie baasiste," passim.

115. *Daily Star* (Beirut), March 18, 1971.

116. Ba'ath Party Provisional Regional Command Statement, FBIS, November 17, 1970, pp. F-1 to F-4. Jebran Chamieh, ed., *Record of the Arab World (Documents, Events, Political Opinions)* (Beirut, March 1971), pp. 1584–85.

117. Jesse W. Lewis, Jr., "Syria Makes Cautious Overture to West," Washington *Post,* August 26, 1971, pp. H-1, H-7. Reduction of the police role should not be taken to mean that Assad has reduced the level of security forces protecting the regime. On the contrary, he has added Special Forces (of about 30,000 men) led by his nephew, Adnan Assad, to the Defense Squads led by his brother Rifaat Assad. Both clearly are regime security forces. "Syrian Front: Tense but Calm."

118. Nyrop et al., *Area Handbook,* p. 165; Ma'oz, "Attempts at Creating," p. 404. Ba'ath secularism has returned to the emphasis on the importance of Islam in Arab culture.

119. Thus, the Ba'ath is scarcely a coherent and effective political organization any longer. See Lewis, "Syria Makes Cautious Overture."

120. Balta, "La Syrie baasiste"; "Syria: The New Cabinet"; Cooley, "Syria Opens Windows."

121. *Jaish al-Shaab,* October 1974, p. 3. Similarly, the disengagement agreement was defended as an Israeli retreat, an Arab victory. *Al-Ba'ath,* June 3, 1974, p. 1.

122. See, for instance, Assad's interview by Milhelm Karam, *Al-Bayraq,* February 21, 1974, p. 1; his earlier interview in *An-Nahar,* March 17, 1971, p. 1; "Is It a War of Attrition?"; Petran, *Syria,* p. 201; "Syria's Crucial Position in Mideast Situation," *Arab World* 21, no. 5129 (February 5, 1974): 11–12; Seymour Topping, "Egypt and Syria Divided on U.S. Peace Proposals," New York *Times,* December 18, 1974, pp. 1, 17.

123. "Syria's Ayoubi Demands Israel Get off Arab Land," *Christian Science Monitor,* March 12, 1973, p. 2.

124. For example, see the interview with Syrian Information Minister George Saddiqni, *Svenska Dagbladet,* August 9, 1974, p. 3.

125. See Foreign Minister Khaddam's statement in "Saudi Arabia and Kuwait Give Syria Pledge on Oil Embargo," New York *Times,* February 5, 1974, p. 3.

126. The disengagement agreement meets this criterion by being tied to Resolution 242, which Syrians view as requiring withdrawal from all occupied territories. In other words, the ambiguity of the resolution has been employed to bring about a disengagement agreement acceptable to both Israel and Syria.

127. Israel destroyed Kuneitra before withdrawing in 1974. To rebuild it would be expensive, especially with Israeli guns on surrounding hills threatening the new city. Topping, "Egypt and Syria Divided," p. 17; FBIS, June 26, 1974, p. H-9; *Al-Ba'ath,* September 17, 1974, p. 1.

Second, it should be recalled that Kuneitra's population increased to some extent because the area was militarized. Many inhabitants were armed forces personnel and dependents. With the present order of battle, it is unlikely that many military dependents will move to Kuneitra, in effect beyond the front lines. Many other inhabitants were farmers, tending land still occupied by Israeli troops. The proximity of the front is a disincentive to resettlement in Kuneitra for all former inhabitants, particularly since Israeli military forces are ensconced on the surrounding hills. *Al-Ba'ath,* September 17, 1974, p. 1.

128. As both sides recognize, the pressure of a sizable Syrian population in the Golan would add to the costs Syria would have to bear if hostilities broke out again.

129. John K. Cooley, "Syria Hopes Kissinger Brings Pullout Solution," *Christian Science Monitor,* February 26, 1974, p. 2. The fact that Israel has set up 30 new settlements in the Golan, several of them built on the remains of Syrian towns, is well known in Syria and does not facilitate negotiation. See John K. Cooley, "Syria-Israel Disengagement: Soviets Take Part This Time," ibid., February 1, 1974, p. 1.

130. It should be pointed out that Assad, even before his coup, was in favor of reducing the level of confrontation. "Syria could no longer afford the luxury of threatening Israel and playing at extremism; 'it would be better,' [Assad] said, 'to refrain ... from ... gratuitous acts of provocation which the enemy could use as a pretext to challenge the Syrian Army and force upon it a battle which it is in no position to undertake....' " Kerr, "Hafiz Asad," p. 699.

131. See Khaddam's press conference, March 13, 1971, in Chamieh, ed., *Record of the Arab World,* pp. 1586–87, in which the foreign minister avers that war will be necessary because Israel is not amenable to peaceful settlement: "The Arabs have tried to pursue a course leading to a peaceful settlement." Assad had just previously suggested that Syria was ready for negotiations. "The Soviet Union and the Arab World (3)," *An-Nahar Arab Report* 3, no. 23 (June 5, 1972): "Backgrounder."

132. John K. Cooley, "Syria Joins Arab 'Peace Policy,' " *Christian Science Monitor,* March 10, 1972, p..3.

133. Walter Laqueur, *Confrontation: The Middle East War and World Politics* (London: Wildwood House and Abacus, 1974), p. 54. Also see "Hussein's Peace Efforts," *An-Nahar Arab Report* 4, no. 6 (February 5, 1973): 3. Virtually all sources on October War planning indicate the limited objectives intended by the Arab combatants.

134. U.S. Congress, "The Middle East Between War and Peace," p. 28; Raymond H. Anderson, "Syrians Cautious on Hopes for Talks," New York *Times,* March 1, 1974, p. 7. Assad has, however, stressed that Syria is engaged in peace talks, not negotiations. FBIS, October 30, 1973, pp. F-1 to F-6, *Al-Ba'ath,* September 17, 1974, pp. 1, 7.

135. Minister of Information Ahmad Iskandar Ahmad, October 11, 1974; FBIS, October 18, 1974, p. H-3.

136. "Growing Isolation," *An-Nahar Arab Report* 1, no. 14 (June 8, 1970): 1.

137. See "Embarrassing Partner," ibid. 3, no. 49 (December 4, 1972): 1.

138. Also see al-Lawzi, "The Disengagement," pp. 20–22. Sadat's treatment in Syria following the Egyptian-Israeli disengagement agreement was very cool. Bernard Gwertzman, "Kissinger Is Given Syrian Proposals on Opening Talks," New York *Times,* January 21, 1974, pp. 1, 6.

139. "Saudi Arabia and Kuwait Give Syria Pledge on Oil Embargo," New York *Times,* February 5, 1974, p. 3.

140. "Syria: Ball Starts Rolling," p. 1.

141. Joseph Kraft, "The Divided Arab World," Washington *Post*, April 16, 1974, p. A-17.

142. "Disengagement Accord: Syrian Precautions"; "Syria: Moscow Helps Out," *An-Nahar Arab Report* 3, no. 29 (July 17, 1972): 3–4.

143. "Syria's Crucial Position," p. 11; *Svenska Dagbladet,* August 9, 1974, p. 3; Henry Kamm, "Syrian Guns Seen in Political Role," New York *Times,* March 21, 1974, p. 11. Also see Assad's speech to the Ba'ath, April 17, 1974; FBIS, no. 68 April 18, 1974, pp. H2-H4.

144. Topping, "Egypt and Syria Divided," p. 17; Raymond H. Anderson, "Damascus Is Linking Disengagement to Recovery of All Golan Territory," New York *Times*, February 25, 1974; "Syria's Ayoubi," p. 2. See the interview of Assad, by Arnaud de Borchgrave, *An-Nahar*, June 3, 1974, p. 1. However, Syria has used a firm hand to ensure Palestinian approval.

145. As we have indicated, the most important individual in the regime after the president is his brother. It must be assumed that Rifaat's views are weighed on a variety of important issues. However, the reservations of Tlas and Khaddam are important to the extent that they reflect the feelings of significant publics.

146. Although it has been suggested that Egypt was weaker after Nasser's death and that Syria joined the Federation of Arab Republics to strengthen Egypt. Leonard Binder, "Transformation in the Middle Eastern Subordinate System After 1967," in Michael Confino and Shimon Shamir, eds., *The U.S.S.R. and the Middle East*, p. 259.

147. The best analysis of these relations is Jureidini and Hazen, *Six Clashes*.

148. The intervention followed from Syrian determination not to be the new home of the guerrilla forces (not to turn a Jordanian-guerrilla conflict into a Syrian-guerrilla conflict), the urge of the Alawis to demonstrate their "revolutionary virtue," and a direct concern about the Palestine movement. See Jureidini and Hazen, *Six Clashes*, p. 157; and Stephen Oren, "Syria's Options," *The World Today* 30, no. 11 (November 1974): 474.

149. Binder, "Transformation," pp. 256–57; Kerr, "Hafiz Asad," p. 705; Petran, *Syria*, pp. 253–54; Cooley, "Syria Opens Windows," p. 5; John K. Cooley, "Syria Chides U.S. Leadership," *Christian Science Monitor*, November 19, 1971, p. 10. Those who seek perfect consistency as the key to explanation of government motives will be frustrated in this case. The Syrian blockage (closure of borders) had deleterious effects on several economies. Maintaining the blockade at some cost to Syria must appear a matter of principle. Yet, immediately before the July 1971 clashes, Syria seized and confiscated a large shipment of arms destined for the Palestinian guerrillas, apparently at least partially because allowing completion of the transaction through Syria would have imperiled relations with the Amman regime. Moreover, Syrian efforts to improve these relations were not interrupted by the border closure. "Arab Borders: Brotherly Blockades," *An-Nahar Arab Report* 3, no. 36 (September 4, 1972): "Economic Brief"; "Syria-Jordan: A Much Needed Detente," ibid. no. 50 (December 11, 1972): 2–3; Kerr, "Hafiz Asad," p. 705; Petran, *Syria*, pp. 253–54.

150. John K. Cooley, "Syrian Move Brings Praise—and Apprehension," *Christian Science Monitor*, December 4, 1972, p. 4; Jim Hoagland, "Syrian Leaders Call on Hussein to Join Battle Against Israel," Washington *Post*, December 6, 1972, p. A-19; "Syrian-Jordanian Border Reopened to Facilitate Battle," FBIS, December 1, 1972, p. F-1; 'Amid Khuli, "Why Were Our Borders with Jordan Opened?" *Al-Ba'ath*, December 3, 1972, p. 3. However transparent this rationale with regard to the (un)likelihood of Jordan's actively joining any near-term military effort against Israel, it is certainly true that the economic consequences of the closed borders were undermining the Arab anti-Israeli boycott and were forcing the Jordanian government to deal increasingly (and more publicly) with Israel. "Arab Borders: Brotherly Blockades."

151. "Consolidating Trend," *An-Nahar Arab Report* 6, no. 24 (June 16, 1975): 1–2; "Closing the Ranks," ibid. no. 25 (June 23, 1975): 2–3; "Prospects for Disengagement," ibid. no. 34 (August 25, 1975): 1–2; "Facing the Future Together," ibid., pp. 2–3; "Serious Determined Effort," ibid. no. 35 (September 1, 1975); "Economics and Oil," ibid. nos. 36 (September 15, 1975) and 37 (September 22, 1975): "Chronology"; Syria-Jordan Supreme Commission, Joint Statement, July 30, 1975; Elizabeth Picard, "La Syrie du 'redressement' et les chances de paix au Proche-Orient," *Politique étrangère* 61, no. 2 (1976): 174–75; Fehmi Saddy, *The Eastern Front: Implications of the Syrian/Palestinian/Jordanian Entente and the Lebanese Civil War* (Alexandria, Va.: Abbott Associates, 1976), pp. 9–16.

152. Heroes of the Return was the name of the commando group based on Habbash's Arab National Movement.

153. John K. Cooley, *Green March, Black September,* p. 139. For a discussion of the evolution of the Palestinian organizations, their activities, and ideologies, see el-Rayyes and Nahas, eds., *Guerrillas for Palestine;* Quandt, Jabber, and Lesch, *The Politics of Palestinian Nationalism;* and Jureidini and Hazen, *The Palestinian Movement.*

154. El-Rayyes and Nahas, eds., *Guerrillas for Palestine,* pp. 49–52.

155. Ibid., pp. 44, 47.

156. Ibid., p. 51; "The Resistance Movement in Crisis (3)," *An-Nahar Arab Report* 13, no. 21 (July 31, 1972): "Backgrounder."

157. "Arms from Peking," *An-Nahar Arab Report* 2, no. 27 (July 5, 1971): 1–2; "Mediator Needed," ibid. no. 28 (July 12, 1972): 2–3; Petran, *Syria,* 253–54.

158. El-Rayyes and Nahas, eds., *Guerrillas for Palestine,* p. 145.

159. Ibid., pp. 144–45. The restrictions became even tighter in mid-1973 ("Syria and the Palestinians," *An-Nahar Arab Report* 4, no. 23 [June 4, 1973]: "Backgrounder"); but these later restrictions probably were directly related to the October War, which by then was already in the planning stage. In January and February, stories concerning alleged Syrian "incitement" of villagers against the commandos circulated. These rumors probably grew out of the increased restrictions, but one cannot discard the idea of a government-inspired or -spread canard. See "Hussein's Peace Efforts," *An-Nahar Arab Report* 4, no. 6 (February 5, 1973): 3; "The Commandos: Plan for Action," ibid. no. 7 (February 12, 1973): 4.

160. "A Front Reopened," *An-Nahar Arab Report* 3, no. 38 (September 18, 1972): 1.

161. "Syria and the Palestinians"; "Cairo Summit: Splits and Alignments," *An-Nahar Arab Report* 4, no. 38 (September 17, 1973): 1–2.

162. "Lebanon-Commandos: New Formula Sought," ibid. 3, no. 27 (July 3, 1972): 3–4.

163. U.S. Congress, in "The Middle East Between War and Peace," p. 29. See the interview of Assad by Arnaud de Borchgrave, *An-Nahar,* June 3, 1974, p. 1.

164. R. D. McLaurin and Mohammed Mughisuddin, *Cooperation and Conflict: Egyptian, Iraqi, and Syrian Objectives and U.S. Policy* (Washington, D.C.: American Institutes for Research, 1975), p. 235. These views are based on discussions with a variety of individuals in the Middle East.

165. Saddy, *The Eastern Front,* pp. 16–35; Paul A. Jureidini and William E. Hazen, *Lebanon's Dissolution: Futures and Consequences* (Alexandria, Va.: Abbott Associates, 1976); Enver Koury, *The Crisis in the Lebanese System: Confessionalism and Chaos* (Washington, D.C.: American Enterprise Institute, 1976); Kamal S. Salibi, *Crossroads to Civil War: Lebanon 1958–1976* (Delmar: Caravan Books, 1976); Pierre Vallaud, *Le Liban au bout du fusil* (Paris: Librairie Hachette, 1976). The best journalistic analysis available in English is *An-Nahar Arab Report,* most of the 1975–76 issues of which deal in substantial part with the Lebanese crisis.

166. That Sa'iqa and PLA units were sent in should not be misconstrued. The units were increasingly composed of Syrian troops. This deception was necessary for a variety of reasons, but primarily to enable the Israeli government to avoid domestic pressures to intervene in order to safeguard Israeli security.

167. Hafez Assad's remarkable speech to the Syrian provincial councils gives an excellent explanation of his government's perception of the Lebanese situation and reveals many details not widely known before. The speech is reprinted in FBIS, July 21, 1976, pp. H-1 to H-23.

168. See "Disengagement Accord: Syrian Precautions."

169. The rationale for Iraq's withdrawal of its forces from Syria was the exigencies of the Kurdish and Iranian problem. Syria accused Iraq of "engineering separate developments to abdicate [its] pan-Arab responsibilities." *Al-Ba'ath,* February 24, 1974, p. 3.

170. Cooley, "Syria Opens Windows," p. 5; "Syria-Jordan: A Much Needed Detente," pp. 2–3; Holmstrom, "Syria," p. 13; Petran, *Syria,* pp. 253–54.

171. The important point here is that Assad may attack Egypt over such tactical differences, but will simply agree not to agree with the Saudis. The major public disagreement has been in

Lebanon, where Saudi Arabia could not idly watch Syria destroy the Palestinian movement. Thus, Riyadh terminated its subsidy to Syria—although Saudi money continued to reach Damascus secretly. In October, Saudi Arabia removed its military contingents in Syria, but the most important Saudi contribution to Syria—oil—continued. Saudi Arabia's public dismay at Syrian attacks on the Palestinians in Lebanon covered private sympathy for the Syrian approach and an agreement that the PLO should not again be allowed to acquire the level of power it reached in Lebanon or in Jordan before 1970.

172. "The Soviet Union and the Arab World (3)"; Lenczowski, *Soviet Advances in the Middle East* (Washington, D.C.: American Enterprise Institution, 1972), p. 117.

173. John K. Cooley, "Russian Test in Syria," *Christian Science Monitor,* September 13, 1973, p. 4.

174. "The Soviet Union and the Arab World (3)."

175. Ibid. The Soviet Union and Eastern Europe have provided ten times as much economic aid to Syria as either international organizations or the United States. See U.S. Central Intelligence Agency, *Communist Aid to Less Developed Countries of the Free World, 1975,* ER 76-10372U (July 1976), table 8; U.S. Agency for International Development, *U.S. Overseas Loans and Grants and Assistance from International Organizations: Obligations and Loan Authorizations, July 1, 1945–June 30, 1975* (Washington, D.C.: AID, n.d.), pp. 27, 180. It should be pointed out that trade with the socialist countries does represent a very sizable portion of Syrian foreign commerce: in 1973, about one-third of Syrian exports went to, and about one-fifth of imports originated from, the socialist countries. Economist Intelligence Unit, *QER: Syria, Lebanon, Cyprus—Annual Supplement 1974* (London: EIU, 1974), p. 13.

176. "Syria and Russia: Pink Balloon," *The Economist,* October 7, 1972, p. 37.

177. "Syria: New Policy Lines"; "Bakr in Moscow: A Reply to Sadat," *An-Nahar Arab Report* 3, no. 38 (September 18, 1972): 2–3.

178. "Syria: New Policy Lines"; "Syrian-Libyan Relations."

179. Soviet Jewish emigration has become a problem, because a substantial proportion of Soviet Jews who emigrated to Israel settled in the occupied Golan Heights. "Syria: Military Moves," *An-Nahar Arab Report* 4, no. 20 (May 14, 1973): 1.

180. Pressure frequently has been used to moderate Syrian demands or policies, but recently the Soviet Union has been more concerned to protect distinctly Soviet interests.

181. "Joint Syrian-Soviet Communique Backs Syrian Right to Liberate Occupied Land as USSR Aid Is Promised in Military and Economic Fields," *Arab World* 21, no. 5779 (April 17, 1974): 2–3; "Is It a War of Attrition on the Golan?"; "Disengagement Accord: Syrian Precautions"; "Syria: A Waiting Game."

182. McLaurin and Price, *Soviet Middle East Policy.*

183. Drew Middleton, "Syria, with Forces Built up Since '73, Maintains Alert Stance in Golan Area," New York *Times,* July 21, 1975, p. 4; "Healing the Rift," *An-Nahar Arab Report* 7, no. 23 (June 7, 1976): 2–3; "The Issue of Soviet Arms Supplies," ibid., "Backgrounder."

184. Lewis, "Syria Makes Cautious Overtures," pp. H-1, H-7.

185. "Disengagement Accord: Syrian Precautions"; *Svenska Dagbladet,* August 9, 1974, p. 3. At the same time, it should be recognized that Syria has less bargaining power than Israel and occupies a more desperate position. Thus, Syria must be more tentative for the present, as Assad's opposition to the ending of the oil embargo exemplifies. See "Arabs Lift Oil Embargo on U.S. with Libya and Syria Dissenting," *Middle East Economic Survey* 17, no. 22 (March 22, 1974): 1; "Syria: A Waiting Game."

186. *Al-Thawrah,* June 5, 1974, p. 1; James F. Clarity, "Syria Says She Shifted U.S. Attitude," New York *Times,* June 6, 1974, p. 3. Another domestic argument used to justify relations with the United States was the need for flexibility in foreign affairs, a position that contrasts sharply with Jadid's. See *Al-Ba'ath* and *Al-Thawrah,* June 11–15, 1974; "*Al-Ba'ath* Defines Syria's

Foreign Policy," *Arab World* 21, no. 4218 (June 12, 1974): 5; "Flexibility of the Syrian Foreign Policy," ibid. no. 5219 (June 13, 1974): 11–12.

187. Petran, *Syria,* p. 234.

188. Dale R. Tahtinen, *The Arab-Israeli Military Balance Today* (Washington, D.C.: American Enterprise Institute, 1973), pp. 4–10.

189. Stockholm International Peace Research Institute (SIPRI), *The Arms Trade with the Third World* (Stockholm: Almqvist and Wiksell, 1971), pp. 545–49; Jacob C. Hurewitz, "Changing Military Perspectives in the Middle East," in Paul Y. Hammond and Sidney S. Alexander, eds., *Political Dynamics in the Middle East,* p. 90.

190. "Grechko's Tour: Longer Term Hopes," *An-Nahar Arab Report* 3, no. 21 (May 22, 1972): 2. Some of the additional items Syria wanted may have been available in return for the conclusion of a treaty like those signed with Egypt and Iraq. It is rumored that Assad refused such an offer.

191. David Hirst, "Soviet Arms Airlift to Syria Seen as Bid to Recoup Loss," Washington *Post,* September 25, 1972, p. A-16; Marilyn Berger, "Moscow Sends Syria Latest Tanks, MIG-21s," ibid., September 28, 1972, p. A-28; Jim Hoagland, "150 More Soviet Advisors Reported in Syria, Airlift Ends," ibid., October 6, 1972, p. A-25; "Syrian Arms—More Political than Military," *Christian Science Monitor,* October 3, 1972; "Syria and Russia: Pink Balloon," p. 37.

192. William Beecher, "Syria Said to Agree to Soviet Build-up at 2 of Her Ports," New York *Times,* September 14, 1972, pp. 1, 18; "Syrian-Libyan Relations."

193. "Syrian Front: Tense but Calm"; "Syrian Budget: Decreased Defense," *An-Nahar Arab Report* 4, no. 6 (February 5, 1973): 2.

194. John K. Cooley, "Syria Seeks Arab Prestige with New Blows at Israel," *Christian Science Monitor,* January 10, 1973, pp. 1, 5.

195. John K. Cooley, "Syria Complains to U.N. of Israeli Air Invasion," *Christian Science Monitor,* September 15, 1973, p. 2.

196. See International Institute of Strategic Studies, *Strategic Survey 1973* (London: IISS, 1974), pp. 16–20.

197. Henry Kamm, "Syrian Guns Seen in Political Role," New York *Times,* March 21, 1974, p. 11; "Syria's Crucial Position in Mideast Situation," *Arab World* 21, no. 2159 (February 5, 1974): 11–12; "Syria: Ball Starts Rolling."

198. Hafez Assad; FBIS, April 8, 1974, p. F-2. ". . . In this field, namely the field of political struggle, daily political action is intermingled with daily military action." Ibid., March 11, 1974, p. F-3.

199. International Institute of Strategic Studies, *The Military Balance 1974–1975* (London: IISS, 1974), pp. 37–38; Dale R. Tahtinen, *The Arab-Israeli Military Balance Since October 1973* (Washington, D.C.: American Enterprise Institute, 1973); Seymour Topping, "Egypt and Syria Divided on U.S. Peace Proposals," New York *Times,* December 18, 1974, pp. 1, 17; Bordwiec, "Syria Opening Doors," p. A-6.

200. Bordwiec, "Syria Opening Doors."

201. However, there is widespread Arab recognition that sophisticated Soviet weapons systems are less advanced than their U.S. counterparts. R. D. McLaurin, "The Soviet-American Strategic Balance: Arab Elite Views," forthcoming article.

7

PEOPLE, PROCESSES, PRESSURES

Foreign-policy processes are expressions of political culture, including political institutions and their stability. However, the decision-making process by which foreign-policy choices are made also reflects the external environment. Because the proximate threat of major war is very salient, regional foreign-policy issues, particularly those relevant to such potential conflicts, enjoy much greater elite attention in the four states we have studied—especially in Egypt, Israel, and Syria—than in most other developing countries.

Similarly, the recurrence and level of violence associated with Middle East wars have underscored the importance of superpower sponsorship in terms of the provision of military matériel. Thus, Egyptian, Iraqi, Israeli, and Syrian relations with the United States and the Soviet Union are also of central importance in the political system.

In this chapter, we shall briefly compare the ways in which the people, processes, and pressures we have examined forge foreign policy.

PEOPLE

That individuals play a greater role in decision making in the Arab states than in Israel is hardly surprising, for on the whole government is less representative—certainly much less directly so—than in Israel. In Egypt, Iraq, and Syria, decisions on key issues—indeed, the general lines of foreign policy—are determined by a handful of individuals.

Although Sadat is the principal formulator of Egyptian foreign policy, he typically consults with other major leaders in the executive and legislative branches. The National Council—including the vice-presidents, the prime minister and his deputies, the ministers of war and supply, the director of intelligence, the national security adviser, and the secretary-general of the Arab Socialist Union (ASU)—is the usual forum for executive branch consultation. Legislative consultation is less formalized, discussions usually being limited to important members of People's Assembly and ASU committees.

Consultation is more visible, more institutionalized, and far broader in Egypt than in Iraq or Syria, partially because the Egyptian government is more bureaucratized and partially because the president has less complete control of the entire legitimate political system in Egypt. Nevertheless, Egypt's foreign policy accurately reflects Sadat's views. Both in dealing with the two superpowers external to the Middle East and in regional relations, Sadat has changed the course of Egyptian policy. The reorientation of Egypt's relations with the United States and the Soviet Union is a function of his belief that the involvement of American private enterprise is a sine qua non of Egyptian development, as well as of his (representative) views that the Arab world has more in common with the West than with the Soviet Union. Egypt's policies toward Israel also reflect Sadat's recognition that Israel is "here to stay," that the Jewish state cannot be defeated by the Arabs, and that a settlement (that returns the Sinai) is necessary to allow Egypt to deal with its real enemy—poverty.

In Iraq, as in Egypt, the voice of one man is dominant. Saddam Hussein Takriti, although he shares responsibility for foreign-policy decisions with the other members of the Revolutionary Command Council (RCC), is much the most active Council member in foreign-policy matters. His pragmatic approach to the realization of Iraqi interests is seen in the reduction of hostility with Iran (clearly the stronger of the two countries), the signing of a border accord with Saudi Arabia, the Iraqi proposal of a joint defense arrangement for the Persian Gulf, diminished support for regional insurgencies, and the spectacular growth of commerce with the West.

Syrian foreign policy is even more clearly dependent on the views of one individual—Hafez Assad. As in Iraq, Syrian Ba'ath institutions are used to legitimize decisions reached by the leadership; and Ba'athist rhetoric clothes and camouflages pragmatic policy values. Because Assad so completely dominates key foreign-policy decisions, policy outputs reveal his views. Assad seeks to control forces of the eastern front with Israel—including Palestinian, Lebanese, and Jordanian, as well as Syrian, resources, both political and military —in order to improve the chances of reaching a settlement he feels his regime can afford to accept. The Assad government is characterized by a determination to pursue long-term goals—such as a settlement with Israel—despite short-term costs.

The role of individuals in Israeli foreign policy is significantly more complex than is the case in any of the three Arab countries we have considered. While each Arab government has shown stability and a substantial degree of control, the current Israeli government is less stable and more subject to domestic political dissent.

Following the October War and Israeli national elections in December 1973, the Ma'arach (Labor Alignment) was forced to form the first minority government in Israel's history. With the resignation of the Golda Meir government in April 1974, and the election of the Rabin government by a divided Labor leadership, Israel has been left with a weakened and fragmented leadership.

The most important figures in Israeli foreign-policy formulation are the three key ministers—Yitzhak Rabin (prime minister), Shimon Peres (defense minister), and Yigal Allon (foreign minister). Because of their differing backgrounds, personalities, and different constituencies within Israel, they have divergent policy perspectives. In addition, they have developed a set of increasingly bitter personal antagonisms that have affected the government's formulation of policy. It is important to note that while none of the three key ministers alone appears to have the ability to negotiate on behalf of Israel, at least the prime minister and defense minister have the personal ability to block policy initiatives. Thus, policy making in the vital security area continues to hinge on the interpersonal relationships of these three ministers.

One of Rabin's key problems within the Labor party is that he has no widespread support or constituency, as did his predecessor. Although he claims to represent the "center" of the Labor movement, he has been attacked by both the right and far left of the party.

Defense Minister Shimon Peres is more popular than the prime minister. He represents the pragmatic right wing of the Labor party, the Rafi faction, and has advocated security and settlement policies closer to the mainstream of Israeli public opinion than those of the prime minister. Although Peres has the popular support and image to become prime minister, he lacks sufficient support within the Labor party leadership to challenge Rabin directly at this time. Such a challenge cannot, however, be ruled out in the near to intermediate term.

Least popular and weakest politically of the three key ministers has been Foreign Minister Yigal Allon. Holding office largely because of his lack of association with the "failures" surrounding the outbreak of the October War, Allon represents the left wing of the Labor party and has, at best, limited support within the government and public alike. He holds the most accommodation-oriented views of the three key ministers, and has attempted to promote Israeli policy flexibility that would increase settlement prospects. It is, however, increasingly unlikely that Allon's views will be adopted by the present government, or that Allon would become prime minister in any new government.

In sum, the degree of dissension among the major figures and their constituencies in the Israeli government impedes bold or concerted initiatives. The pre-1970 position of the Arabs and Israel has been reversed: today it is the Israeli government that may not be able to agree on reasonable and realistic settlement terms.

PROCESSES

We have examined at some length the foreign-policy mechanisms of Egypt, Iraq, Israel, and Syria. In the three Arab countries, key decisions are made by individual leaders; and the formal processes of foreign policy are used to channel necessary information to these leaders and to legitimize and disseminate decisions. The press, tightly controlled in Iraq and Syria, and substantially controlled in Egypt, is primarily an agent for the dissemination of regime views and policies. In all of the Arab countries—but particularly Syria —the views of specific interest groups within the population are weighed at least as heavily as international considerations in determining the appropriate policy option. Intelligence operations are closely tied to the executive, and focus far more on domestic than on regional or global challenges to the regime. However, the openness of Israeli society in some respects compensates for limited foreign intelligence operations. Generally, the intelligence collection, dissemination, and analysis functions are not given the same priority in Egypt, Iraq, and Syria as in Israel, as far as foreign affairs is concerned.

Military policy in the three Arab states is also a function of the views of key leaders and therefore is relatively well integrated with foreign-policy goals at the strategic level. The military is well represented in decision-making councils in Egypt. In both Iraq and Syria, the military is permeated by personnel who serve as intelligence agents, in effect maintaining surveillance over the military for the regime. Security policy is an integral part of foreign-policy choices by Saddam Hussein and Assad, with only implementation issues left to military staffs. Even in important decisions on effectuating policy, Assad's and Saddam's overall views guide the planning process. Little is known of Iraqi decision chains. In Syria, the information and control channels are only partly a function of formal organization; they are largely dependent upon the informal but pervasive network of Alawis at all levels and in all service branches.

Israeli foreign-policy formulation is the product of the interaction of three key ministries—the Ministry of Defense, the Foreign Affairs Ministry, and the Office of the Prime Minister—and the relationship of those ministries to the civil service and the IDF.

Although the Agranat Commission recommended a number of institutional changes within Israel, on the basis of its analysis of the events preceding the outbreak of the October War and the conduct of the war thereafter, the government has only begun to effect some of these changes. The Commission recommended changes in the Office of the Prime Minister, the Defense Ministry, the Foreign Ministry, and Israel's intelligence establishment, and the integration of these elements into the conduct of foreign affairs and security policy.

At the highest policy levels, Prime Minister Rabin generally failed to carry out a recommendation calling for the establishment of an Israeli National Security Council, or to provide for integrated crisis management and policy making in the security area. Top-level policy making continues to operate on a highly personal and ad hoc basis. In leaving the Rabin administration, both Information Minister Aharon Yariv and General Ariel Sharon, security adviser to the prime minister, indicated this shortcoming.

In an effort to overcome a lack of policy planning capability and to prepare for interim settlement negotiations in February 1975, a high-level "think tank" was organized on an interministerial basis. The mandate of this group was to formulate alternative policy proposals; it did function for a time during the spring of 1975, but has since lost most of its key numbers.

Within the ministries related to the making and implementation of security and defense policy, as well as Israel's intelligence services, various efforts at analysis, policy planning, and policy support have been undertaken. Most advanced in this area is the Defense Ministry, where a long-range strategic planning capability has been undertaken to support the defense minister's efforts; a planning branch has been developed within the framework of the IDF General Staff to coordinate activities and military force planning; and efforts have been made to upgrade the analytical capabilities of Israeli military intelligence.

At the same time, Israel's external intelligence service, Mossad, has created its own analytical support system to augment its collection and operational capabilities. The orientation of these efforts has been to upgrade Israel's early-warning capability, and not to produce analyses of the Arab world that could support a more settlement-oriented policy.

Within the Israeli Foreign Ministry a new analytical support unit designated MMT has been created to support the foreign minister, largely in his struggle with the defense and prime ministers. The structure is similar to the U.S. State Department's Bureau of Intelligence and Research, although it is currently unclear that anything useful will be forthcoming from the new organization.

The least advanced area in the defense and security field continues to be the Office of the Prime Minister. Rabin has failed to resolve bureaucratic problems between himself and the defense minister or to implement any of the changes recommended by the Agranat Commission. Rabin continued to rely on his security adviser—who has since resigned—and now depends upon his military assistant and several close aides, without adequate analytical support or coordination with the other key ministries. Coordination among the Office of the Prime Minister, Defense Ministry, and Foreign Ministry, as well as with Israel's intelligence community, appears to be limited at best; and it is difficult to determine the extent to which the available intelligence data are disseminated among these organizations. Indeed, distribution of intelligence between the Defense Ministry and Office of the Prime Minister has become a political issue within Israel.

PRESSURES

Each of the four Middle Eastern polities we have studied regularly considers several constituencies' views and interests in the formulation of foreign and defense policy. Strong governments are more independent of such groups than weak ones are, but all must assess the likely impact on these publics of alternative courses of action.

Egyptian political culture has evolved in such a way that a great deal of leeway is given the president in dealing with foreign affairs. Electoral contests and public opposition generally focus on domestic issues. The principal pressure groups Sadat must consider in making major foreign-policy decisions are the military, the ASU (and, within the party, the three *minbars* recently established), and, to a lesser extent, the workers and peasants (who together control 50 percent of the seats in all elected political bodies in the country).

Iraqi interest groups, such as the Kurds, the Communists, the military, and the Shiites, are more cohesive than their Egyptian counterparts. The views of these groups, as well as their likely reactions to various policy options, are carefully weighed by the RCC. The strength and stability of the Iraqi Ba'ath has, however, allowed the regime considerable latitude in policy.

Until very recently, no Syrian leader had sufficient control of the many factions, regions, interest groups, and classes to formulate or implement a coherent, forward-looking foreign policy. Although many outsiders describe Assad's hold on Syria as tenuous, we feel his regime is—or at least perceives itself as—relatively secure. Consequently, Assad has been able to allow a greater degree of domestic "dissent" and non-Ba'ath representation, and to take initiatives in regional politics that are contrary to the views of important groups.

The Alawi minority dominates Syrian policy, which favors long-term Alawi benefits and regime security. Religious pressures are the greatest potential problem the Assad regime must face, but they have not prevented the government from taking positions certain to inflame this societal division. Assad's view is that the resolution of major outstanding international problems, such as the Arab-Israeli conflict, is necessary to bring about the economic development and social progress required to maintain social harmony and Alawi control.

REPRISE

The Arab defeats of 1948, 1956, and 1967 tended to push the unstable Arab world toward polarization in both regional and global foreign relations. Most of the primary confrontation states turned increasingly to the Soviet Union (as the only great power not sympathetic to Israel) to rearm and to rebuild war-shattered societies. The dichotomy between "traditional" and "progressive" or "revolutionary" states grew in both rhetoric and political reality. "Radical" movements and regimes suggested that the traditional regimes were primarily responsible for the Arab defeats, and that the social, economic, political—and hence, military—potential of the Arab world was unrealized as a result of these "anachronistic" leaders.

By the 1970s, however, it became apparent that revolutionary movements were foreign to the Arab masses, that ideology played a marginal role in the lives and views of most Arabs. The traditional regimes played an increasingly active and vital role in regional foreign policy, especially after 1972, and the leading Arab "progressive" regimes—although revolutionary rhetoric continued—began to take more and more pragmatic roads to the achievement of their foreign-policy goals. Indeed, after the October War, Arab governments seemed to recognize and exploit more visible signs of domestic traditionalism. In foreign policy, continued espousal of "revolutionary" ideology was accompanied by increasing interaction with the United States and the West and distance from the Soviet Union.

The degree of change in Israel since 1948 has been much less than in the Arab states. For all of the debate and turmoil that has characterized Israel in the post-October War period, real shifts in the mode and extent of influence on the military and political decision processes are few. Surprisingly, in view of the strong public demand for "new leadership" following the October War, relatively little change has taken place anywhere in the military or the political leadership. Thus, we can conclude that although the potential for change is great, the political leadership has not presented any new viable alternatives from which to choose, and the public has effectively failed to force changes in either leadership or policy.

An opportunity for change existed in the 1973 elections, but little was realized. One-third of the members elected to the Eighth Knesset are new, but they in no way make for new leadership or new policy. The "old guard" of the Ma'arach remains; and the Knesset continues to be essentially powerless and dominated by the executive, which in turn is dominated by the prime minister. At this level, public opinion was able to force some change by securing the resignations of Golda Meir and Moshe Dayan. In some ways Rabin, and even Peres, represent "new leadership," although the Mapai and the other parties are still in the hands of the established leadership.

The change in the Office of the Prime Minister, as well as the Defense Ministry and Foreign Ministry, has created some indications of new views; but these appear to be more of process than of policy. Government policy has tended to shift leftward in accepting accommodation, despite the mood of the electorate. This shift would seem to be explained by the pressures of the strategic situation, perceived pressure from the United States, and a need for the government to "buy time" to restore the IDF and search for a political settlement.

Polarization of Israel's voters toward force-centered and accommodation-centered modes, as demonstrated in the 1973 elections, has served both to lessen the gap between left and right and further to reduce the impact of the minor fringe parties. Since these parties have had virtually no influence over policy making, their demise would have no direct impact on policy; but it could help give Israel a two-party system, which might have a substantial impact.

Arab elites are as aware as their Israeli counterparts of the significance of the impact of foreign events on domestic matters; but the greater stability in the Arab world and instability in the Israeli coalition reduces the vulnerability of the former, as it increases that of the latter, to domestic pressures.

Although poverty in the Arab world is far from eradicated (and oil deposits are located in sparsely populated countries), Arab leaders today are more optimistic than in the past about development prospects. One of the major impediments to development, in their view, is the Arab-Israeli conflict. Israel, however, has seen its economic position erode rapidly since 1973. Economic and social concerns may yet be the strongest force for peace in the Middle East.

Abu Jaber, Kamel S. *The Arab Ba'th Socialist Party.* Syracuse, New York: Syracuse University Press, 1966.

Adams, Michael, ed. *The Middle East: A Handbook.* New York: Praeger, 1971.

Adamson, David. *The Kurdish War.* London: George Allen and Unwin, 1964.

Adomeit, Hannes. "Soviet Policy in the Middle East: Problems of Analysis." *Soviet Studies* 27, no. 2 (April 1975): 288–305.

Akzin, B. "The Role of Parties in Israeli Democracy." *Journal of Politics* 17, no. 4 (November 1955): 507–45.

Alexander, Lewis M. "The Arab-Israeli Boundary Problem." *World Politics* 6, no. 3 (April 1954).

Allon, Yigal. *The Making of Israel's Army.* London: Vallentine, Mitchell, 1970.

_____. "The Making of Israel's Army: The Development of Military Conceptions of Liberation and Defense." In *The Theory and Practice of War: Essays Presented to B. H. Liddell Hart on His Seventieth Birthday.* Edited by Michael Howard, pp. 335–71. London: Cassell, 1965.

_____. *Masakh Shel Hol* ("Curtain of Sand"). Tel Aviv: Ha'kibbutz Ha'meuhad, 1959.

Alnasrawi, Abbas. "The Changing Pattern of Iraq's Foreign Trade." *Middle East Journal* 25, no. 4 (Autumn 1971): 481–90.

Antonovsky, Aaron. "Classification of Forms, Political Ideologies and the Man in the Street." *Public Opinion Quarterly* 30, no. 1 (1966): 107–19.

Arfa, Hasan. *The Kurds: An Historical and Political Study.* London: Oxford University Press, 1966.

Arian, Alan. *Hopes and Fears of Israelis: Consensus in a New Society.* Jerusalem: Jerusalem Academic Press, 1972.

_____. *Ideological Change in Israel.* Cleveland, Ohio: Case Western Reserve University Press, 1968.

Arian, Alan, and Aaron Antonovsky. *Voting and Ideology in Israel.* Jerusalem: Jerusalem Academic Press, 1972.

Avneri, Uri. *Israel Without Zionists: A Plea for Peace in the Middle East.* New York: Macmillan, 1968.

Badre, Albert Y. "Economic Development of Iraq." In *Economic Development and Population Growth in the Middle East.* Edited by Charles A. Cooper and Sidney S. Alexander, pp. 160–207. New York: American Elsevier, 1972.

Bakali, M. "A New Page in the History of Iraq: The Significance of Achieving Unity and Cooperation Between the Arabs and the Kurds." *Review of International Affairs* (Belgrade) 21, no. 482 (May 15, 1970): pp. 23–25.

Bar-Zohar, Michael. *Ben Gurion: The Armed Prophet.* Englewood Cliffs, N.J.: Prentice-Hall, 1968.

Bechtold, Peter K. "New Attempts at Arab Cooperation: The Federation of Arab Republics, 1971–?" *Middle East Journal* 27, no. 2 (Spring 1973): 152–72.

Beeri, Eliezer. "A Note on Coups d'État in the Middle East." *Journal of Contemporary History* 5, no. 2 (1970): 123–30.

————. *Army Officers in Arab Politics and Society.* New York: Praeger, 1970.

Begin, Menachem. "Conceptions and Problems of Foreign Policy." *Ha'Uma* (March 1966): 462–70.

Bell, J. Bowyer. "Israel's Nuclear Option." *Middle East Journal* 26, no. 4 (Autumn 1972): 379–88.

Ben-Gurion, David. *Israel: A Personal History.* New York: Funk and Wagnalls, 1971.

————. "Israel's Security and Her International Position Before and After the Sinai Campaign." In *Government Yearbook 5720, 1959/60,* pp. 9–87. Jerusalem: Government Printing Office, 1960.

Ben-Porat, Yeshoyahu, et al. *Ha'Michdal* ("The Omission"). Tel Aviv: 1973. Translated as *Kippur.* Tel Aviv: Special Edition Publishers, 1974.

Ben-Tzur, I. "The Neo-Bath Party of Syria." *Journal of Contemporary History* 3, no. 3 (July 1968): 161–81.

Bill, James A. "The Military and Modernization in the Middle East." *Comparative Politics* 2, no. 1 (October 1969): 41–62.

Binder, Leonard. "Transformation in the Middle Eastern Subordinate System After 1967." In *The U.S.S.R. and the Middle East.* Edited by Michael Confino and Shimon Shamir, pp. 251–71. Jerusalem: Israel Universities Press, 1973.

————. "Political Recruitment and Participation in Egypt." In *Political Parties and Political Development.* Edited by Joseph La Palombara and Myron Weiner, ch. 8. Princeton: Princeton University Press, 1966.

Birnbaum, Ervin. *The Politics of Compromise: State and Religion in Israel.* Teaneck, New Jersey: Fairleigh Dickinson University Press, 1970.

Bitar, S. "The Rise and Decline of the Baath." *Middle East International* (London) no. 3 (June 1971): 12–15.

Blanc, Haim. *Communal Dialects in Baghdad.* Harvard Middle Eastern Monograph Series, X. Cambridge, Massachusetts: Harvard University Press, 1964.

Boulding, Kenneth E. *Conflict and Defense: A General Theory.* New York: Harper and Row, 1962.

_____. "National Images and International Systems." *Journal of Conflict Resolution* 3, no. 2 (June 1959): 120–31.

Brecher, Michael. *Decisions in Israel's Foreign Policy.* New Haven: Yale University Press, 1975.

_____. *The Foreign Policy System of Israel: Setting, Images, Processes.* New Haven: Yale University Press, 1972.

Brodkey, Robert M., and James Horgen. *Americans in the Gulf: Estimates and Projections of the Influx of American Nationals into the Persian Gulf, 1975–1980.* Washington, D.C.: American Institutes for Research, 1975.

Buchanan, J., and Gordon Tullock. *The Calculus of Consent.* Ann Arbor: University of Michigan Press, 1962.

Burrell, R. M. "The Persian Gulf." *Washington Papers* no. 1 (1972).

Campbell, John C. "The Soviet Union and the United States in the Middle East." *Annals of the American Academy of Political and Social Science* no. 401 (May 1972): 126–35.

_____. "The Arab-Israeli Conflict: An American Policy." *Foreign Affairs* 49, no. 1 (October 1970): 51–69.

_____ and Helen Caruso. *The West and the Middle East.* New York: Council on Foreign Relations, 1972.

Cass, Alain. "Cool Head in Damascus." *Middle East International* no. 60 (June 1976): 6–8.

Confino, Michael, and Shimon Shamir, eds. *The U.S.S.R. and the Middle East.* Jerusalem: Israel Universities Press, 1973.

Cooley, John K. *Green March, Black September: The Story of the Palestinian Arabs.* London: Frank Cass, 1973.

Cooper, Charles A., and Sidney S. Alexander, eds. *Economic Development and Population Growth in the Middle East.* New York: American Elsevier, 1972.

Copeland, Miles. *The Game of Nations.* London: Weidenfeld and Nicolson, 1969.

Dagan, Avigdor. *Moscow and Jerusalem: Twenty Years of Relations Between Israel and the Soviet Union.* London: Abelard-Schuman, 1970.

Dann, Uriel. *Iraq Under Qassem: A Political History 1958–63.* New York: Praeger, 1967.

Dawisha, A. I. "The Transnational Party in Regional Politics: The Arab Ba'th Party." *Asian Affairs* 61, no. 1 (February 1974): 23–31.

Dayan, Moshe. *Mappa Hadasha—Yehassim Aherim* ("New Map—Other Relations"). Haifa: Shikmona, 1969.

———. "Israel's Border and Security Problems." *Foreign Affairs* 33, no. 2 (January 1955): 250–67.

Dekmejian, R. H. *Egypt Under Nasser: A Study in Political Dynamics.* Albany: State University of New York Press, 1971.

——— and M. J. Wyszomirski. "Strategic Perceptions and the Arab-Israeli Conflict." Paper read at the annual meeting of Middle East Studies Association, Boston, November 6–9, 1974.

De Rivera, Joseph H. *The Psychological Dimension of Foreign Policy.* Columbus, Ohio: Charles E. Merrill, 1968.

Devlin, John. *The Ba'th Party: A History from Its Origins to 1966.* Stanford: Hoover Institution Press, 1976.

Dowty, Alan. "Israeli Perspectives on Nuclear Proliferation." In *Security, Order and the Bomb.* Edited by J. Holst. Oslo: Universitetforlaget, 1972.

Dzirkalis, Lilita. "Present Soviet Policy Toward Third World States." Paper presented at Southern California Arms Control and Disarmament Seminar, Santa Monica, California, November, 1971.

Eagleton, William, Jr. *The Kurdish Republic of 1946.* London: Oxford University Press, 1963.

Eban, Abba. "Reality and Vision in the Middle East." *Foreign Affairs* 43, no. 4 (July 1965): 626–38.

Edmonds, Cecil J. "The Kurdish National Struggle in Iraq." *Asian Affairs* 58, no. 2 (June 1971): 147–58.

———. "The Kurdish War in Iraq: A Plan for Peace." *Royal Central Asian Journal* 54, no. 1 (February 1967): 10–23.

———. *Kurds, Turks and Arabs: Politics, Travel and Research in North-Eastern Iraq.* London: Oxford University Press, 1957.

El-Rayyes, Riad N., and Dunia Nahas, eds. *Guerrillas for Palestine: A Study of the Palestinian Commando Organizations.* Beirut: An-Nahar Press Services S.A.R.L., 1974.

———. *The October War: Documents, Personalities, Analyses and Maps.* Beirut: An-Nahar Press Services S.A.R.L., 1974.

Eshkol, L. *B'havlei Hitnahlut* ("In the Pangs of Settlement"). Tel Aviv: 1966.

Eytan, Walter. *The First Ten Years: A Diplomatic History of Israel.* New York: Simon and Schuster, 1958.

Fein, Leonard J. *Politics in Israel.* Boston: Little, Brown, 1967.

Feron, James. "Yigal Allon Has Supporters, Moshe Dayan Has Disciples." New York *Times Magazine,* April 27, 1969.

Freedman, Robert O. *Soviet Policy Toward the Middle East Since 1970.* New York: Praeger, 1975.

George, Alexander L. *The "Operational Code." A Neglected Approach to the Study of Political Leaders and Decision-Making.* Santa Monica, California: RAND Corporation, 1967.

Glassman, Jon. *Arms for the Arabs: The Soviet Union and War in the Middle East.* Baltimore: Johns Hopkins University Press, 1975.

Goldman, Nahum. "The Future of Israel." *Foreign Affairs* 48, no. 3 (April 1970): 443–59.

Graham, R. "Iraq and Iran: The Struggle Sharpens." *New Middle East* no. 45 (June 1972): 14–16.

Gray, Albert L., Jr. "Egypt's Ten-Year Plan: 1973–1982." Paper presented at the Middle East Studies Association annual meeting, Boston, November 7, 1974.

Groennings, Sven, E. W. Kelley, and Michael Leiserson, eds. *The Study of Coalition Behavior: Theoretical Perspectives and Cases from Four Continents.* New York: Holt, Rinehart and Winston, 1970.

Guriel, B. "Ideological Origins of the Soviet-Egyptian Alliance." *New Middle East* 17 (February 1970): 17–23.

Gutmann, Emanuel. "Some Observations on Politics and Parties in Israel." *India Quarterly* 17, no. 1 (January–March 1961): 3–29.

Guttman, Louis. "Whither Israel's Political Parties?" *Jewish Frontier* 28, no. 12 (December 1961): 32–40.

Haddad, George. *Revolutions and Military Rule in the Middle East: The Arab States.* New York: Robert Speller and Sons, 1971.

Halpern, Ben. "The Role of the Military in Israel." In *The Role of the Military in Underdeveloped Countries.* Edited by J. J. Johnson. Princeton: Princeton University Press, 1962.

Halpern, Manfred. "Egypt and the New Middle Class: Reaffirmations and New Explorations." *Comparative Studies in Society and History* 11, no. 1 (January 1969): 97–108.

Hammond, Paul Y., and Sidney S. Alexander, eds. *Political Dynamics in the Middle East.* New York: American Elsevier, 1972.

Hansen, Bent. "Economic Development in Egypt." In *Economic Development and Population Growth in the Middle East.* Edited by Charles A. Cooper and Sidney S. Alexander, pp. 22–91. New York: American Elsevier, 1972.

Harik, Iliya. "The Single Party as a Subordinate Movement: The Case of Egypt." *World Politics* 26, no. 1 (October 1973): 80–105.

Harkabi, Yehoshafat. *Palestinians and Israel.* Jerusalem: Keter, 1974.

_____. *Arab Attitudes Toward Israel.* New York: Hart Publishing Co., 1972.

Harsanyi, John C. "Rational Choice Models of Political Behavior vs. Functionalist and Conform-
ist Theories." *World Politics* 21, no. 3 (July 1969): 513–38.

Hart, Parker T. "Where We Stand." *Annals of the American Academy of Political and Social
Science* 402 (May 1972): 136–42.

Hazen, William E., and Peter A. Gubser. *Selected Minority Groups of the Middle East: The Alawis,
Berbers, Druze and Kurds.* Kensington, Maryland: American Institutes for Research, 1973.

Hazen, William E., and Mohammed Mughisuddin. *Middle Eastern Subcultures: A Regional
Approach.* Lexington, Massachusetts: D. C. Heath, 1975.

Heikal, Mohamed. *The Cairo Documents.* New York: Doubleday, 1973.

––––––. *The Road to Ramadan.* New York: Quadrangle, 1975.

Hermann, Charles F. *Crises in Foreign Policy-Making.* China Lake, California: Project Michelson,
1965.

Herzog, Chaim. *The War of Atonement.* Boston: Little, Brown, 1975.

Higgins, Rosalyn. *The Middle East (United Nations Peacekeeping, 1946–1967: Documents and
Commentary, Volume I).* New York: Oxford University Press, 1969.

Hilan, Rizkallah. *Culture et développement en Syrie et dans les pays retardés.* Paris: Editions
Anthropos, 1969.

Hinnebusch, Raymond A. "Local Politics in Syria: Organization and Mobilization in Four Village
Cases." *Middle East Journal* 30, no. 1 (Winter 1976): 1–24.

Hoffman, Stanley. "A New Policy for Israel." *Foreign Affairs* 53, no. 3 (April 1975): 405–31.

Holmstrom, David. "Syria—Unity, Liberty and Socialism." *Middle East International* no. 22
(April 1973): 11–13.

Holsti, O. R. "Cognitive Dynamics and Images of the Enemy: Dulles and Russia." In *Enemies
in Politics.* Edited by D. J. Finley, O. R. Holsti, and R. R. Fagen. Chicago, 1967.

Holt, Peter M., ed. *Political and Social Change in Modern Egypt.* London: Oxford University
Press, 1968.

Hopkins, Harry. *Egypt the Crucible: The Unfinished Revolution in the Arab World.* Boston:
Houghton Mifflin, 1969.

Hottinger, A. "How the Arab Bourgeoisie Lost Power." *Journal of Contemporary History* 3, no.
3 (1968): 111–28.

Howard, Harry N. "The United States and the Middle East." In *The Middle East in World
Politics: A Study in Contemporary International Relations.* Edited by Tareq Y. Ismael, ch. 5.
Syracuse: Syracuse University Press, 1974.

_____. "The United Arab Republic." *Current History* (Philadelphia) 58, no. 1 (January 1970): 8–12.

Howe, Irving, and Carol Gershman, eds. *Israel, the Arabs and the Middle East.* New York: Quadrangle Books, 1972.

Hudson, Michael C. "Developments and Setbacks in Palestinian Resistance Movement 1967–1971." *Journal of Palestine Studies* 1, no. 3 (Spring 1972): 64–84.

_____. "The Palestinian Arab Resistance Movement: Its Significance in the Middle East Crisis." *Middle East Journal* 23, no. 3 (Summer 1969): 291–307.

Hunter, Robert. "The United States in the Middle East." In *The Middle East: A Political and Economic Survey.* Edited by Peter Mansfield, pp. 90–100. London: Oxford University Press, 1973.

Hurewitz, Jacob Coleman. *Middle East Politics: The Military Dimension.* New York: Praeger, 1969.

_____, ed. *Soviet-American Rivalry in the Middle East.* New York: Columbia University Press, 1969.

Hussein, Mahmoud. *Class Conflict in Egypt: 1945–1971.* New York and London: Monthly Review Press, 1973.

"Iran-Iraq: Documents on Abrogation of the 1937 Treaty Concerning Shatt al-Arab Waterway." *International Legal Materials* 8, no. 3 (1969): 478–92.

"Iraq: Statement of Four Parties." *World Marxist Review Information Bulletin* (Toronto) 8, no. 12 (1970): 35–38.

Ismael, Tareq, ed. *The Middle East in World Politics: A Study in Contemporary International Relations.* Syracuse: Syracuse University Press, 1974.

Israel. *Agranat Commission Report* (1975).

Jabber, Fuad. "Not By War Alone: Curbing the Arab-Israeli Arms Race." *Middle East Journal* 28, no. 3 (Summer 1974): 233–47.

_____. *Israel and Nuclear Weapons.* London: Chatto and Windus, 1971.

Jalal, F. *The Role of Government in the Industrialization of Iraq.* London: Frank Cass and Co., 1971.

Joiner, Charles A. *The Fedayeen and Arab World Politics.* Morristown, New Jersey: General Learning Press, 1974.

Jureidini, Paul A. "The Abiding Threat of War." Forthcoming article.

Jureidini, Paul A., and William E. Hazen. *Lebanon's Dissolution: Futures and Consequences.* Alexandria, Virginia: Abbott Associates, 1976.

————. *The Palestinian Movement in Politics.* Lexington, Massachusetts: D. C. Heath, 1976.

————. *Six Clashes: An Analysis of the Relationship Between the Palestinian Guerrilla Movement and the Governments of Jordan and Lebanon.* Kensington, Maryland: American Institutes for Research, 1971.

Jureidini, Paul A., R. D. McLaurin, and Mohammed Mughisuddin, eds. *The Prospects for Joint U.S.-Soviet Peacekeeping in the Middle East: A Conference Report.* Kensington, Maryland: American Institutes for Research, 1973.

Kalb, Marvin, and Bernard Kalb. *Kissinger.* Boston: Little, Brown, 1974.

Kaylani, Nabil M. "The Rise of the Syrian Ba'th; 1940–1958: Political Success, Party Failure." *International Journal of Middle East Studies* 3, no. 1 (1972): 3–23.

Kelidar, Abbas. "Religion and State in Syria." *Asian Affairs* 61, no. 1 (February 1974): 16–22.

Kerr, Malcolm H. "Hafiz Asad and the Changing Patterns of Syrian Politics." *International Journal* 28, no. 4 (Autumn 1973): 689–706.

————. "Nixon's Second Term: Policy Prospects in the Middle East." *Journal of Palestine Studies* 2, no. 3 (Spring 1973): 14–29.

————. *The Arab Cold War, 1958–1967: A Study of Ideology in Politics.* 3rd ed. London: Oxford University Press, 1972.

————. "Regional Arab Politics and the Conflict with Israel." In *Political Dynamics in the Middle East.* Edited by Paul Y. Hammond and Sidney S. Alexander, pp. 31–68. New York: American Elsevier, 1972.

————. "The United Arab Republic: The Domestic, Political and Economic Background of Foreign Policy." In *Political Dynamics in the Middle East.* Edited by Paul Y. Hammond and Sidney S. Alexander, pp. 195–224. New York: American Elsevier, 1972.

Khadduri, Majid. *Arab Contemporaries: The Role of Personalities in Politics.* Baltimore: Johns Hopkins University Press, 1973.

————. *The Role of Ideas and Ideals in Politics.* Baltimore: Johns Hopkins University Press, 1973.

————. *Political Trends in the Arab World.* Baltimore: Johns Hopkins University Press, 1970.

————. *Republican Iraq: A Study in Iraqi Politics Since 1958.* London: Oxford University Press, 1969.

Kimball, Kent Lorenzo. *The Changing Pattern of Political Power in Iraq, 1958 to 1971.* New York: Robert Speller and Sons, 1972.

Knorr, Klaus. *The War Potential of Nations.* Princeton: Princeton University Press, 1956.

Kohler, Foy D., Leon Gouré, and Mose L. Harvey. *The Soviet Union and the October 1973 Middle East War: The Implications for Detente.* Miami: Center for Advanced International Studies, University of Miami, 1974.

Koszinowski, Thomas. "Syrien und der vierte arabische-israelische Krieg." *Orient* 15, no. 1 (March 1974): 24–28.

_____. "Korrektur der Korrektivbewegung?" *Orient* 14, no. 2 (June 1973): 83–85.

_____. "Die innepolitische Entwicklung in Syrien seit der Machtergreifung des Ba'th im März 1963." *Orient* 13, no. 3 (September 1972): 123–38.

_____. "Die Bildung der Progressiven Nationalen Front in Syrien." *Orient* 13, no. 2 (June 1972): 95–100.

Koury, Enver. *The Crisis in the Lebanese System: Confessionalism and Chaos.* Washington, D.C.: American Enterprise Institute, 1976.

"The Kurdish Revolution After Eight Years." *Kurdish Journal* (Langley Park, Maryland) 6, no. 3 (September 1969): 87–90.

Lall, Arthur. *The U.N. and the Middle East Crisis, 1967.* Rev. ed. New York: Columbia University Press, 1970.

Laqueur, Walter. *Confrontation: The Middle East War and World Politics.* London: Wildwood House and Abacus, 1974.

_____. *The Struggle for the Middle East: The Soviet Union in the Mediterranean—1958–1968.* New York: Macmillan, 1969.

_____. *The Road to War: The Origins and Aftermath of the Arab-Israeli Conflict 1967–68.* London: Weidenfeld and Nicolson, 1968.

_____, ed. *The Israel-Arab Reader: A Documentary History of the Middle East Conflict.* 2nd ed., rev. New York: Citadel Books, 1970.

Lenczowski, George, ed. *Political Elites in the Middle East.* Washington, D.C.: American Enterprise Institute, 1975.

Levy, Avigdor. "Strategic Forecast: Trends in the Development of the Balance of Power in the Middle East." Unpublished paper, 1975.

_____. "The Syrian Communists and the Ba'th Power Struggle, 1966–1970." In *The U.S.S.R. and the Middle East.* Edited by Michael Confino and Shimon Shamir, pp. 395–417. Jerusalem: Israel Universities Press, 1973.

Lewis, Bernard. "The Arab-Israeli War: The Consequences of Defeat." *Foreign Affairs* 46, no. 2 (January 1968): 321–35.

Luttwak, Edward N. "The Defense Budget and Israel." *Commentary* (February 1975): 27–37.

Magnus, Ralph H., ed. *Documents on the Middle East.* Washington, D.C.: American Enterprise Institute, 1969.

Ma'oz, Moshe. "Alawi Military Officers in Syrian Politics." In *The Military and State in Modern Asia.* Edited by H. Z. Schiffrin, pp. 277–97. Jerusalem: Academic Press, 1976.

————. "Syria Under Hafiz al-Asad: New Domestic and Foreign Policies." *Jerusalem Papers on Peace Problems* no. 15 (1975).

————. "Attempts at Creating a Political Community in Modern Syria." *Middle East Journal* 26, no. 4 (Autumn 1972): 389–404.

March, James G., and Herbert A. Simon. *Organizations.* New York: John Wiley and Sons, 1958.

Marr, Phebe Ann. "Iraq's Leadership Dilemma: A Study in Leadership Trends, 1948–1968." *Middle East Journal* 24, no. 3 (Summer 1970): 283–301.

McLaurin, R. D. "The Soviet-American Strategic Balance: Arab Elite Views." Forthcoming article.

————. "Soviet Policy in the Persian Gulf." In *Conflict and Cooperation in the Persian Gulf.* Edited by Mohammed Mughisuddin. New York: Praeger, forthcoming.

————. "Arab Perceptions of the Superpower Military Balance." Paper presented at the annual meeting of the International Studies Association, Toronto, 1976.

————. *The Middle East in Soviet Policy.* Lexington, Massachusetts: D. C. Heath, 1975.

McLaurin, R. D., and Mohammed Mughisuddin. *Cooperation and Conflict: Egyptian, Iraqi, and Syrian Objectives and U.S. Policy.* Washington, D.C.: American Institutes for Research, 1975.

————. *The Soviet Union and the Middle East.* Washington, D.C.: American Institutes for Research, 1974.

McLaurin, R. D., and James M. Price. *Soviet Middle East Policy Since the October War.* Alexandria, Virginia: Abbott Associates, 1976.

Mezerik, A. G., ed. *The United Nations Emergency Force (UNEF): 1956—Creation, Evaluation, End of Mission—1967.* New York: International Review Service, 1969.

————. *Kuwait-Iraq Dispute, 1961.* New York: International Review Service, 1961.

Moore, Clement Henry. "Authoritarian Politics in Unincorporated Society: The Case of Nasser's Egypt." Paper presented at the 1972 annual meeting of the American Political Science Association, Washington, D.C.

Munro, Sir Leslie. "Can the United Nations Enforce Peace?" *Foreign Affairs* 38, no. 2 (January 1960): 209–18.

Niv, D. *Battle for Freedom: The Irgun Tzva'i Le'umi.* 3 vols. Tel Aviv.

Nyrop, Richard F., Beryl Lieff Benderly, William W. Cover, et al. *Area Handbook for Syria.* Washington, D.C.: Foreign Area Studies Division, American University, 1971.

O'Brien, Patrick. *The Revolution in Egypt's Economic System: From Private Enterprise to Socialism, 1952–1965.* London: Oxford University Press, 1966.

Oren, Stephen. "Syria's Options." *The World Today* 30, no. 11 (November 1974): 474 ff.

Page, Stephen. *The U.S.S.R. and Arabia: The Development of Soviet Policies and Attitudes Towards the Countries of the Arabian Peninsula, 1955–1970.* London: Central Asian Research Centre, 1971.

Pajak, Roger F. "Soviet Military Aid to Iraq and Syria." *Strategic Review* 4, no. 1 (1976): 51–59.

Palit, D. K. *Return to Sinai: The Arab Offensive, October 1973.* New Delhi: Palit and Palit, 1974.

Paltiel, K. Z. "The Progressive Party: A Study of a Small Party in Israel." Ph.D. dissertation, 1964.

Peres, Shimon. *David's Sling.* London: Weidenfeld and Nicolson, 1970.

_____. *Ha'shlav H'ba* ("The Next Stage"). Tel Aviv: Am Ha'safer, 1965.

_____. "Outlines for an Israeli Foreign Policy." *New Outlook* (September 1963): 14–19.

Peretz, Don. "The War Elections and Israel's Eighth Knesset." *Middle East Journal* (Spring 1976): 111–25.

_____. "The United States, the Arabs, and Israel: Peace Efforts of Kennedy, Johnson and Nixon." *Annals of the American Academy of Political and Social Science* no. 401 (May 1972): 116–25.

Perlmutter, Amos. *The Military and Politics in Israel.* London: Cass, 1969.

_____. "The Israel Army in Politics: The Persistence of the Civilian over the Military." *World Politics* 20, no. 4 (July 1968): 606–43.

Petran, Tabitha. *Syria.* New York: Praeger, 1972.

Picard, Elizabeth. "La Syrie du 'redressement' et les chances de paix au Proche-Orient." *Politique étrangère* 41, no. 2 (1976): 169–80.

Pranger, Robert J. *American Policy for Peace in the Middle East, 1969–1971: Problems of Principle, Maneuver and Time.* Washington, D.C.: American Enterprise Institute, 1971.

Quandt, William B. "United States Policy in the Middle East: Constraints and Choices." In *Political Dynamics in the Middle East.* Edited by Paul Y. Hammond and Sidney S. Alexander, pp. 489–525. New York: American Elsevier, 1972.

_____. "The Middle East Conflict in U.S. Strategy, 1970–1971." *Journal of Palestine Studies* 1, no. 1 (Autumn 1971): 39–52.

_____, Fuad Jabber, and Ann Mosely Lesch. *The Politics of Palestinian Nationalism.* Berkeley: University of California Press, 1973.

Quester, George. "Israel and the Non-Proliferation Treaty." *Bulletin of the Atomic Scientists* 25, no. 6 (June 1969).

Rabinovich, Itamar. *Syria Under the Ba'th 1963–66: The Army-Party Symbiosis.* Jerusalem: Israel Universities Press; New York: Halsted Press, 1972.

Reisman, Michael. *The Art of the Possible: Diplomatic Alternatives in the Middle East.* Princeton: Princeton University Press, 1970.

Riker, William H. *The Theory of Political Coalitions.* New Haven: Yale University Press, 1962.

Rosenne, Shabtai. "Basic Elements of Israel's Foreign Policy." *India Quarterly* 17, no. 4 (October-December 1961): 328–58.

Rubinstein, Alvin Z. "Egypt Since Nasser." *Current History* 62, no. 1 (January 1972): 6–13.

Rugh, William A. "Arab Media and Politics During the October War." *Middle East Journal* 29, no. 3 (Summer 1975): 310–28.

Saab, E. *La Syrie ou la révolution dans la rancoeur.* Paris: Juilliard, 1968.

Sadat, Anwar. *Revolt on the Nile.* New York: John Day, 1957.

Saddy, Fehmi. *The Eastern Front: Implications of the Syrian/Palestinian/Jordanian Entente and the Lebanese Civil War.* Alexandria, Virginia: Abbott Associates, 1976.

Safran, Nadav. "Arab Politics, Peace and War." *Orbis* 18, no. 2 (Summer 1974): 377–401.

―――. *From War to War: The Arab-Israel Confrontation 1948–1967.* New York: Pegasus, 1969.

Salibi, Kamal S. *Crossroads to Civil War: Lebanon 1958–1976.* Delmar, N.Y.: Caravan Books, 1976.

Schif, Zeev. *October Earthquake.* Tel Aviv: University Publishing Projects, Ltd., 1975.

Schmidt, Dana Adams. *Armageddon in the Middle East.* New York: John Day, 1974.

Seale, Patrick. *The Struggle for Syria.* New York: Oxford University Press, 1965.

Sella, Amnon. "Soviet Military Doctrine in the October War." Unpublished ms., 1974.

―――. "Soviet Training and Arab Performance." Jerusalem *Post* Magazine, February 8, 1974, pp. 6–7.

―――. "The Soviet Union in the Middle East." Unpublished MS, 1974.

Seymour, Martin. "The Dynamics of Power in Syria Since the Break with Egypt." *Middle Eastern Studies* 6, no. 1 (January 1970): 35–47.

"Shatt-al-Arab—Iraq and Iran," *Arab World* (New York) 16, nos. 3–4 (March–April 1970): 14–20.

Smith, Harvey H., et al. *Area Handbook for Iraq.* Washington, D.C.: U.S. Government Printing Office, 1971.

―――. *Area Handbook for the United Arab Republic (Egypt).* Washington, D.C.: U.S. Government Printing Office, 1970.

Snyder, Glenn H. *Deterrence and Defense: Toward a Theory of National Security.* Princeton: Princeton University Press, 1961.

Soffer, Gad. "The Role of the Officer Class in Syrian Politics and Society." Ph.D. dissertation, American University, 1968.

Stewart, D. "Egypt in Search of Religious and Political Community." *New Middle East* nos. 52–53 (January–February 1973): 19–22.

Stockholm International Peace Research Institute. *The Arms Trade with the Third World.* Stockholm: Almqvist and Wiksell, 1971.

Suleiman, Michael W. "Attitudes of Arab Elites Toward Palestine and Israel." *American Political Science Review* 67, no. 2 (June 1973): 482–89.

_____. "Syria: Disunity in Diversity." In *Governments and Politics of the Contemporary Middle East.* Edited by Tareq Y. Ismael, pp. 213–30. Homewood, Illinois: Dorsey Press, 1970.

Tachau, Frank, ed. *Political Elites and Political Development in the Middle East.* Cambridge, Massachusetts: Schenkman, 1975.

Tahtinen, Dale R. *The Arab-Israeli Military Balance Since October 1973.* Washington, D.C.: American Enterprise Institute, 1974.

_____. *The Arab-Israeli Military Balance Today.* Washington, D.C.: American Enterprise Institute, 1973.

Thoman, R. "Iraq and the Persian Gulf Region." *Current History* 63, no. 1 (January 1973): 21–25.

_____. "Iraq Under Baathist Rule." *Current History* 62, no. 1 (January 1972): 31–37.

Torrey, Gordon H. "Aspects of the Political Elite in Syria." In *Political Elites in the Middle East.* Edited by George Lenczowski, pp. 151–61. Washington, D.C.: American Enterprise Institute, 1975.

_____. "The Ba'th—Ideology and Practice." *Middle East Journal* 23, no. 4 (1969): 445–70.

Ullman, Richard H. "After Rabat: Middle East Risks and American Roles." *Foreign Affairs* 53, no. 2 (January 1975): 284–96.

U.S. Agency for International Development. *U.S. Overseas Loans and Grants and Assistance from International Organizations: Obligations and Loan Authorizations, July 1, 1945–June 30, 1975.* Washington, D.C.: AID, n.d.

U.S. Central Intelligence Agency. *Communist Aid to Less Developed Countries of the Free World, 1975.* ER 76-10372U. July 1976.

U.S. Congress, Senate, Committee on Foreign Relations. *Foreign Assistance Authorization.* S.3394, 93rd Congress, 2nd Session, 1974. Washington, D.C.: U.S. Government Printing Office, 1974.

———. "The Middle East Between War and Peace: November–December 1973." Staff report prepared for the use of the Subcommittee on Near Eastern Affairs. 93rd Congress, 2nd Session. March 5, 1974.

U.S. Department of State. "Summary of a Conference: The Psychological Impact of the Seventeen Day War." 1974.

Valland, Pierre. *Le Liban au bout du fusil.* Paris: Librairie Hachette, 1976.

Van Dam, Nikolaos. "The Struggle for Power in Syria and the Ba'th Party (1958–1966)." *Orient* 14, no. 1 (March 1972): 10–20.

Van Dusen, Michael H. "Syria: Downfall of a Traditional Elite." In *Political Elites and Political Development in the Middle East.* Edited by Frank Tachau, pp. 115–55. Cambridge, Massachusetts: Schenkman, 1975.

———. "Political Integration and Regionalism in Syria." *Middle East Journal* 26, no. 2 (Spring 1972): 123–36.

———. "Intra- and Inter-Generational Conflict in the Syrian Army." Ph.D. dissertation, Johns Hopkins University School of Advanced International Studies, 1971.

Vatikiotis, P. J. "The Politics of the Fertile Crescent." In *Political Dynamics in the Middle East.* Edited by Paul Y. Hammond and Sidney S. Alexander, 225–66. New York: American Elsevier, 1972.

Wagner, A. R. "A Rational Choice Model of Aggression: The Case of the Six Day War." In *International Yearbook of Foreign Policy Studies 1975.* Edited by Patrick J. McGowan. Beverly Hills, California: Sage Publications, 1975.

———. *Crisis Decision-Making: Israel's Experience in 1967 and 1973.* New York: Praeger, 1974.

———. *Political Change and Decision-Making in Israel: The Aftermath of the October War.* Beverly Hills, California: A. R. Wagner & Co., 1974.

Wakebridge, Charles. "The Syrian Side of the Hill." *Military Review* 56, no. 2 (February 1976): 20–30.

Wakin, Edward. *A Lonely Minority.* New York: William Morrow, 1963.

Waterbury, John. "The Crossing: From the Bar Lev Line to Geneva." American Universities Field Staff, *Reports,* Northeast Africa Series 18, no. 6 (December 1973).

———. "A Note on Egypt: 1973." American Universities Field Staff, *Reports,* Northeast Africa series, 18, no. 4 (July 1973).

Wenner, Lettie M. "Arab-Kurdish Rivalries in Iraq." *Middle East Journal* 17, nos. 1–2 (Winter and Spring 1963): 68–82.

Whetten, Lawrence L. *The Canal War: Four Power Conflict in the Middle East.* Cambridge, Massachusetts: MIT Press, 1974.

Yodfat, Aryeh. "The End of Syria's Isolation?" *The World Today* 27, no. 8 (August 1971): 329–40.

──────. "The U.S.S.R., Jordan and Syria." *Mizan* 11, no. 2 (April 1969): 73–93.

Zidon, Asher. *Knesset: The Parliament of Israel.* New York: Herzl Press, 1968.

PERIODICAL SOURCES REGULARLY CONSULTED

Al-Ahram. Cairo. Daily.

An-Nahar. Beirut. Daily.

An-Nahar Arab Report. Beirut, An-Nahar Press Services S.A.R.L. Weekly.

The Arab Economist. Beirut, Center for Economic, Financial and Social Research and Documentation S.A.R.L. Monthly.

Arab Report and Record. London. Bimonthly.

The Arab World. Beirut. Daily.

Christian Science Monitor. Boston. Daily.

Foreign Broadcast Information Service, *Daily Report.* Washington, D.C. Daily.

Ha'aretz. Tel Aviv. Daily.

Jerusalem *Post.* Daily.

Journal of Palestine Studies. Beirut, Institute of Palestine Studies. Quarterly.

Kayhan International. Teheran. Daily and weekly.

Keesing's Contemporary Archives. London, Keesing's Publications. Weekly.

Los Angeles *Times.* Daily.

Ma'ariv. Tel Aviv. Daily.

The Middle East. London. International Communications, Inc. Monthly.

Middle East and African Economist. New York. Monthly.

The Middle East and North Africa. London, Europa Publications. Annual.

Middle East Economic Digest. London, Economic Features, Ltd. Weekly.

Middle East Economic Papers. Beirut, American Univeristy of Beirut. Annual.

Middle East International. London. Monthly.

The Middle East Journal. Washington, D.C., Middle East Institute. Quarterly.

The Military Balance. London, International Institute for Strategic Studies. Annual.

New Middle East. London. Monthly.

New York *Times.* Daily.

Strategic Survey. London, International Institute for Strategic Studies. Annual.

Syrie et monde arabe. Damascus, government of Syria. Monthly.

United Nations Statistical Yearbook. New York. Annual.

UNESCO Yearbook. New York. Annual.

Wall Street Journal. New York. Daily.

Washington *Post.* Daily.

Washington *Star.* Daily.

R. D. McLAURIN is a research scientist with Abbott Associates. A graduate of the University of Southern California, Dr. McLaurin completed his Ph.D. at the Fletcher School, Tufts University. Author of *The Middle East in Soviet Policy* and numerous other studies and articles on related subjects, he was formerly employed in the Office of the Assistant Secretary of Defense (International Security Affairs) and was later on the staff of the American Institutes for Research.

MOHAMMED MUGHISUDDIN, a native of Pakistan, has traveled widely in the Middle East, and has lectured and taught on the Middle East at numerous educational institutions throughout the United States. Dr. Mughisuddin did his undergraduate work at the American University, Washington, D.C., where he also received his Ph.D. Currently a research scientist at Abbott Associates and an adjunct faculty member at the American University, Dr. Mughisuddin is editor of *Conflict and Cooperation in the Persian Gulf* (forthcoming) and coauthor of *Middle Eastern Subcultures: A Regional Approach*. He also has written or contributed to a number of other books and studies on the Middle East.

ABRAHAM R. WAGNER travels frequently to the Middle East. Dr. Wagner was educated at Syracuse University and the University of Rochester, where he received his Ph.D. Author of *Crisis Decision-Making: Israel's Experience in 1967 and 1973,* Dr. Wagner was the director of the NHA Policy Group before leaving to form his own research firm, Analytical Assessments Corporation. He lectures widely across the United States and is a consultant to the departments of Defense and State. He also served in the Israel Prime Minister's Office in 1973–74.

RELATED TITLES

Published by

Praeger Special Studies

*SOVIET POLICY TOWARD THE MIDDLE EAST SINCE 1970
Robert O. Freedman

POLITICAL CULTURE IN ISRAEL: Cleavage and Integration among Israeli Jews
Eva Etzioni-Halevy
with Rina Shapira

CRISIS DECISION-MAKING: Israel's Experience in 1967 and 1973
Abraham R. Wagner

THE ARAB BOYCOTT OF ISRAEL: Economic Aggression and World Reaction
Dan S. Chill

MIDDLE EAST ECONOMIES IN THE 1970s: A Comparative Approach
Hossein Askari
John Thomas Cummings

*Also available in paperback as a PSS Student Edition.

SAINT JOSEPH'S COLLEGE, INDIANA

DS63.1 .M25   ISJA
McLaurin / Foreign policy making in the Middle East : domest

3 2302 00090 2207

DS   Foreign policy making
63.1   in the Middle East
.M25